BATTLE AXES

BATTLE AXES

A HARD ROCKIN' HISTORY OF POINTY GUITARS

SEAN KELLY

ECW

Published by ECW Press
665 Gerrard Street East
Toronto, Ontario, Canada M4M 1Y2
416-694-3348 / info@ecwpress.com

CERTIFIED CANADIAN PUBLISHER

Editor for the Press: Michael Holmes
Copy editor: Kathryn Lane
Cover design: Michel Vrana
The cover artwork is based on photographs courtesy of Jackson/Charvel Manufacturing, Inc.

LIBRARY AND ARCHIVES CANADA CATALOGUING IN PUBLICATION

Title: Battle axes : a hard rockin' history of pointy guitars / Sean Kelly.

Other titles: Hard rockin' history of pointy guitars | Hard rocking history of pointy guitars

Names: Kelly, Sean, 1972- author

Identifiers: Canadiana (print) 20260175072 | Canadiana (ebook) 20260178713

ISBN 978-1-77041-794-6 (softcover)
ISBN 978-1-77852-555-1 (ePub)
ISBN 978-1-77852-556-8 (PDF)

Subjects: LCSH: Electric guitar—History. | LCSH: Rock musicians—Interviews.

Classification: LCC ML1015.G9 K35 2026 | DDC 787.87/19—dc23

This book is funded in part by the Government of Canada. *Ce livre est financé en partie par le gouvernement du Canada.* We also acknowledge the support of the Government of Ontario through the Ontario Book Publishing Tax Credit, and through Ontario Creates.

Canada Ontario ONTARIO CREATES

PRINTED AND BOUND IN CANADA

PRINTING: MARQUIS 5 4 3 2 1

CONTENTS

FOREWORD

> John Hughes movies. Big hair and parachute pants. Hair metal and new wave. All of these popular things that emerged from the '80s evoke so much fond nostalgia, proving it was an electrifying time to be alive. And just as much as the wild and wacky was a prevailing constant, the decade was also a catalyst in radical innovation for electric guitars. From locking tremolos to higher-output pickups (it was all in its nascency), there was no limit to how far you could modify a guitar. Guitar shapes were reimagined and finished in flashy paint jobs and outrageous graphics that made the electric guitar the ultimate symbolic accessory of a rock star.

What you just read is an excerpt from a review that I wrote about a Jackson guitar for *Guitar World* magazine. I chose the following snippet as the overarching theme because I believe it perfectly encapsulates the powerful history detailed ahead in Sean Kelly's brilliant book about pointy guitars. To which I say,

Read this book!

Sure, it might be tempting to dismiss the detailed descriptive narratives and personal stories about these pointed guitars, which often resemble a glaive more than a six-string, simply because one could argue the subject matter is so niche. But guess what? You're going to find the passionate players who still wield these battle axes believe they are as momentous today as they were then. To which I say,

Read this book!

Let me be clear: I was no fan of pointy guitars. All those exaggerated cutaways and elongated headstocks found on guitars from B.C. Rich, Dean, and others never really appealed to me growing up. Instead, I lusted after the classic, elegant curves of Fender and Gibson instruments that I continue to play today. But truth be told, my narrow-minded view shifted after I witnessed two specific events. The first was seeing Aerosmith's Joe Perry and Brad Whitford in the kitschy movie *Sgt. Pepper's Lonely Hearts Club Band*, brandishing pointy B.C. Rich guitars while portraying a villainous band. Here was a perfect example of art imitating life; seeing these two with sharp-edged guitars that I'd never seen before made them appear even more menacing and badass. The second was seeing a young rising star by the name of Randy Rhoads playing the eye-catching Concorde guitar (an inspired, angular V-model he designed with Grover Jackson), which would ultimately be refined as one of the most renowned models in the Jackson guitars stable. Even now, I believe Rhoads never anticipated how popular and far-reaching his visionary instrument would become. All you need to do is read about the many famous artists and musicians who play a version of that asymmetrical guitar today. To which I say,

Read this book!

In closing, the seismic shift these extreme shapes and their designers caused in guitar manufacturing cannot be overstated. Armed with features like razor-sharp contours, pointy tips, overwound pickups, and evolving locking-vibrato systems, these avant-garde instruments were more than a stylistic statement. Their forward-thinking innovations streamlined guitar design, resulting in sleeker and more ergonomic shapes optimized for blistering speed. If you think about it, the multitude of heavy-metal and hard-rock guitarists who championed these supersonic road racers early on were not only rebelling against the status quo but were also trailblazers, fundamentally changing the perception of what is traditional and propelling heavy music into the future. Ultimately, these inspirational guitars served as the foundation for all the exhilarating music we love to listen to over and over. And isn't that the point?

Read this book!

— Paul Riario, tech editor, *Guitar World*

INTRODUCTION

A STARTING POINT

Toronto's Queen Street Viaduct carries traffic across the Don River, bringing commuters from the city's east end into its downtown core. The aphorism "this river I step in is not the river I stand in" is emblazoned in large metallic letters, arching over Queen Street at the bridge's eastern end. It is likely the only phrase I will ever read by the Greek philosopher Heraclitus (no offense, dude) but I have contemplated it many times over the years as I traveled across the Don from my east-end home to a myriad of gigs and recording sessions in the center of the city. Call me crazy but I think this phrase applies directly to this book. *Battle Axes* was meant to be a *historical* document on pointy guitars, but as I researched, wrote, and considered the many voices interviewed for this story, my intentions would change as swiftly as the water under old Heraclitus's feet.

Don't get me wrong — I have tried desperately to be a pointy-guitar historian for months on end. But as I should have realized after writing my previous two books, I am the last person who should ever be giving a linear *historical* account about anything. The truth is, I have very little control over which details stick in my brain. For example, I can't remember the wood that was used to make my own signature model SK-2 Exquire guitar (fluorescent pink and very pointy). According to the man who designed and built it, Canadian luthier par-excellence Les Godfrey of Godfrey Guitars, it was poplar, with a walnut neck and an ebony fingerboard. Yet, for some reason, I *can* remember that Mick Mars was quoted as saying, "To play metal, you have to know how to play guitar," in an ad for the Kahler tremolo system in some guitar magazine I read in the early '80s. I don't recall any of the model details of the shiny silver device that Mick had fitted on the beautiful (and terrifyingly pointy) white B.C. Rich Warlock he was playing, but I remember those words rang so true — simultaneously obvious, cliché, and awe inspiring.

I also recall feeling that a full-page advertisement dedicated to this one very particular component of the electric guitar made the Kahler tremolo system (or "vibrato system" if we're being technically accurate) seem very special. The way it gleamed, the way it caught the stage lights. It was sexy as hell, and I wanted one, preferably on a pointy guitar like Mick was rocking. I'd find out later on that that simple yet ingenious device could turn a ringing, low E-string note into a revving motorcycle (à la the intro to Mötley Crüe's "Kickstart My Heart") or a dive-bombing fighter jet, targeting our ears and souls (think of the devastating final note of Eddie Van Halen's solo guitar masterpiece "Eruption") by slackening and tightening the tension of strings in ways subtle, torturous, and all points in between. How many times has a well-placed whammy-bar dive bomb saved my ass from the perils of my own lack of imagination at the end of a flailing guitar solo?

I would come to learn that for many guitarists I admired, a tremolo system was just one of many components that could be utilized in the customization of a guitar, allowing them to amplify the sounds that were in their heads and hearts. For the hard-rockin' guitarists of the '70s and '80s, and the talented luthiers and guitar designers that came along in the wake of the early electric-guitar pioneers of the 1950s, it was this never-ending pursuit of mixing and matching parts that added up to a much more rocking sum.

Now, of course, in this book there *are* going to be details about many types of pointy guitars. And there is going to be solid factual research on people, places, and things. At the very least, I'm going to try and point those of you interested in the minutiae of guitars (and in my experience, that is a majority of my guitar playing, making, and loving friends) to places where you can find those exacting details.

Alas, in the end, I have to surrender to who I am, how I write, and ultimately, focus on how pointy guitars make me *feel*. As I spoke with a varied

collection of passionate and highly experienced guitar experts, many of those feelings were subject to change as more was revealed about the people and practices responsible for bringing these pointy masterpieces of guit-art (I won't ever use that term again, I promise) into our collective consciousness. While the chapters in this book will ultimately reveal the guitars to be the main focal point, there will be instances where these instruments might just be one piece of a greater musical moment, like a classic recording or iconic live performance.

I've never once purchased or craved a guitar based on an intellectual understanding of its components and construction. I have, on many occasions, purchased guitars because their geometry, their color, or the graphics painted on their bodies shocked me with the same electric excitement and joy that I felt when watching and listening to my hard rock and heavy metal guitar heroes. Sometimes I bought them because they sounded great and played well, but I wanted to play 'em more if they were pointy.

My own guitar collection of 56 instruments (a modest collection for a guy writing a book about guitars; an excessive amount to my feng-shui practicing and long-suffering wife) is made up of a handful of guitars of considerable value, but most of my guitars lack the qualities or origins to be deemed truly collectible. They inhabit a space someplace in the mid- to higher-end spectrum of mass-produced guitars. They were purchased primarily as tools of spiritual inspiration, a kind of affordable connection to simpler days and the guitar heroes of my heavy metal youth. I will speak of the importance of my handcrafted custom guitars in the book, as they offer an entirely different kind of playing experience, especially when considering the inspirations and motivations of the craftsmen and visionaries who created instruments that have become iconic pieces of great cultural importance, sometimes even beyond the music world.

I am proud to say that none of my guitars are "all show and no go"; they all must earn their keep in my life as a professional musician. However, most of my guitars would fail to raise the interest of the serious guitar collectors I follow (with no small degree of envy and gear lust) on social media.

Of course, the sonics and playability of an instrument are of high importance, but it is the contention of this book that the shape and look of a guitar plays a similarly important role in terms of inspiration and the connection between artistic intention and audience appreciation. When performance and visual aesthetic come together in a way that satisfies the player, it's like King Arthur finding Excalibur. (Maybe that's why Dean Guitars was so successful with an ad that featured a beautiful woman coming out of the water — more to come on that particular magic moment.)

This book is driven by my love, fascination, and desire for the wildly customized pointy guitars played by my musical heroes in the '70s and '80s.

These angular, graphically ordained instruments were thrust into our faces and burned into our brains in the visually driven era of music videos, glossy rock magazines, and smoke-bomb polluted concert spectacles that I talked about at length in my previous book, *Don't Call It Hair Metal*. When I first contemplated playing a power chord, I knew I wanted to play it on a pointy guitar hanging off my scrawny, 11-year-old frame.

In the many conversations I had for this book, I came to see many parallels in the origin stories of some of the world's most famous purveyors of pointy guitar magic, both in their rises and in their falls. But you can't keep a good man — or a good brand — down, and in some way or another these battle axes have lived to fight many more days. In my friend Sean Barrette's excellent book *Heartstrings — First Guïtars*, I shared the story of how I came into possession of my first guitar:

> My first electric guitar was purchased on December 21, 1984, and appeared underneath my family's Christmas tree 4 days later. It was purchased for $55, with an additional $3.85 tagged on for Provincial Sales Tax at the Bargain Bonanza Flea Market, located at 915 Cassells Street in North Bay ON. I know all of this because I found the receipt for the guitar shortly after the passing of my father this year, whose name was on the "Sold To" portion of the bill.
>
> The guitar bore a serial number of A00036, with the word "Japan" stamped onto the plate securing the body to the neck, and these are the only details I can offer with regards to its manufacturer's identification. The guitar itself was a thin-line, hollow-bodied, double-cutaway model, spray painted in a metallic pink/purple flake, with double "F" holes, and two strange single coil pickups that could be flipped in and out of phase via plastic toggle switches. The bridge was a Bigsby knock off, but it came with no vibrato arm. As far as I can tell, the body is made of particle board. But hey, it came from the five-and-dime, and I played it 'til my fingers bled.
>
> I'm holding it now as I write this, and it takes me back to the mystery, magic, and possibility that this instrument offered me on my nascent playing journey. The first piece I learned to

> play on it was the guitar solo for "We're Not Gonna Take It" by Twisted Sister. In 2015, 30 Years after I received that guitar for Christmas, I would be playing that song and performing alongside its composer (and one of my heroes) in a 40-show run of Dee Snider's Rock N Roll Christmas Tale at Toronto's Winter Garden Theatre.
>
> I feel so blessed to have found the receipt for this guitar. As much as it represents the beginning of a dream that has taken me around the world as a musician, it also represents the love of a father for his son (even if he didn't quite understand why his son wanted to grow his hair so long), the unending support of family, and the power music has to connect us.
>
> — Sean Kelly (Sean Barrette, *Heartstrings*.)

I look back with a deep sense of affection at my relationship with that first guitar, and it still hangs proudly on the wall of my studio here in Toronto. A lot of hours were spent mastering rudimentary scales and wrenching my left hand to form the crippling barre chords that would become my stock in trade. It was a good and faithful servant, even if getting the beast into any semblance of being in tune was an exercise in futility. But I have to be honest here. For all the hours of playing I put into that instrument, and the enormous debt of gratitude I felt I owed to my parents, the guitar I received on that Christmas morning of 1984 was not the guitar I really wanted.

The object of my Yuletide desire was a nondescript copy of Gibson's famous Flying V model, one I had come across in either the *Sears Christmas Wish Book* or the *Consumers Distributing Fall/Winter* catalog, both publications being a prime inspirational source for stoking the fires of Christmas yearning for Canadian boys and girls angling for a place on Santa's nice list. (If only I knew how many naughty situations those electric guitars would help me find just a few years later!)

Ah yes, that flying V. With its space-age angles, it looked like a rocket ship designed to launch me a thousand miles into space, far beyond the atmosphere of my preteen Northern Ontario isolation. The flying V in the catalog was created by Harmony, a Chicago-based company formed in 1892 by German immigrant Wilhelm Schultz. How would he have reacted to his company making copies of guitars that would destroy all concepts of what conventional stringed instruments should look like? Those Norse god–inspired thunderbolts being used by German bands like the Scorpions and Accept to play heavy metal music was about as far removed from a Schumann piano piece (but pretty close to Wagner, in parts) as you could get. The first Harmony stringed instruments were small acoustic guitars with gut strings, violins, and mandolins — nothing you would see Rudolf Schenker playing with the Scorpions on MuchMusic or MTV.

Chicago was at the center of America's industrial boom in the late 1800s and early 1900s, a central hub for manufacturing thanks to its location for shipping product via the Great Lakes or by rail. Harmony made a name for itself as a company that was able to put playable instruments in the hands of thousands of aspiring musicians who were taking advantage of the new mail-order business model (developed in Chicago), which changed shopping and consumer behavior around the world. Companies like Montgomery Ward and later Sears (who distributed the first Harmony guitars via catalog around 1897 and bought the company in 1916), played a big part in the distribution of guitars, and the rise in guitar makers, across America.

In an article for Guitar.com, Justin Beckner highlighted a policy that would play a major role in the perception of guitar consumers for years to come:

> MW pledged to sell only American-made guitars because, the catalogue claimed, American-made guitars were a superior product. Imported guitars, said Montgomery Ward, would crack or split due to climate changes, while American guitars would not. Perhaps this was the kernel of what would grow into a huge legend around the quality and reliability of American guitars the world over.

That Harmony flying V, though not quite as flashy with its wood-grain, tobacco-sunburst finish, was evocative of the guitars I saw and heard in the hands of K.K. Downing of Judas Priest, Carlos Cavazo of Quiet Riot, Wolf Hoffmann of Accept, or any other number of MTV (or in my case, the Canadian equivalent, MuchMusic) stalwarts who were burning up the charts as fast as they were burning up their fretboards in those early days of pop metal's commercial dominance.

The V looked like it could be an accessible gateway to the more extreme guitar shapes that were lighting my soul ablaze like the Guild X-79 model that

Jay Jay French of Twisted Sister was popularizing in iconic videos like "We're Not Gonna Take It," the futuristic Guild X-100 Bladerunner that Joe Perry rocked in the ground-breaking "Walk This Way" (a 1986 collaboration with hip hop pioneers RUN DMC that both revitalized a tired and drug-addled Aerosmith and brought hip hop to a much wider audience), or the death-defying Guild X-88 that Mötley Crüe's Mick Mars was wielding to sleazy and terrorizing effect in the "Too Young to Fall in Love" music video.

It would take me many years to acquire my first fully pointy guitar, although there were a few pointy adjacent guitars along the way: a 1987 Series A Super Strat with a headstock that could take your eye out and a 1988 Yamaha RGX that I bought because of an ad I saw with Triumph's Rik Emmett that promised a guitar with "No Borders. No Boundaries," which rang true to me, considering Rik's versatility as a player, the magic power of a credible endorsement in full effect. But these guitars were still very much based on the Fender Stratocaster shape, which is arguably still the most popular electric guitar shape of all time. (That shape, as we will come to see, found a way to carve out some real estate in the heavy-metal market and, near the end of the '80s, actually conquered it.) But my first authentically pointy acquisition was the cherry-red 1967 Gibson Flying V re-issue that I bought in Calgary, Alberta, while on the road with my band 69 Duster in 2000. It had once belonged to guitar monster Reed Shimozawa, who would come to prominence as guitarist for Canadian '90s neo-glam rockers Zuckerbaby and go on to work with Wide Mouth Mason, One Bad Son, and many more.

You see, over the years I had quite a few obstacles that stood in the way of me getting those pointy guitars in my hands, even during the '80s commercial heyday. To my parents, the idea of their well-behaved, mild-mannered son playing electric guitar was already a bit of an oddity and cause for concern, and I was constantly battling against challenges from well-meaning adults and authority figures (like my guitar teacher) who understandably wanted me to have guitars that were both classic in their aesthetic and of high-quality construction. Clearly, as a fully integrated member of the music video era, my interpretation of "classic" was bound to be wildly different from previous generations, and whatever constituted "quality" was a concept that was far beyond my scope of understanding at the time. Still, it bothered me that the instruments I coveted, like those glorious neon pink and yellow B.C. Rich Warlocks and Mockingbirds that I saw Poison guitarist C.C. DeVille wrestling into submission in the "Talk Dirty to Me" video, were considered to be somehow less worthy based on their looks, or the looks of the players who had them in their hands.

Now, in truth, looking cool while jumping in front of a mirror was much more of a priority to me than how I actually sounded, because sounding like the electric guitar gods in bands like W.A.S.P., Autograph, Loudness, Kiss, or any other hard rock or heavy metal confection of the mid-80s just seemed like something completely out of reach. And by the time I was actually good enough to be out playing in front of audiences, guitarists like Slash and Izzy Stradlin from Guns N' Roses with their Gibson Les Pauls and 175s, and Yngwie Malmsteen with his army of classic Fender Stratocasters were making vintage cool again amongst young players (never mind what was just around the corner with the dawn of the grunge era in the '90s and the rejection of anything that remotely brought the visual and sonic excess of the previous decade to mind). Those beautifully angular and exotic guitars didn't come into my life until the early 2000s, once I had truly come to understand that my artistic happiness was only going to be found by fully embracing my '80s hard rock influences — and ultimately, the influence of the glam rock artists who came before in the '70s. How gratifying it was when my acceptance of my authentic musical self led not only to my first solo record deal, but also to my first major guitar endorsement with B.C. Rich Guitars. I had discovered that the tonal qualities I coveted in my more traditional shaped Les Paul and Fender Esprit guitars could be found in the visually exciting shapes of the B.C. Rich Mockingbird (like the one C.C. picked up in that Poison video and *talked to me* through!), the edgy and controversially named Bich, and the classic and classy Eagle.

Quality in electric guitars comes down to so many factors. There are myriad combinations of types of wood, electronics, hardware, and — of course — design. How do the people who design and create guitars prioritize sonic, visual, and ergonomic considerations? Do these pointy guitars that I love so much come with the sacrifice of playability and great tone? Or do these shapes that veer away from more universally accepted classic shapes like the Gibson Les Paul or ES-335 and 125, or the Fender Telecaster and Stratocaster, actually offer enhancement and sonic variety? Throughout the writing of *Battle Axes*, I reached out to luthiers and designers to discuss these factors and the evolution of the pointy guitar from an expert's point of view as well as to delve into the artistic intention behind guitar design in general.

But the heart and soul of this story is an exploration of the talismanic qualities of guitars that I consider to be iconic, the craftsmen who make them, and the impact of the guitarists who play them. Clearly, one doesn't choose to play a B.C. Rich Warlock or a Washburn Stage series A-20 just to fade into the background. I spoke with as many players as I could from famous guitar heroes to passionate hobbyists (and players who fall somewhere in between) to find out what excites (or maybe even disgusts) them about pointy guitars. And yes, like my two previous books, the focus will be on the musical genre and periods I am most passionate about, the hard rock of the '70s and '80s. I also took the opportunity to place these instruments in their musical context, diving into some of the great albums and songs that were elevated by all manner of six-string razors.

In order to trace the evolution of pointy guitars as they relate to the heart of this book, we need to go back to the 1950s to see where this phenomenon truly began. There are three shapes in particular that connect to almost every variation I talk about, but — full disclosure — I am compelled to admit that I sacrificed total comprehensiveness to my own selfish interest in the guitars and music that *I* want to write about. That being said, I have done my best to get as many brands, styles, and shapes in there as I could. I know there are people out there playing or lusting after a guitar that gives them the same thrill that I get from my Akira Takasaki designed Killer Exploder or my ESP Edwards Random Star, and I want to know about it. After all, like the music we listen to, the guitars we play become more valuable and meaningful to us when we can share the joy they bring to our lives with a like-minded community. I love that an electric guitar, a relatively simple concoction of wood, wire, plastic, and paint, can be turned into a divining rod that leads me to the waters that slake my spiritual thirst. This occurs when the instruments are infused with the passion and creativity of the luthier and the designer, the marketing savvy of the company bringing the guitar to market, and the inspiration of the player who makes it sing. While that quenching of thirst may be one that I experience uniquely, it is enriched when shared with my fellow obsessives be they band mates, fans, or — as I like to call all of the people who share my passion for rock n roll — friends.

Electric guitars, especially those pointy ones, have been my portable companion for many years now, helping me navigate the demands of everyday life while pointing me towards that magical, spiritual state where my world resonates at the frequency of the music of the spheres.

Ok, let's leave this heady stuff and get into the pointy headstocky stuff — time to grind the battle axes!

CHAPTER 1

WHAT'S THE POINT OF A POINTY GUITAR?

There is no doubt about it — strapping on an electric guitar is a portal into a world of cool. But "cool" has always been a subjective thing, and while a Les Paul, Stratocaster, or Tele can surely get you to that place in classic style, the player who arms themselves with an altogether more protrusive instrument seems to be making a statement that takes the term to its outer limits. I asked some industry vets and hard rock luminaries just what it meant and felt like to sling one of these pointy children of the guitar revolution on massive arena stages across the world. What *is* the point of these pointy guitars?

> Whether it's the Charvel Star guitar, the Explorer, the Flying V, in my opinion, these guitars are the epitome of, let's say, the big rock of the '80s, the hard rock that we love. I'm much different than the older guys that revere the Les Paul and Stratocaster as being the essence of rock and roll. For me as a kid, man, it was when I saw Eddie Van Halen with a star guitar in 1980, I was like, woah — that was the coolest thing! And then finding out that on *Van Halen I* that Ed mostly used that '75 Ibanez Explorer [Destroyer], and it was like, man, there was always something about those guitars that spoke to me immediately.

> Seeing Paul Stanley with the Flying V or Ace with the Explorer, it was always that dream where I said, "I'm going to have one of those guitars." And luckily, that's happened numerous times for me.
>
> — Steve Brown of Trixter

How does it make you feel to have a pointy guitar in your hand when facing down an arena packed with ten thousand screaming fans?

> It makes you feel like a rock star. I mean, you got this long pointy thing, and it's, yeah, it's not your normal, typical Fender from the '50s. [Pointy guitars] have more of a space age, modern feel, and they seem to really accentuate the idea of a rock star on the stage.
>
> — Steve Plunkett of Autograph

> All of those guitars, you know, the Flying V, the Ibanez Iceman, they're really kind of awkward to play. It was really more of an image thing with a lot of them. It was like trying to be a bit different, especially in the '80s. These guitars were a little like a weapon actually. It's like some kind of sci-fi weapon. And I think that was the whole idea, to be quite honest!
>
> — Phil Collen of Def Leppard

I very much relate to this — like a light saber or a hockey stick, a pointy guitar feels like an extension of my preteen self, weaned on the abundance of early fantasies offered to us in the 1970s and early '80s. A pointy guitar can make me feel like some combination of Mick Mars, Joe Perry, Luke Skywalker, the Mighty Thor, and Buffalo Sabre Gilbert Perreault, characters who were identifiable by their flashy style and their superhuman abilities. A pointy guitar can be just the right musical accessory for presenting that avatar in public.

> I think you have to want to stand out from the crowd. I think you wanna be unique. And I think no matter if it's someone like an Albert King or Lonnie Mack, who's like a blues artist that wants something different than an ES-355 like B.B. King's

Lucille or something like that, or a Michael Schenker or a Lenny Kravitz, these types of instruments lend themselves to that rock and roll abandon, that kind of take no prisoners kind of attitude. Rock and roll — it's energy, it's movement.

— Aljon Go, product manager,
Gibson Brands, Kramer, and Epiphone

When I was 11, I fell in love with two things musically: Flying Vs and Ace Frehley. My first electric guitar was going to be a V or a three-pickup cherry Les Paul Custom that gushed smoke come hell or high water. My dad took me to the Long & McQuade in Brampton and got me what we could afford: a used black El Degas Lawsuit–era LP. (I wish I still had it — it was Japanese and played way, way better than anyone in 1977 realized.) That's the electric I learned on and played until I had saved enough money to buy a *real* made-in-the-USA sienna burst Stratocaster at 16.

By the time I bought that Strat I had fallen for all things punk. Pointy guitars were anathema, and I was conflicted — I loved the way guitars like Explorers and Warlocks looked, but my Miss Clairol–blue-black punk-monkey mind wouldn't let me put my hands on something with too many straight, sharp body lines. The Strat was a compromise: a classic "rock" guitar shape I could play punk *or* metal on. (I quickly had it modded with a DiMarzio Super Distortion bridge humbucker and Floyd Rose. It was an awesome guitar — I sold it through a classified ad in 1990 to have beer money at university and it's a huge regret. I would pay just about anything to have it back and I look for it on Reverb and Kijiji about once a month.)

And that's continued — the guitar-shape conflict inside me — to this day: there are a dozen electric guitars in this house, but I have never had one that's pointy. It's funny, you've really made me think about this for the first time. (I've almost pulled the trigger on a Gibson Moderne a couple times, but something's stopped me.) Sitting here now, I think I deserve to have the pointy experience.

— Michael Holmes of Queen Beach Killer Cat

> I was just never into the straight-ahead Strat shape, and I've never liked those guitars for me personally. I always liked the big, long, pointy guitars that some of those '70s bands, especially the English guys like Ian Hunter, Ariel Bender, and Pete Overend Watts played in Mott the Hoople.
>
> — Steve Plunkett

I wondered what pointy guitars and pointy-guitar-playing guitarists inspired some of the people I talked with for this book?

> Especially growing up, I was really into the pointy guitars, something that didn't look like a doctor or a lawyer would be playing any time soon. I always loved the Explorer shape, so it was kind of a no-brainer that the first time I was to buy a really good quality guitar, I was gonna get a shape that I really liked. Up until then, I could just buy what I could afford, and what I could afford was really just junk. I just had really no choice in what the shapes were, or what kind of guitars they were. It was basically just a charity type of thing. But, when I saw that Jackson had that shape [the Kelly model], I just said "Wow, that's the one." And I think that I first got into those shapes, these Explorer shapes, because when I was a kid, I loved the very first Def Leppard album. And on the back, Pete Wills is playing a Hamer Explorer [Standard], and I was a big Runaways fan, and Lita Ford played a Hamer Explorer [Standard] back then. So those two just looked the coolest thing I ever saw.
>
> — Marty Friedman of Megadeth

> One of my first and biggest influences, and I don't necessarily play or sound anything like him, is Michael Schenker, and he always played a Flying V, and I always loved that. I loved his style. I loved his soul, and I loved the fact that he played a V, and it was different. And then when Randy Rhoads came on the scene and I saw his Vs, his Jackson Rhoads model, and the [Karl Sandoval] Polka Dot V, I loved his style and I love the fact that he played a V as well. Those are two of my biggest influences,

> most definitely. I would say that might have contributed subconsciously to me playing flying Vs as well.
>
> — Michael Sweet of Stryper

> Well, I think, the first that comes to mind is always Randy Rhoads. I think probably everybody will give you that answer. When I think of pointy guitars, I always think of Jacksons. And, you know, I consider this a pointy guitar (motions to his blue Jackson soloist used on Skid Row's multimillion selling debut) because it's got a pointy headstock. And the first time I saw those was when Warren DeMartini of Ratt knocked over those wine glasses on that fucking table in the video for "Round and Round" with his headstock! I was like "That's fucking cool. I want one of those, man."
>
> — Scotti Hill of Skid Row

> I saw a picture of Randy Rhoads with the Polka Dot Sandoval Flying V and that was a game changer — a life changer — for me.
>
> — Steve Brown

> Randy Rhoads and Michael Schenker, with a shoutout to Pete Willis and Matthias Jabs.
>
> — Angus Clark of Trans-Siberian Orchestra

Wild-shaped guitars are clearly not for everybody, for a variety of reasons. But even though some players, like my friends Gilby Clarke and Rik Emmett, have found the more traditional shapes of the Les Paul or the Telecaster suits them better, that doesn't mean that they can't (or haven't in their past) appreciate the power and presentation of a properly appointed pointy ax.

> Michael Schenker really was the king of the Flying V, in terms of looking cool. As far as the Explorer, what an odd, odd shape. You know? I mean, everything about it says that it shouldn't work, but there are certain guys that can pull it off. Rick Nielsen from Cheap Trick just made that guitar work and everything. It just never really worked for me. And as a matter of fact, I had B.C. Rich Mockingbird Supreme . . . we're talking, like, 1978 I had one.

And I got it for one reason, Rick Derringer. Rick Derringer had one when he was on a solo tour. I saw him play it, and I was like, "Oh my god. What is that?" I worked at a music store back then, and it was one of those guitars that came in used. It was the '76 Mockingbird Supreme, so it had the cloud inlays and everything. And I had to actually put it on layaway and make payments until I had enough payments where I could take it home and then keep the payments going. And I had that guitar for years. I actually had two Les Pauls, the Mockingbird, and a Tele at that time.

And my house was broken into by a bunch of drug addicts, and they stole that guitar. We're talking, like, maybe '78, '79. And oddly enough, after that, I moved to Hollywood and was playing with Candy. And at that time, I only had two guitars. I had a Les Paul and the Telecaster that survived the theft. And I was living in Hollywood, and I got a call from an old friend, and he says, "I think I found your Mockingbird!" And it had been five years. It was in a pawnshop, and he saw it. He knew I was the only person around town that had a Mockingbird, so he knew it was mine. I called the store, and sure enough, it was mine. I had the police report and the serial number. He paid one hundred and fifty dollars for it. I gave him one hundred and fifty dollars and I got the guitar, and when I got it back five years later, I started playing it and I thought "This guitar is too easy to play." It was a very well-made guitar. It was just too easy. I was so used to a Les Paul and a Telecaster at that point. I was pulling strings out of tune and stuff like that. I ended up selling it after I got it back after five years.

— Gilby Clarke of Guns N' Roses, Heart, and MC5

Attitude. It's attitude when Dean [Zelinsky, founder of Dean Guitars] makes a guitar and goes, "I'm gonna make it so that it's crazy, sexy, and weird, and then people are gonna see it, and they're gonna go crazy, sexy, and weird!" And the guitar player is gonna be playing it, and *he's* gonna be a guitar player that plays with attitude. And that's a really cool thing that goes all the way to making a Baby Z model that sticks out in three directions with triple binding in a flame sparkle finish. It's also attitude when [late, great Jazz guitar legend] Ed Bickert goes, "Look, I don't polish my guitar. I just play it until I've gone all the way through the finish, and that finish is orange because I smoke all the time, and my hand's orange, and the air is filled with nicotine." I used to love Gibson guitars that had white binding that was now orange because it had been played in bars for years when everybody smoked back in the old days, and all of the Gibsons would get that orange color in in the finish. Eventually, guitar guys were going, you know, "*That's* attitude. I think I need to add a little bit of orange to the lacquer just so that it'll have that orangeness that makes an old guitar look vintage and cool." It's all just attitude. And, I think that's what guitar players want to project, and they just make their choices. You make a choice when you're 18 that you wouldn't make when you're 28, that you surely won't make when you're 38, 48, 58, 68. Attitude changes. And I remember when I was full of testosterone jumping around up on arena stages and going, "Yeah, Dean Guitars — that would be pretty cool." You know? That would be pretty cool. Then you go, okay. I don't need that cool anymore. My idea of cool is something different now, which is why I'm a Tele guy.

— Rik Emmett of Triumph

Once the King Kobra thing ended, which is where I used my Jackson Star more than anything else, it felt natural to sort of leave that in the past, where it belonged, and to get down to a more — I don't know if organic is the right word, but that's sort of how it felt, you know, going back with the Les Paul in BulletBoys. I mean, the funny thing is that after I kind of abandoned the Jackson after King Kobra, I busted it out during the sessions for our second BulletBoys record, and I couldn't believe how good that guitar sounded! I mean, it just blew away all the other guitars I was using. And if you listen to that record, I mean, cranked up my Jose [Arredondo-modded Marshall amp] a little bit more, and the combination of that and this guitar with this really heavy, meaty sound, it just sounds tortured, you know, it sounds like my amp is just screaming "Please save me. Give me some mercy here." And I just love that.

— Mick Sweda of BulletBoys,
King Kobra, and the Rockett Mafia

Well I knew about the odd shapes early on just because of Kiss — they all played one at some point, you know? Ace played an Ibanez Destroyer. Right? And Paul played a Firebird, and he played a Flying V. Michael Schenker played one with UFO in the '70s, Pete Willis from Def Leppard had the Hamer Explorer [Standard]. I recognized those things early on in the '70s, even with bands like Molly Hatchet, Allen Collins in Lynyrd Skynyrd, and Rickey Medlocke in Blackfoot. And Rick Nielsen and Cheap Trick, with the Hamer Standards and the blue Ibanez Iceman on the cover of *Budokan*. The clothes, the guitar, the whole band look was part of the whole package. In Cheap Trick, Rick and Bun E. Carlos had the nerdy, funny look, and the other guys [Robin Zander and Tom Petersson] were the cool, sexy dudes. But Rick Nielsen clicked with [those guitars].

— Billy Rowe of Buckcherry and Jetboy

What does a pointy guitar say about the player who plays one?

I think it's a metal attitude. It's the spirit of the distorted electric guitar in a shape! It's a demonstration of the strength we feel onstage with an electric guitar in our hands! I got a B.C. Rich Warlock that I used when I was in the band Heaven, it was cool! I think when I got my first Jackson Warrior on the Gutter Ballet Tour with Savatage, that kinda officially popped my "pointed cherry"!

— Chris Caffery of Savatage and Trans-Siberian Orchestra

A pointy guitar says, "This person is fully committed to rocking you to the ground and is well past giving a single fuck about anything else."

— Angus Clark

> I think it says that the player has a bit of flash and attitude and does not conform to the standard ideas of what a guitar is supposed to be. Mötley Crüe, W.A.S.P., and Jefferson Starship were the bands that made me want to own a B.C. Rich guitar when I was a young teenager.
>
> — Nick Walsh of Slik Toxik

> I'd say in the '80s a pointy guitar meant you were forging new ground and being modern, if you didn't have a pointy headstock on your guitar back then, you looked dated. I recently found a receipt for a purple B.C. Rich Ironbird that I owned for less than a month before trading it back to the store for an Ibanez superstrat. Some of those guitars looked great on a wall at a music store, but on me they looked ridiculous — and forget about them fitting on a guitar stand!
>
> — Stacy Stray of Die Mannequin and Robin Black and the Intergalactic Rock Stars

> Guitars are a fashion statement as much as a functional musical instrument. I think that's part of the reason they're so cool. I mean, no offence to other musicians but your instrument is definitely not as badass as ours. It's really no different than the clothes you wear or the way you choose to style your hair. You're telling people how you wish to be perceived. A Jazzmaster is a statement too, just a different one than a Warlock.
>
> — Reed Shimozawa of Zuckerbaby, Wide Mouth Mason, and One Bad Son

For some artists, a pointy guitar is just another color in a palette that embodies a wholistic love of guitar culture in general. For all the beauty of a wild body shape, an eye-popping graphic or paint job, or a classic vintage finish, one of the '80s most iconic players reminds us what truly lies at the heart of any instrument, no matter what shape or trimmings it possesses.

> A perk of being in Kiss was that I could ask the makers of these great guitar brands to create something unique. I wasn't

trained in art, but I did like to draw. My first attempt at a unique guitar was the Charvel in purple that was used in the "Tears Are Falling" video and the Asylum Tour. It just used some geometric shapes, (I always loved Art Deco) and I think it's really an intriguing design. The Zebra Jackson design was fun to see go from paper to a real guitar, and then there was the B.C. Rich Ironbird in blue, with its angular-shaped graphic lines and lighting bolt inlays. The radioactive symbols for my B.C. Rich ST-III were a natural idea because [they matched] my stage suit. At times I challenged ESP to try some things on some Horizon model guitars. Did they make me play better? Of course not. Did it add something exciting to the fact that Kiss was a very visual band, yes. Guitars are living art. An awesome graphic, or metal flake design, is very appealing. But then again, a handsome Black LP Custom always has a "wow" factor, as does a beat-up Gibson sunburst LP JR. This is why the guitar industry is so powerful. It brings up amazing emotions, not unlike the vintage and new automobiles we love. I never forget the concept of guitars being living art, but most importantly for me, they are tools for me to create great music with.

— Bruce Kulick of Kiss

Metal players have always kept the torch alive for pointy guitars. It seems every heavy band has one guitarist sporting the Randy Rhoads Jackson. Nowadays it seems a bit retro and ironic, like Rivers Cuomo from Weezer rocking a mullet and playing a Jackson Rhoads after the pandemic. You got a sense he was just having fun and reliving his youth, and hey why not? Our teenage years were the best time for electric guitars, especially the ones you couldn't play sitting down!

— Stacy Stray

And with these words of revelatory pointed wisdom, we begin our journey at a factory in Kalamazoo, Michigan, in the late 1950s.

CHAPTER 2

TAKING FLIGHT – THE GIBSON FLYING V, EXPLORER, AND FIREBIRD

Tom Petty said "even the losers get lucky sometimes." In the case of the Gibson Flying V, it just happened to take a decade or two.

The cover of Tom Petty and the Heartbreakers debut album features the now iconic sailor's tattoo logo, with one of those "weird" Flying V guitars piercing a heart, the group's name written on a stylized banner. Petty was purportedly loathe to share a connection with the hard rock bands of the '80s, many of whom would also claim the Flying V as a crucial part of their image, but there is no doubt that the connective thread between Petty's brand of stripped down '60s inspired rock n roll and the hard rockers who were his commercial contemporaries is the cool toughness that choice of instrument represents — a sense of badassery, if you will.

The Flying V feels and looks like the guitar of choice for the victorious outlier. The smirking, slightly leering Tom Petty who appears on that album cover comes across as both compelling and repellant. Like the older kid in high school that sold hash outside the arcade, we are attracted to the undeniable "cool" of it all, but wary of the implied menace.

It's fitting that the Flying V might be considered an outsider's instrument, because like most outsiders, it was at some point underestimated, and perhaps even deemed unworthy of love or attention.

> If you think about it, you know, Gibson were the first ones. I think all of the pointy guitars are derivative of the Flying V and the Explorer at the end of the day. The shapes may have been exaggerated here and there, but they're all from that template. But those early Flying Vs and Explorers were a massive failure. You know, they came out in one year and just died, which is why they're so collectible these days.
>
> —Jay Jay French of Twisted Sister

In this chapter, we are going to go back to the instruments that most players, collectors, and fans of pointy guitar culture widely acknowledge as the inspiration for the wild shapes that would follow: Gibson's Flying V, Explorer, and Firebird models.

> I'm such a fan of the Gibson Flying V. It just represents rock and roll abandon to me. I've identified with that instrument for a number of years. If you're looking at players that wanna stand out, that want to be aggressive, but just also want this kind of classiness about it, I think you can't go wrong with a Flying V, an Explorer, or a Firebird.
>
> —Aljon Go, product manager,
> Gibson Brands, Kramer, and Epiphone

Let's take a look at how these strange models came to exist as variations on an already "out there" concept, the electric guitar itself.

In 1958, Gibson had long since been established as a company known for high quality, American-made stringed instruments. The company was founded by Orville Gibson, and set up in Kalamazoo, Michigan, around 1895. (Fun fact: The Kalamazoo that Poor Boy is "twang[ing] the rhythm out" in Creedence Clearwater Revival's "Down on the Corner" is a reference to a budget brand of instruments created by Gibson. As we'll see throughout this book, many companies would come to issue lower-budget instruments under different brand names, with some going on to become highly collectible, while others not so much.)

Tony Bacon tells us in his beautifully written and thoroughly detailed book *Flying V, Explorer, Firebird: An Odd Shaped History of Gibson's Weird Electric*

Guitars that up until 1958, Gibson had created guitars following a classic design template of "familiar rounded outlines to the body, with an upper and lower 'bout' straddling a waisted midsection." In what might be considered an allusion to the overtly sexist marketing of some pointy guitars in the '80s, Bacon goes on to say that "it was this classic symmetrical shape that led to the cliché about a guitar being like a woman's body. This was the shape the instrument had enjoyed for some time, since its roots in earlier centuries. Every guitar more or less copied the template."

After the Chicago Musical Instruments company bought a controlling interest in Gibson in 1944, Bacon tells us that the company began developing a series of models with a pioneering cutaway design, breaking the "timeless outline" to offer players greater access to the upper playing range of the guitar. Electric guitars were becoming more in demand, as their amplification provided an opportunity for the guitarist to step out as a soloist in any number of ensembles. The ES-175 (ES standing for Electric Spanish) appeared in 1949 and marked Gibson's first electric guitar with a pointed cutaway, followed by the Super 400 CES and the L-5 CES. These guitars were outfitted with coveted P-90 single coil pickups, and later the more powerful alnico pickups. The development of new pickup technology would come to play a big part in the evolution of the sound of the electric guitar, and would become particularly important in the overall marketing push of guitars in the '70s, '80s, and beyond.

While the electric guitar story begins with the amplification of more traditionally shaped and designed hollow-body instruments, this story is about the extreme variation of *solid body* guitars. The introduction of the solid body guitar was a radical concept in and of itself. In 1950, *The Purchaser's Guide to the Music Industries*, a sales book published by *The Music Trades* magazine, revealed a bold new design by the Californian company Fender Fine Electric Instruments — a thin, cutaway electric guitar called the Esquire, with a shape similar to those being produced by Gibson. But unlike any Gibson guitar, the Esquire had a solid body — a major innovation. "The newest thing in Spanish guitars — fine action, new tone, perfect intonation," boasted the ad. As Bacon writes, "It was the first of its kind to be sold commercially, and it would change guitars, guitar playing, and music." In addition to the solid body, the Esquire had all six string tuners on one side of the headstock, as opposed to the three-per-side headstocks found on other six-string guitars. It would be a design element we would come to see a lot more of on many of the pointy guitars of the '80s, for practical and aesthetic reasons. As we will investigate later, headstock design would come to play a controversial — even polarizing — role in the electric guitar's development.

In 1950, Ted McCarty, a music executive who had joined Gibson in 1948 from the famed Wurlitzer company, was appointed as the president of the Gibson company. Along with having a hand in overhauling how manufacturing was handled at the factory, he was a major contributor of design ideas. He was keeping an eye on this new solid body that his competitor Leo Fender was bringing to market and set about coming up with something that could top what Fender was offering.

The Gibson response was to create an instrument that would become one of rock n roll's definitive instruments. The original Les Paul model, known today as the Gold Top, was introduced in 1952. With its unique tone-wood combination of a mahogany body and carved maple top, a striking sonic balance of warmth, clarity, and sustain was achieved.

> We designed that guitar because Leo Fender was having some success making solid body guitars. We worked about a year and came up with what we thought was a very fine guitar. I asked Mr. Berlin, "Who's going to sell it for us? We've got to have this guitar on display, because we think it's finer than anything Leo Fender has made." Then I said, "What about Les Paul," because at the time, he and Mary [Ford] were at the top of the charts. I knew Les and had been trying to get him to play Gibson guitars, because he was an Epiphone man.
>
> — Ted McCarty (*Vintage Guitar* magazine, April 1999.)

Artist endorsements of musical instruments would play an important marketing role, and the Les Paul name helped Gibson's electric guitar sales increase exponentially. By 1953, 63 percent of Gibson's guitar sales were electric models.

While Gibson was expanding, so too was Fender, buoyed by the success of the Esquire. The guitar went through some refinements and was renamed the Broadcaster. But, when the Gretsch company complained that that name would cause confusion with its Broadkaster banjo and drumkit, Fender was forced to change the moniker again and landed on the Telecaster. With the growing popularity of television, *Telecaster* suggested an instrument and company born of and representing the future.

In 1951, Fender brought the Precision bass to market, and in doing so, made an immeasurably important aesthetic contribution to electric guitar design. While the Telecaster had a single horn cutaway, the Precision had two horns, which provided greater balance to the instrument and, just as crucially, a futuristic look that served as the template for the design of the Fender Stratocaster, arguably the world's most famous and copied electric guitar shape.

> The Stratocaster was a stunner. It seemed in some ways to owe more to contemporary automobile design than traditional guitar forms, especially in the flowing curves of its beautifully proportioned body. It defiantly moved away from the classical symmetrical guitar template, bravely throwing the shape forward with offset, opposed cutaways. It was the embodiment of tailfin-flash '50s American design . . . It seemed excitingly new and it had a modern space-age name. Gibson had to compete.
>
> (Tony Bacon, *Flying V, Explorer, Firebird*, 14.)

Since marketing plays such a big part in the popularity of the guitars we will talk about, let's hear some hype direct from the horse's mouth, or in this case, the horse's website.

> The Fender Stratocaster is the quintessential electric guitar — a worldwide archetype; the basic form that leaps to mind at the very mention of the phrase electric guitar even among those who don't play. Maybe that's because it was so well designed to start with that it has existed largely unchanged for 60 years now, allowing it to become an ingrained form in the minds of successive generations.
>
> (Jeff Owens, Fender.com)

Undoubtedly, the Stratocaster, the Telecaster, and the Gibson Les Paul represent the holy trinity of solid body electric guitars. Of these three, it is the Stratocaster that would lend itself best to various pointy appointments, all the while maintaining its perpetually classic-yet-forward-looking shape. However, players like Mick Mars of Mötley Crüe and Izzy Stradlin of Guns N' Roses were known to rock Telecaster-shaped bodies with pointy headstocks (Kramer and ESP respectively), and Canadian rocker Aldo Nova had his 1984 signature Les Paul Standard fitted with a droopy, Gibson Explorer–style or hockey-stick headstock.

One of the most important contributors to the overall sound of hard rock and heavy metal is Seth Lover. Lover joined the Gibson team full time in 1952. A radio and electronics expert who worked for the U.S. Navy, Seth was given the daunting task of finding a way to eliminate, or at least reduce, the unwanted hum and interference that resulted from standard single-coil guitar pickups. While these pickups produce a beautiful, singing, and highly musical sound, the hum that can arise when volume increases can be distracting and unpleasant. And let's face it, learning how to control volume is more than half the battle cry in hard rock and metal. Being a fan of the sound of single coil pickups myself, I can speak firsthand to the frustration and unpleasantness that arises when your bandmates and sound technicians shoot you a sharp cut-eye as you struggle to conceal the cacophonous buzzing arising from your side of the stage.

Working off the humbucking choke coil found in Gibson amplifiers at the time, Lover reasoned that a similar approach might provide a similar result. As Tony Bacon says in his book, two coils with opposite magnetic charges are wired together so that they are out of phase resulting in a pickup less likely to pick up extraneous noise while also producing a powerful clear tone. These early pickups are greatly desired by collectors and have come to be known as PAF pickups, standing for "Patent Applied For." As it turns out, Lover was not the first person to come up with the idea of a humbucking pickup; Ray Butts came up with a similar idea for the Gretsch music company, the highly regarded Filter'Tron humbucking pickup.

Going back to the gauntlet that Leo Fender had thrown down with his space-age Stratocaster, McCarty and Gibson answered with wildly inventive takes on the solid-body electric guitar — the Flying V, the Explorer, and the Moderne. This Modernistic trio, conceived in the spring of 1957 in advance of a national musical instrument trade show, was Gibson's attempt to bring attention to the company by creating guitars that were shockingly new and outlandish. While the question of who did what is a matter of some historical debate, there was a team of people from various departments who, through their ideas, sketches, engineering, and woodworking expertise, brought these ground-breaking instruments to life. It's interesting to note that the Modernistic guitars, which would come to be used by some of the most reckless musicians in rock and heavy metal, were a result of careful corporate planning and project co-ordination, a collaborative design think tank. The design team included chief woodworking engineer Larry Allers, final assembler Rem Wall, assistant treasurer and personnel manager Julius Bellson, vice president of sales Clarence Havenga (also known as Mister Guitar), and the aforementioned Seth Lover, who has laid claim to coming up with a number of inventive design shapes for Gibson, including the Flying V.

Gibson filed three patents in June of 1957 for "ornamental design of a string instrument, as shown and described," and these simple design patents were far less detailed than the usual invention patents that focused on meticulous drawings and wordy descriptions and claims.

> McCarty told me that he patented three new designs, for the guitar that became known as the Moderne, Flying V, and Explorer because he "knew what Leo would do" — presumably meaning he expected that a Fender Flying-V type model might follow."
>
> (Tony Bacon, *Flying V, Explorer, Firebird*, 16.)

The first Gibson patent (181,865) was for the design that ultimately became the Explorer. This particular version would become known as the Futura, essentially an Explorer with a narrower waist and a split headstock shaped like an offset V. (We'd see the influence of this headstock shape in the designs of Dean Zelinsky of Dean Guitars in the late '70s.) The hockey-stick headstock that would later inspire many future headstock designs would come later in the Explorer's design process.

The second patent (181,866) was for a design that wouldn't see production until the early 1980s — the ill-fated Moderne. I was never a fan of this shape, that is until I saw one of my guitar heroes, Bruce Kulick of Kiss and Grand Funk Railroad fame, playing one in the early 1990s.

United States Patent Office

Des. 181,865
Patented Jan. 7, 1958

181,865

STRINGED MUSICAL INSTRUMENT

Theodore M. McCarty, Kalamazoo, Mich., assignor to Gibson, Inc., Kalamazoo, Mich., a corporation of Michigan

Application June 20, 1957, Serial No. 46,674

Term of patent 14 years

(Cl. D56—9)

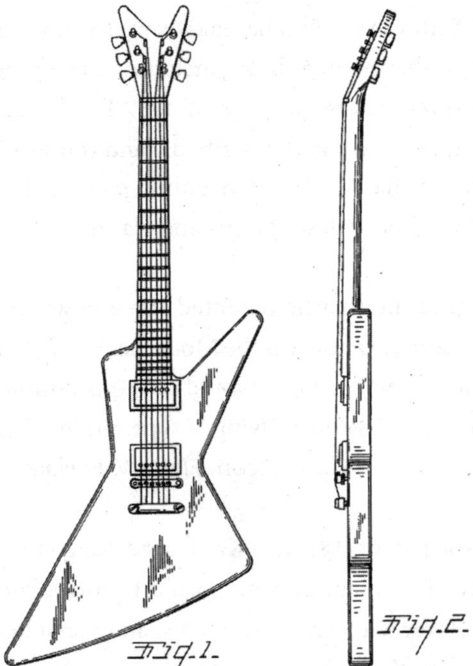

Fig. 1 is a top plan view of a stringed musical instrument showing my new design, and

Fig. 2 is a side elevational view thereof.

The back of the article is substantially plain.

I claim:

The ornamental design for a stringed musical instrument, as shown and described.

References Cited in the file of this patent

UNITED STATES PATENTS

D. 17,888	Darbyshire	Nov. 22, 1887
D. 155,881	Evers	Nov. 8, 1949
D. 162,521	Crowle et al.	Mar. 20, 1951
D. 175,328	Van Pelt	Aug. 9, 1955
1,208,077	Ashley	Dec. 12, 1916

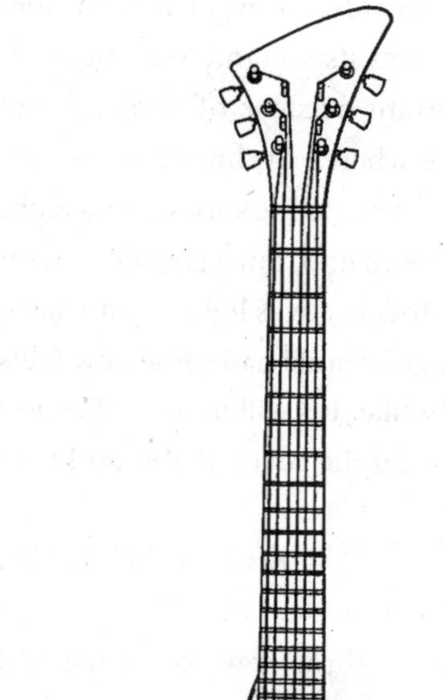

Fig. 1.

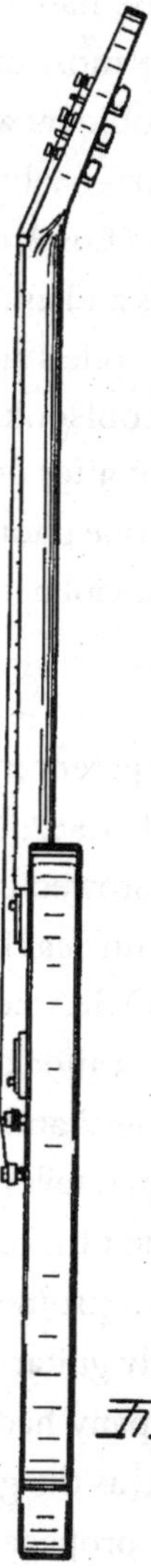

Fig. 2.

> Now the Moderne, in a way the ugly duckling of the three designs, is sort of a Gumby looking shape because of the headstock. The use of my 1983 Korina in black with gold hardware was sort of a necessity. Norman's Rare Guitars in Reseda at the time had a few black ones in stock. I bonded with one, but the most important reason was its weight. Very light on the shoulder, which was important because of a very crazy accident — a broken collar bone when a car hit me crossing a street in Los Angeles — that forced me to look for guitars eight pounds and under. Not impossible to find, but a challenge with some models and brands. The Moderne was light — and black so it's cool looking. It did sound good and I had some new frets put in it after owning it a short while. It's still in my collection and in one photo shoot with Kiss for the cover of *Pollstar* I held it like a violin.
>
> — Bruce Kulick of Kiss

The third patent in the group of these three new "ornamental designs" was number 181,867, the guitar that became known as the Flying V (a name reportedly bestowed upon the guitar by the aforementioned Seth Lover).

While it's unclear if all three of these guitars made their first appearances at the 1957 North American Music Merchants (NAMM) show, there is at least one photo of a mocked up Futura. Tony Bacon suggests that it was likely both the Flying V and Moderne made appearances as well, and that coveted feedback from retailers may have been the reason that the ugly duckling, the Moderne, didn't make it into production.

In Gibson's promotional trade magazine, the *Gibson Gazette*, the Flying V was the only guitar of the three patented designs to be featured, implying that the company had evaluated feedback from retailers and guitarists and deemed the V as the guitar most likely to find commercial success. Firing up the space-age propaganda machine, the *Gazette* declared,

> Russia has her satellite, perhaps to the embarrassment of the US, but the Gibson folks have come forth with their own "first" — the futuristic Flying V guitar. The swept-back, tapered

United States Patent Office

Des. 181,867
Patented Jan. 7, 1958

181,867

STRINGED MUSICAL INSTRUMENT

Theodore M. McCarty, Kalamazoo, Mich., assignor to Gibson, Inc., Kalamazoo, Mich., a corporation of Michigan

Application June 27, 1957, Serial No. 46,764
Term of patent 14 years
(Cl. D56—9)

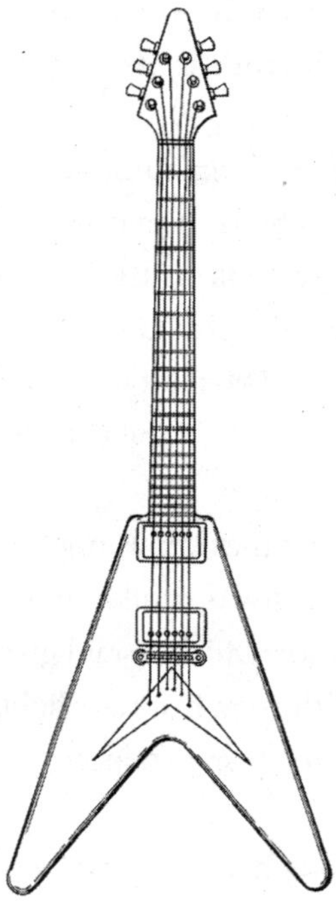

Fig. 1

Fig. 2

Fig. 1 is a top plan view of a stringed musical instrument, showing my new design, and

Fig. 2 is a side elevational view thereof.

The back of the article is substantially plain.

I claim:

The ornamental design for a stringed musical instrument, as shown and described.

References Cited in the file of this patent

UNITED STATES PATENTS

D. 17,888	Darbyshire	Nov. 22, 1887
D. 155,881	Evers	Nov. 8, 1949
D. 162,521	Crowle et al.	Mar. 20, 1951
D. 175,328	Van Pelt	Aug. 9, 1955
1,208,077	Ashley	Dec. 12, 1916

> lines of this really forward-looking instrument will be a real asset to the combo musician with a flair for showmanship.

I think it's safe to surmise that heavy metal maniacs like James Hetfield and Kirk Hammett of Metallica chose the Gibson Flying V not only for its sonic properties and playability factors, but also to add a little flair to their fire-breathing heavy metal "combos."

The Flying V came equipped with a humbucking pickup which, as the *Gibson Gazette* article claimed, "generates more power and creates greater clarity and sustaining tone while reducing hum from outside interference," qualities that would also be appealing to heavy metal and rock guitarists playing through stacks of cranked amplifiers at ear-bleeding volume.

> The V's mahogany body and neck, twin humbuckers and classic 24.75" scale length account for its huge sustain and skull-crushing tone. That said, it's as tonally versatile as the Les Paul, SG and others but it just looks right in a metal setting.
>
> (Ed Mitchell, "The Guitars That Built Rock: The Gibson Flying V.")

Another feature of the Flying V was that it was made from Korina wood (also known as limba), chosen because it was similar in quality to mahogany, a popular tone wood, but lighter in color, which would give the guitar a blond appearance, favored by the players of the day. Korina is lighter than mahogany and is easy to cut and shape because it doesn't splinter.

> The new Flying V's Korina body had two "legs" making the V shape, and these had gently rounded ends and formed a rounded 'crotch'. There was a very subtle curving of the squared shoulders where the neck joined the body. There was a deep rout cut into the front of the body, intended to stop the guitar slipping should the musician choose to play it sitting down."
>
> (Tony Bacon, *Flying V, Explorer, Firebird*, 23.)

> Given its looks, and pedigree as a Weapon of Metal Destruction, the Gibson Flying V should have been forged by some Norse

> God from molten lava and lightning bolts or some such. Its radical V-shaped body and arrow-profile headstock met the needs of rock and metal players looking for an eye-catching beast.
>
> (Ed Mitchell, "The Guitars That Built Rock: The Gibson Flying V.")

While it would eventually come to be known as, arguably, the electric guitar most closely associated with heavy metal thanks to iconic players like K.K. Downing of Judas Priest and Rudolf Schenker of the Scorpions — and even more so with his younger brother and one-time Scorpions bandmate, Michael, who would go on to inspire thousands of young metal heads to pick up a V thanks to his melodic and technically flawless precision lead guitar playing with bands UFO and MSG — it was actually a pair of blues guitarists who came onboard as early adopters of the Flying V.

Lonnie Mack used his V to great effect on his instrumental recording of Chuck Berry's "Memphis," and he can even be seen with it on the cover of his 1963 album *The Wham of That Memphis Man*. Mack is considered a pioneer of rock guitar soloing, and his thick, clean yet aggressive tones on "Memphis" are some of the earliest recorded examples of what the Flying V could do sonically.

Albert King wrangled gut wrenching, stinging blues guitar tones out of his '59 Flying V on his 1967 classic *Born Under a Bad Sign*, an album that would form the bedrock of the blues-inspired hard rock guitar stylings of players like Eric Clapton, Gary Moore, Paul Kossof of Free and many more. King even inspired great '70s blues rockers like Johnny Winter and Mountain's Leslie West to pick up a Flying V, though their guitar images would come to be more closely associated with other Gibson models, the Firebird and the Les Paul Junior, respectively.

The Gibson Flying V would get another shot at relevance when Gibson re-issued the model in 1966, thanks to the exposure provided by television appearances by Dave Davies of the Kinks, who picked one up in an American music store in 1965 while on tour, looking for a replacement for his Guild Starfire, which had been lost by an airline in transit. Davies paid the princely sum of two hundred dollars for the odd shaped instrument that had been left to collect dust, and a quick in-store airing of the proto-metal riff that kicks off the Kinks classic "All Day and All of the Night" was enough to convince Davies that he had found something special.

> That's how I came across the Flying V. In those days, you only carried one guitar each; we didn't have the luxury of four, five, or six each. I saw this funny looking guitar case in the back of a shop and opened it, and it was a Flying V. Then we were doing "Shindig!" and I thought it would look cool, so I put my arm through the V.
>
> — Dave Davies of the Kinks (*Vintage Guitar*, August 2023.)

Yes, Davies famously played his Flying V high on his chest, shoving his arm through the space between the lower bout wings of the V (the crotch, as it were); fortunately, this visually awkward approach to playing the instrument never caught on. God knows how many future metal heads would have shunned the Flying V had players like Michael Schenker taken such a dorky approach to the strumming of this treasured heavy metal talisman. But I guess when you're responsible for playing the riff on the recording to "You Really Got Me," you can play your guitar any way you bloody well please. Besides, to be fair to Davies, it's not like there were any manuals out there to see how to deal with this odd, unwieldy beast of an instrument.

All that aside, players like Marc Bolan of glam rock pioneers T. Rex, Keith Richards of the Rolling Stones, Paul Stanley of Kiss, and Mick Ralphs of Bad Company all figured out how to make the Flying V look hotter than hell and cool as ice in the '70s. Even Jimi Hendrix took his '67 V, complete with psychedelic paint job, to soaring heights of spaced-out blues-rock ecstasy. The "Love Drops" Flying V now hangs in New York's Metropolitan Museum of Art, the Met, with the following description of its unique accoutrements:

> Though known for playing Fender Stratocasters, Jimi Hendrix played this Gibson Flying V extensively from 1967 to 1969. He probably used it on his 1967 BBC Radio 1 sessions and 1968's Electric Ladyland, notably for his solo on "All Along the Watchtower." Hendrix modified the nut and strap button and painted the instrument himself using nail polish. When Hendrix gave the guitar to Mick Cox of the Irish band Eire Apparent in 1969, Cox refinished it in black and removed the original design. In the 1990s, session musician Dave Brewis acquired the instrument and restored Hendrix's original paint job.

Former Kiss guitarist Bruce Kulick, the man who kept Kiss's pyrotechnic flame (and fame) burning bright for over a decade starting in the mid-80s, was often seen with a Gibson (and as we'll see later, other iconic brands) in his gifted hands.

> I was always a fan of the Gibson line of guitars. I thought that the Flying V was a great design, seeing Hendrix play one. With Kiss it started with an off white 1983 Korina V, that appeared in some photos of me, as well as a yellow V-90 model. The '90s V-90 was a very lightweight ax, and featured in the video for "Unholy" our first single from *Revenge*. I did some club dates with it when we promoted the release. Standing and playing a Flying V is much easier than sitting, that's a fact! I also had a natural finish Korina V from 1983 that I used when Kiss did a promo performance for Monday Night Football!
>
> — Bruce Kulick

The Gibson Explorer was next in line, and it was designed as a companion instrument to the "already famous Flying V," according to the April–May issue of the *Gibson Gazette*. While the Explorer's body shape was different, it shared a similar design layout, with two humbucking pickups, each with a separate volume control, three-way toggle pickup selector, and a solitary tone knob. It was also very close in construction to the Flying V, with its 22-fret rosewood fingerboard, 24¾-inch scale length.

The Explorer had a slightly wider "waist" than the patented Futura, and an early version featured the same split-V headstock. Rick Derringer, who would go on to be associated with a number of pointy guitars over his storied career with Steely Dan, Johnny Winter, and as a solo star, owned one of these split-V headstock Explorers. Ultimately, Explorers would go on to have the now famous drooping headstock, which would become very closely associated with many pointy guitars to follow. These headstocks would come to be known as "hockey-stick headstocks" and would inspire the future headstock designs of companies like Kramer, Jackson, Ibanez, and many more to follow.

> The shape of the Explorer's body . . . was anything but conventional, and was perhaps even more radical than the Flying V. It's

> a pleasing mix of angularity and modern straight lines, with a wedge-shaped base and an elongated horn pushing beyond the lower cutaway.
>
> (Tony Bacon, *Flying V, Explorer, Firebird*, 28.)

The Explorer takes up a lot of real estate and, while more physically diminutive (but sonically *huge*) players like former Def Leppard guitarist Pete Willis and Runaways' ax mistress Lita Ford have wrestled and tamed the beast, it does seem to make a proportionate fit for musicians of a grander physical stature.

> Now the Explorer is such a great shape, perfect for a tall guitarist like me. First, I owned a Gibson Custom shop model from the early '90s and posed with it for many photos. Then I asked ESP Guitars in Japan to make me a white and black one with a mirror pickguard. I asked for Gibson vintage specs, and they came out amazing. They were featured quite a bit in my Kisstory from the *Revenge* era. Traveling with that model is not easy; the angles required make them need a very large guitar case, but just look at me on the cover of *Alive III*, with my angular body playing my black ESP Explorer. Symmetry at its best!
>
> — Bruce Kulick

Some speculate that the Explorer was named after America's first satellite, Explorer 1, a reference to an exciting future yet to be discovered. Fitting, because like the Flying V, the Explorer was another sales flop and wouldn't find acceptance among guitarists until later in that exciting future promised by the space-age hype of the late 1950s.

> Well, the earliest Explorer I ever saw being used on stage was Don Preston, who was Leon Russell's guitar player. I saw him play that Explorer at the Fillmore East at one of the greatest shows I've ever seen. I've seen everybody you can imagine, and I've seen thousands of shows. But the single greatest night of rock and roll in my life was that Leon Russell concert at the Fillmore. I've seen Hendrix and Zeppelin many times, all of them in their prime, and they're all great. But this night, this

> particular night, Don Preston was there, and I remember just saying to myself, man, that guy's playing an Explorer. You know, how cool! So that's the first time I ever saw one in use, and that was '69, '70, around there.
>
> — Jay Jay French

The Explorer has a lot of the same sonic qualities as most other Gibson-style solid-body models with a 24 ¾-inch scale, set neck, humbucking pickups, and stop tailpiece. It has the sustain of a Les Paul, and the midrange howl and bite of the SG or Flying V. The Explorer seems to respond very well to both active pickups like the ones made famous by EMG (think of James Hetfield's highly compressed and tight rhythm tone in Metallica) as well as the more dynamically open sound of the classic PAF pickups (like Allen Collins of Lynyrd Skynyrd on the cleaner side, or Dave Grohl of the Foo Fighters on the heavier rock side). "Some players feel that the extended lower bass bout and extra body mass below the bridge enhance its bass response, but that could just be a psychologically influenced observation," says Chris Gill on GuitarWorld.com.

Eric Clapton had a modified '58 Explorer that has been the subject of some contentious debate. One unique feature of the guitar that grabbed his interest was the shortened bass bout (the upper back horn). Clapton initially believed that this came as a result of the guitar being an original prototype, but that theory was eventually tossed out, as the guitar turned out to be modified by the previous owner. Perhaps this is why, in a famous ad for Music Man amplifiers, Clapton has the upper back horn of his Explorer obscured by his billowing shirt sleeve; to misquote a John Hiatt lyric, it must have broken his heart to be a star with a mutilated (but still perfectly fine sounding) guitar.

The Edge from Ireland's most famous musical export, U2, is another famous Explorer player, having obtained his on a family trip to America.

> In 1978, a seventeen-year-old Irishman went on a vacation to New York City with his family. He had just recently joined a new music group and on the trip had his eyes open for any guitar stores in the city where he might acquire a new instrument with which to play in the band. He had a certain guitar in mind, but upon entering Stuyvesant Music Inc he happened upon

something that caught his eye, "I just picked it up in the store and it felt so great, this is it. I actually went in to buy, I think I was going to buy a Les Paul, but I just fell in love with this guitar."

It was of course a second run model 1976 Gibson Explorer, and the young man was none other than The Edge. Once he played it, he knew he had to have it, and though it cost him

> a small fortune $248.40, he gladly plunked it down on the counter and made his way out of the store. Once he made it back to Ireland, his bandmates were a bit bewildered by the [sight] of his latest acquisition as he was to recall, "I brought it back and I was slightly like . . . it's a little strange looking . . . are the guys in the band gonna look at it and go 'what?' . . . there's a few strange looks for the first day, but everyone just loved the sound of it. I think it became like a signature look, no one else was playing Explorers at that point, and so quite soon it became the thing we were famous for. Apart from a few other things obviously."
>
> (Iconic Axes.)

From the early U2 classic "I Will Follow" through to later smashes like "Beautiful Day," that Explorer has been an important part of the Edge's guitar arsenal, giving sonic weight and thick yet chiming clarity to his imaginative use of guitar effects.

Two of the most famous Explorer players in hard rock and heavy metal are James Hetfield of Metallica and Matthias Jabs of the Scorpions, each of whom encapsulates the most famous traits of the instrument — the ability to deliver thick yet articulate midrange punch for power chords, and chest-pounding riffing (Hetfield), as well as stinging, singing, sustain-drenched lead guitar solos (Jabs). Concertgoers could expect to see a myriad of Gibson Flying Vs and Explorers in action when Hetfield or Jabs were on stage with their respective guitar partners (Kirk Hammett and Rudolf Schenker), — as well as other company's variations on these classic axes. Sure, the odd humbucker-equipped Stratocaster or Les Paul would be broken out as the years progressed, but those classic Gibson shapes are the ones most closely associated with these tandem guitar terrors.

With only 22 Explorers purported to be made between '58 and '59, they are some of the most collectable and expensive guitars in the world. In 1959, with only 17 Flying Vs and 3 Explorers shipped, these modern designs for Gibson seemed destined to be window display curios for most retailers; instruments that might draw attention to guitars that could actually sell.

Gibson would dust itself off from the failure of the V and Explorer (with the Moderne not even going into production, although Billy Gibbons may or may not have an "original" prototype one, depending on who you talk to, and your appetite for mysterious conjecture) and turn its attention to improving its factory via a $400,000 expansion, with a focus on reviving their Les Paul models while also pushing the new low-end solid-body Melody Maker guitars introduced in 1959. While initially considered student models, they were still high-quality instruments with great playability and tone and are now highly coveted.

The Les Paul Junior, Standard, and Custom models were given a makeover with a sharp, modern, double-cutaway design. When Les Paul found the instruments to be lacking and requested that his name be removed from the line, these thin bodied, double cutaways were dubbed the SG series (for Solid Guitar). While these models are undoubtedly considered classic shapes, their pointy horns do give them a distinctively wicked look. The SG's most famous proponent in hard rock music is Angus Young from AC/DC, who has rocked them exclusively throughout the Australian group's 50-plus year journey along the "Highway to Hell." Players like Glen Buxton and Michael Bruce from the Alice Cooper Band; Jake E. Lee of Ozzy Osbourne, Badlands, and Red Dragon Cartel fame; and Carlos Cavazo from heavy metal's first Billboard chart-toppers Quiet Riot are just a few hard rockers who have helped to associate the SG's shape with the devil's favorite music. If not exactly a pointy guitar, the Gibson SG is most certainly pointy adjacent.

The SG acquired its new name in 1963, the same year a bold new design came roaring down Gibson's drag strip. Still trying to win the space race with Fender in 1962, Gibson president Ted McCarty hired outside designer Ray Dietrich, a legendary automobile designer and company owner who had worked with Lincoln, Ford, and Chrysler, to create the Gibson Firebird guitar, as well as the Thunderbird bass, an instrument that could rival the success Fender was having with their Precision and Jazz basses.

> Fender owned the electric guitar market in the early '60s. Gibson on the other hand couldn't catch a break. The single cutaway Les Paul models went the way of the dinosaurs — in favor of the new SG body models — while the Flying V and Explorer tryouts had been received with all the enthusiasm of the Sinclair C5. Even Gretsch and Rickenbacker were kicking Gibson's arse

> thanks to Beatles John and George. They desperately needed a win.
>
> (Ed Mitchell, "The Guitars That Built Rock: The Gibson Firebird.")

The Firebird and Thunderbird series built upon foundations laid with the failed Explorer designs, but delivered them in a sexier, more rounded contour, with a distinctive firebird logo on the pickguard suggesting the elegance and showy appeal of a high-end automobile. Four Firebird designs were offered, the I, III, V, and VII; the Thunderbirds were numbered II and IV, picking up some of the sequential slack, but there was never a number VI.

> At its launch in late 1963, the "reverse" Firebird was available in four formats, kicking off with the single mini-humbucker-loaded I model as used by Eric. This no-frills edition came spec'd with a volume and tone knob and a combined bridge / tailpiece, although you could order it with a vibrato unit. Production costs were kept in check with an unbound rosewood fingerboard and simple dot inlays.
>
> Next up was the twin-pickup version — the confusingly named Firebird III — which had two volume and two tone controls and a three-way pickup selector toggle switch. It came with the same combined bridge / tailpiece as the Firebird I but the vibrato unit was standard issue.
>
> The Firebird V also featured two mini-humbuckers with the four controls and three-way switch, but the hardware was upgraded to a deluxe vibrato with an engraved cover plate and a tune-o-matic bridge. The single bound rosewood fingerboard was pimped with trapezoid fingerboard inlays. . . . The final model in the range was the Firebird VII, the real purty three-pickup top-of-the-line edition with the same gold hardware, bound ebony fingerboard and block inlays found on the Gibson Les Paul and SG Custom models.
>
> (Ed Mitchell, "The Guitars That Built Rock: The Gibson Firebird.")

Of important structural note is that these were the first Gibson solid-body designs to feature "through neck" construction. A multilaminate mahogany and walnut section ran through the length of the guitar from the headstock to the strap button, with two mahogany wings glued on completing the shape.

> The body shape was sleek and asymmetrical, coming something like an Explorer with curves — there's no mistaking that angled parallelogram — although the Firebird was an altogether more exciting design. The elongated shape had a horn-less upper section that makes the lower horn appear to stick out further than it really did. The result was an almost-unbalanced but quite appealing look, and it was that that led to these original models becoming known among collectors and players as the 'reverse body' or simply 'reverse' Firebirds.
>
> (Tony Bacon, *Flying V, Explorer, Firebird*, 36.)

The reverse headstock design on the Firebird and Thunderbird was unusual at the time, and like the drooping hockey-stick headstock of the Explorer, would go on to be a major influence on pointy guitar culture in years to follow. The low E-string fed the furthest tuner, the opposite to how a traditional Fender headstock was fed. The tuners were Kluson banjo-style tuners that protruded from the back of the headstock — a weird and, frankly, unwieldy choice, but one that I have come to find intriguing as a Firebird owner.

> Why are these guitars described as "reverse" Firebirds? Well, unlike a Fender Strat, which has a longer body horn on the bass side of the neck and a short horn on the treble side, the Firebird's layout is reversed with the longer horn closest to the floor. That's not the only unusual thing about the F-bird. The headstock is also reversed — something that became all the thing in the hair metal and spandex '80s — it plays host to a set of chunky, and borderline bloody useless, banjo tuners. Even by '60s standards this guitar was a bit weird.
>
> (Ed Mitchell, "The Guitars That Built Rock: The Gibson Firebird.")

The Firebird series marked the first time Gibson offered custom colors, an option Fender had been offering since 1956, using DuPont paint to flash up the standard brown, blond, or sunburst finishes.

> Fender were riding the crest of the surf music craze with the Stratocaster, Jaguar and Jazzmaster models. And it wasn't just about the sound. In the late '50s, Leo Fender and his crew had the brilliant idea of offering their guitars in custom DuPont paint, the same glossy stuff used to finish cars rolling out of Detroit. This made their already futuristic guitars look sexy as hell. You see, Gibson stuff came in gold or black . . . and eventually, cherry sunburst. Alternatively, you could order your Fender in hues like Lake Placid Blue, Dakota Red, Shoreline Gold, Sherwood Green Metallic."
>
> (Ed Mitchell, "The Guitars That Built Rock: The Gibson Firebird.")

With the ascent of the Firebird and Thunderbird instruments, Gibson began offering finishes such as Cardinal Red, Ember Red, Frost Blue, Golden Mist Poly (metallic), Heather Poly, Inverness Green Poly, Kerry Green, Pelham Blue Poly, Polaris White, and Silver Mist — "ten beautiful Gibson custom colors — one will suit your personality perfectly," as the pamphlet attests. These acrylic lacquer colors, inspired by the flashy automobiles of the day, offered players "that finished, professional touch — the extra drama and flair that sells a combo!" The idea that a player's instrument could serve as an avatar for their personality and as a crucial part of their art would go on to have an incredible impact on the future of electric guitar marketing and, cynically, how to make an instrument saleable.

While these new models sold in higher numbers than the Explorer, Gibson found that the instrument was a challenge to make — and an expensive challenge at that — due to its through-neck design and the potential for breakage where the head met the neck, as well as the time-consuming intricacies of the carving and routing for electronics. There were also rumblings from Fender that the Firebird was a bit too close for design comfort to their Jaguar and Jazzmaster models. In 1965, Gibson adopted a more conventional body shape for the Firebird, essentially flipping the original design to create what would come to be known as the Non-Reverse Firebird. These came with different pickups, the famed P-90 single coils, a glued in neck, and a more traditional, Fender-style headstock and tuners. This new line was notably less expensive but still failed to deliver the commercial home run Gibson was hoping for. To this author's heavy metal eye, the non-reverse body shape doesn't deliver the same heroic punch and seems more suitable for the jangly eccentricities of alternative rock, or even the grunge scene that would come to cast a shadow over hard rock and heavy metal in the '90s. It's funny how such a seemingly simple alteration in geometry can shape an entirely different emotional reaction to an instrument. I shudder a bit every time I pass a Non-Reverse Firebird in a music store, probably because it reminds me of an old Fender Mustang or Jazzmaster in the hands of someone like Nirvana's Kurt Cobain or Mudhoney's Mark Arm in those days when grunge music had impaled my beloved hard rock and metal upon the pointy headstocks of a bygone era. Still, in the hands of Brian Jones from the Rolling Stones, Steve Winwood in his days with Traffic, and blues great Clarence "Gatemouth" Brown, a Non-Reverse Firebird can erase those painful grunge memories and evoke an undeniable classic sense of cool.

Alright, back to happier pointy guitar memories.

The late, great Steve Clark of Def Leppard was the first player I can recall who inspired a desire to acquire a Firebird of my own. As Simon Bradley of *Guitarist Magazine* in the U.K. so perfectly stated in 2002, Clark was "easily the coolest man to have ever wielded a Gibson Firebird in anger." Steve had a number of the beauties, including a gorgeous cardinal red VII model outfitted with a Kahler tremolo system, and a 1964 single pickup Firebird I that was nicknamed Lorelei (after his fiancée at the time, Lorelei Shellist), and according to DefLeppard.com served as Steve's "songwriting guitar." There was also a Lorelei II that was taken out on the road for live shows, and it may be surmised that this is the two pickup model that Steve used to breathtaking effect during his solo-guitar spot on the 1987–1988 world tour for the *Hysteria* album, captured in the stunning concert video *Live: In the Round, in Your Face*.

The in-the-round setup of an open stage in the center of an arena's floor offered every spectator a front-of-the-stage view and was perfectly suited for the young, fully energized Def Leppard. (You'd have to be young and fully energized to run around a stage of that size, especially considering the grueling schedule of over two hundred shows performed on that particular run!)

Hearing Steve's graceful and elegiac prelude to the Leppard classic deep cut "Gods of War," his high-water mark as a composer and riff writer. The image of Steve with his low-slung Firebird hung around his neck, staking out his claim on that magical night in Denver, Colorado, a moment forever captured on celluloid, made me a Firebird fan for life. The futurism of the elongated shape that seemed to bend space and time mirrored the way Steve's use of the Kahler tremolo bent his guitar strings in a cascade of droning notes that filled the arena air, blending into the plumes of cigarette and pot smoke to create a heavy metal Narnia that I could explore through the portal of my VCR and well-worn VHS copy of that show. It was a world where maybe, one day, I could play guitar on a stage like that. Sadly, Steve Clark slipped this mortal coil on January 8, 1991, but it is no mere cliché to say that his spirit lives on as the embodiment of the perfect rock-n-roll guitar hero.

As fate, destiny, or just dumb luck would have it, I would one day get a chance to acquire a Gibson Firebird through an endorsement, and play it on arena stages, including a few dates opening for Def Leppard with my band Trapper. Our amazing lead vocalist, Emm Gryner, was a long-time friend of the band, and one of the few people invited into their tight inner circle as a musical collaborator. On our first date in Montreal at the famed Bell Centre arena, I made a point of walking around the backstage area with my tobacco-finished Firebird around my neck, looking at the multitude of road cases emblazoned with the Def Leppard logo and making my way up the ramps to the massive stage for our soundcheck. Images of Hysteria-era Def Leppard flickered on the digital screens in the background, looming large over us as we lived our arena rock fantasies — fantasy becoming reality and, for me, Montreal, Quebec, becoming Denver, Colorado. We were playing with one of our favorite bands, friendly ghosts of our pasts still informing our hard rocking present, with a Gibson Firebird slung low on my frame. Thank you, Steve Clark.

The funny thing about a Firebird is that it doesn't really *sound* the way it *looks*. Firebirds come equipped with mini-humbucker pickups, and they provide a sound that is a mix between a Gibson PAF humbucker and a Fender Telecaster, giving it a slightly thinner tone with more high end, although still not as sparkly or bright as a Tele or Stratocaster. I acquired my Firebird as part of an endorsement deal that I secured while playing guitar for Grammy award–winning, multiplatinum Canadian superstar Nelly Furtado. I was so thrilled to get a Firebird to live out those Steve Clark–Def Leppard inspired arena rock dreams, but was very surprised when I plugged my gorgeous guitar (albeit very neck heavy, which made holding it and keeping it in tune a bit precarious!) into my Marshall JCM800 that the tone was less than desirable — very squishy, and lacking the power and punch I was looking for. This, of course, was another lesson along the path of my career. Each guitar is unique, and sometimes the best approach is to let the instrument tell you what it wants to do, rather than to expect an instrument to be perfect in an application it's not designed for.

Then again, I wouldn't be writing this book if people like Eddie Van Halen, Grover Jackson, Wayne Charvel, and many more innovators took that tack — customization lies at the heart of the pointy guitar story. But for Johnny Winter, perhaps the most famous and inspirational Firebird player, it was a perfect visual and musical fit.

> I was initially attracted to the Firebird because I liked the way it looked . . . and when I played it I discovered I liked the way it sounded, too. The Firebird is the best of all worlds. It feels like a Gibson, but it sounds closer to a Fender than most other Gibsons. I was never a big fan of humbucking pickups, but the mini-humbuckers on the Firebird have a little more bite and treble.
>
> —Johnny Winter (Ed Mitchell, "The Guitars That Built Rock: The Gibson Firebird.")

I once saw my friend Gilby Clarke playing a Firebird live in concert at Toronto's Massey Hall, a deviation from his usual Les Paul or Telecaster:

> Johnny Winter was the Firebird guy. I really do believe that Johnny Winter can make anything sound good. I had a '76 a long time ago that was stock. It was black. And why I got rid of it, I'll never know — I probably didn't have enough money and just sold something. [*laughs*] But a Firebird does have a different sound. There is a bit more "clang" to it, you know?
>
> — Gilby Clarke of Guns N' Roses, Heart, and MC5

Tom Keifer, lead vocalist and guitarist for the Philadelphia-based, Bon Jovi–discovered blues and roots-inspired hard rock band Cinderella, has been known to play a number of classic Gibson instruments, including a gorgeous red Firebird VII, which was inspired by his love of Johnny Winter.

> I didn't even realize how big he was in my life until the news [of Winter's recent passing] hit me . . . I started thinking back, and to be honest, I am still kind of broken up about his passing. He was a huge influence on me — that blues element and the slide guitar and the amount of fire that he had in his playing and singing. And certainly his use of the resonator guitar, the National Steel, was something that he really inspired me to pick up. And the day after he died, I had an epiphany in that as much as I have always named him as an influence and always realized what an influence he was, it kind of dawned on me that he was one of the biggest — if not the biggest — in terms of some of the things that were unique to Cinderella like the slide guitars and resonator guitars and the bright fiery tone of the Gibson Firebird [guitar] that I have been playing for years.
>
> — Tom Keifer of Cinderella (*Lithium Magazine*, 2014.)

Phil Manzanera is another famous Firebird player; his crystalline and elegantly compressed guitar lines reveal themselves in high fidelity on Roxy Music albums like *Stranded*, *Siren*, and *Avalon*.

> What's particularly good about this guitar is it's always been great for recording. The tuning aspect is not brilliant, but for recording purposes . . . it just likes going onto analogue tape. And so this was used in quite a lot of the Roxy songs — I'd use this for something on every album.
>
> — Phil Manzanera of Roxy Music
> (Jamie Dickson, *Guitar World*.)

Companies like Hamer, Jackson, and ESP would later go on to take the famous Firebird shape and modernize it with pointy headstocks, different pickup combinations, locking tremolo units, and other hard rock and metal accoutrements for players like Robbin Crosby of Ratt and Slash from Guns N' Roses, creating instruments whose sonics matched the wild yet sensuous shape of the Firebird. On the Thunderbird bass side, players like Tom Hamilton from Aerosmith, Tom Petersson of Cheap Trick, Pete Overend Watts from Mott the Hoople, and perhaps the most famous Thunderbird (literally) high flyer of '70s hard rock, Pete Way of UFO, would make the instrument a ubiquitous outlier bass on stages around the world, influencing latter-day hard rockers like Nikki Sixx of Mötley Crüe, Brian Wheat of Tesla, and Eric Stacy of Faster Pussycat to rise from up from the ashes of obscurity and soar into the blue skies of rock-n-roll fame. It's safe to say that these '80s rockers may have been inspired by more than just Pete Way's sound and stage swagger. As the late, great Way wrote in his biography *A Fast Ride Out of Here: Confessions of Rock's Most Dangerous Man*:

> Nikki Sixx [of Mötley Crüe] told me that I was his hero and how he used to watch me do this and that, and would copy me. . . . It was an odd feeling for me, being viewed as a kind of elder statesman and also to see Nikki get up to pretty much all of the things that I had done what seemed almost a lifetime earlier with UFO. I really am talking about as much excess, women, booze and drugs as one can possibly imagine.

And so, from experiments ranging from total failures to moderate successes, the space-age vision of Gibson's futuristic Flying V, Explorer, and Firebird models would set the stage for a wild-shaped guitar renaissance in the 1970s that would see companies like Hamer, Dean, B.C. Rich, and Ibanez build upon these classic designs (with sometimes litigious results) and ultimately usher in the pointy-guitar explosion of the 1980s.

CHAPTER 3

HAMER GUITARS — LOOKING BACK, POINTING FORWARD

The pointy guitars of the '80s sometimes get a bad rap, as if they're garish aberrations of the early Modernistic Gibson designs of the '50s. And to be honest, by the end of the '80s the market was saturated with them, and one could understand why some people felt this way. Pointy guitars had become something of a marketing cliché, an accessory deemed necessary to fit the expectations of record companies, music television networks, and guitar magazine ads. Luthier Dave Reimer has opinions about how '80s hard rock grew into an oft maligned stereotype.

> Music can be like that, where people are afraid. "Oh, our last record really did well, I'm afraid to change." Then you're not making rock n roll, my friend. It isn't rock n roll. Initially, that's what a pointy guitar meant — innovation and excitement. And then it almost instantly didn't mean anything anymore. If you're just strapping it on because it's the thing to do to make you look like the band that just had the hit record, and if you're spraying up your hair and putting on your pointy guitar to be like somebody else without any soul, you're missing the whole point. And

> the original point of making that V and the Explorer was to do something different.
>
> — Dave Reimer of Lee Aaron's band and founder of Reimer Guitars

Looking at the '70s, there is a logical line of evolution in guitar making that runs parallel with what was happening in rock music as it built upon its past to become something new. As rock moved into the '80s, it became louder, bigger, brighter, and more technically demanding. The popularity of angular axes really started in the late '60s and into the '70s, as players like Dave Davies, Jimi Hendrix, Rick Derringer, Michael Schenker, Rick Nielsen, Allen Collins, Keith Richards, Paul Stanley, Ace Frehley, Johnny Winter, and more were seen with Vs, Explorers, and Firebirds on stages around the world. The popularity of these instruments continued to grow fed by a desire among intrepid young guitar builders and enthusiasts wanting to capture the original quality of craftmanship found in Gibson and Fender guitars before the companies were taken over by bigger corporations. For Dave Reimer, who has played with Bryan Adams, Headpins, Barney Bentall and the Legendary Hearts, and with me in Lee Aaron's band, "It was a way to take the past and move it into the future."

> These people [musicians and guitar makers] were all individuals who were not afraid to keep moving, to look for the next thing. They didn't phone their masters and ask "What's selling? Let's do that!" They didn't write a song and say, "Oh this will be a hit because it's like *this*." It was like, "Let's just be different." And that's the best of America to me — there was so much amazing innovation. The original point of the making of the V and the Explorer was to do something different. And the minute you've lost that spirit, you've lost what the guitar is.
>
> — Dave Reimer

By the 1970s, working musicians in the know were seeking out '50s Les Pauls, Stratocasters, Telecasters, and — most relevant to this book — Flying Vs and Explorers for their superior playability and sound. To most musicians, older guitars were still being referred to as "used" guitars, but to the tone-chasing savant guitarist these guitars were *vintage*.

Paul Hamer of Chicago, Illinois, was one of those young guitarists who fell under the sway of the Beatles on that magical Sunday night in 1964 when four young mop-tops turned the *Ed Sullivan Show* stage into a platform unmatched — even by social media standards — to this day. A few weeks later, after scrounging money from his paper route and his mother generously donating some S&H Green Stamps, he was the owner of a Harmony acoustic guitar. Frustrated by the antiquated guitar instruction of the '60s, which involved an agonizingly slow process of teaching notes first, rather than those glorious full chords that the Beatles had been strumming, the guitar went in the closet for a few years, until an offer of free lessons from the Village School of Folk Music lit the fire for Paul once again. (Another young musician by the name of Dean Zelinsky was also a student at the school — take note of that name.)

Ask any rock music historian about influential, perception-changing musical events in America, and you will likely hear mention of the fabled Woodstock Music and Art Fair. Bearing witness to not only the folk music of Arlo Guthrie and Joan Baez he already loved, but the powerful electric guitar sounds of Mountain, Johnny Winter, the Who, and finally Jimi Hendrix, a young Paul Hamer (one of only eighteen thousand who actually paid to see the event, as opposed to the estimated "half a million strong" gate crashers that Joni Mitchell sang about) had fundamentally changed.

Upon finishing high school and abandoning college after one semester to pursue musical interests, Hamer would go on to take a position with the U.S. Postal Service, the result of successfully completing a civil service exam prior to attending college. His successful interview was no doubt helped by his decision to tie his radical long hair into a ponytail and drop it down the back of his coat. The steady income that a mailman's salary provided him afforded Paul the ability to purchase and resell high-quality electric guitars. Scouring pawnshops and music stores in the seediest parts of the Chicago area, Hamer unearthed hidden treasures that could be sold through a growing network of guitar traders who were hip to this still underground scene, who understood that the value of vintage instruments were ever-growing in the estimation of the budding rock stars who were starting to fill arenas and concert halls all over America.

Hamer had followed a tried-and-true path — acquire an electric guitar, find like-minded friends, start a rock-n-roll band. But where some changed the course of history by going on to become famous rock stars, Paul's path led him to begin seeking out, buying, and selling old guitars to English rock bands like Wishbone Ash, who toured the U.S., hungry to devour all elements of American culture, including hard to find American-made guitars. Ultimately, Paul would open his own music store and take a DIY approach to learning how to repair guitars, becoming the first official warranty repair provider for Gibson outside of the factory. Through this process of deep diving into the inner workings of the Gibson guitar-making process, Paul was inspired to build his first guitar, combining the handcrafted quality of those early Gibsons with a forward-thinking desire to create something new. He aimed for vintage quality with modern appointments for the modern player seeking their own take on a vintage sound.

It was Gibson's failed Explorer shape, seen in the hands of Leon Russell's guitarist Delaney Bramlett at a mid-70s music festival in Iowa, that inspired the first Hamer electric guitar. Paul fell under the sway of the angles and lines of the Explorer. As fate would have it, a young band from Illinois by the name of Fuse was on the bill that day. Fuse featured in its ranks two young musicians, guitarist Rick Nielsen and bassist Tom Petersson, who would go on to loom large in the history of Hamer guitars. Eventually Nielsen and Petersson would form Cheap Trick, a rock band that in many ways mirrored the vintage-inspired yet forward-thinking aesthetic of Hamer guitars; a band whose love of the British adaptation of American blues was combined with the burgeoning power pop of late-era Beatles and the heavy rock of bands like the Who and the Move. It's safe to say that both Cheap Trick and Hamer have, for the most part, followed a course of putting quality of craftsmanship and adherence to artistic purity ahead of crass commercial concerns.

> There was something about Hamer and the association with Cheap Trick, because they were kind of genre busting. They came along just as punk rock was about to happen. They certainly weren't a punk band, but they had a lot of those same kind of attitudes or, you know, it was rock that was on the edge. Something about Hamer reviving the '50s outlaw guitar, which those Explorers were. Nobody played them, and if you did, somebody would have thought you were some kind of alien space guy.
>
> — Dave Reimer

A long-standing connection has existed between Paul Hamer and Rick Nielsen from back in Paul's high school days, when he would see Rick and Tom Petersson playing as Grim Reaper at the Electric Theatre in Chicago. That band would become Fuse, which landed a deal with Epic Records before morphing into Cheap Trick. Nielsen had access to high-quality instruments through his parents, who owned a music store, which was the Midwest importer of the Mellotron, an early tape-based keyboard heard on Beatles albums that could emulate various orchestral sounds. Seeing Nielsen and his band on stage with '50s Gibson Les Pauls, a Hammond B-3 organ, and a tower of Sound City amplifier stacks made an impression on Hamer.

In 1972, Nielsen and his wife were living in Philadelphia and expecting their first child. Nielsen, now playing with a band called the Nazz, was looking to sell his '50s Les Paul sunburst to raise some money, just as Hamer had sought out Rick's father to get his number to see if the boys in Fuse were interested in selling any of that beautiful vintage. The result of this connection was a transaction that arguably changed the course of pointy guitar history. For a sum of $2500 (a healthy amount of money back in '72!), Rick sold Paul that '50s sunburst. As Nielsen states (with his characteristic acerbic wit) in his foreword to Steve Matthes and Joe Moffett's absolutely excellent resource *The Ultimate: An Illustrated History of Hamer Guitars*:

> Paul's purchase of the guitar financially allowed me to move back to Rockford so our first son could be born there. Paul's reselling of it offered the seed money for Hamer Guitars. And now, nearly 40 years later, I'm almost to the point of forgiving the both of them.

Jol Dantzig is the other key player on the early Hamer team. Jol was born into a musical family in Chicago, Illinois, and received early training on the piano and violin before having an electric guitar epiphany when he heard "Greensleeves" being played by a camp counselor on an amplified electric guitar. As a kid fascinated with cars and the mechanics of how things work, it was transformative to the point of Jol pushing his parents to get him his first electric guitar, a Fender Duo-Sonic. More inspiration followed as Jol's musical tastes developed from the early instrumental rock of the Ventures, to the inevitable discovery of the Beatles catalog, and then on to the darker, rougher sounds of the Rolling Stones. Asking his local music store to find him a teacher who could instruct him in the dark arts of rock n roll, Jol would soon come under the tutelage of a young Mike Bloomfield, who would go on to inspire countless hard-rock guitarists with his own electric take on Chicago blues.

Dantzig's growing obsession with rock-n-roll guitar aligned perfectly with his interest in fast cars and the mechanics of how they worked. It was at a local hobby shop in Evanston, Illinois, where Jol met Gary Gand, a fellow long-haired music-and-car afficionado and mutual friend of Paul Hamer. It was Gand's father, Bob, who offered Hamer his free lessons at his Village School of Folk Music in Deerfield, Illinois.

As Matthes and Moffett tell us in *The Ultimate*, the offer came as a way of saying thanks for a ground-breaking precedent that had been established thanks to the efforts of Paul Hamer's father, an attorney who had successfully fought a policy set out by Deerfield High School that essentially banned boys from having "extreme hair styles, work jeans, sweat shirts and heavy boots." Mr. Hamer's argument that the policy infringed on constitutional freedoms protecting individual expression directly resulted not only in the reinstatement of Paul Hamer and Gary Gand to their high school classes (both having been kicked out for their refusal to cut their hair), but also effectively ended prohibitive school dress codes across the country.

And so, in a moment when rock n roll, electric guitars, fast cars, and social subversion met, Gary Gand suggested Jol Dantzig as a bass player to Paul Hamer in their band Bunion Stew (gotta love those '70s band names). Bunion Stew would play around the Midwest nightclub scene, becoming acquainted with great players who would later become well-known Hamer-guitar endorsers. Like Hamer, Dantzig had an entrepreneurial spirit that saw him seeking out pawnshop guitar prizes that he could purchase, clean up, and then sell to suburban garage-band kids for a tidy profit. When Bunion Stew ran its course, Hamer looked toward becoming more involved in the business of selling guitars. In 1972, Hamer opened Northern Prairie Music with partner Craig Hendee. The shop served as a retail store for used guitars, a repair shop, and a studio for music lessons. Many of the used instruments the store was selling needed set up and repairs, and it was here where Hamer honed his skills through trial and error. Dantzig, who was now a technician for Music Dealer Service in Chicago, would stop by and help with some of the repair work. Paul's interest in banjos, mandolins, and bluegrass would meld with Jol's electric guitar expertise and his love of hard rock music like Black Sabbath, Free, and Humble Pie. The repair and finishing side of the business became more and more appealing to Hamer, and he began making significant orders from Gibson's factory in Kalamazoo, Michigan, for authentic binding and finishing materials. A skilled elder craftsmen named John "Monty" Montgomery was brought into service to apply his knowledge of woodworking and instrument repair, and Hamer credits his skill, patience, and good-humored nature as a teacher for Hamer Guitars' ultimate success. As Dantzig was hanging around the store more and more, and because he was earning enough money with his other ventures (which included working as a machine shop foreman, selling used guitars for profit, and gigging), he was able to take advantage of an offer to join Northern Prairie Music as a partner, at a time when the company was well-positioned for success.

The timing and place setting were perfect for Northern Prairie to capitalize on the nascent market for vintage instruments. They were located close to a major American metropolitan market with a very active music scene — Chicago. In the early '70s, the general perception of the now Norlin-owned Gibson and CBS-owned Fender was that the quality of the instruments had suffered in the name of mass production and cost-cutting efforts that sacrificed quality to increase the volume of guitars going out the door. When Gibson noticed that Northern Prairie was ordering a vast amount of supplies, Paul and Jol were invited to the factory in Kalamazoo to discuss the possibility of Northern Prairie becoming the first official Gibson warranty and repair facility outside of the Gibson factory. While initially very excited to meet some the craftsmen who had worked on the coveted guitars of the '50s, the duo were shocked at the rate at which guitars were being manufactured and sent out for retail, with little concern for quality control. It seemed to Hamer and Dantzig that Gibson had become out of touch with what higher profile, professional musicians were looking for in a quality guitar.

Despite the importance guitar repair held for the business, and the love and care they put into that work, the main thrust for Northern Prairie was still vintage instrument sales, and it was through these sales that Paul Hamer would develop relationships and devise systems for connecting with high-profile rock-guitar players of the '70s and '80s.

> To this end, Hamer had developed an effective means of gaining access to shows. For example, he knew the location of the stage door in an alley behind the Aragon Ballroom and he and any of his friends would simply walk in with briefcases, business cards, and guitar cases as if they belonged there, usually stating they were bringing instruments for the band. Appearing "authorized" they were never questioned by security, who were more concerned with the front entrances. Once the bands arrived, Hamer and his comrades would be quickly ushered back to the dressing rooms and would be given passes to come and go as they pleased. . . .
>
> Dantzig's stint as a tech at Music Dealer Service, a company that did repairs for all the stores in Chicago as well as the big touring acts, came in handy at this point as well. "Music Dealer Service had concert sound systems and manufactured the cabinets too. Three days a week I'd drive their 28 ft truck for pickups and deliveries, which gave me access to a lot of stores and concert venues. You meet the security people as a professional — it was very helpful to meet musicians. Between Paul and I, it was cake to get into a show."
>
> (Steve Matthes and Joe Moffett, *The Ultimate*, 25.)

With these types of hookups at major venues in the Chicago area, Hamer and Dantzig were developing a reputation as being the go-to vintage guitar guys, providing instruments for bands like Jethro Tull, UFO, Wishbone Ash, Humble Pie, Rick Derringer, and Savoy Brown, as well as the great Jeff Beck.

> I was taking vintage guitars and amps backstage to sell to the big touring acts. They were our best customers. When we started making guitars we brought them along as well, just to make our vintage shop more interesting to the players. We weren't thinking about starting a guitar company, but as we started getting orders from rock stars I thought there was a market for them. In the beginning my partner Paul and I were just going out to shows, and because I was a gigging musician, I knew how to talk to the guitar players. This is when

> the marketing guys at the big companies were still in their "jazz-in-suits" mode. We were tuned in to what was going on, and that appealed to rock players — I spoke their language and, unlike the big company people, I took these musicians seriously.
>
> —Jol Dantzig, Hamer Guitars

When Jan Akkerman, guitarist for the popular Dutch progressive rock band Focus, sought out Paul Hamer's assistance in swapping out some guitar pickups and adding a maple top to his Les Paul Recording model, the result was not only an amazing sounding guitar, but a visually pleasing one, thanks to its bound top and cherry sunburst finish. With Monty's suggestion to add a flame-maple veneer top and Akkerman playing the guitar on recordings and in concert halls around the world, Hamer and Dantzig had proof of concept. Players wanted guitars with quality that harkened back to the glory days of Gibson and Fender during the 1950s, but were also open to guitars with a classic but decidedly new look.

When Hamer, Dantzig, and Montgomery put together a custom flying V (with a body made by another local builder, Jim Beach, and a flamed-maple top by Hamer), it wasn't quite the tonal success that Akkerman's modified Les Paul had been, but it was another step in the right direction and a realization that it would be easier to start building these concept guitars from scratch.

But just before that, another more important modification was to take place. In 1973, Dantzig designed and built himself a flying-V bass that would set him apart with an instrument that looked more like something a lead guitarist would use. With the help and guidance of Monty, Hamer took a Gibson EB-3 bass, cut it down, and added flying-V wings, while also sharpening its headstock to a point. Flashy crown inlays were put into the fingerboard, and the instrument was painted black with white binding, creating a visually stunning outline. A tremolo arm completed the look, and Dantzig's use of the instrument with his band Heartbreaker would get live music fans (and other musicians) talking. Hamer and Dantzig would also start showing the unique instrument to their growing client base of rock stars backstage, laying the groundwork for the formation of a company that could satisfy the growing market for guitars that embodied vintage quality, but didn't come with a vintage price tag.

> I was obsessed with vintage guitars, actually before most people had ever heard that term in the electric guitar world. I loved the rebellious look of the Flying V, and I wanted a bass version. Nobody made one at the time so I had to make one myself. It all grew from there. The Explorer and V were just badass designs, and we wanted to make them more diverse.
>
> — Jol Dantzig

The flagship model of the company that would become Hamer guitars featured a mahogany body, a flamed-maple top, the fast-playing, slim neck of a Les Paul or an SG, and an Explorer body. This first Explorer-shaped Hamer (later versions would be called the Standard) had a body and neck built by Jim Beach. It was powered by Gibson PAF pickups from a 1958 Flying V, and had a Gibson stop tailpiece and tune-o-matic bridge. With a couple more modifications (slightly angled Grover tuners, tone controls that ran parallel to the neck as opposed to the lower bout), the first guitar to bear the Hamer logo, #0000, was born. All Hamer guitars built in Monty's basement would come to be known as *four-digit Hamers*.

When Hamer brought the guitar to a Wishbone Ash concert, guitarist Andy Powell loved it but was only interested in flying Vs at the time. However, bassist Martin Turner was inspired by the shape, and Hamer #0001 was built for him, using old Gibson Thunderbird pickups from the Kalamazoo factory. Martin Barre of Jethro Tull, a Les Paul man through and through, was tempted by the allure of Hamer's Explorer shape, and also because he saw, heard, and felt a similar quality to his old Gibsons, which he was reluctant to take out on the road. Cheap Trick guitarist Rick Nielsen would snag Hamer #0000 from Paul, as he waited for his order — #0004 — to be completed. (For a wonderfully complete overview of the cataloging and details of these early guitars, Steve Matthes and Joe Moffett's *The Ultimate: An Illustrated History of Hamer Guitars* is a must read.)

> Of course, there was Rick Nielsen, who at the time wasn't known outside of the club scene that I was playing in as well. He was a friend, and fellow collector. Rick got one of the very first guitars we finished a bit after we built my V Bass. Some of the first people we sold guitars to were Mick Ralphs, Martin

> Barre, Tommy Bolin, and a whole bunch of other early 1970s bands who have come and gone. The list is so endless that when I sometimes look at the sales records it sort of blows my mind. Then when Cheap Trick became the biggest band in the world in the late '70s, that's when people really started to learn about Hamer. Before that it was sort of an "insider" club with touring guitarists. Even Roy Buchanan bought a couple!
>
> —Jol Dantzig

Barre and Nielsen would become important endorsers of these early Hamer guitars, along with hard rockers like Rick Derringer and Lita Ford of the Runaways. While orders initially came in for Hamer guitars from relationships built over the years with Northern Prairie Music customers and from music shop owners who were hearing about the guitars from customers who had seen them being played in concert by their rock-n-roll heroes, Hamer and Dantzig realized they had to secure national distribution and take a proactive approach to marketing. Through modest promotional means, Hamer took out print ads in guitar and music magazines featuring Martin Barre's sunburst flame-top standard. The once-rejected futuristic shape of the Explorer was standing out, just as the energy of '70s hard-rock culture was taking root. Hamer's tagline *The Ultimate*, credited to Rick Nielsen, was being emblazoned on T-shirts, print advertising, and guitar catalogs, further cementing the impression that Hamer guitars were high-quality instruments that looked every bit as great as they sounded. Capturing the good looks of these instruments for early ads and catalogs was photographer Rich Kwasniewksi, whose rock-star images appeared in influential music magazines like *Creem* and *Circus*.

As someone who would go on to a career making world class instruments and also as a very successful professional musician, Dave Reimer was inspired by these ads, which conveyed the spirit of Hamer as much as they did the quality of their products.

> I just liked where it was coming from. I love the design. The attitude was, this didn't exist, let's make this happen. That's what's really influential to me. Making the couple of clones [Dave makes beautiful high-end Explorer replicas as well as unique

> designs] that I do now . . . it's the spirit of it that drives me to do it. It's not because I think it's the greatest guitar ever built. It just represents all these things that were inspiring to me as a kid, which was to take little bits from everything, whether you're doing that with a song that you're writing, whether you're doing that with what kind of clothes you're going to wear on stage, or what kind of instrument you're going to play. It's not like any kind of retro vibe. If you're stuck precisely in an era, people just go, "Yeah, yeah. It's like a costume." Who cares that you look like John Lennon? But if you look like John Lennon, Elvis Presley, and David Bowie at the same time, well, then that's something different. I think Hamer had that for me. Plus, they had great ads. At my early age, I probably didn't even realize I just loved black and white photography when I saw those ads. There's just something edgy, you know? Something about the logo, something about everything they were doing just said "This is the best. We're the best. We're rocking." It's the ultimate, man.
>
> — Dave Reimer

The association of Hamer with Cheap Trick could not have been more perfect for the time. Cheap Trick was a band that combined the best qualities of the British rock that came before them (the Beatles, the Move, the Who, ELO, Led Zeppelin) with a sardonic, art-rock delivery that was smart enough to charm the critics, heavy enough for the rockers, catchy and commercial enough for the American public at large to digest. Mind you, it would take a fluke success with a live album recorded in Japan, *Cheap Trick at Budokan*, to break through in America, taking the best of the three studio albums (their self-titled debut, *In Color*, and the masterful *Heaven Tonight*) and delivering the songs with the explosive energy of their reputation-building live shows. Hamer and Cheap Trick were a brand and a band seemingly made for each other; both looked back to bring things that were ahead of their time into the future with a bold new perspective. Cheap Trick were the perfect ambassadors for the odd guitar shapes of the past: "Mommy's alright, Daddy's alright. They just seem a little *weird*."

> I think that the appeal was to look more aggressive — to stand apart from the "old-time" look of the mass-produced guitars. As

> I'm sure you know, the V and Explorer were super rare guitars and a lot of people that we showed our instruments to had never seen them before, so it made an impression. As it always was and still is, musicians are influenced by what they see around them so it was a natural thing that the angular guitars started to become popular at last.
>
> —Jol Dantzig

The late '70s saw Hamer grow from a custom shop into a true production company with the creation of the Sunburst double-cutaway model, another modern vintage-design inspired by the double-cutaway Les Paul Junior. While in no means a pointy guitar, many hard rockers would come to love the Sunburst's double-cutaway mahogany body, humbucking pickups (DiMarzio PAF), with the same electronic as the Explorer-shaped Standard. Unlike other Hamer models, the Sunburst would come with a fixed bridge with six adjustable saddles on a fixed metal plate. The bridges came from Mighty Mite, an aftermarket guitar-parts company that we will hear more about on our pointy guitars journey.

While the Sunburst would be available only in a sunburst finish for the first year of production, the first opaque-finished Sunburst model in black came in 1978. This started a trend of flashier versions of traditional shapes created in the Hamer custom shop that, while not necessarily fully pointy, features certain *accoutrements* of pointy guitars. Famous Sunburst players included Johnny Ramone, Andy Summers of the Police, and James Honeyman-Scott, musicians whose endorsements of Hamer guitars showed that the company had an eye for artists beyond power rock, tapping into a more diverse pool of genres like punk and new wave.

It was around this time that Hamer endorser Tom Petersson of Cheap Trick suggested creating a 12-string bass to Paul and Jol, with the intention of helping the band fill in the sonic holes inherent in a four-piece group with ambitious arrangements. Hagstrom had already come to market with the H8 8-string bass, which Petersson was familiar with and, while having a 12-string bass made was always Petersson's goal, Hamer and Dantzig felt that there would be too much tension for a guitar neck to handle, and opted instead for a 10 string model. This first 10 string was taken out on Cheap Trick's first trip to Japan, and was subjected to a full on R-and-D test before a 12-string version was attempted.

> Petersson took the bass with him to Japan and decorated it for the live shows with long streamers, which he tied to the headstock. At one show, Petersson leaned over the audience and a fanatical young female audience member grabbed onto the streamers, refusing to let go. When Petersson pulled the bass back, the girl, still holding on, was pulled off the floor and out of the crowd. After that, Hamer and Dantzig had to concede that if the neck could withstand the tension of 10 strings and a young girl dangling from it, they could certainly build a neck that could handle the two additional strings.
>
> (Steve Matthes and Joe Moffett, *The Ultimate.*)

I had the pleasure (well not physical pleasure, they weigh a ton!) of playing a Hamer 12-string bass when my band Crash Kelly toured the U.K. with Cheap Trick pop metal acolytes Enuff Z'Nuff in 2003. On one occasion, I deputized for Chip Z'Nuff on bass at a soundcheck while he grabbed a few more hours of sleep on the tour bus. I can still remember the powerful clang of those thick, telephone wire, doubled-up bass strings as their vibrations punched through the air. I felt like I was cradling an entire orchestra in my arms — it was power-pop heaven and rock-n-roll hell all at once.

It should be noted that the initial 12-string basses that Hamer built featured a Seymour Duncan "quadrophonic" humbucking pickup and special electronics that could deliver the instrument's signal in stereo. The first Quad bass 12-string caught the eyes and ears of Jethro Tull's John Glascock and the Who's John Entwistle (who had his built in the Explorer-inspired Standard shape). Players like Chip Z'Nuff, Pearl Jam's Jeff Ament, and dUg Pinnick of King's X would carry on the legacy of the Hamer 12-string bass, a truly formidable instrument.

As demand for Hamer guitars increased, the company moved to a new facility that could accommodate the equipment needed to automate certain parts of the production process (cutting bodies, carving necks, etc.). The Hamer Special was a stripped-down version of the Sunburst, retaining the same hardware, wood, and electronic materials, but with a pared down visual aesthetic (no binding, simpler fretboard inlays).

The Special's success prompted the investigation of a new (actually, an old) model design. With the rise in popularity of heavy metal bands like the Scorpions, UFO, and Judas Priest, all with members playing Flying Vs, Hamer introduced the Vector series. It had the same electronic control layout as previous Hamers and was offered with either a solid mahogany body or a flamed-maple veneer top. The Vector differed from the Gibson Flying V in that its headstock differed from a classic '58 style Gibson headstock, and utilized the smaller headstock found on the special model. Hamer changed back to the traditional V headstock design in 1984 after deciding the look was completely wrong for the lines of the V body shape, but I personally love the quirkiness of the smaller, more traditional headstock design juxtaposed against the Vs radical body shape. It screams early '80s guitar to me.

The emerging sounds of new wave and pop rock production in general, with guitarists beginning to explore pedals and electronically processed sounds, inspired the design of the Hamer Prototype. By adding a unique pickup design that allowed both a humbucking pickup (big rock sound) and a single coil pickup (brighter, cleaner sound) to be mounted within the same pickup ring, Hamer created an instrument that appealed to '80s players looking to carve out a space in a frequency spectrum that was beginning to get crowded by low-end keyboard frequencies, drum machines, and samplers.

The Prototype was Hamer's first all original design, and through the early '80s the company experimented with a number of different pickup configurations. Its slightly offset double-cutaway shape, thinned-out, pointier treble-side horn, and comfortable back belly cut, addressed the visual and practical modernity of what was happening in music. The Cruisebass was the low-end option of this particular shape, and Pretenders bassist Pete Farndon (who played a Cruisebass with the popular at-the-time red-and-white rising sun graphic) and the Cars' Benjamin Orr (who acquired an 8-string version) were two notable players

It's fitting that the final variation of the Prototype guitar was the SS model, Hamer's first signature model for Billy Idol guitarist Steve Stevens. Just as Rick Nielsen and Cheap Trick were the perfect representatives for Hamer's reinterpretation of classic designs that were ahead of their time, Steve Stevens was perhaps the best person to represent the next phase of truly original designs.

> Perhaps it seems only natural that a guitarist of the calibre of Steve Stevens has his own guitar line, but the Hamer SS model is the product of a relationship built on mutual respect

> that dates back to Steve's pre-Idol existence. About five years ago, Hamer Guitars was building instruments for Kiss, and in talking to their management the subject of a great new talent came up. "So after hearing this guy, we made him a few guitars that were basically stock," explains Hamer's co-founder and chief scientist Jol Dantzig, "a bright pink stock special and a bright orange Explorer with a full-scale neck but a mini-body and peg head. Steve was interested in wild colors and modifying existing models — black parts and binding, not too far ahead of his time."
>
> (Jon Tiven, *Guitar World*, May 1986.)

Like Hamer, Stevens had mastered the techniques of earlier and varied influences, and was adept at a number of guitar styles ranging from jazz, fusion, and funk to all variations of rock. He was able to express these styles with a bold and original sonic palette that married effects, whammy bar wizardry, ray gun–inspired bloops and bleeps, and the dazzling hard-rock lead guitar techniques of the day. When combined with Billy Idol's Jim Morrison swagger, Elvis croon, and Johnny Rotten sneer, the result was some of the most exciting and immaculately produced and performed music of the '80s. Idol classics like "White Wedding," "Rebel Yell," and "Eyes Without a Face" are techno-rock masterpieces that sound as fresh and vibrant coming out of speakers today as they did in the '80s. Stevens was more than just a lead guitarist to Billy Idol, he was a de facto music director. While his undeniable technique speaks to his virtuosity, his incessant quest for new sounds and the quality of his parts reveal the depth of his musicianship, something Dantzig knew would need to be considered when building an instrument for him.

> As Steve and Jol got friendlier, and the nature of Mr. Stevens guitar experimentation revealed itself, these two began playing more with the electronic configuration of the guitars. [Jol Dantzig explains,] "When it comes to playability, Steve knows exactly what he wants and can articulate it in a way that goes straight onto the drawing board. But the sonic thing is different — he talks more like a musician or a producer. So the

> musician part of me has to translate terms like 'more cut' and 'transparent' into the number of pickup winds."
>
> (Jon Tiven, *Guitar World*, May 1986.)

Having hooked up with Hamer through a relationship with Kiss manager Bill Aucoin (Stevens provided guitar work on Kiss drummer Peter Criss's second solo album, and Aucoin would go on to manage Billy Idol as well), Stevens was the recipient of a bright orange Standard at three-quarter size and a bright pink Sunburst with a three-coil pickup arrangement that suited the guitarist's stylistic flare. The Prototype SS was based on the model's existing layout, but was tweaked by shortening both horns of the guitar, giving it a pointier SG look and feel.

> On his first fully customized guitar, the controls were moved around on a pink Sunburst and featured a triple-coil pickup at the bridge plus humbucking arrangement. But this was only a preview of what was to come — an upside-down Prototype with specially wound pickups to meet the musical requirements ("Ballsy and shimmering") of guitar perfectionist Stevens. "Some guitar companies have arrangements with their artists that are more or less endorsements in name only, and they could give a fuck about input as long as they get to use the artist in their ads. Hamer's whole approach has been that if we get the finest players to let us know what they want in a guitar, and we can make them happy, then we can make the best guitars around. Period. Steve has been a vital part of Hamer r&d, not just a musician who gets his name on the guitar."
>
> The real start of the Steve Stevens model as an entity unto itself came around the time of Steve's appearance with Billy Idol on Saturday Night Live in January, 1984, a show for which Jol had delivered a white pearl Prototype with a shortened bottom horn. This guitar was destroyed by a truck two weeks later, and Dantzig and Stevens sat down on road cases before a gig and discussed the possibility of building the SS. "He came up with both shortened horns and the cracked Day-Glo pattern

> looking like Barney Rubble's shirt" explains Dantzig, "and we played around with different woods, different fingerboards, maple necks, finally emerging from the lab with the definitive Steve Stevens guitar. I thought I was a perfectionist, but Steve is even pickier than I am. Thank goodness for that — the combination of what he wants to hear, and what my skills have allowed me to deliver, has produced an instrument that could only have been born from the combination of his musical way of thinking with Hamer's more technical approach. I'm very proud of this guitar, and I know Steve is, too."
>
> (Jon Tiven, *Guitar World*, May 1986.)

With Aucoin's management acumen to assist, Stevens worked out a deal to market this new-look Prototype as the Steve Stevens model, the most famous being the Steve Stevens Raygun, which Stevens cradled on the May 1986 cover of *Guitar World* magazine. Finished in jet black, with on-board hot-pink push buttons for those intergalactic bleeps and bloops of Stevens's ray-gun sound, his name writ large in hot-pink signature script on the lower bass-side bout, and an equally hot-pink Hamer logo emblazoned on the headstock, this Floyd Rose– and HSS pickup–outfitted beast stands as a sonic and visual testament to the outlandish design style of the '80s that still retains an element of class.

Derry Grehan, guitarist for multiplatinum, Canadian rock band Honeymoon Suite, did his part to spread the word about the Hamer Prototype SS on tour and in videos that were staples of MTV and the Canadian equivalent, MuchMusic.

> The guys at Hamer came out to a show and asked me if I'd like one. And, yes, I got the pink Steve Stevens one, which I thought was badass. That's the guitar I used on "Feel It Again," on the clean part. Unfortunately, that one got stolen with all the others in New Jersey.
>
> — Derry Grehan of Honeymoon Suite

While Hamer was indeed courting guitarists of a variety of genres, the '80s bread that was coming in with the company's success was still largely buttered by the endorsement of hard rock and heavy metal players who were gaining new levels of popularity. Dantzig mentions the importance of these relationships to the Hamer brand, and the value of getting to know the players as people, and the very personal preferences specific to each guitarist.

> Some of the best times were offstage, and there are too many to recount here. One of my favorites was working with Ken Downing [K.K. Downing] and Glenn Tipton. Because of their appearance I was a little intimidated to meet them, even though I really don't get starstruck. I had a meeting with them, and they showed up at the hotel in pleated pants and pastel colored Izod shirts. They asked if I could get them a tee time! They were big-time golfers, and from that point on we really hit it off, so to speak. Great guys, and we had a wonderful relationship. They had very particular things that they needed the guitars to do, and I worked very closely with them to design the guitars as opposed to what I normally did, which was to design stuff, and then show models to artists. I've played onstage with quite a few of our endorsing artists, including Ken and Glenn, Steve Stevens, James Honeyman-Scott, the guys in Def Leppard, Gary Moore, and a bunch more I can't remember.
>
> — Jol Dantzig

The Blitz guitars and basses were Explorer-shaped with solid one-piece mahogany bodies. The guitars featured the classic hard rock–heavy metal two DiMarzio humbucker pickup combination. Eventually, the Blitz guitars were ordered with requests for Floyd Rose and Kahler systems, like the yellow and black zebra model that Mötley Crüe guitarist Mick Mars was known to brandish live on the Shout at the Devil Tour. Crüe bassist, Nikki Sixx, is one of the most famous users of the bass model, and he could be seen alternating between his Ferrari-red Blitz and the various B.C. Rich Warlock basses that could survive the abuse he hurled at them as one of hard rock's most aggressive live performers.

Def Leppard bassist Rick Savage was also a keen supporter of Hamer basses:

> My first pointy was a Hamer Blitz bass back in 1981. I visited the Hamer factory when we were playing Chicago, and they had it made for me. I was blown away by its shape but even

> more by the outrageously bright yellow color. As a 20-year-old I really felt like a proper rock star playing it! Hamer guitars were very kind and supportive back in the '80s and I loved playing their basses. They epitomized the vibe and nature of that era. I kind of went to a more traditional shape once I started playing the five-string. Sadly (on the recordings) none of them were pointy but, for the record, the first three albums were Fender Precisions, while *Hysteria* was a mix of Precision, ESP (I think), and samples. I don't play them much these days, but I still keep a couple of my original Hamer Scarab basses and the Blitz bass.
>
> — Rick "Sav" Savage of Def Leppard

Bon Jovi guitarist Richie Sambora could be seen rocking custom sunburst and opaque black Hamer Standards on tour and in videos from Bon Jovi's sophomore release *7800° Fahrenheit*. While the monster success that would come from 1986's *Slippery When Wet* album was still around the corner, Sambora's blend of traditional blues-based classic-rock vocabulary and blistering post–Van Halen speed and firepower made him an ideal representative of the Hamer ideal. Like Hamer, Sambora was grabbing hold of the best of the past and building it into something new, something that would appeal to an audience hungry for high-performance attitude.

The Phantom was the product of a collaboration with Andy Summers from the Police who was looking for a guitar that built upon the Protoype's two-pickups-in-one-pickup-ring concept by adding the option of going to a Tele single coil in the neck position. The A5 was the fifth iteration and the version that Andy approved, thus the sensible name. One of the first production guitar synthesizers, the A7, was a reference to Andy's desire to access the sounds from the Roland GR-700 synthesizer. Elliot Easton was a Phantom fan, as was Mike Wanchic of John Cougar Mellencamp fame.

Glenn Tipton of Judas Priest was heavy metal's most famous Phantom player, and his GT version arrived in 1984 with a single humbucker pickup and a six-in-line headstock that differed from the 3+3 version on other Phantoms.

Around 1984 Glenn moved to Hamer Guitars and started using a custom Hamer Phantom made by Jol Dantzig (Hamer Guitars technical director). This guitar was fitted with one EMG humbucker, a Kahler tremolo, and one volume pot. A signature model of this was developed and sold to public from '84 to '86.

The Hamer Phantom GT featured a contoured body with double offset cutaways and a pickguard. The neck had 22-frets (24.75 inch scale), a rosewood fingerboard, dot inlays and was made of mahogany (changed to maple in 1985).

Other appointments were a Kahler flat-mount 2300 C locking tremolo and a single Hamer Slammer pickup. The Phantom GT had a limited production run from 1984 to 1986. Glenn's personal models feature Duncan or EMG pickups.

> Glenn has traditionally favored Strat-shaped guitars, and the GT is sort of a combination of different models we've made for him in the past. It features a custom-wound Seymour Duncan humbucker, and we designed the double cutaways so that he has unobstructed access to every fret.
>
> — Jol Dantzig (Hamer Guitars technical director)

> For me, a guitar has to assist my role as a performer, and the Hamer GT does that.
>
> — Glenn Tipton (GlennTipton.com)

Tipton's guitar partner in Priest, K.K. Downing, played a stripped down, one humbucking pickup Vector with the more classic Gibson-style headstock.

Judas Priest had progressed considerably from their earlier prog- and psych-inspired proto-metal days, and in a way, these new guitars can be seen as an extension of those changes. Certainly, by the time they had reached their 1986 Turbo album, the guitars had become much pointier, and their sound much more modern as they began incorporating drum machines and guitar synthesizers into their ultra-melodic pop-metal confections. By that point, Downing had added four custom-made mini Vs with a Scepter headstock, and Tipton was playing an ultra-pointy, non-production model custom Hamer GT.

> For the Turbo / Fuel For Life tour in 1986, Hamer introduced a new non-production model called the GT Custom. Its black angular body loosely resembled a Gibson Explorer.
>
> This guitar features a maple fretboard with black dot inlays, two Duncan and EMG humbucking pickups, a Kahler locking tremolo and a white stripe outlining the body shape.

"The GT is my own design and it looks a bit strange, but there's always method in madness. For me anyway, this is a great thing, because onstage, I still play some stretch stuff, so I need to get the guitar at this angle and as you can see, it just fits nicely to me."

"So this was all tailor-made. It's got a very narrow neck which is how I like to play. But the beauty of this guitar is we can do anything onstage, you know, play with our teeth or jumping around, and then I can just find the right position to play. So it's got a certain nice line to it, but it's very functional and it also balances the guitar. If you ever tried to design guitars, they can look very good, but they can be top or bottom heavy, but with this guitar, it's really nicely balanced and it's always in a good position to play."

— Glenn Tipton (GlennTipton.com)

Both Savage and Sixx — who were rocking Blitz basses — were integral to the "Hamer Rocks Hard" advertising campaign that also featured action shots of heavy metal heavy weights like Glenn Tipton (Phantom GT signature model) and K.K. Downing (Vector KK signature model) of Judas Priest, Fernando von Arb (with his Scarab II) and Mark Kohler (Blitz) of Switzerland's number one rock export Krokus, and Steve Stevens (with his Prototype "SS" model). All were featured in action shots sporting full rock-n-roll regalia, centered on backdrops of Day-Glo colored graphics and stylized script that was designed to be projected through the eyes and deep into the heavy-metal hearts of guitarists the world over looking to inject some of that flash into their own guitar collections.

By the time we got to the mid-1980s we'd been using some endorsement advertising and just word of mouth to get our message out. The guitarists who used our guitars were actually responsible for spreading the word among their peers, and in magazines. When MTV hit big, it just happened to coincide with a lot of bands I'd been working with. For a while it was like we owned MTV. Our message was just emphasizing that we understood the music and the musician, and that the guitars were prolevel stuff. I actually met Floyd Rose when he and his wife were making the trems in their home, and we were the first "production" guitars to use them. I tried to keep finding new ways to make the guitars better, cooler, and more interesting.

—Jol Dantzig

Before I fell under the spell of Steve Clark's Gibson Firebird, the iconic body shape of that guitar was burned into my brain courtesy Ratt's Robbin Crosby and Mötley Crüe's Nikki Sixx. Standing at 6'5" and 6'1" respectively, Crosby and Sixx had the physical stature to pull off the Hamer Firebird's larger body, and the more rounded curves suited the commercial hard sounds that Ratt and the Crüe were exploring on their 1985 multiplatinum releases *Invasion of Your Privacy* and *Theatre of Pain*. While Crosby was most widely seen playing Jackson Firebirds, Hamer did try to woo him away from Grover and Co. by working with him to design a Hamer guitar version of their Firebird. Hamer had already received massive exposure with the bass version of the Firebird thanks to Nikki Sixx's use of it on the Welcome to the Theatre of Pain Tour, and in hit MTV videos for "Home Sweet Home" and "Smokin' in the Boys Room." (Although it should be noted that Sixx opted to use a much pointier B.C. Rich Warlock bass to bust through the boys' room's wall in the video, despite rocking his Firebird for the musical segments of the video.) Crosby did order a number of Hamer Firebirds, in red opaque, pink and black, and a bunch in white. The guitar initially had a 22-fret neck, but later was made with 24 frets when it went into its limited production; *The Ultimate: The Illustrated History of Hamer Guitars* tells us that fewer than two hundred were made.

It struck me in looking back on both Steve Clark and Robbin Crosby's influence on me, and on '80s rock music in general, how many similarities there were between the two. Both were statuesque, golden-maned rock gods. Both were riff masters and rock music composers of the highest order, perhaps not as technically proficient as their guitar duo counterparts (in Steve's case, the flash-fingered Pete Willis and then Phil Collen, and in Robbin's the virtuosic Warren DeMartini), but both more than capable of delivering the perfect, melodic lead break at the perfect moment. Both Steve and Robbin played for the song, filled the stage with their swagger and presence, and truly embodied the myth of the rock-n-roll guitar hero. Sadly, they also shared a taste for the darker elements of the rock-n-roll lifestyle that would ultimately claim both of their lives far too soon. But those sad stories have been written and told many times, and I choose today to remember them as the gods of war and the wanted men they will always be in the memories of those who cherished their music.

Steve Brown from Paramus, New Jersey, sold millions of records with his own band, Mechanic (MCA) recording artists Trixter, and he also deputized in Def Leppard at the behest of his pal Phil Collen when Lep guitarist Vivian Campbell needed time off for health reasons.

> In late 1990, I signed on with Hamer Guitars. I became a Hamer Guitar endorser and Jon Dantzig and I hit it off immediately. And I was always such a fan of Hamer, because of you know, early Def Leppard. Steve Clark, and Pete Willis played those cool Hamer Explorers. Rick Savage in Leppard was playing the Hamer bass, the Blitz. And, of course, Rick Nielsen from Cheap Trick is one of my biggest influences as a songwriter. You know, he had tons of Hamers.
>
> Hamer was great, they built me some beautiful guitars, and in 1991 or '92 they built me an awesome flying V Hamer that was influenced by one that Jeff Watson had built. It had 24 frets, and a, you know, like, plain maple top. There are a bunch of pictures of it online, it had a Floyd Rose on it, and it had the LED lights. It had a switch that turned on red lights in the fret-board. That was a beautiful, beautiful guitar. I wish I still had that, but I sold it to this big Hamer collector about 20 years ago. He bought, like, my three custom Hamer guitars that they built for me, and he made me an offer I couldn't refuse.
>
> — Steve Brown of Trixter

Steve mentions the influence of Night Ranger guitarist Jeff Watson, a guitarist who, alongside bassist and lead vocalist Jack Blades, and fellow six-string slinger Brad Gillis (the guitarist who famously stepped up to fill the shoes of the departed Randy Rhoads in the Ozzy Osbourne band with panache, grace, and rocking style) are strongly associated with the Hamer brand in my eyes. All three played a variety of Hamer models, even though both Watson and Gillis are more likely to be associated with a classic Gibson (Watson's Les Paul Gold Top) and Fender (Gillis's legendary red 1962 Fender Stratocaster).

Night Ranger had racked up a number of million-plus selling albums, fueled by hit songs like "Sister Christian," "Sentimental Street," "Four in the Morning," and "Goodbye." But it was hard rockers like "(You Can Still) Rock in America" and "Don't Tell Me You Love Me" that cemented the reputations of Watson and Gillis as rock virtuosi, each with a distinctive style based on a mastery of specific techniques. For Watson, it was his eight-fingered fingerboard tapping that allowed him access to a pianistic approach that expanded his melodic and harmonic reach, and enabled him to lay out flurries of high speed, legato passages. For Gillis, it was his mastery of the whammy bar and an ear for intonation and touch that rivaled the mastery while also suggesting the influence of Jeff Beck. In Gillis's hands, the Floyd Rose tremolo system (of which he was an early adopter) becomes a tool of Hendrixian expression, unparalleled in the hard rock community. His jaw-droppingly melodic solo on the aforementioned "Sister Christian" is a masterclass in motif and singing, soaring, nuanced melodic rock guitar playing.

By 1989, Night Ranger were ready to release their heaviest album to date, the Keith Olsen produced *Man in Motion*. The objective was simple — phasers and six-string lasers on stun. Hamer was there with instruments to support an album that, while not as commercially successful as past endeavors like *Dawn Patrol*, *Midnight Madness*, and *7 Wishes*, featured guitar playing that pushed hard against the perceived limits of pop metal with a heavier sounding and more technically demanding approach.

> Jeff Watson's beloved Gold Top is today safely locked away in the recording studio built into the attic of his suburban San Francisco home. While he does own a custom copy of that workhorse guitar, he recorded all the electric guitar parts on *Man in Motion* with a prototype double-cutaway instrument built for him by Hamer. "It's one of the most beautiful and finest-playing guitars I've ever owned," he says. "It's really resonant. In fact, Allan Holdsworth, who hates wooden guitars now, played it and said that it's one of the finest wooden guitars he's ever played, so that's a pretty nice compliment. The neck is also absolutely incredible. It's got twenty-seven frets, and that's how I can get so high up there; at the end of the solo in 'Love Shot Me Down,' those are just pulls up that fretboard."

> The custom-built, 25-inch scale instrument, modeled roughly after Hamer's first production model, the Sunburst, has a light-density, straight-grained Mahogany body with an arched, broad-leaf maple top.
>
> The hard rock maple neck is constructed with a neutral centerpiece flanked by two counter-grained outer pieces; the resulting "stress" prevents twisting. The ivory bound ebony fingerboard extends to its twenty-seventh fret beneath the three treble strings, where it butts against a P.J. Marx single-coil pickup. A P.J. Marx humbucker sits in the bridge position alongside a tune-o-matic-type bridge and a fine-tune tailpiece.
>
> Because he used a Les Paul for such a long spell, Jeff finds that certain stylistic characteristics he's developed necessitate his exclusive use of Gibson-style guitars. "Although the action's pretty low on the Hamer," he explains, "I can still get my really wide vibrato happening on it. I can't play a Strat, though. I can't play Brad's guitar to save my life, because of the way the neck's mounted to the body. I need a mount where the neck goes off at an angle, so I have the high bridge to get my hand around on it. But this guitar is great; I'm having a second one made to go on the road." Jeff also plans to tour with his custom Hamer doubleneck ("the Flying 'W!'") and a commissioned copy of his Guild F412BLD acoustic twelve-string.
>
> (Matt Resnicoff, *Guitar World*, February 29, 1988.)

In speaking with Resnicoff for the same article, Gillis detailed his use of the Floyd Rose as a personal stylistic tool, using specially designed Hamer "stressed" necks, with two counter-grained maple slabs fixed to a neutral centerpiece to help prevent twisting on his beloved '62 Strat, and offered a classic example of a high-end, 1980s rock guitar signal chain.

> At the time, Eddie Van Halen had just arrived, and people were imitating his use of harmonics and his divebomb effects. I started doing just the opposite — the pull-ups — like the one you hear at the end of the first solo in "Don't Tell Me You Love Me," that pull-up harmonic at the third fret on the G

string, with the big wiggle on the end. It's something I continued to work with. Then, one day I accidentally banged my guitar and it made a fluttering sound. That's when I started doing that cricket sound, which is the result of the fluttering of the bridge; if you flick the end of the bar on a floating unit like a Floyd Rose, it'll shake back and forth. The fewer springs you have in the back, the wider a flutter you'll get out of it. So I went down to three springs, and every time I bang that thing it flutters real nice."

One of the more heralded figures in whammy-bar artistry, Brad today can barely speculate what shape his playing might have taken had he not discovered the bar. He's installed a Floyd Rose unit on every electric guitar he owns, including the old, black Les Paul Custom he used with Ozzy Osbourne, a mini-guitar and his workhorse 1962 Stratocaster, which he's outfitted with prototype P.J. Marx pickups and built-in, wireless effects-switching and transmitter systems. Brad recorded *Man in Motion* with that Stratocaster ("It's got the sound!"), and used select Hamers for certain rhythms.

His main amplifier for the sessions was his stereo Mesa/Boogle Mark IIC Simulclass, which he ran through various Marshall and Boogie bottoms. Although his rack contains an assortment of effects, including Yamaha SPX90s and a Roland DEP5 processor, they were all routed out of his system for the recording, and all processing was added at the board. "I did use an ADA MP-1 preamp for some harmonic stuff," he notes, "like when the guitar comes in on 'Don't Start Thinking'; that's a real clean, ADA tone with my out-of-phase rhythm pickup, and it sounds really good. I'm not quite sure how I'll recreate that stuff live. I may see if I can get the Boogie clean enough, but it doesn't have the sound that the ADA does."

Brad's also brooding over the prospect of touring with one of several custom, three-piece Hamer necks fitted to the body of his favorite Strat. Although he's been working with Hamers, and has a Scarab model on order, he's not yet completely sold on the idea of mixing vintage with new blood. "We're working

> on him," sighs Jol Dantzig of Hamer Guitars, who confers with Gillis and Watson on design ideas and refinements. "You've gotta take Brad one step at a time."
>
> (Matt Resnicoff, *Guitar World*, February 29, 1988.)

While it may have been tricky to get a reticent Gillis to shake familiar guitar habits, he sure looked comfortable rocking a very pointy Hamer Scepter, my all-time favorite Hamer guitar shape. A modernized take on the Standard's Explorer-inspired body, the model was beveled with contrasting colors (in Gillis's case in glossy black and red) and featured eye catching boomerang inlays on an ebony fingerboard. The pointiness of the guitar is nicely offset by the six inline headstock, which offers a more rounded, hockey-stick contour. This top of the line Hamer, for all of its pointiness, still retains an elegance about it, perfectly shaped and sized for the forward thinking '80s rocker. Night Ranger bassist Jack Blades was known to play a number of Hamer models, including one co-designed with bassist Kip Winger, the Impact.

> Professionals like Brad Gillis, Jack Blades, and Jeff Watson rely on the superior sound and playability designed into every Hamer instrument. So if you're serious about your sound get your hands on a Hamer and taste a little success for yourself.
>
> (Hamer guitar ad, 1987.)

Skid Row, another massive New Jersey success story, were known to rock hard with Hamer, as well as with Kramer, Spector, and Jackson models, all which the band played with a blend of soulful proficiency, classic hard rock finesse, and bratty, snot-nosed punk attitude. Band co-founder Snake Sabo plays a red Standard in the video for their breakthrough hit "18 and Life" off of their 1989, multiplatinum self-titled debut. Scotti Hill, Sabo's guitar partner, employed a number of Hamer models, including a gorgeous blue 1991 mini Firebird custom and one of Hamer's entries into the Superstrat arena — a Californian — that met an early and violent demise, a victim of a crime of rock n roll passion.

> There are pictures of me floating around with a what they call the Standard, I believe, the double cutaway. I had one of those

with a Floyd Rose on it. It was gorgeous. I've gone through a couple of periods where I've cleaned house, and all those Hamers are gone. I don't have any of them anymore. But at one point, I had three. I had that one, and, and since we're talking about pointy guitars, these will qualify but they're a little rounder. I had two Firebirds.

They made me the first Firebird that was a full-size Firebird shape, and it was super top heavy. It was beautiful . . . this beautiful blue. They were very generous. They made me a shorter version of it with one pickup and a smaller body. I should've never have gotten rid of those because they were really unique. I think a friend of mine who is a Hamer collector has those. My friend Steve. They also made me a Californian, a beautiful green Californian that, in the heat of a giant rock show, got smashed and knocked over with a bunch of gear — we trashed the stage. Now that Californian, what ever became of it, is a giant mystery. And my friend, Steve, who is the Hamer collector, he has been on a mission to find the remains of that guitar for decades. The last time I saw that guitar it was backstage at Alpine Valley. It was in two pieces. And, as a matter of fact, there's video of me smashing it into a speaker cabinet that was laying on its back on the floor. You're just a dumb kid, doing what you think you're supposed to be doing. Yeah. But I wish I had that now.

— Scotti Hill of Skid Row

In the latter half of the '80s into the '90s, Hamer jumped into the Superstrat arena with models like the aforementioned Californian, its predecessor the Chaparral, the bolt on neck Centaura, and the last design Paul Hamer would help to create, the Virtuoso!, before leaving the company that bears his name in 1987. Hamer knew it had to keep pace with companies like Kramer and Jackson who were dominating the market, and Hamer responded in kind, while still keeping an eye towards the quality and versatility that high-calibre players of the day demanded, players like Vernon Reid, Doug Boyle of the Robert Plant band, and even Steve Steven's replacement in the Billy Idol band, Mark Younger-Smith.

Clearly, as evinced by this piece of copy from a 1990 ad in *Guitar World* magazine, Hamer still had a specific clientele in mind — the pro guitarist.

> Attitude. It's the secret ingredient in a successful formula. It's the way a musician injects personality and excitement into the music, no matter what style they play. We thought you'd like to meet some of the pros who count on our attitude to help them express theirs.
>
> Eddie Martinez: Known for his trademark "crunch" chords and solid funk chops. His Hamer-ized sound has helped propel artists like Robert Palmer, Stanley Clarke, Mick Jagger, and Steve Winwood.
>
> Jeff Thall: While on the Bryan Ferry tour, Jeff has been called on to touch upon numerous styles and textures during Bryan's atmospheric set.
>
> Tommy Williams: Bought his first Hamer while playing the clubs in New York. Now he's the guitarist and musical director for Debbie Gibson. On stage and in the studio, Tommy's Hamers have been with him every step of the way.
>
> Stevie Salas: From producing and playing on tracks for Bootsy Collins, the Tubes, and Was Not Was to touring with Rod Stewart, Stevie counts on Hamer's versatility to get the job done.
>
> For over a decade Hamer has been the choice for serious musicians. That's because we only build professional quality instruments. The very same guitars you see here can be found at your authorized Hamer dealer. Now that's the Hamer attitude.
>
> — The Professionals' Choice . . . Make It Yours.

Other models and variations would come along, each a testament to the enduring quality and innovation built on a love of the past, but never slavishly chained to it. Ownership would change hands over the years, but a thread of spiritual continuity still ran through this most innovative of boutique brands — until it didn't.

> In the beginning, I was more of a Gibson fan — I loved the fat sound of a humbucker guitar. Even though I grew up on

the Ventures, I had moved away from the Fender thing. I still loved the 1950s Fender stuff, but I wasn't interested in making Stratocaster clones. I regarded the set neck guitars as much more sophisticated in design and construction — much more difficult to build properly. So that's what I wanted to do, not make Fender-type bolt-on guitars, which I viewed as kind of a Lego project. I always gravitated to the highest form of the art, so pitched-back headstocks, neck pitch and glue joint neck-to-body were what I wanted to do. Now, I've come to love the simplicity of the bolt on guitar as much as the sound they make. True, anyone can make a bolt-on guitar, that's why everyone does, but there is beauty in their simplicity. In the 1980s, I designed a number of great bolt-on designs that intentionally weren't just EVH clones either. I never really sought to reach the biggest, trendy market, I just did what I liked and tried to make it so well that I could be proud of my work. It was the work that mattered, not the success. Steve Stevens was partially responsible for us moving in that direction. He was obsessed with Ed Van Halen, and wanted to get that vibe, so naturally I accepted the challenge. I thought, "Okay, I'm going to make the most killer bolt-on guitars ever." And that's what we did, but what really happened is that we diluted the brand by doing that.

After we sold the company to Kaman Music their sales force insisted on a pure Fender clone. I designed guitars that improved on the Fender thing, but that was the beginning of the end. We made a ton of them, and they were great guitars, but they sat in the stores because they lacked the one thing that people wanted — the Fender name on the headstock. I carried on for a while, then left the company until they brought me back to try to save it.

The last decade or so was really the golden era. We upped the ante on quality and pursued perfection like never before. The designs were undeniably Hamer, and we had a shit ton of endorsers who loved them, but it was too late, and the salespeople didn't get it. We'd started the whole boutique, high-end category, and dropped the ball by trying to go down market

> when everyone else went upmarket. They threw away a legacy brand. So now with my own guitar brand I just do what I want and don't have to think about sales tactics and the latest trend, or what bands are "hot" anymore. People accept what I do, and they come to me trusting my aesthetics and design philosophy. I'm fine with that, and I love what I do.
>
> —Jol Dantzig

Dave Reimer has his own take on the Hamer attitude. It's an attitude that has seen the value of the company's classic guitars soar in value in recent years on the vintage market:

> I think that the Hamer attitude was a little warmer, a little bit more organic. . . . Hamer was all about you know, if you think a '59 Les Paul is cool, well, try that shaped like an Explorer. Now you're Clapton *and* you're something new. You're everything that was before, yet you have a lantern just shining into the future. You could be both at once. That's what Hamer is to me, in that time. You weren't leaving anything behind, but you were fucking moving ahead.
>
> — Dave Reimer

CHAPTER 4

DEAN GUITARS AND THE DAWN OF ARENA ROCK

> I was tired of going to concerts and seeing the same old guitars. It bothered me to death to see an act open up with the players appearing out of smoke on a stage with 100,000 watts of light, laser beams and everybody suited up like you'd only see at a rock performance, and here'd be the guitarist playing something that was designed before rock was. My idea was to have a stage look with a radical body style so brilliant that they would light up on stage.
>
> (Dean Guitars catalog, 1981.)

The motivations of Dean Zelinsky, founder of Dean Guitars, draw obvious parallels with the vision that Paul Hamer and Jol Dantzig shared for Hamer Guitars. The goal was to take the body shapes and high quality of Gibson's early Flying V and Explorer models and add customizations and features found on Les Pauls (flamed-maple tops, binding, ebony fingerboards, and upgraded pickups — in this case the popular DiMarzio Steve's Special humbuckers) in order to create instruments of a higher quality than what Gibson was putting out at the time; guitars that would meet the high-performance needs of guitarists intent on sending louder riffs and faster licks to the upper rafters of a stadium. This was the dawn of arena rock, and Dean Guitars were there to *show* the audience how to listen.

> I feel like I was born to build guitars because I grasped everything very early. And not only how to build them, but what a guitar was. What made it special, and what made another guitar *not* special? I had an innate ability to understand the innuendo of guitars, which actually came out in my guitar building, because I added a lot of innuendo.
>
> — Dean Zelinsky

Innuendo would go on to play a key role in how Dean Guitars would seep into the consciousness of the guitar-buying public. Dean's marketing campaigns traded upon Zelinsky's perception of the instrument's connection to sexual attraction. While rock n roll certainly has its purists who engage in its practice purely for musical and artistic reasons, there is no denying that players all over the world — and let's face it, mostly male players — have sought out and reaped the social benefits of wielding an electric guitar. Dean Guitars was one of the first companies (B.C. Rich was another) to blatantly associate their instruments with the possibility of becoming more sexually desirable.

> I knew that sex appeal was the way to sell guitars. The hot chick sells guitars, but I also knew the hot chick had to be really hot, like, Playboy quality. The ad that I pulled off that changed my life is called the "girl in the water" ad.
>
> She was a girl who flew in to shoot a *Playboy* cover. The photographer I used was Barbie Benton's brother. Barbie Benton was Hugh Hefner's girlfriend at the time, and her brother worked in the studios in Chicago, and he used to shoot ads for me. I got him to shoot that ad. He shot other ads, but that was the first one he probably shot for me. He pulled off an amazing shot, which made an amazing ad. I'll give using women maybe forty percent of the credit. The woman we used and the shot we pulled off, that was way beyond just using girls in an ad. I mean, I've seen this girl in hundreds of lovely pictures. She's never looked this good.

> There were three hundred photos I had to pick from roughly, and there were two photos of this caliber that could've made the ad, you know, that were this hot, and I picked between the two. I think using girls is one thing, but nobody did it as effectively as I did, and I think it was that one shot that I pulled off that changed everything. It was a game changer for me. But I will tell you, society has changed. And what used to be acceptable [no longer is] . . . but you can't take it out of your DNA.
>
> — Dean Zelinsky

My friend Reed Shimozawa, a highly in-demand guitarist in the Canadian music scene, describes how a dean guitar ad would impact his life in a full-circle way:

> One day I came across an ad in *Guitar Player* magazine for Dean Guitars. It wasn't the now infamous Dean girl photo, it was Elliot Easton and he was holding the most amazing guitar I'd seen up to that point in my life, the ML. Half V, half Explorer, it was everything I was obsessed with all wrapped up in one glorious coffee table–sized instrument. I began to collect photos and clippings of Dean Guitars and the people who played them. This was in the early '80s, so we are talking old school scissors and tape collecting. I wrote a letter to Dean requesting a catalog and price list. My response came from the Canadian distributor and enclosed was a full color pamphlet which I laminated and probably still have somewhere. I had no idea how I would ever find the means to buy a guitar like this but I knew that I would. My salvation was my high-school girlfriend, who was not wealthy but had a good job and believed in me for some unknown reason. For my surprise birthday gift in '82 or '83, we drove two hours to Calgary to Mother's Music, the only Dean-authorized dealer in Alberta. I had carefully planned out every spec of my dream ML, and we placed a special order. It was a black ML Standard with a bound headstock. If memory serves, the total price was about one thousand seven hundred dollars which was a lot of money at that time, especially for a couple of

> teenagers. I'll never forget the day we got a call saying the guitar had arrived, months later. Man, I loved that guitar. My friends and I would stare at it in awe like it was Excalibur freed from the stone. I played some of my earliest public performances with that guitar and it always made me feel kinda special when I took it out of its massive case. Keep in mind this is all long before Dimebag had made that shape his signature look. Eventually, as I became more and more obsessed with Eddie Van Halen, the ML fell out of favor, and I traded it or sold it to get something with a Floyd. Fast forward 20 years. I'm working at the guitar store in Calgary where I spent a chunk of my adult life. A customer comes in, walks right up to me and says, "I have a guitar that you want." I'm susceptible to this kind of opener, and he proceeds to put a giant case on the counter and opens it to reveal a vintage Dean ML. My Dean ML. Exactly as I last saw it. Yeah, I bought it back.
>
> — Reed Shimozawa of Zuckerbaby,
> Wide Mouth Mason, and One Bad Son

Dean Guitars would go on to feature beautiful women to sell guitars throughout their run, and while these sexy and salacious ads may have been responsible for the initial attraction to the brand, it was the quality of the instruments that kept players coming back for more.

> I can build guitars in my sleep, okay? I mean, they're not easy things to build. When everybody started importing, and you had guitars that were made offshore, you had Gibson guitars made by Norlin, you had Fender guitars made by CBS, everybody said they weren't good, but nobody could tell you why they weren't good.
>
> I always told people that guitar building is like two chefs cooking. You give two chefs the same ingredients and the same recipe. One can make an infinitely better meal. And it's the things that aren't written down on the recipe sheet, the way one chef does something that makes the one meal better. You know what I mean? Yeah. And I've always said that about guitars. It's all how you shape

> the body, shape the neck, round over the binding — little innuendos in guitar building that give your brand its signature. And that was what was lost when companies like Gibson sold to other people — the innuendo of guitar building goes away.
>
> — Dean Zelinsky

When Dean speaks of innuendo, I believe what he is getting at is how each of the elements of his guitar craftsmanship work together to suggest the sensuality and quality that he strives for in his work:

> It takes a visionary to build a guitar. I mean, anybody can build a guitar, and anybody can go overseas and go to Korea or Indonesia today, and get a decent guitar built. But they're not gonna have all the innuendo of guitar building like they would if a real guitar maker fronts the company.
>
> — Dean Zelinsky

Dean started his company in 1976, at the tender age of 19. Knowing that musicians were seeking out higher quality, feature-loaded, instruments better than what the corporately minded, Norlin-owned Gibson and CBS-owned Fender were offering, Dean put his innate skills as a woodworker toward the task of satisfying that need.

> I started playing guitar at the age of nine and repairing guitars at fourteen. Before I knew it, I was buying old vintage instruments and rebuilding them. . . . I began thinking about building my own guitars when I began to see the big guitar companies losing touch with the performer.
>
> — Dean Zelinsky (*Dean News*, Summer 1981.)

Comparisons between guitars and cars came up quite a bit in my conversation with Mr. Zelinsky — they make sense. When it comes to customizations, Dean guitars were absolutely designed in the spirit of the hot rod.

> I always said, back in the day, you had to kinda pick a lane. In America, we have Ford or GM, you know? Two different types

> of approaches to cars. Guitars were the same way, Gibson and Fender. I was always in that Gibson lane, so I was really well aware of what they're doing. Norlin had taken over and the guitars that Gibson were making were not good.
>
> — Dean Zelinsky

Vs and Explorers were becoming more popular thanks to the reissue efforts of the big boys at Gibson, but Zelinsky was intent on building guitars based on those designs and loading them up with the good stuff. At the same time, he wanted to create something that was unique, something that would set his instruments apart from other companies, guitars that were different from companies like Ibanez, who were bringing to market high-quality copies of Gibson's futuristic '50s shapes.

> Probably one of the strongest reasons I began manufacturing my own models though, was the need I saw for a good "stage guitar". Most companies weren't combining the best manufacturing features and probably for no other reason than to cut costs — after all, R & D can be a good portion of your overall budget.
>
> — Dean Zelinsky (*Dean News*, Summer 1981.)

In late 1976, Zelinsky worked night and day to get his guitar factory up and running. He hired Zan Skolnick to be the marketing director of his new company, and set about the monumental task of not only building guitars to show at the upcoming NAMM show on January 21, 1977, but also developing effective marketing materials in a pre-digital age in order to prime the pump of retailer interest in advance of the show. The result of this effort was an ad that ran in the back of a music trade magazine prior to the show, featuring three Dean guitar creations.

> NAMM was approaching and one day my mother, who very often worked in the office, comes back in the shop and says a guy named Jerry Ash is on the phone. Jerry owned Sam Ash Music which was the biggest music store chain in the country with seven stores. Guitar Center was not all that big back then. Keep in mind, I'm 19 years old, starting a guitar company and

> now I'm on the phone with The Largest Music Retailer in the World . . . and he called me! We had a nice conversation and he said he was going to come by my booth at NAMM. He went on to say, "if your guitars are as good as you say they are, I'm going to buy them!" Jerry was a sharp businessman, and being cutting edge on new products was a big part of his success. Apparently reading the classifieds in the back of magazines was part of his M.O.
>
> — Dean Zelinsky ("The History of Dean Guitars," MikesGig.com.)

Inspired by the Flying V, as well as the split-V headstock that was found on the earliest Gibson Explorers in the '50s, Dean developed a headstock concept that would infamously become known as the BFH — Big Fuckin' Headstock. By creating his headstock in the shape of a symmetrical V, Zelinsky hit upon a signature look that could be instantly recognized from the back of a stadium as a design that was all his own. This headstock adorned four models that would go on to become iconic designs. The Explorer-shaped Z, the Flying V–shaped V, and a guitar that would merge both of these space-age shapes into one incredible hybrid, the Dean ML, named after, and inspired by, the passing of a childhood friend, Matthew Lynn. The ML was Zelinsky's first truly unique design, and was soon followed by the brilliant E'lite model, and its upgraded three-pickup, block-inlay version, the Cadillac. The E'lite was a mix of the lower bout of a Les Paul and the upper-bout wings of an Explorer with the Flying V–inspired BFH headstock thrown in, a holy trinity of classic Gibson hard-rock axes formed into one slick rock-n-roll weapon, and could be found in the hands of rock hotshots like Kerry Livgren and Rich Williams of Kansas, Ric Ocasek of the Cars, John McFee of the Doobie Brothers, Nancy Wilson and Howard Leese of Heart, and Sheron Alton of Toronto. Eventually, all Dean models with this shape would come to be known as Cadillacs, and these instruments were perhaps the most literal visual representation of the back-to-the-future spirit of post-Gibson pointiness.

With the interest of the biggest music retailer in America spurring him on, Dean and his skeleton crew of family and friends set about the task of getting a targeted goal of 10 guitars built and ready to display. Zelinsky also had to build a modular booth to display the guitars on at the trade show, one that could fit into the Chevy van he would be taking, along with his pal Keith Fisher (who helped him build that booth), across the country from the wintery environs of blustery Chicago into the sunnier climes of Anaheim, California.

> It was a grueling drive, about 30 hours, and because of all the prior challenges, the calendar didn't allow any time for stopping. Keith and I needed to drive straight through taking turns driving and sleeping. I remember there was a time we simply couldn't go any longer. We pulled over and both fell asleep for about two hours and then got back on the road.
>
> The van had two seats up front and that was it. It was freezing cold driving west from Chicago at that time, these vans had no insulation and never heated well. The heat blowing from the dashboard barely reached the two front seats. There were two circular vents on top of the dashboard for defrosting the windshield. I cut out the louvers in the passenger side vent, which perfectly fit a Shopvac hose that I stuck into the hole. Keith and I took turns putting the hose under our jackets to keep warm until we hit warmer weather. Not sure how I thought the guitars finished with nitrocellulose lacquer would survive the cold, but it obviously was not on my radar.
>
> We were headed to my aunt's house near Anaheim. She was a college professor who invested in Orange County homes and had a house for us to stay in until we checked into the hotel suite.
>
> We pulled up to my Aunt's house the Wednesday afternoon before the show, totally exhausted from our long journey. We unpacked the van only to find that all the guitars — AFTER ALL THAT WORK AND ALL THAT PREP — had finished cracked and checked!! My first NAMM show had suddenly became a NIGHTMARE!
>
> — Dean Zelinsky ("The History of Dean Guitars," MikesGig.com.)

Like any of the challenges Zelinsky faced in bringing his vision to life, he soldiered on and found a way to have instruments ready for display and demonstration at that trade show, even if they weren't in the same pristine condition they were prior to leaving Chicago. It's hard to fathom that a 19-year-old Dean Zelinsky, fresh out of high school, could walk away from the three-day trade show with a remarkable $45,000 in sales, but this was indeed what happened. Perhaps this was a testament to the wide-eyed innocence of the times, but more likely it was the incredible quality of instruments that the young entrepreneur and luthier was bringing to market. Of course, the pre-NAMM marketing advice proffered by Zan Skolnick didn't hurt either.

The Dean Guitar 1977 catalog gave retailers looking for the next big thing in guitars the following description of Zelinsky's outlier take on Gibson's wild-child designs.

> Dean Guitars' new solid-body instruments, introduced at the 1977 NAMM Western Market, embody the high-quality materials and craftsmanship usually limited to custom instruments. All models feature distinctive head, body, and neck designs. The neck, specially created for the high speed playing that guitarists want today, is up to 3/8ths of an inch thinner than models of other major manufacturers and is molded into the body in such a way that it's "good to the last fret." Fingerboards are of ebony or rosewood on a standard 22-fret scale and dotted with abalone. The mahogany body is topped with two-piece curly maple which is quarter-sawn to enhance grain qualities. Electronic equipment is set directly into the wood.
>
> Components include two specially-made DiMarzio super distortion humbucker pickups, a 3-way toggle switch, two volume controls and one master tone control. All hardware is precision cast, high quality brass or chrome-plated steel. Pickguards are optional. All models are available in Cherryburst, Brasiliaburst, or Opaque black.

What really got the Dean machine rolling was its first high-profile customer — a player who, alongside his successful band, was whetting the appetites of hard-rock loving listeners with a penchant for progressive music.

Kerry Livgren of Kansas was not only the first rock star to play my guitar, he literally bought the first guitar I ever shipped. And I didn't figure that out until about five years ago.

The NAMM show was in California, West Coast, '77 Anaheim. And all the guitars that I brought cracked — the finishes cracked. Disaster of a show, but I sold $45,000 worth of guitars. I just took orders. The first guy to come by my booth and give me an order was Jerry Ash, Sam Ash Music, which is the biggest store in the country at the time. So literally the first dealer I ever took on was Sam Ash Music. We hadn't shipped any guitars till the June show. We were physically working out manufacturing problems because everything leading up to the Anaheim show was about trying to tool a factory. At this point, you're only partially tooled, but you're getting your prototypes to the factory. Now (after the NAMM show in Anaheim) you got orders. I got $45,000 worth of orders. Now I really have to manufacture guitars. I have to tighten up my tooling and my procedures and hire employees and do all that stuff. So that took us another five months.

So now we're heading into the June show with a new batch of guitars that were ready to roll. Now we can produce, we can manufacture guitars. So the first batch of manufactured, ready to ship guitars were at the June show in Atlanta. Now Kansas had hit big with the big song, "Carry on My Wayward Son." They had all moved to Atlanta because they married flight attendants, and the flight attendants were all based in Atlanta.

The June NAMM show is happening. Someone tells me Kerry Livgren's at the show, and next thing I know, he's at my booth! So, I say, come on in, and he played a guitar. He's playing a guitar in my booth, we have a conversation, and then he split.

We exchanged phone numbers. Not cell phone numbers. [*laughs*] So, the show ends on a Sunday. I'm back at my office, and I get a phone call.

"Hey, Dean. It's Kerry from Kansas. I want you to know I played every guitar at the show, and I like yours the best. Can I get that guitar?" [the tobacco Z] We had just shipped the

> guitars back from the show. Then he says, "You know, my manager says I'm at a place in my career where I shouldn't have to pay for guitars." I said, "Yeah . . . I get it. But I'm in a place in my career where I need to charge for guitars." [*laughs*] Because I was literally just about broke at that time. I was like scraping the bottom. It had been so long trying to tool the factory and do everything. It cost a fortune to launch the company. I said, "Tell you what, I'll sell it to you for $400." He says, "Yeah, but I'm leaving for a tour. I need it right away." I said, "I'll ship the guitar today, just put a check in the mail." He said okay, so I shipped him the guitar and a few days later, the check showed up.
>
> — Dean Zelinsky

> The way it's sculpted out . . . the way it hangs on your body . . . the total feel and aggressive sound makes Deans the essence of a great rock n roll guitar.
>
> — Kerry Livgren (1981 Dean catalog.)

Over the course of a phone call, a tobacco sunburst Dean Z guitar was on its way to a life of stadium shows with one of the most visible arena-rock guitar players of the '70s. Soon after, Livgren's guitar partner in Kansas, Rich Williams, would also start playing a Dean. A pretty great start.

Harkening back to Dean's use of beautiful women in guitar ads, it seems Zelinsky's understanding of innate human desires and appetites informs not only the commercial side of his enterprise, but the actual creation of the instruments themselves. Beyond the initial sense of attracting the serious guitarist to his instruments through their looks and a perceived association with virility, there had to be form, function, and an exceedingly high level of quality that could sustain a lifelong relationship between the player and the guitar. Dean knew he had to foster a belief within a prospective customer that a Dean guitar was worthy of the investment, that a Dean guitar was cool, and you could be cool too, if you were cool enough to drop your money on one.

> Your DNA is preprogrammed to be able to tell or see if something's sexy. That's not something that you learn. You know?

Nobody looks at a Ferrari and a Buick and says, "Hey, that Buick is really cool." You know what I mean? And the same thing with your taste in women. I mean, in the old days when you were allowed to use models and stuff, people used attractive models. It wasn't what you were used to — they didn't look like your mom. You know, you're used to your mom.

I saw Flying Vs and Explorers, and they didn't look like everything else, and they didn't look like round body guitars, and they were cool. The other thing that was happening is, arena rock's starting to happen. We're coming out of an era when the Beatles came to America, and they didn't even have sound systems big enough to support them [in large venues]. That's in '64. Okay? I'm saying that the system wasn't ready for this movement that was gonna happen. And they're playing Shea Stadium in New York, and they're using speakers you'd probably use in your backyard.

Rock n roll as we knew it during the late '70s and '80s was way different than what had happened prior. And I felt the guitars were behind the curve. I saw a V and an Explorer and I lit up. It lit me up when I saw those guitars.

I said this in my earliest years, guitars were part of rock n roll fashion. What the guitar player was holding in his hands was equally important, or more important than anything they were wearing. And the thing about a rock star is, they don't look like you. Nowadays, they do. Guys go on with jeans and a T-shirt, like Dave Grohl. But back in the day, *everybody* dressed up, and they weren't dressed like people on the street. And the guitar was an added feature, and I was prepared — "I'm gonna make the guitars of the time."

Listen, the Les Paul — it's an iconic guitar. I still couldn't really critique the Les Paul today as far as the design. It's kinda modeled after a woman's body. It's kinda sexy. But, you know, there was just room for a whole lot more.

And that was kind of my approach, but my approach was twofold. One was the design aspect, just beauty, but there had to be something under the hood in terms of how it was made.

At this point, Dean drops a bit of knowledge that fits perfectly with the back-to-the-future concept that plays such a big part in the evolution of pointy guitars, and really, guitars in general:

> I'll never forget that at one point, when DeLorean's stock tanked and the company was in trouble, and DeLorean got busted for cocaine. All of a sudden, you could buy a DeLorean for $14,000. They were, like, $30,000 [before that]. So I said, "I'm gonna go buy a DeLorean." I went to a DeLorean dealership, and I drove the thing. It was a pig. [*laughs*] It was the worst designed car — it had no engine. It was a Renault six cylinder. It wasn't as fast as my mother's Monte Carlo. And I left. I can't buy this car. You know what I mean? When I say it had to have something under the hood, that was a perfect example of something that had some "show" but no "go," you know? So, my guitars were gonna have "show" and they were gonna "go." [*laughs*]
>
> — Dean Zelinsky

Speaking of cars, hearing a certain Boston-based band that was taking late '70s arena rock in a decidedly new-wave direction on the radio for the first time prompted Zelinsky to think they might be just what he needed to help spread the word about his forward-thinking designs.

> The Cars were unique. There's a handful of songs you hear in your life where you say, "This is new." The *chunk chunk* of those guitars . . . everyone chugs today, but at the time it was really new and catchy, and I just felt like these guys needed my guitars. They needed my guitars and, probably equally, I needed them. The band was just what I needed. [*laughs*] I felt the band was gonna be big and I wanted them to have my guitars. And that's a great time to get a band when they're on the way up. You know what I mean? You get a nice ride. [*laughs*]
>
> — Dean Zelinsky

Really, it's hard to think of a player more suited to the role of Dean-endorsed artist than the Cars guitarist Elliot Easton. The Roy Thomas Baker–produced

1978 self-titled debut had a forward-thinking modern rock song that deftly straddled the line between pop songcraft, cutting edge sonic technology, and the best rock maneuvers from the previous decades. Tracks like "Just What I Needed," "My Best Friend's Girl," and "Good Times Roll" were clean, precise, and cutting edge without ever being sterile, their new-wave keyboard and electro-drum cool tempered with the organic heat of Easton's impeccably crafted guitar parts. Credit to drummer David Robinson, bassist/vocalist Benjamin Orr (who could be seen playing a Dean ML bass), rhythm guitarist/vocalist Ric Ocasek (who also rocked Dean ML and Cadillac models), and keyboardist Greg Hawkes, who all contributed to a contemporary, modern pop sound that could rock as hard as it could techno-shock. The Cars were a case of technology *enhancing* the sound of the band, rather than *becoming* the sound of the band.

If ever a player served the song with his guitar solos and riffs, it's Elliot Easton. Easton could take Chuck Berry's double stops, James Burton's country-inspired twang, a jazz guitarist's understanding of harmony and melodic playing that follows the chord changes, and a seemingly endless vocabulary of rock guitar moves to create a style that was both varied and identifiable. To this day, seeing the Cars in concert is the only situation where I remember the audience cheering wildly after almost every solo, as if they were miniature hit songs within a hit song. With Easton's playing on the Cars' stellar debut, as well as on smash albums like *Candy-O*, *Panorama*, *Shake It Up*, *Heartbeat City*, and beyond, the past was brought screaming into the present to reveal a future of musical possibilities, achieving much the same spirit as Dean Zelinsky's player-centric guitar designs.

> Dean brought me an ML during the *Candy-O* sessions and I put it right to work. . . . The first song I used it on was "Since I Held You," and I liked it a lot. Now, people kind of laugh about the pointy headstocks and funny-shaped bodies, but the Dean was a really good guitar, and I really enjoyed playing them. They had fantastic tones, felt great, and had great necks.
>
> — Elliot Easton (*Vintage Guitar*, March 2018.)

Guitars, cars, women — a theme that would take holistic shape in what may be Dean Guitars' most famous endorsement relationship. In the early

1980s, ZZ Top was a loud and proud product of the great state of Texas, a bad and nationwide power trio known for its adherence to the principles of the great blues musicians who preceded them (ZZ Top sound a lot like B.B. King, don't it?), but also to the sonic-guitar explorations of Jeff Beck, Eric Clapton, and Jimi Hendrix. (The band's founder, Billy Gibbons, had opened for Hendrix's first headlining tour of the U.S. with his psychedelic band the Moving Sidewalks.) ZZ Top's vocalist and guitarist, Gibbons was an acolyte of the tone seekers who came before him, and — not unlike Zelinsky — a chef who could take different ingredients from the past and cook up delicacies that smacked of futurism. Like the proper rock-n-roll Anglophiles they were, ZZ Top signed with London Records shortly after the disbanding of the Moving Sidewalks and released *ZZ Top's First Album* in 1971. Bassist/vocalist Dusty Hill and drummer Frank Beard (who had played together in American Blues) rounded out the trio. The band followed up that first album with 1972's *Rio Grande Mud*, and then with a string of hit albums, like the masterpieces *Tres Hombres* (1973) and *Fandango!* (1975), which yielded the classic radio hits and live staples "La Grange," "Beer Drinkers & Hell Raisers," and "Tush," each of which featured searing guitar tones smokier than Texas BBQ emanating from Gibbons's impressive arsenal of classic guitars. To this day, these recordings contain some of the most sought after sounds in rock n roll, high water marks for tasty licks and suck-the-meat-off-the-bone tone.

Beyond their musical reputation as a band that could swing, shuffle, *and* rock with the best of them, ZZ Top was also winning fans with their sly and sassy lyrical content. Lowdown never sounded as upscale as it did when Gibbons drawled about the "nice girls" of La Grange (a famous Texan den of iniquity) or, in "I'm Bad, I'm Nationwide" from 1979's *Degüello*, the fine fox in the front (and three more in the back) of his Cadillac.

Degüello was the first album ZZ Top recorded for Warner Bros. after their run with London Records ended with the *Tejas* album (1976). Their first effort for Warner Bros. was a platinum hit, which yielded two other classic singles — "Cheap Sunglasses" and "I Thank You." When the band went to support the album on their European tour, they performed on BBC2's Old Grey Whistle Test, where they were introduced to the synthesizer sounds of another band who was in the studio that day, Orchestral Manoeuvres in the Dark (OMD). Taken by the English band's stage presence and technological savvy, ZZ Top started experimenting with new maneuvers of their own, both choreographed and sonic. The beginning of that experimentation can be heard on 1981's *El Loco*, with keyboards and drum machines melding with the band's southern-fried boogie and shake. But the even more intense interpolation of these past and present ideals on the band's next release would see ZZ Top become one of the most important visual and musical representations of the MTV generation. And they were playing Dean guitars when they did that.

> It's quite a story. I've told this Billy Gibbons story a gazillion times, but, Billy, he was my friend before he ever played my guitars, and he used to call me up and we'd just talk, you know? This is before cell phones, when you were in your house or in your office with a cord. [*laughs*]
>
> But anyhow, we used to talk and one day, I said, "Let me build you a guitar." And I built him the guitar and I shipped him the guitar. It was an ML guitar, which, by the way, to this day he never played live, that one guitar. And, you know, we'd talk blah blah blah and one day, he calls me. He's in the studio recording [1983's *Eliminator*], and he says, "This guitar just sounds amazing — the whole record is your guitar!" And that was verified by not only him, but . . . his producer and manager, Bill Ham, told me this. And then I just recently read something about the engineer in the studio said that whole album was done on that Dean guitar and how amazing it was.
>
> I was hanging with Billy. He was calling me up, and I said, let me make you guitars for the tour. There was all this stuff going on that I was a part of. I was just a young kid just doing what I do, you know, building guitars.
>
> It had to be, like, two, three years ago, I watched this documentary on ZZ Top, and I learned so much about what was going on at that time that I wasn't aware of. Gibbons was hanging in Europe and hanging in discos and clubs, and he was all upset because nobody was dancing to ZZ Top music. The whole *Eliminator* record was born out of that. First of all, MTV was new and video was making bands. Bands had to embrace video, so that was one thing. But the music was

born out of dance music. And next thing you know, Gibbons tells me he's got a Fairlight, which was a $50,000 sequencing keyboard. Before there were $400 sequencing keyboards, the only sequencing keyboard you could get, I think, was a Fairlight worth 50 grand. So that whole record was done on the Fairlight.

But he's hanging in Europe, hanging in the clubs, and he's orchestrating this record. And I'm just in Chicago getting — I don't wanna say marching orders, but we were talking about guitars. You know? I didn't know what was going on.

You can't take this to the bank, but my best recollection is that the guys didn't get along. Billy told me, "We really get together for records and tours, and then we go away." That's how the whole long beard thing started because they were on hiatus and they hadn't seen each other. And then when they said, "Okay, we gotta get together and make a record," the two guys hadn't seen each other in a year or two, and they both had beards down to their stomach. But the point is, they would make the records. Those guys [bassist Dusty Hill and drummer Frank Beard] would come, play their parts, and then they would leave, and Billy would orchestrate. This is the story — that he kinda finished the record. And I think they used to put drum tracks in and then Frank would come in and play the drums to the beat of the music that Billy wrote with the electronic drums. When he made the *Eliminator* record, they all came and did their parts, and when they heard the album, they weren't on it, you know? And I guess that's the story.

I'm getting away from guitars now, but the point I'm making is that Billy orchestrated this album. It was based on this whole desire to get people to dance to ZZ Top music. Sequencing was huge, and electronic drums were huge because that's what was going on in the discos. And I'm making guitars. Then the next thing after the record's done, he literally told me to come see him down in Houston. I heard the record in its raw form, you know, on tape in his car.

> I think I heard it before [they added] all the sequencing. I remember hearing "Legs" and not remembering all that sequencing stuff in it. But, anyways, I heard the record, and then they were getting ready for the tour.
>
> I said, "Billy, why don't you let me make you some guitars for the tour?" The tour was really cool and high-tech, and I made really cool guitars. He wanted them painted fluorescent. He was putting UV lights in the spots, and the guitars were lighting up like they had lights in them on stage. So, he kind of took that whole dance theme — they got dressed up and they took it on the road. My guitars were a part of it.
>
> — Dean Zelinsky

Eliminator is a triumphant mash up of hard rock guitar hooks, hook-laden sing-along choruses, and highly danceable rhythms. All the aspirational attitude and juke-joint joy of the techno grooves and Texan tones of "Legs," "Gimme All Your Lovin'," "Sharp Dressed Man," and "Got Me Under Pressure" resulted in a timeless, high-society backyard bbq of an album.

In a way, the '80s were a reinvention of the spirit of the '50s. The space-age ideals of the latter era might have been a little too far-fetched for the consumer to grab on to, but by the time the '80s rolled around, the appetites of the masses had caught up. And, with the dawn of MTV basically showing people how to listen to music, ZZ Top was at the vanguard of this whacky futurism, playing fuzzy Dean guitars that they could spin around their belt buckles!

> Right. Well, they embraced videos. The tour started happening, they had the videos going, and they had this new look and this new sound. Also, tours got way more interactive. It used to be you see a band play and they had some props on stage and stuff. The laser light show started coming in.
>
> They had huge screens with video playing on screen and stuff like that. The shows were becoming way more theatrical, I guess, for lack of a better word.

But as Zelinsky says, under the hood you've still got something that can deliver tone that's good enough for a band that's built their career on great guitar sounds.

> Well, if Billy Gibbons used your guitar to do a whole record in 1983 or whenever that record was made, you had a great sounding guitar.
>
> There's a handful of guys that were known for tone and he was one of them. You know, ZZ Top had their own sound. He had an arsenal of guitars at his disposal. So, if Billy played your guitars, they were special.
>
> — Dean Zelinsky

Gibbons was responsible for getting another rocker, in this case a red one, to use a Dean guitar on arena stages. Sammy Hagar is no stranger to pointy guitars. Gibson Explorers, Jackson Kelly and Rhoads models, and the iconic, red Dean ML he is holding as he parachutes onto the White House grounds on the cover of his platinum album *VOA* are all connected to my perception of Hagar as a tireless live performer and, for all of his obvious vocal prowess, as an almost equally talented guitarist. When I think back to seeing Hagar on the 5150 Tour, his first tour as vocalist for Van Halen in 1986, his guitar playing and the guitars he used remain as vivid a memory as anything that else that transpired at Toronto's CNE Stadium stage that night. Considering it was Eddie Van Halen on lead guitar, that is truly saying something.

In fact, when I was performing in a musical theater production a few years back, I spoke about Hagar's impact on me to such an extent that it inspired my fellow guitar slinger, Gino Del Sole, to get his first pointy guitar.

> The purchase of my first and only *real* pointy guitar was inspired by yourself, Sean! We were performing Rock of Ages [a musical] in the spring of 2023 when you stated that you wished to get a red Jackson Rhoads V like the one Sammy Hagar plays. I happened to go to Long & McQuade in North York the next day for something unrelated and spotted an unfinished one. I believe I sent you a pic and offered to finish it in red for you. You passed on the idea (thankfully!) and it was then I had a lightbulb moment! I could get it and finish it myself with the

> Randy Rhoads–style Concorde theme. I was excited about my new project! It came out great and I play it to this day.
>
> — Gino Del Sole, "first call" musical theater and session guitarist, Toronto.

Sorry, this is a chapter about Dean — we'll get to that Jackson guy later. Just how did Sammy Hagar come onboard with Dean, again?

> Through Billy Gibbons. They were on the *Eliminator* tour. And Billy said they were gonna be playing Miami. He said, "Why don't you come to the show?" So, I flew to Miami. We were staying at the Fontainebleu. And we were at the pool bar. This was maybe the day of the show or the day before the show.
>
> And we're out at the pool, and there's the three of us sitting at the bar, me and Billy and Sammy. And Billy turns to Sammy and goes, "How come you don't play a Dean guitar?" [*laughs*] And Sammy says, "Because Dean never made me one." Billy literally goes back to his room, comes back with this briefcase because he used to carry Dean catalogs in a briefcase. [*laughs*] He sat down, and the three of us worked out which guitar he was gonna get.
>
> It turned out he wanted the Baby Z. And then he said, "I'm playing Chicago in a few months." He says, "Deliver it." I said, "Fine." So, I went to the show with the guitar. I met with him, and he put the guitar right on stage. He literally got in front of I don't know how many thousands of people and he says, "Dean Zelinsky just built me this guitar. And I'm gonna play it. If it's great, I'm gonna keep playing. If not, I'm gonna crash and burn it." [*laughs*] I didn't know too much about Sammy Hagar. He picked up the guitar and he was climbing the rafters with it. He was flying all over the stage with the guitar, and that's how it all happened.
>
> — Dean Zelinsky

Hagar's use of a custom Dean ML guitar on the aforementioned *VOA* album cover and 5150 Tour, and most importantly, in the video for Sammy's signature song "I Can't Drive 55" makes him an important part of Dean's association with world-class stadium rockers.

By 1984, Dean had introduced a slimmed down version of the V and Z models that would become known as the Baby series. They had also moved to a smaller headstock design, which would be referred to as the "shrimp fork," which better accommodated locking tremolo units and improved intonation. These smaller models were perfect for players who wanted to retain the scale length and feel of the Standard models, but could benefit from the lighter weight, a real plus for an artist who was beginning to employ more stagecraft and choreography into their live-concert and video performances.

Just as ZZ Top had found their greatest commercial success with the 20 million-plus selling *Eliminator* thanks to the use of iconic video imagery (Gibbon's custom red 1933 Ford Coupe, the image defining beards and shades, the cool as ice Playboy models), Heart made an even more radical visual and musical transition in the '80s, which rocketed them to the top of the pop charts.

Sisters Ann and Nancy Wilson had found substantial success in the '70s with a deft blend of Led Zeppelin and folk-inspired hard rock music, a fixation on Beatles-inspired songcraft and harmony, and a vocal blend that could only come from siblings. Alongside guitarists Howard Leese and Roger Fisher, bassist Steve Fossen, and drummer Michael Derosier, the Seattle-born group had taken their highly dynamic mix of acoustic and electric guitars and Ann Wilson's soaring vocal chops to the upper reaches of the album charts and dominated the album-oriented radio (AOR) waves with efforts like *Dreamboat Annie, Little Queen, Dog & Butterfly* by following their muse and honoring the influences that most deeply resonated with them to create a sound that fit perfectly with the expansive tastes of '70s rock audiences. The band entered the '80s strong with the *Bébé le Strange* album, but by that point tastes were changing and, as rock n roll became more streamlined and compact thanks to the impact of punk and new wave, Heart struggled to find solid commercial footing with their follow-up albums *Private Audition* (1982) and *Passionworks* (1983). Both albums failed to reach the gold and platinum heights of their predecessors, and marked the end of their relationship with Epic Records. Despite the band taking on a simpler, hard rock–based guitar sound, these albums simply lacked the production power that was coming from other acts competing for the same AOR real estate.

In 1985, the band saw a move to Capitol Records, and a chance to remain in the major-label record game provided they were willing to go along with the direction suggested by the record company and their producer, Ron Nevison. The result was 1985's self-titled, 5-million-selling smash album *Heart*, and a radical departure from their warm, organic sound of the past. The Heart lineup had changed on the previous recording to include some new members — drummer Denny Carmassi and bassist Mark Andes. Both members brought with them not only formidable performance chops, but a willingness to adapt to the visual and musical changes that would see Heart become one of the most visible entities of the MTV era.

Delicate and deft acoustic guitar intros, warm tube-driven organic amplifier tones, and gooey and chewy analog effects and synthesizers were now replaced with cool and crisp digital reverbs, heavily processed electric guitars, Simmons electronic drums, and thick keyboard pads. Many die-hard Heart fans would argue that this was a denigration of the earlier aesthetic that had made Heart special, but millions of rock fans embraced the hit songs like "What About Love" (a cover written by Jim Vallance and members of the band Toronto, including Dean endorser Sheron Alton) and "Nothin' at All," while guitarist/vocalist Nancy Wilson could be seen sporting a blue-burst Dean Standard Z in the video for "These Dreams," and a pink burst Dean Baby Z in the clip for rocker "Never."

Howard Leese and Nancy Wilson had been flirting with pointier guitar shapes since the dawn of the '80s. Leese has an enviable vintage guitar collection with numerous classic Gibson modernistic shapes, including some gorgeous Firebird VII's from 1964 and '65, and a '58 Flying V that was used to record the rhythm guitar tracks to '80s Heart classics "What About Love" and "Alone."

While Leese is most closely associated with vintage Gibsons, Fenders, and PRS models, he also endorsed Washburn A-20 guitars along with Wilson for a spell, and could be seen taking a Dean ML for a spin in live-concert situations. And while one is most likely to see Wilson playing classic Gibson and Fender models these days, the ubiquitous nature of video in the mid-80s will always tie her to Dean guitars.

The band was now in full makeup and regal dress that would be fitting of seventeenth-century French royalty, a mix of crushed velvet and spandex, along with breath-confining bustiers for the Wilson sisters. By all accounts, it was not the happiest of times for the Wilsons, who struggled with the imposition of male-influenced image consultations, body-shaming and framing, and an ever-growing feeling of artifice. On the other hand, the pomp and grandeur of these videos actually saw the men and women in the band as unified in their look. For all of the overt sexuality foisted upon the Wilsons, the boys in the band were at the very least blurring the lines of gender and what constitutes the visual representation of the traditional male. Howard Leese and Mark Andes were no strangers to wild-looking guitars in Heart videos, and clearly the shapes and finishes of Nancy Wilson's Dean guitars played a role in the overall presentation.

> The guitars were part of the fashion and it helped. I'm not gonna take credit for anything, but I think they saw my guitars [and thought] the carpet had to match the cushions. It was part of the look. People were gravitating to my guitars because of the look. They were saying *I need that look*, and then they loved the sound.
>
> — Dean Zelinsky

In a letter to retailers in the Dean 1983–84 catalog, Zelinsky highlighted the features of the Hollywood series of guitars, which included the Baby models, as well as his take on the Stratocaster shape, the Bel Aire.

> The Hollywood Guitars are the hottest rock guitars ever. Designed with today's performer in mind. They're available in two models, the Hollywood and the Hollywood Z (as pictured on the reverse side).
>
> The necks are made of rock hard maple shaped especially for the ease of high speed playing. The fingerboards are made of high quality rosewood for the smoothest playability and have 24 frets for a full 2 octaves (25½" scale). The pickups are two specially made Dean humbuckers designed for incredible sustain and tonal quality.
>
> The Hollywood models are available in three beautiful high gloss finishes. Choose from a brilliant Pearl Red, Pearl White, or Jet Black.

> Finally, both the Hollywood and the Hollywood Z are available with either a flat mount bridge or the New Accutune*™ locking tremolo system. The Accutune system locks above the nut and has fine tuning on the bridge which enables you to divebomb the vibrato and come back in perfect tune.
>
> Find out why these and thousands of other performers play Dean Guitars. ZZ Top, Def Leppard, Iron Maiden, Loverboy, Triumph, The Cars, Kansas, Heart, John Cougar Band, John McFee (The Doobie Bros), Gary Moore, Sammy Hagar, Jefferson Starship, Toronto, Savoy Brown, Shalamar . . . People who live the Rock n Roll Dream . . . These are the people we build guitars for.
>
> — Dean Zelinsky, President

Reading the list of bands that used Dean Guitars, all of whom are now classic-rock radio staples, hits me with an immediate feeling of the innocence and naive excitement of the new arena-rock era. Before huge video screens, LED lights, and lasers made every seat in a stadium feel like the front row, performers had to fight for the attention of the punter with the nose-bleed seats, and a Dean guitar was a tool that could aid and abet in this quest. I can only imagine how exciting and rewarding it must have been for these musicians to be holding in their hands Dean's embodiment of their own musical ideals, an amplification of the musical promises of the decades before. It must have been equally thrilling for the audience members of the time, discovering something new and exciting with each concert — innovations in light, sound, staging, wardrobe. And in the case of the bands above, revealed through the haze of pot smoke and dry ice, a Dean guitar with a Big Fuckin' Headstock, homed in on your very rock-n-roll soul.

I asked Zelinsky if there was anything that he looked for in a Dean Guitars–endorsed artist? Were there particular traits that he was looking for?

> You always want a rock god. You want a guitar idol. You know, this was the era of arena bands. I wanted everybody. If I liked them, I really wanted them. If I didn't like them, you know, I kinda wanted them. [*laughs*] I used to spend a lot of time going backstage.

> I don't know what genre the Pretenders and all those bands were — kind of that new wave–type stuff? And it seemed like Hamer was always after those people, and I just didn't really care for the music. It's easier when you know the players to go knock on their door. New wave wasn't my thing, and we didn't chase that market. All the guitar idols were playing hard rock.
>
> — Dean Zelinsky

Canadian guitarist Rik Emmett was one such guitar idol, and his band Triumph was a pioneer in arena-rock production, taking lights, lasers, pyrotechnics, and sound reinforcements to new heights, all the while demonstrating a self-directed and self-managed business acumen that was as impressive as the diversity of the music.

Rik is a world-class player and a lover of the guitar in the purest sense — a musician who can deftly incorporate styles including jazz, classical, folk, British blues rock, and heavy metal in a seamless and fluid manner. Throw in his impressive vocal range, a penchant for writing musically challenging songs with enough hooks to connect with the common man and woman — "Hold On," "Fight the Good Fight," "Never Surrender," "Allied Forces" — plus him being an athletic-performance and a pretty good lookin' cat to boot, and you have the perfect Dean Guitars rock-god endorser.

> There was a guy who had a store in Mississauga called Music City. And he actually became a distributor. And I guess he and Rik Emmett were buddies, you know. Rik Emmett probably used to buy a lot of stuff from him. So, he turned Rik on to Dean Guitars and, at some point there was a phone call, then I made him a custom one. I worked out all the details with Rik. It was a one pickup V, and I remember we put the jack plate on the upper wing. So it's kinda unique in that way — it had a twist.
>
> — Dean Zelinsky

> When I got into Triumph, I got a Gibson Flying V that I had painted all white. I had it repainted because I wanted to come out on the stage at the beginning and make a bold statement. And white guitars make a great statement because if

the spotlights are red, your guitar goes red. If the spotlight goes blue, your guitar goes blue. So, to me, white was this really cool color to have on stage. Mike [Triumph bassist, Mike Levine] had his Fender bass repainted white, and I had a white double-neck and I had a brown Flying V . . . but then I was like, let's put a mirror pickguard on and get it repainted white. It never sounded any good. It was a very dull sounding guitar. You know? You could only ever use the bridge pickup. You could never use the neck pickup. It just was too dark, too woofy. And I had Les Pauls and then I got the (Framus) Akkerman. I was getting into this whole thing of having a guitar tech. I never had that earlier in bar bands. In Triumph, I could be changing guitar every song if I wanted because the tech could be bringing me something new.

My introduction into the Dean thing was through a local guitar retailer at a shop called Music City in Port Credit [Ontario], and that guy was Wally Bieniawski. Wally was a great guy, and he ran the local music store. He became the Canadian distributor for Dean. That was my local store where I'd go for picks and strings and Wally said, "Hey, do you wanna do an endorsement deal?" And I went, "Well, I'm not crazy about those headstocks, man. I kinda want the straight string pull through the nut." And he goes, "No, no, you're gonna look incredible on stage!"

Wally pitched me, and at the time, Dean had already made deals with, the guy in Kansas, Kerry Livgren, and he was playing his guitars and the guy in the Doobie Brothers, McFee, I think, was his name. So I went, "Okay, let me try some. The Cadillac." And then I went, "Okay, I think a flying V would be really cool." And the guy said, "We'll make you a custom one."

Wally had put me on the phone with Dean, and I was talking to him direct. He said, "I'm gonna make you the best flying V that you ever had. It's gonna sound amazing. It's gonna be great." And I went, "Okay, I don't want it to weigh a ton. I want it to look really nice, white with all this black, triple binding and a DiMarzio in the back, and a jack on the upper bout." Because

> I wanted to be able to prop it without anything getting in my way, you know? If it's on the lower bout, then you've got the cable that you're dealing with. Where does it go? Now, I was only one year away from going wireless, when it wouldn't have mattered necessarily. Although, I probably would've had them customize it with the thing on the upper bout so that I could put the pack on the strap, and then I would be rocking.
>
> And then Wally had given me a stock red one that I think I used at the US Festival for a song. It was like a mini explorer [Baby Z] that had a Kahler on it. That Kahler was a really good whammy because it had the infinite [*imitates long, slow dive bomb sound*]. Very smooth. The thing I didn't like about the Kahlers was that when you went into high positions and you bent strings, because they were on rollers instead of just a clean saddle, then your sustain would go away because you were literally pushing the string up against the roller at the bridge. I'm not keen on this. I like the tone to be really singing in the high positions. And you needed fixed saddles for that to happen.
>
> I asked Dean if he could make me one with some really nice maple — maple neck, maple body, maple flame. And he made me one of those, and it was great. It was a really nice guitar. But only one pickup and a fixed bridge. It was really good.
>
> — Rik Emmett of Triumph

In my chat with Zelinsky he told me a funny story about being invited to a video shoot, which highlighted the largesse of visual presentation that was taking hold of the music industry at the time.

> I remember they had a big album, *Allied Forces*, and they had a song called "Magic Power." And for the video, they built this huge flying-V stage. I got invited to come up there when they were shooting the video. And it was kinda cool, but I think they screwed up something, and the video didn't come out as great as they wanted. But I remember being up there and seeing them play my guitar on this flying-V stage, that was kinda cool.
>
> — Dean Zelinsky

Not being able to imagine what could possibly go wrong with a band performing on top of a giant flying V–shaped guitar, I asked Rik for his recollections of the "Magic Power" video shoot.

> We did a series of songs on a sound stage down in west Toronto in Etobicoke. And they built this stage that was a giant flying V. And, I thought it was gonna look amazing. You know? And when the guy talked to me, I think Philip Kaufman might have been the name of the director-producer guy. I'm not sure. But, you know, when he pitched me, he'd said, "Oh, this is gonna be amazing. It's gonna have lights in it and Gil will be on a drum riser back at the point where the V comes together and Mike will be back there. But you can walk all the way up the neck right to the headstock, and it'll be great." I think Dean probably might have been a little unhappy that they made the headstock more like a Gibson V headstock, and not the [signature Dean split-V] headstock. I think they went, well, that's a little too complicated for us to build, we're gonna make it this way, so Dean might have been disappointed in it.
>
> When we got there and we saw it, it was like too thick. Like, they'd made it too high. It wasn't gonna look like a guitar. I said to the guys, it looks like a birthday cake. [*laughs*] And then we started calling the video "birthday cake in space." [*laughs*] We were already mocking it before we'd even shot the video. We were going like, "I don't know about this."
>
> Now, there's something you have to understand about Triumph. Anybody that, you know, you've been telling stories to about the band. We were very much our own entity. We managed ourselves, and we were very sort of prideful about being in charge of our own destiny.
>
> We've got money from the record company, but we're really executive producers of our own videos. And, we're telling the guy this is what we wanna do, but he's telling us, no, this is what *I* wanna do, and this is how I'm gonna do it. And you guys don't understand the technical thing here. I'm gonna shoot the thing, but it's green screen, and then I'm gonna make

it [look like it's] a spaceship flying through space. And then we're gonna get the girl to — you know from the song, she gets the magic power from her radio. We're gonna shoot all this background stuff and then she's gonna turn into a dancer that gets up on the stage with you and she's gonna dance. MTV is gonna love this!

I'm going, I don't know, man. Sounds like it could be really hokey.

Anyways, long story short, we start to look at the roughs and we went, this is brutal. This is terrible. Like, we're gonna have to kill this. In the Triumph documentary, there's some footage of it, and they show it to people like Sebastian Bach [Skid Row], and they show it to the guy in the *Trailer Park Boys*, and they're going, "What the fuck is this?" [*laughs*] Birthday cakes in space. And I'm killing myself laughing because I remember us killing the video. Like, no. You can't send it to MTV. We don't want it to be shown. So, lots of people didn't ever see it.

We did have one for "Allied Forces" that didn't have the girl in it and stuff. So, for a certain period of time, we allowed that one to be shown. It had a kid that played a video game. He was shooting flying-V spaceships. It was hokey. It was corny. It was bad.

And then we did "Say Goodbye" because we thought it was gonna be a single later on in the record. I don't think we ever put it out as a single, which is too bad. I think "Magic Power" kinda caught on, and then "Fight the Good Fight" just became this kind of anthem. And we didn't even have a video for it. But it didn't matter. We were getting tons of airplay.

That album was weird. It was like, there were pockets. In California, the song "Ordinary Man" got played in rotation like it was "Stairway to Heaven." It got a ton of album play out of four or five stations in California. So, that was a weird thing because we would go and play there, and then it wasn't in the set. We didn't play it live. And everybody expected they were going to get to hear it, but the band never learned it to play it live. All we ever did was "Magic" and "Fight" from that album.

— Rik Emmett

So far in this book we have heard how having a recognized rock star was crucial to spreading brand awareness of and confidence in the guitars a company was bringing to market. But what benefits, if any, did being associated with a guitar brand bring to the artist? Did the promotional efforts of the company help with artist visibility?

> I think it did, to a certain degree. But I think the other thing that helped was that now you've got your picture in a guitar magazine ad, and there's more awareness now of you. You're not just the guy writing a guitar column. Now you're turning into somebody . . . you're getting a profile in another way. Trade shows, posters in stores, you know, those kinds of things.
>
> At the same time, Triumph was also a band that was one of the pioneers in the area of corporate tour sponsorship. I'll tell you a Dean story. This is a pretty good one. We were playing in Philadelphia, and we were playing a smaller kind of theater on the *Never Surrender* tour.
>
> We weren't playing the hockey rink. It was one of those old vaudeville places that had a stage, and then you went up a fire escape-y kind of staircase, and there were dressing rooms on the third floor, on the fourth floor, on the fifth floor, going up the staircase. And, after the gig, we had to do a photoshoot for Converse running shoes. They were gonna be our tour sponsors.
>
> So this was early in the tour. And after the gig, our hair is a little bit sweaty and not so good, and we're tired and we're, you know, a little goofy. But we have to go up to this dressing room that they've made to be like this — graffiti on the walls and with bulbs in the sockets around the mirror, you know, that kind of a dressing room look. And, you know, now we're all supposed to sit and huddle together, and, oh, they've got a guitar on a stand with an amp, the Dean Baby Z maple guitar, which I've never played on stage. I've just had it delivered.
>
> But, I'm going, "Hey, Dean guitar in a poster. This will be really cool." So, I got the Dean guitar on the stand, and then we have to put on Converse running shoes. We're all gonna wear

the running shoes. But they don't have any in my size. I'm a seven, seven-and-a-half, and all they've got are nines and nine-and-a-halfs. I put on the shoes, and they just look like clown shoes to me. [*laughs*]

So we're sitting in this room, and we're doing the shoot. And at one point, I sort of hold up my foot, and I say to the other guys, "Fucking look at this." [*laughs*] "It's like a fucking clown shoe." And everybody starts laughing. And they take a picture, and when we get to pick which picture [to use for the poster], we go, "That's the one we want." That poster went up in every shoe store that sold Converse shoes, with the Dean Z in it.

So being in ads, I don't think it helps you sell product, but I do think over the long haul, it's helping awareness, and so that in the end, that's all that matters. You're just trying to raise the profile of the band, and you're taking advantage of a sort of Hollywood and demographics. The bigger question you're asking, I think, is "Does it help if you have a string endorsement? Does it help if you have a guitar endorsement? Does it help if you have an amp endorsement?" Yes. And one leads to another, which leads to another. It's all part and parcel of the game that you have to play. Now, I do think there's a critical element in this, and I think it has to do with quality.

So, you know, when Triumph makes a Pepsi deal, it's not necessarily that we're saying Pepsi is a great quality thing. It's not like you're endorsing a Rolex watch. It's a carbonated beverage. But if it's the same carbonated beverage that's giving Michael Jackson a deal and all these other high-profile artists, and you're getting one too, then people go, "Jeez. They must be a really high-profile act." In Canada, that had a huge [impact] for us. Here's Triumph in Pepsi ads all across the country as part and parcel of the tour, you know, it matters. And then, of course, with the money that you're getting to underwrite tour support, we were able to get ourselves a private jet. And then when you shoot video, you make sure you get the private jet moments in the video so that on MuchMusic, they're going, "Look, Triumph's got their own private jet." And all of this stuff ends up meaning that people get this impression of very high end, very high quality.

Now, you know, when we made a deal with Converse running shoes, they're a big company and they're global. And Converse running shoes are still hip to this day. So we didn't really do ourselves any damage by being associated with a running shoe company that's gonna be around forever, an institution of sorts. It's a good thing. When I picked deals with guitar companies, string companies, I did want to be associated with quality.

So in the early stages with Dean, for example, it was important to me to check out the guitars. I need to go and meet this guy in Chicago. I need to go and see how it works before I say yes. I don't want to say yes unless I feel like the guy's gonna make me great guitars.

— Rik Emmett

In our chat for the book, Rik regaled me with one more tale of the intertwining of corporate sponsorship and rock n roll, in this case involving a guitar that was the literal manifestation of this union of art and commerce:

The Budweiser guitar. So, Triumph is going out on a tour, I tried this out on a tour, and Budweiser is going to be the tour sponsor.

And in the early stages of the tour, a guitar arrives. Dean is making these guitars, and it's just a Dean logo on a neck that's attached to a body that's shaped like the Budweiser bow tie logo — it's misshapen. It's very, very weird on the strap. There's too much weight of the body in front of the pickup, so the pickup doesn't sound any good. It's honky and thin and bright, and it just sounds like shit. And they're made in Korea. Dean has got a deal with Taiwan or Korea or someplace, and if you wiggle the neck too much, the neck moves on the bolts. It's not good. It has one of those really, really cheap vibrato bars, like on a two-hundred-dollar Strat.

So I go, "This is awful." So I think the first day or second day, I said alright, here's what's gonna happen. Get the laser guys to run a fiber-optic strip around the logo, and I'll play it for "Rocky Mountain Way" in the set, you know, because it's the kind of song where intonation matters the least, and I'll bang the shit out of it. And, at a certain point, we can do a laser cue where you turn off all the lights, but you flash the neon guitar. Like, you know, we'll have the neon sign flashing. So, we did that for a while. The guitar now had this plastic clear tape all the way around holding the fiber-optic strand that ran all the way around the guitar. Piece of spaghetti, kind of. So, I did that for a while, but the guitar would just not stay in tune, like, not even for three minutes. So now, we're maybe a week and a half in, something like that, on the tour. Budweiser is still hedging. They are giving us some money for radio advertising, but the big money hasn't kicked in yet, and we're waiting. Where's the big money? Is the big money coming?

But the woman that had set up the deal is having a big party in Saint Louis, I think, because that's where their head office is. So, all the Budweiser execs are at the meet and greet after the show. And everybody's milling about, having drinks, and a guy comes up to me and he says, "Hey, Rik. I understand you don't like the Budweiser guitar." And I went, "Yeah they're really shitty." He goes, "Yeah. I know they are. Listen, they've hired me as a consultant to build you the guitar that will be the guitar of your dreams." And I went, "Well, it can't be the shape of the logo." And he said, "That's the one stipulation that I cannot change." And I went, "Well, then you and I know it's just never gonna work." And he goes, "Yeah. I know that."

Now, the guy is from, like, Saint Louis Music Dispatch, a large company, and this guy is a legit guitar builder. And because Budweiser's got more money than they know what to do with, they've hired this guy as a consultant. He's gonna build Rik Emmett the Budweiser guitar that's gonna be the greatest Budweiser guitar ever.

He said, "Just, Rik, just tell me what you want, and I'll get it done. That's how this works." And we're at a party, and I've had a couple of beers. I go, "Okay. This is what I want. I want African ebony fingerboard. I want Madagascar blah blah blah for the body. I want the latest Floyd Rose, and I want this, and I want that, and I want these pickups, and I want blah blah blah." So I named all of the most expensive parts you could possibly [think of] and I go, "I want it to be a red metal-flake finish."

So the guy goes, "Okay. Great." The tour goes out, and we're about 12 weeks in now, maybe longer. You know, 20 weeks in. And we're on the last leg of the tour.

We're in California. We're going up the coast. And we're gonna end in, like, Long Beach or something. And my wife, you know, never came out on tour ever, but she's flown out because what we're gonna do is rent a car, and we're gonna drive up the coast because I'm thinking this is the last big tour I'm ever gonna do with Triumph. And so we're gonna celebrate. We're gonna drive up to Carmel and San Francisco.

So a guy comes to me after soundcheck backstage, and he goes, "Rik, there's a package here for you." And I go, "Okay." I go to the meet and greet area backstage, and here's this giant box, and it weighs a fucking ton. I open it up, and it's a case. And I open up the case, and it's the Budweiser guitar. And it's everything that I ever asked for. I can't believe it. It's got every detail, and the guitar must be worth just in parts alone, 10 K. And I go to pick it up, and it weighs 18 pounds. It's like a coffee table. Yeah. And I go, "Oh, man. I'm never gonna be able to play this." And it's the last night of the tour.

A key part of the story — Budweiser has long since pulled the plug on whether or not they're gonna come through with the money. We never really got the big tour sponsorship.

The contract was never 100 percent fulfilled. It only got to be about, you know, 37 percent fulfilled. Gotcha. Part of the different obligations. We never got all the money we were supposed to get. So it never really panned out. But the guitar shows up. [*laughs*] So I've got this guitar hanging on my wall of shame. [*laughs*]

— Rik Emmett

While Dean would introduce the Mach 5 model as another unique pointy proposition, the company also introduced guitars that were more in line with the superstrat aesthetic that was becoming more popular in a post–Van Halen world. Was the Bel Aire model, and later the Signature and Eighty-Eight models, a response to what was happening with the changing guitar tastes and techniques as the decade progressed?

> A little of this, a little of that. It was in the fact that [the Bel Aire] had a humbucker in the bridge. The Bel Aire was supposed to wear several hats. Remember I talked about the Gibson and the Fender lane? I was down the Gibson lane, never down the Fender lane, and that was a market I wanted try my hand at.
>
> I literally took a Fender Strat pickguard, put it on a piece of paper, and drew a guitar around it. But I did my thing, I just tried to make it sexier. It was the first thing we really started importing. We had to cut cost, cut our pricing. I went with the company ESP Guitars, when nobody had heard of them. I went and met with those guys in Japan.
>
> I had them making my necks and supplying all my electronics and hardware and pickguards and everything. We were just making the guitar — the bodies — in Chicago and throwing on all this ESP supplied stuff, including the neck, trying to hit a price point. I was wearing a few hats. One was competing against some of the import stuff. One was trying to get into the Fender market — the superstrats.
>
> The Bel Aire kinda crashed and burned because Fender had been building guitars in Japan for the Japanese market. I think they had FujiGen building their guitars. Actually we sold a boatload of Bel Aire. I mean, it was my most successful trade show with the Bel Aire. But by the time the guitars were hitting the streets, Fender came out with a $399 strat made in Japan. And it was half the price of the Bel Aire. I mean, it's Fender, and it's half the price. These days cheap Fenders are a dime a dozen, but in those days, Fenders went from $700 or $800 to all of a sudden down to $399, and that was a game changer.
>
> — Dean Zelinsky

In a tale we will hear a few times in this book, attempts to grow his company in a way that could compete with changing market tastes and a move away from U.S.-based manufacturing in general would take its toll on Zelinsky's initial vision for Dean Guitars.

> The Bel Aires were towards the end of our factory in the USA — We eventually closed the factory, I think, in '86.
>
> And then we went import until '91 with the Hollywood line and some other stuff, the Eighty-Eights. And then in '91, I took my hiatus from '91 to 2000. This whole import thing happened in our country where everybody just decided, or Ronald Reagan decided, we're not gonna make anything anymore and it impacted our industry. I mean, it rocked every industry, I'm sure, but it rocked the guitar industry really bad. You know, I didn't get into the guitar industry because I was an incredible businessman and I went to Wharton School of Business and I could make a lot. I got into it because I could build great guitars. And, yeah, I was business savvy, and I had to deal with all those aspects of it. But I didn't get in the business so I could go to an office, send a telex to a factory in Korea and say, you know, send me a container of compromised pieces of wood that look like guitars. It just got to a point where you couldn't manufacture in America. It got to a point where it was just a race to the bottom, and you just couldn't manufacture a guitar in America and make a buck. Every company got rocked, by the way. I got rocked, Grover Jackson ended up selling his company. Bernie Rico from B.C. Rich sold his company. He got out. Kramer had a huge one. They all went bust. Gibson got sold twice.
>
> — Dean Zelinsky

Dean Guitars was sold to Oscar Medeiros of Tropical Music, who owned the brand from 1986 to 1995, and in that time focused mainly on the Latin market. In 1997, Elliott Rubinson, President and CEO of Armadillo Enterprises, and an entrepreneur and bassist known for his work with Michael Schenker Group, Uli Jon Roth, and Nitro's Michael Angelo Batio, built a successful music retail and supplier called Thoroughbred Music, which, in a twist of fate, he would sell to Sam Ash Music in 1999, so that he could focus his attention on Dean. Zelinsky would return in 2000 to Dean Guitars as a consultant, and he was key in bringing back some major artist relationships to the company and re-establishing the Dean brand in the hard rock and heavy metal guitar market.

One of the guitarists who he worked with at the time was a player who kept Dean Guitars alive during a period when they were not even visible in the U.S. market. Dimebag Darrell Abbott (formerly Diamond Darrell) was the guitarist in Pantera and later Damageplan. Pantera were proud fans of the '80s hard rock and heavy metal that came before them, and Darrell (along with his drumming brother and partner in both bands, Vinnie Paul), waved the flag high for their heroes in a time when grunge and alternative music had all but made the excesses of '80s rock obsolete. In a time when a shredding guitar solo was as far from cool as you could get, Dimebag Darrell was a fleet-fingered anomaly in a sea of down-tuned, seven-string sludge. Pantera managed to retain and exceed all the levels of aggression necessary to compete in the nu-metal arena, without turning their back on their heavy metal heritage. Tragically, Dimebag Darrell was shot and killed by a deranged fan on December 8, 2004, while performing at Alrosa Villa nightclub in Columbus, Ohio.

> I knew Darrell when he was 16 years old. I used to host these guitar contests in various places, and I hosted one down in Dallas. And this kid kept coming in with his mother and blowing everybody away and winning the contest, and his name was Diamond Darrell. Darrell Abbott. So, I met him back then. The unfortunate thing is that — I was like God to him. Okay? I mean, he'd be like, he loved my guitars.
>
> You know, his Dean from Hell [Abbott's heavily used Dean ML] has I-don't-know-how-many million miles on it. And, he just respected me because he needed what I was selling.
>
> To be Dimebag Darrell, he needed that feel, he needed that body, he needed all that stuff. And I needed Darrell. So we kinda communicated on this wavelength between Chicago and Dallas without ever having to talk. You know what I mean? I was building something. He understood what I was building. He wanted that.

He became a fan of the brand before he was famous. And I became a fan of him because I knew that he was this great guitar player. But, you know, in those days, we embraced arena guys. You know? I regret that I just didn't go down and take care of the dude. Just load him up with guitars. He did it anyways, but I'm just saying, we didn't embrace guys at that [club] level. It just wasn't a thing.

But like I said, everything worked out great between him and I over the years, but the timing was just terrible. So anyhow, '89 to '94 is when [Pantera] broke and he was really ready for the prime time. And I was out of the business. I was closed down and the brand was basically inoperative, and then it got acquired in '97. And I went back in 2000 to work for the company. Like I said, the timing was bad. He ended up going to Washburn. Washburn thought they were gonna put him in a Strat or a Tele or something, and he said, "Fuck you," and he pulls out his Dean from Hell and goes, "This is what you're building." And Washburn said, "We gotta modify that."

So they kinda modified it and made the D-3, which was, you know, an ML with a shorter leg and a slightly different headstock. Oscar, who owned Dean Guitars at the time, wasn't having it, and he cut a license deal. So, Darrell had a 10-year deal with Washburn, which was up in 2004.

I went back to Dean Guitars as a consultant in 2000. Kind of a full-time consultant, and I'm the one who brought Darrell back to the company, so we did have our time, you know, to do Dimebag Darrell stuff. But he died three weeks after we signed that contract. The Dimebag thing is a very long saga that is still going on.

— Dean Zelinsky

Dean Guitars would see a number of high-profile rock and metal players with signature models during Rubinson's tenure running the company, including Michael and Rudolf Schenker, Rik Emmett, Megadeth's Dave Mustaine, Mountain's Leslie West, Michael Angelo Batio, and Arch Enemy's Michael Amott. The Dean Razorback model, designed by Dimebag Darrell, is a much pointier and extreme version of the classic Dean ML that initially inspired Dimebag, and would be played by high-profile players like Zakk Wylde of Ozzy Osbourne and Black Label Society fame and who now plays guitar with Pantera in tribute to his fallen friend. In 2016, after Elliott Rubinson's passing from cancer, his son Evan Rubinson became President and CEO of Armadillo Enterprises, and the company would carry on selling classic Dean designs as well as pointier variations like the Stealth, Razorback, and Tyrant models. Dean has since been embattled by lawsuits from Gibson guitars and the Dimebag Darrell Abbott estate, both of which I'm going to avoid getting into here.

There will be plenty of time for talk about lawsuits later on in this story. Besides, salacious legal stories are not why I'm writing this book, and I want to stay close to the source of original inspiration. I would say that Dean does, too. He is still incredibly active, and as the current owner of Dean Zelinsky Private Label Guitars he continues to innovate and do what he does best — make incredible guitars. Zelinsky's run from 1976 to 1986 will forever be remembered as a combination of high-quality guitar building, instrumental design innovation, and savvy marketing that embodied the spirit of the early days of arena rock and MTV.

> My son told me when he grew up that saturation is validation. If people are seeing your product in enough different places, that's validation. Saturation is getting them in stores, getting them in the magazines, getting them in rock stars' hands, getting them on videos. Each of those things are pieces to a big puzzle that, you know, builds brand.
>
> — Dean Zelinsky

CHAPTER 5

WASHBURN AND THE POINTY GUITARS OF QUIET RIOT

Just as the Flying V and Explorer took time to catch on with the guitar buying public, it took a whole lotta tryin' for Quiet Riot just to get up that Hollywood hill to the top of the rock-n-roll mountain. Unlike the Flying V or the Explorer, however, it's hard to make an argument that Quiet Riot was, in its first incarnations, a band ahead of its time. Even though it held in its ranks a genuine virtuoso in guitarist Randy Rhoads and a natural born, motormouthed rock star in vocalist Kevin DuBrow, Quiet Riot was a band *out of* time, chasing and aping the ghosts of glam-rock past as hipper, edgier new-wave artists, like the Knack, were coming into their own with skinny ties and slimmed down, ultra-catchy power-pop arrangements.

The band did manage to amass an impressive following in the L.A. club scene, and even secured a Japanese recording contract, but the two albums the band released with CBS/Sony Records Japan seemed like relics from a glam-rock era that was past its best-before date. When Randy Rhoads was ultimately snapped up by ex-Black Sabbath vocalist Ozzy Osbourne and whisked away to England, soon to be followed by Quiet Riot bassist Rudy Sarzo, it appeared the writing was on the wall for these California dreamers. Despite Van Halen being signed to a deal by Warner Bros. Records and launched into the stratosphere, hard rock and heavy metal seemed dead on arrival in the late '70s in Los Angeles. Punk was the new rebel music, and new romantic synth-pop from England — think Duran Duran, Spandau Ballet, and Culture Club — was turning a well-mascaraed eye towards American pop audiences. But, as this hilariously poignant online sales description from an Australian vintage guitar shop "points" out, all was not lost. (And yes, I do scour the world looking for pointy guitars.)

> In the early 1980s, punk was on its last legs, and new wave was storming up the charts. Some kids still wanted to rock, not in a nihilistic punk way, and not in a haircut new wave way . . . These kids longed for wild long hair, makeup, Corvettes and non sensical lyrics about drinking and staying out all night. There was one band, maybe seen as the least likely to achieve success at the time, who steamrolled the US charts, taking Glam Metal from the underground, into the cassette decks of every fast car in America. The name of that band was Quiet Riot, and their guitarist Carlos Cavazo didn't just rock your Daddy's guitar, he rocked a black Washburn A-10.
>
> (EchoTone.com.au)

The Washburn guitar mentioned here will get a deep dive soon enough, but first let's explore the sonic landscape of this exciting time of change in rock culture.

The new wave of British heavy metal (NWOBHM) was bubbling up in the U.K., with bands like Saxon, Judas Priest, and Iron Maiden melding old-school classic hard-rock riffage with the energy and DIY enthusiasm of punk rock. These NWOBHM bands — who often wielded Flying Vs and Explorers — were also making in-roads at concert halls State-side, and American musicians were taking notice.

Hard rock music received one of its biggest facelifts from the musical marriage of Ozzy and Randy Rhoads. Ozzy gave Randy a platform and the opportunity to develop his innate composition and performance chops by pairing him with a dream team of veteran musicians like Bob Daisley and Lee Kerslake in the Blizzard of Ozz band, while young engineer-turned-producer Max Norman helped Randy to dial in a sound that would inform hard rock records for years to come, with the assistance of a very special and pointy flying V guitar designed and built by Los Angeles luthier Karl Sandoval, a former employee of Wayne Charvel. This was the famed Polka Dot V that would feature on Ozzy's stunning debut album, *Blizzard of Ozz*.

> I got the call from Randy in June/July of 1979. He had seen George Lynch playing a tiger-striped V guitar that I built for him, the Supro V, and had gone backstage to ask George where he got it. George told him to call me and we set up a time for Randy to come out and work on the design. You have to remember that everything was custom back then; these were one-offs, built to order. Randy showed up with Kevin DuBrow, since this is right before Ozzy, when he was still with Quiet Riot. Kevin was really excited and kept telling Randy that he should do this, and do that, and make it look this way. At one point I just turned to Randy and said, "Look man, this is *your* guitar. You tell me how you want it and I will do my best to make it happen." Randy had already sketched a few rough ideas of what he wanted, beginning with the V shape that I'd done for George. He wanted it to be like a combination of Gibson and Fender, playing similar to his 1972 Gibson Les Paul Custom but with a Fender-style tremolo.
>
> — Karl Sandoval ("The Birth of the Randy Rhoads Sandoval Dot V," DiMarzio.com.)

There is no doubt that Randy's leaving Quiet Riot was a blow to DuBrow, but it can also certainly be argued that Rhoads's work on *Blizzard of Ozz* and the equally dynamic and exciting *Diary of a Madman* helped establish the template for commercially accessible pop-metal songs that also featured bold and fiery displays of guitar pyrotechnics, ultimately setting the table for Quiet Riot's future success.

Randy's massive impact on pointy guitar culture will be explored in greater detail in chapter 12 of this book, but this chapter will deal largely with the man who would come to fill the guitar slot for the recording of Quiet Riot's 1983 opus *Metal Health*. This album, released on February 28, 1983, would kick the doors wide open for commercial heavy metal in America, ultimately knocking the Police's monster *Synchronicity* album out of the number one slot in November of that same year.

Carlos Cavazo was born in Atlanta, Georgia, on July 8, 1957. His father would have a considerable musical influence on Carlos, exposing him to the world of classical music. This exposure provided Carlos with a musical vocabulary that informs his lead-guitar style, and a musical analysis of his highly melodic and technically deft playing reveals an understanding of classical harmony and composition techniques.

> I started playing guitar in 1966, believe it or not. I was only nine years old, and my dad got me a guitar for my birthday because I wanted one. He got me some lessons too, so I started learning how to read music. My dad used to listen to classical music, which kinda got me into it. In the late '70s, I started really getting into it. I got myself a classical guitar, a nylon string guitar, because the one my dad got me was a steel string. For classical, you have to have nylon, so I got myself one and started reading out of classical technique books and learning by ear too. But I have been playing classical for a long time, steadily since, like, the early '80s, I would say. And I'd practice flamenco techniques and tremolo techniques, and play pieces by Barrios, Tárrega, and Albéniz.
>
> I think a lot of the guitar players in the '80s were classically influenced. You could tell. Eddie Van Halen probably started it all with his use of classical scales. And Brian May of Queen, he used classical scales. People like Yngwie Malmsteen, Randy Rhoads, myself, and all kinds of people were trying to fit classical scales into rock music, which kind of fits with the tritones and the minor key stuff.
>
> — Carlos Cavazo of Quiet Riot

> Quiet Riot's music thrives on throbbing rhythms, so my classical background doesn't show in the song-writing; it's only noticeable during my solos. In fact, I wanted to put a classical piece on *Condition Critical*, but I scratched the idea since it didn't fit

> in with the rest of the songs. The kids just want to hear rock and roll.
>
> — Carlos Cavazo (*Guitar World*, November 1984.)

The obvious musical touchstones of the *Metal Health* album are the cover of Slade's hit "Cum On Feel the Noize" (originally released almost to the day, 10 years earlier on February 23, 1973) and the genre-enforcing title track "Metal Health (Bang Your Head)." This second track was a re-worked version of the song "No More Booze" from Cavazo's previous band, Snow, and one of the guitars Carlos played in this popular '70s Hollywood club circuit act was a gorgeous custom '70s, red-and-white striped Charvel Explorer with a Telecaster neck that comes with a good story.

> I had a Gibson Explorer back in the '70s when I was in Snow, and then I had a Charvel Explorer that Grover helped me put together. He had given me the parts too. And I ended up selling that Charvel back in the early '80s. Some guy wanted it really bad, and I sold it to him. I don't remember how much I sold it for, maybe $3,400 or something like that. Just a couple of years ago, the guy got a hold of me. And he wanted to give me the guitar back. I said, "I'll give you whatever you want for it. Name a price, I'll give you the money." And he says, "No, I wanna give it to you." He gave it back to me, and I have it now. Those Explorers were the first pointy guitars I had, and then I ended up getting some Flying Vs after that. I have a King V from Jackson, the super pointed one [designed for Robin Crosby from Ratt.]
>
> — Carlos Cavazo

"Cum On Feel the Noize" and "Metal Health (Bang Your Head)" would become staples of music video and radio stations around the world, ultimately propelling *Metal Health* to sales of over ten million copies worldwide (with six million of those being sold in the United States alone), and both featured blistering and iconic solos from Cavazo. In the case of ubiquitous radio smash "Cum On Feel the Noize," he incorporates smooth, legato scalar passages and anthemic major-scale merriment that heightens the euphoria of the participatory rock agenda laid out in the track. On "Metal Health (Bang Your Head)," it's a combination of high octane, '70s American muscle-car blues rock moves and angular modern dissonance redolent of late romantic and early modern classical composition techniques that set an ominous tone more than suitable to, as the track implores, waking the dead; it set heads-a-bangin' (voluntarily, I might add) into high school lockers across the heartland.

> What I try to do when I make a solo is have it mean something, and not just be a bunch of wailing licks that kinda go in one ear and out the other. You want something that's memorable, something they can sing along with, like the "Cum On Feel the Noize" solo. Throw in a little bit of this, a little bit of that, a few tricks, and a little bit of melody. I try to do a little bit of everything in my solos if I can.
>
> — Carlos Cavazo

As much as those two songs were the most listened-to cuts on my well-worn cassette of *Metal Health*, there was one other track that I believe had, in an overall sense, a bigger impact. Big enough to title this book after.

"Battle Axe" is an unaccompanied solo guitar composition for electric guitar, the first of its kind I had ever heard. I wouldn't become aware of Eddie Van Halen's "Eruption" until a few years later, after seeing Eddie's solo spot on the 5150 Tour with Sammy Hagar. (The tour where Sammy was rocking those pointy Jackson and Dean beauties.) I was thrilled to realize that this piece of guitar heaven had been recorded on Van Halen's 1978 debut album, and that I could revisit the magic of Eddie's finger-tapped arpeggios, tremolo-picked speed licks, and gorgeous brown-sound guitar tone, unaccompanied and free of any other musical instrument distractions or barking frontmen, over and over again with a simple drop of a needle, or a well-executed rewinding of a cassette.

But back in 1983, Carlos was the first guitarist I had ever heard being captured in such an exposed and unaccompanied way on tape. My 11-year-old self had so many questions: Why was there a song with no words? Where were the drums? Why was this scaring me, and why did I keep rewinding it over and over again? *Metal Health* had a claustrophobic, taboo, and even icky feeling to it for me. I chalk that up to a couple of factors: the dark album artwork featuring a mental patient bound in a deep wine-red straitjacket, his face covered by an imposing iron mask, and the spelling of the word *cum* in "Cum On Feel the Noize," something that, in a pre-internet world devoid of easily accessible pornography or proper sex education, I had yet to fully comprehend.

But there was also something about the sonic quality of this booming-yet-bright decidedly *un*healthy sounding record that also made you feel like you were listening within the confines of an insane asylum. (It was produced by Spencer Proffer at his Pasha Music House in Hollywood, which was in essence a glorified commercial jingle studio.) The album's addictive creepiness was heightened by '70s artifacts like the disco-metal groove of "Don't Wanna Let You Go," and the chorus pedal–effected guitar and bass tones of "Thunderbird," a heartfelt piano-based tribute to DuBrow's fallen bandmate and best friend Randy Rhoads, who had tragically died in a plane crash.

Don't get me wrong, I have come to love and appreciate these songs and sounds for what they are — performances by musicians who came up in the '70s, and who were applying the musical principles of the classic rock that came before them, while simultaneously adopting the new effects and harder-edged, more overtly distorted and saturated tones of the '80s. But a lot of *Metal Health* does remind me of *Dynasty*-era Kiss, a heavy-metal-monsters-under-a-disco-ball vibe.

Now, getting back to "Battle Axe," this was something that flat out frightened me. It creeps up on you with a dramatic, stuttering and sputtering staccato, minor-scale guitar riff that crescendos to a spiky peak, and then slices and dices its way through the speakers with a motif based on the Phrygian mode, a minor scale with a flattened second degree that is used in many Spanish and flamenco classical guitar pieces. (In a tip of the toque to my Northern Ontario upbringing, I used to mispronounce "Phrygian" as the "friggin'" scale.) Carlos then proceeds to move through some aggressive and angular variations, fast and furious tremolo-picked arpeggios and wailing string bends, like a heavy metal version of Rodrigo's Concierto de Aranjuez. Cavazo moves through sophisticated melodic key changes and Bach-inspired arpeggiated figures, before applying some classic Ace Frehley pickup-switching stutter effects, ultimately ending in a flurry of hammer-on diminished-scale trills, rapid pentatonic-scale picking, and a series of scrapes and slides. Like a battered and blood-soaked warrior, "Battle Axe" ultimately comes to a *ritard*, collapsing into one last glorious power chord, squeezed of every last bit of tone and sustain through a series of whammy bar articulations, and fades out as the conquering hero stumbles towards some imagined heavy-metal Valhalla.

When asked about what he remembers from the recording of "Battle Axe," Carlos's humility and laid-back demeanor stand in stark contrast to the bombast the listener experiences when hearing the track:

> You know, it's been a long time — more than 40 years. I just remember playing what I would do live. Just laying it down the best I can and, you know, hoping something comes out of it. I couldn't say I was 100 percent satisfied with it, but the producer [Spencer Proffer] liked it a lot. The energy level was right, he said. I think a lot of times [artists] are not 100 percent satisfied with the things they do. I thought I could have maybe gotten it a little bit better.
>
> — Carlos Cavazo

In this, my age of innocence, and with a limited preteen budget, the only evidence I had of what Quiet Riot looked like came from the miniscule images of their faces on the buttons that adorned the straitjacket on the cover of my *Metal Health* cassette. I had no idea what kind of musical instrument could make the types of sounds I was hearing on "Battle Axe," as MuchMusic, the Canadian equivalent of MTV, wasn't on air yet, and I had no clue as to where I could find information about bands like Quiet Riot and Def Leppard, bands that had supplanted Michael Jackson's *Thriller* to be the object of my burgeoning musical desires.

Enter one Troy Prior, the smartest kid in my elementary school — he was also the coolest and the toughest, which is entirely unfair, upon reflection.

For a middle-school music project that I can't actually remember completing myself (no doubt my efforts were sporadic and unfocused), Troy had created a stunningly detailed bristol-board masterpiece on the aspects of making a sound recording, and on that board was a poster of Quiet Riot's Rudy Sarzo and Carlos Cavazo rocking on stage, with the bold proclamation "Heavy metal's hottest new band going for gold with Washburn" emblazoned underneath bassist Sarzo's splayed-legged rock pose, a lean and mean Cuban-American rock machine in black tights, red boots, a sleeveless shirt, and the obligatory heavy-metal sweatband on his wrist. He was wrestling a badass Force 40 electric bass into musical submission. But the real moment of transcendent revelation for this student of St. Joseph Elementary Catholic School came in seeing Carlos Cavazo in the background, hoisting his black, pointy Washburn A-20V Explorer towards the sky, his slight frame, skin-tight stripy shirt, and spiky-yet-longish blond hairdo perfectly aligned with the sleek angles and compact size of the heavy-metal weapon he was holding in his hands. *This* was the "six-string razor" that vocalist Kevin DuBrow was comparing his own innate metal-manhood to in the lyrics to "Metal Health (Bang Your Head)." More importantly *this must have been* the guitar that was making the sounds I was becoming addicted to on the *Metal Health* album. This glorious Washburn A-20 guitar was the *Battle Axe*.

Turns out it wasn't.

> The guitar I played on "Battle Axe" was a black Charvel Telecaster. The one I used a lot in the '80s on tour — it was that same guitar. Unfortunately, that guitar was stolen from me, but, thankfully, the great people at Jackson-Charvel made me another replica of that original one. At that point, Grover Jackson had taken over Charvel. I only met Wayne Charvel maybe a couple of times, but I knew Grover a lot better. He did a lot for my career. Somebody introduced me to him, and I asked him, "Could I get an endorsement and work with you?" He believed in me so he said, yeah. He would give me stuff, sometimes for free, sometimes, at cost. At the beginning, you know, I was nobody, but Grover gave me really good deals on guitar parts and stuff that I needed, which helped me out a lot.
>
> — Carlos Cavazo

Frank Gryner is a producer, recording engineer, and video creator who has worked with Rob Zombie, Methods of Mayhem, A Perfect Circle, Def Leppard, ELO, Alice Cooper, Ian Hunter, and many more musical luminaries. He is also a great guitarist and one of my most valued musical collaborators. Here, he provides some insight on why the guitars we see our heroes playing on stage or in magazine ads may not always be the guitars they use when recording their albums.

> Most of my career has been spent in recording studios through an era where pointy guitars were certainly frowned upon. Few of them found their way into the studio over the tuning stability and solid tone of a good fixed-bridge Les Paul. Even high-profile guitarists would set aside their flashy custom models when it came right down to it. If it can't be played sitting down and it has a floating bridge, it got relegated to the guitar wall. All this being said, it secretly made me want to play a pointy guitar even more.
>
> — Frank Gryner

It turns out that Carlos wasn't even playing Washburn at the time of the recording of the *Metal Health* album. The Washburns would come later, as a result of Rudy Sarzo's relationship with the company. In the credits for *Metal Health*, the band states that "the following instruments were used in the making of this album," with Sarzo going on to mention his use of Washburn basses, as well as the Roland bass guitar synthesizer that we hear on "Thunderbird." Carlos only mentions one guitar company in these credits, Charvel guitars that were "custom designed by Grover Jackson."

With respect to his tone on *Metal Health*, I asked Carlos what it was, beyond his choice of guitars, that made for a sound that was as aggressive and powerful as any of his hard-rock contemporaries, but could also be sweet, violin-esque, and even vocal-like while soloing.

> On *Metal Health* I was using a '70s Mark II 100 Watt Marshall amp with an MXR Distortion+ box. Duane Baron was the engineer. He's the one who got the tones for me on the board. I got my tone on the amp, and he would get the tone on the board.

> We'd send somebody out into the live room with earplugs, and they would move the microphone in front of the speaker to find the right sweet spot. And I'd be playing, and they'd be moving the microphone [a Shure SM57 or SM58] around. And [when we found the sweet spot] we'd say, "Stop right there!" They would mark that sweet spot with white chalk or paint, so when we would tour, I could have the sound man put the mic in that same sweet spot every time, so it sounded more consistent every night.
>
> — Carlos Cavazo

Other effects and amps used on the album included a Roland Jazz Chorus amp for clean tones, a BOSS Chorus, an MXR flanger, and various studio effects, including delays, reverbs, and a harmonizer to provide width and depth to the sound. Carlos has also been quoted as saying he used a Fender Stratocaster during the sessions. However, a famous live-concert recording shows Carlos rocking a pointy ax that offers a flashier visual representation of what the tracks on *Metal Health* would come to represent in the early days of heavy metal's commercial dominance, and for naive audience members such as yours truly.

Many people believe that May 29, 1983, was the day that the youth of America officially accepted hard rock and heavy metal as the dominant music genre of the era. This was the second day of the US Festival, billed as Heavy Metal Day and featured performances from Quiet Riot, Mötley Crüe, Triumph, Ozzy Osbourne, Judas Priest, the Scorpions, and headliners Van Halen. Pointy guitars abounded on that day: Nikki Sixx of Mötley Crüe with his B.C. Rich Warlock bass, Rik Emmett of Triumph with his Dean Baby Z, K.K. Downing and Glenn Tipton rocking custom Hamer guitars (a Vector flying V and Phantom, respectively), the Scorpions' Rudolf Schenker and Matthias Jabs representing the O.G. pointy scene with a Gibson Flying V and Explorer, and in the pointy-adjacent club, headliner Eddie Van Halen with his iconic Frankenstrat, now sporting a Kramer neck with a pointy beak headstock.

For Quiet Riot's opening slot that day, Carlos played his black Washburn A-20V, the instrument he was holding in the ad that helped me — or so I thought — connect the dots between the sounds I was hearing and the visuals I was seeing, one of many illusions employed by artists of the '80s, as I would come to realize. If you listen to the audio recorded during that performance, there is no denying Cavazo's signature sound. It is there in all of its crystalline, powerful glory, which proves two things: firstly, that these Washburn guitars sounded great, and that ultimately the signature sound of a player rests in their hands and hearts; and secondly, that the guitar is simply a conduit for the sonic imprint of the player, albeit a conduit that can offer different shades, colors, and perspectives.

Washburn entered the electric guitar market in 1978 with the Wing series. These double-cutaway guitars featured thin, somewhat pointy horns and an enhanced lower bout, and were available with a variety of wood, hardware, and finish options. The Eagle, Falcon, Hawk, Raven, and T-Bird guitars, as well as the Scavenger bass, all shared the same general shape and headstock design, and came equipped with two humbucking pickups. Notable Washburn Wing-series players include Bob Marley, whose Washburn Hawk was one of seven guitars he owned, and was reportedly sold to the Jamaican government by his estate for a price estimated between $1.2 and $2 million. The Hawk was the highest-end guitar of the Wing series, with an ash body, maple top, a maple neck-through design with an ebony fingerboard, and power-sustain humbuckers.

Nancy Wilson of Heart was another famous Wing-series player and she endorsed the Eagle in an ad from the early '80s:

> I use my Washburn Eagle for "Straight On" and get a real clean Strat sound . . . the next song is "Even It Up" where I need a real dirty sustaining sound, and it works that way, too . . . it's an incredible guitar! [signed] Nancy Wilson

Washburn's Stage series was introduced shortly after the Wing series debuted. These guitars have more traditional '80s-style appointments with pointy bodies and hockey-stick headstocks similar to, but smaller than, the Gibson Explorer's.

The entry-level A-5 featured a Gibson Firebird-esque cutaway body, bolt-on maple neck, 22-fret maple fingerboard with black dot inlays, matching hockey-stick-style headstock with six-on-one-side tuners, standard bridge, and two exposed humbucker pickups. It also came with single-coil pickups, two knobs and a three-way switch on a metal plate similar to a Telecaster, chrome hardware, and was available in black, candy apple red, or white finish, and was manufactured between 1983 and 1985, according to the *Blue Book of Guitar Values*.

The next step up was the A-10, another Firebird-style cutaway body (made of solid ash), which featured a set rock-maple neck, 22-fret rosewood fingerboard with pearl dot inlay, matching hockey-stick headstock with six-on-one-side tuners, a standard bridge, two Washburn Power Sustain exposed humbucker pickups, four knobs, three-way switch, chrome hardware, and was available in black, maroon, or ivory finish. There was also an A-15 version of this guitar that came with three single-coil pickups. It was manufactured in Japan between 1980 and 1985 (*Blue Book of Guitar Values*).

At the head of the class was the A-20, another Firebird-style cutaway, this time with a solid ash body with bound flame-maple top, three-piece rock-maple and rosewood neck-through body, 22-fret ebony fingerboard with brass target inlay, matching hockey-stick headstock with six-on-one-side tuners, standard bridge, two Washburn Power Sustain exposed humbucker pickups, coil tap, four knobs, three-way switch, chrome hardware, available in black, cherry sunburst, metallic gray with black hardware and red binding, or white with black binding, and manufactured between 1980 and 1985. Vibrato soon became standard, and around 1984, a BBR (black, black, red) version was available with black finish, black hardware, and red binding, inlays, and accents.

An ad for the A-20 featured another Heart member, Nancy Wilson's guitar partner, Howard Leese:

> This year I'm taking mainly custom instruments out on tour . . . except for my Washburn A-20 which is a stock model. That guitar is great . . . just the way it is! [signed] Howard Leese

Washburn would go on to make Sarzo a signature series bass — the Slammer. In a 1984 ad that appeared in various music publications, Washburn invites aspiring heavy metal bassists to "move into the spotlight with Washburn's new Slammer bass. Designed by Rudy Sarzo of Quiet Riot, the Slammer 'Kicks in and delivers!'" The Slammer featured Washburn branded "slap shot" humbucking pickups, on board "Roto tech" EQ system, "fast action," two octave neck, ebony fingerboard with jumbo frets. I can say from experience that these basses played like a dream, as I actually owned one for a number of years, even using it in concert while I was a member of the band Helix (a band who toured with Quiet Riot in the mid-80s). The red-and-black variation of the rising sun graphic decorated my Slammer's sleek, Explorer-meets-charcuterie-board body shape! I sold the guitar about 10 years ago, and even more so than the 1978 Les Paul Custom I sold to help finance my band Crash Kelly's first tour of the U.K., that Washburn Slammer bass feels like the pointy prize that got away.

Washburn's HM Tour series guitars, launched in 1985, were Explorer-based shapes with more extreme horns and points, making for a compact and modern design that paired nicely with the RR Tour series guitars, inspired by original Quiet Riot guitarist Randy Rhoads's famous Jackson RR model. Both came with graphic options reflective of the time (blood spatters, diagonal lines of varying degrees of thickness shooting across the body), as well as the Wonderbar locking tremolo unit, and dual humbucker and SSH pickup configurations. The FV Tour series guitars featured a traditional flying V body shape with Washburn's smaller "hockey-stick" headstock.

A particularly prized pointy gem for pointy afficionados is the AF-40, a signature model for former Kiss guitarist Ace Frehley, who was now fronting his own band, Frehley's Comet. The AF-40 came out in 1987 as part of Washburn's Limited Edition Tour series. *The Blue Book of Guitar Values* describes the AF-40 as having an

> axe shaped solid ash body with pointy ends and large bass bouts and short treble bouts, bolt-on Canadian rock maple neck, 24-fret Carbonite fingerboard, black hockey stick-style headstock with six-on-one-side tuners and lightning bolt, Wonderbar tremolo bridge with locking nut, single high-output coil-tap humbucker pickup, two knobs, one three-way switch, black hardware, Ace Frehley signature on treble bout, available in Black finish with red or silver lightning bolt that goes half way up the neck and accents.

> Sleek, angular, bold styling and high output electronics combine to create the Limited Edition Tour Series . . . The Tour series are the only guitars of their kind to offer the amazing Washburn Transfer neck joint. The sustain is incredible! Harmonics and

> hammer-ons jump off the two octave Carbonite fingerboard with the slightest touch. (Washburn 1987 catalog.)

I had the opportunity to be in a band called Four By Fate for a short while with two members of Frehley's Comet, the late, great bassist John Regan and vocalist, guitarist, and keyboardist Tod Howarth. When I first joined, knowing that we would be playing songs from the Frehley's Comet albums, I tried to no avail to track down an AF-40. It was probably a good thing I didn't spend a lot of money on one for two reasons. The first — the albums that Four By Fate ended up making had little to do with the feel good, melodic pop metal of the Frehley's Comet albums (one of the reasons I left the band). The second reason comes straight from Ace's mouth:

> I got introduced to people at Washburn, really nice people, and they designed this really cool-looking guitar for me. Unfortunately, it didn't sound very good. I started off in Kiss playing Les Pauls which, to me, is the best-sounding guitar in the world. I played the Washburn a few times live and it just didn't have the sustain, it didn't have the output that I wanted, and I ended up putting it aside and going back to Les Pauls.
>
> — Ace Frehley (The Virtual Guitar Show, *Ultimate Classic Rock*.)

For all its cool looks, the guitar just didn't do what Ace needed it to. I'd still love to get my hands on one to find out for myself. There just has to be a way to make an instrument that looks that cool sound good!

The three Washburn guitars from the '80s that I do have in my possession (a 1983 A-5 with delightfully plucky single-coil pickups, a white 1984 A-10 with dual humbuckers, and an FV-20 flying V with three humbuckers and a gloriously smooth Kahler tremolo) all sound fantastic while also satisfying my nostalgic and aesthetic requirement of simply making my life better by looking great on a guitar stand.

My FV-20 is the best of the bunch, and I feel safe in saying that it will most likely be the only Washburn flying V to ever make an appearance on a Top Five Billboard New Age–charting Christmas album. While recording my originally titled *Christmas Guitar* album back in 2008, my co-producer James

ALL ON PAGE: GEORGE ASLAENDER

The Gibson Flying V, Explorer, Moderne, and Firebird models are ground zero for the pointy guitar revolution.

Above: K.K. Downing of Judas Priest and Carlos Cavazo of Quiet Riot rocking arenas with their Gibson Flying Vs.

Below: Rick Nielsen of Cheap Trick with an early Hamer Standard (left) and a Greco RN V-Head model (right).

ALL ON PAGE: PETE DOVE

Clockwise from Left: Rudolf Schenker of Scorpions with one of the many Flying Vs that grace his collection. Rik Emmett of Triumph, Sheron Alton of Toronto, and Nancy Wilson of Heart, were all high-profile Dean Guitars players.

ALL ON PAGE: PETE DOVE

Below: The Guild Bladerunner, a cutting-edge pointy design.

Right: GuitarNutTees rendering of Eddie Ojeda's "bullseye" Charvel model.

AARON GREER/ GUITARNUTTEES.COM

AARON GREER/ GUITARNUTTEES.COM

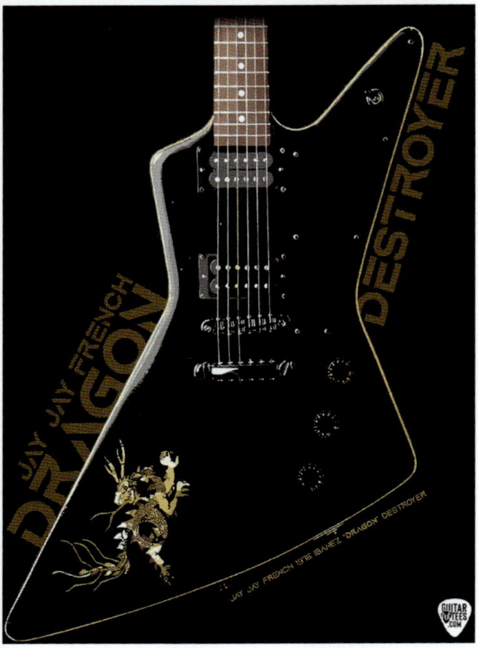

AARON GREER/ GUITARNUTTEES.COM

Above Left and Right: GuitarNutTees rendering of Twisted Sister's Jay Jay French Guild X-79s and Ibanez Destroyer models.

ALL ON PAGE: AARON GREER/GUITARNUTTEES.COM

Guitars from the collections of Jay Jay French and Bruce Kulick, artist renderings by Aaron Greer of GuitarNutTees.

AARON GREER/ GUITARNUTTEES.COM

AARON GREER/ GUITARNUTTEES.COM

AARON GREER/ GUITARNUTTEES.COM

PETE DOVE

Top Left and Right: Winger guitarist Reb Beach's wild Ibanez WRB3 models.

Bottom Left: The Godfey SK-1, a signature model for author Sean Kelly.

Bottom Right: Iron Maiden's Dave Murray with an Ibanez Destroyer II.

ZACH GUNTER

PETE DOVE

Top Left and Bottom Left and Right: B.C. Rich Bich and Mockingbird models from the B.C. Rich Custom Shop.

Top Right: Iron Maiden's Adrian Smith playing an Ibanez Destroyer II.

ZACH GUNTER

ZACH GUNTER

ALL ON PAGE: ZACH GUNTER

Some classic pointiness from the B.C. Rich Custom Shop.

Robertson and I would often take breaks during our sessions to go for sushi in Toronto's lovely High Park neighborhood. Of course, the sushi dinners would also involve a considerable amount of sake, and we would often return to the studio to complete our work in a more relaxed state. On one of these sake-fueled trips back home, James and I popped into Kaos Music on Bloor Street, where hanging in the window display was that wonderful FV-20. I was in no condition to resist its charms, and that guitar came back with us to the session, where the previously and delicately recorded nylon string classical guitar would be decorated with reverb-ensconced whammy bar articulations and ornate flurries of fingers from the flying V that, upon reflection, are quite similar to lines that Carlos Cavazo played on "Cum On Feel the Noize" decades earlier. We did have some explaining to do to my staunchly classical record label when they first heard it, but fortunately the record was a bit of a hit, and the crossover of new age feels with classical and rock is something I am very proud of. Have a listen to "Joy to the World" on your favorite streaming platform, and feel free to judge if I'm right, or if I'm just trying to justify a drunken pointy-guitar purchase. Perhaps duality of mind should be exercised here, and both might be true.

Speaking of purchase justifications, I can remember a time when pawnshops were filled with guitars, many being of the pointy variety, that were built offshore in Asia. I seem to recall a bias against these guitars as being of much lower quality, a result of the mass production efforts that brought them to life in countries like China, Korea, Indonesia, and, at one point, even Japan.

As we have seen in earlier discussions with experts in this book, there is some justification to this opinion. Of course, the master guitar craftsmanship of Japanese guitars is well known. Handmade guitars by companies like Yamaha and Ibanez are state of the art examples of guitar making, but with mass production comes an inevitable removal from the initial inspiration, human touch, and detail of custom-shop work. Even with improving technologies and quality inspections in place to ensure that fret ends don't stick out, that electronics and hardware are functioning properly, or that necks aren't twisted, most inspectors will simply not be able to meet the mass production demands of a factory *and* execute their inspections with the care and detail of a master luthier.

However, there is a Japanese factory name that I have seen in many a guitar want-ad or on sales tags for used guitars in pawnshops and music stores, proudly trumpeting the origins of certain Japanese guitars (pointy and not so pointy) like Washburn, Aria, Westone, Greco, Vantage, Electra, Fresher, Hondo, Fernandes, and many more, pronouncing that the guitar in question was made in the Matsumoku factory.

The factory was known as Matsumoto Mokkou when it was founded in 1951, and in 1971 changed its name to Matsumoku, a combination of the words Matsumoto (the name of the Japanese city in which the factory was based, and Mokkou-jo, which means carpentry.) The company initially produced wooden cabinets, tables, and accessories for sewing machines for Singer Japan. When sewing machine designs became more compact, and reliant on plastic, the company diversified and began making products in other areas. FujiGen Gaki, a well-known and respected stringed instrument manufacturer founded by Yuichiro Yokouchi, requested OEM (Original Equipment Manufacturer) work from Matsumoku, which marked the beginning of Matusmoku's venture into guitar manufacturing. Among the excellent engineers, designers, and craftsmen who worked for Matsumoku was Norikatsu Harayama, who began working for the factory just three months after it was founded, and moved up the ranks to serve as chief engineer in the '60s. His skill as a master craftsman would see him further build Matsumoku's repuatation as a high-quality guitar manufacturer for many brands in the '70s and '80s, before closing in 1987. Mr. Harayama would go on to found the Harayama Guitar Factory, providing OEM for ESP, Kramer, Schecter, DiMarzio, Mighty Mite, Moon, and other brands.

Many of the first pointy guitars that ended up in the hands of young rock n rollers, including my friends Reed and Frank, came from the Matsumoku factory, helping to launch inspiring and inspired careers in music. These gateway guitars were a point of entry to a world of heavy metal dreaming.

> I traded my first electric guitar — a 1960s Teisco knockoff (along with months of bottle collecting money) for a bright red Hondo ZX-100 with a locking whammy bar and a single bridge humbucker pickup. The design was — much like I was, myself — definitely Eddie-inspired. I finally had a *real* guitar that resembled the ones I'd been obsessively staring at in *Guitar World*. I can't remember where it came from. Growing up in rural Ontario in the '80s made it really difficult to get any of the brands that got paraded in front of me in those magazines.
>
> — Frank Gryner

> I believe my very first pointy guitar was a V copy made by Vantage. It was a '67-style V with the large pickguard. I don't think I had it for long, as my memory of it is vague.
>
> — Reed Shimozawa of Zuckerbaby, Wide Mouth Mason, and One Bad Son

I am constantly on the hunt for hidden pointy gems of Matsumoku origin like the Westone Dimension IV model, a smaller bodied, much pointier take on the Explorer, or the uber-pointy Dynasty series, which has a shape that occupies a space between flying V, intergalactic weapon, and alien insect. These models were featured in Westone's 1985–86 catalog and represent that particular brand at its pointiest. Of course, by the late '80s, things were trending towards superstrat shapes, and Westone was no exception as they moved in that direction with models like the Pantera, played by Kirk Pengilly of INXS.

I find it fascinating that a guitar from a factory in Japan can make it to the other side of world, end up in the hands of a rock star in an ad in a magazine or on a concert stage, and leave such an indelible mark of inspiration and influence. As clear as it is that handmade, custom instruments created by highly skilled and inspired luthiers offer details and qualities that mass produced instruments simply cannot, I am very grateful for the import guitars that I have in my collection. Most of them sound and look great, and play just as well. The Matsumoku factory seemed to have both modernity and soul, and that combination of function and affordable access brings me great joy. To paraphrase the great Rush drummer Neil Peart, all of this machinery making modern guitars can still be open hearted. It's really just a question of your honesty — and your inspiration. Even if the guitar in the ad is not the one on the record.

Through his wonderful playing on the ultra-successful *Metal Health*, to his progressively less commercially successful efforts (but increasingly more artistically successful) — 1985's *Condition Critical*, 1986's *Quiet Riot III*, and 1988's bluesier *Quiet Riot* album with new vocalist Paul Shortino — Carlos Cavazo has inspired within me a lifelong commitment to guitar, as well as a lifelong romance with the pointy version. It's a romance that borders on obsession.

Now I'm off to Reverb.com to see if I can get back that Rudy Sarzo Slammer bass, or maybe one of those Westone Dimension IV delights. It turns out that the lust for pointy guitar acquisition, like bangin' your head in the name of *Metal Health*, just might drive you mad.

CHAPTER 6

CARVIN GUITARS AND THE METAL METHOD

In the pointy guitar world, nostalgia can play a very large role in our desire to acquire, with memories of the days when dreams may have been all we could afford. The hours spent wondering what it would be like to play, never mind actually *own*, a real Jackson Rhoads flying V, or a set-neck Carvin V220 with hot M22 pickups, and the Kahler Pro tremolo system was almost as fun as actually picking one up. Almost.

I first became aware of Metal Method mail-order guitar lessons through rock rags like *Hit Parader* and *Circus*. These particular periodicals weren't solely aimed at musicians, but at hard rock and heavy metal fans in general, which might have meant the ads created a bigger impact on me. Something about the inclusive vibrancy of the verbiage made playing heavy-metal guitar seem less threatening and, more importantly, possible.

"It doesn't have to be complicated or confusing to become an excellent Rock guitarist."

It *doesn't*?

"There's no faster way to reach your potential than this."

There *isn't*?

"If you had started taking these lessons when you first heard of them, you would be on stage instead of in the crowd!"

I *would be*?

"Don't just copy the stars, become one!"

Hell *yes*! I'm *in*!

These early ads featured simple, wonderfully executed, hand-drawn illustrations of an early '80s rock guitarist caricature, rail thin in tight black pants, spiky palm-tree hairdo, white boots with Cuban heels, and most importantly, playing Flying V- and Explorer-styled guitars; the V adorned with simple graphics like those that were growing in popularity at the time, the Explorer sporting a whammy bar. These illustrations by Londa Marks, then-wife of Metal Method founder Doug Marks, represent to this day my ideal image of the rock-n-roll guitarist, an image that still inspires feelings of excitement, and even ambition, within me. This combination of clear language and simple but effective imagery felt like a call to arms, and it was a call that many aspiring rockers answered.

In a few years' time, as Metal Method continued to grow, those quarter page ads with the hand-drawn characters became full-page glossy ads, featuring an iconic Doug Marks decked out in full heavy-metal regalia — a custom designed rock shirt, studded arm bands, a massive head of blond hair defying gravity by means of what must have been a case of Aqua Net hair spray, and most strikingly, a white Jackson Rhoads flying V. Doug was an early endorser of this new model, and the text underneath Kristen A. Dahline's photo of the metal maestro proclaims "Doug Marks, Metal Method instructor playing the new Jackson guitar by Charvel. The guitar was designed by Grover Jackson and Randy Rhoads." The address and phone number for Charvel Mfg. at PO Box 245, San Dimas, CA 91773. Seeing that address rang a bell, and sure enough, it is the address that is stamped on the metal neck plate on the back of my Charvel Jake E Lee model signature guitar, and was common with early Charvel model guitars . . . grass roots advertising at its finest.

> My first pointy guitar was a Jackson RR model. It was given to me by Jackson for promotional considerations. It's probably a 1983 model. Serial number: 0213. I was a fan of Randy Rhoads and still remember the first time I saw the RR hanging up in Guitar Center. That inspired me to give Jackson a call. I used one of their guitars in my first full-page Metal Method ads.
>
> I remember going into a Guitar Center and seeing that Jackson Randy Rhoads model. I can still picture it up on the

wall, way up there where you can't pick it up and play it. It was out of reach because at the time, if my memory serves correctly, it was like $1,800 or something ridiculous. And I just started Metal Method, and this was 1982, before I had done any ads with my picture in them in the magazines. It had been cartoon characters up until then, drawn by my wife. But anyway, I saw that guitar and I thought, man, that is so cool. I really, really would like to have that, but $1,800? I was so poor at the time. And I mean, really, really, really poor. It was completely unaffordable. And what little bit of money I had, I had spent on advertising for Metal Method, which started making me some money. I wrote Grover Jackson. Actually, I was mainly in touch with his wife, Joanne. I told them I was planning on doing an ad for Metal Method in magazines. I asked if I could get a guitar, one of those [a Jackson Rhoads], in exchange for doing the ad for endorsement considerations, and they said "Sure."

And I said, "Man, alright! This is awesome — nobody's ever given me anything like that before." Of course, I'm doing something for them in return. But they didn't want to give me one right off the bat because there were so few of them. At the time when I did that ad, there was basically no inventory. So, they said they couldn't give me one yet, but they would build one for me, and they would send me one to use in my first ad, a loaner while they made my guitar. That was the one used in the aforementioned ad. No telling what the history was on that guitar.

— Doug Marks

Turns out that prior to getting his first Jackson, Doug had been using a Les Paul, the same guitar played by one of his heroes, Mick Ronson. Ronson was a gifted guitarist, writer, and arranger famous for his work as foil to David Bowie during the Ziggy Stardust era. Aside from his facility as a musician, Ronson was also blessed with chiseled, Byron-esque good looks and was almost as influential for his shock of blond hair (cut into a fabulous layered shag) and his commanding stage presence as he was for his powerful guitar style. Doug's admiration for Ronson was shared by none other than Randy Rhoads, and you can hear hallmarks of Mick's style in some of the more sonically adventurous aspects of Randy's playing, and certainly in how Rhoads fashioned his image in the earlier part of his career.

> My ex-wife was an artist. She did hair and makeup. She was really into the glam look and she was a big David Bowie fan. I believe that I got my hairstyle at the time from the same place Randy Rhoads got his hairstyle, and that was from Mick Ronson. I thought Mick Ronson looked so cool. And I used a Les Paul that I still own today. In Denver, I would be the only guy in the club with my hair cropped, and the hairspray and that whole deal. It's like we came from the same influences. When I got to L.A., I looked like I fit in, not because I was copying what was going on. I was just bringing the same thing to the party.
>
> — Doug Marks

Here was a state of the art, perfectly molded heavy-metal rocker, and he was offering us the chance to make the heavy-metal guitar sounds that were altering our priorities, igniting our dreams, and scaring the hell out of our parents, all without hearing a single shredded lick from Doug's Jackson's flying Vs. Later ads would show him with a gorgeous red 1986 iteration of Randy's classic ax . . . I'm getting serious GAS (Guitar Acquisition Syndrome) just thinking about it.

> When I went to do the photo shoot for my guitar lessons, the photographer said, "Do you actually play guitar?" because I wasn't really playing, I was just posing, and I said, "Yeah, yeah, as a matter of fact, I do." [*laughs*] "That's what this is all about!"
>
> So that loaner guitar had to go back to the factory, and then I got to go to the factory to pick up my guitar. And that was quite an experience, meeting Joanne and Grover Jackson.

> And then in '86, because I've used their guitars in my ads, they sent me the red Jackson RR model guitar and I used *that* one in ads. I never really thought this much about it, but I *was* a billboard for the pointy guitar. And a lot of people looked at me in my pose and said, "That looks pretty cool." It could have

> been the other way around. I could imagine someone looking at it and going, "Guitar instructor? I'm never gonna use *that* guitar, that's hokey!" or whatever. You know what I mean? They could've taken it that way, but because I *did* look like a rock star in those ads, and the look of the guitar was cool, instead of people looking at it and going, "Oh, a guitar instructor used that." They'd look at it and go, "This guy that kinda looks like Randy Rhoads used that." I'm sure that it popularized and influenced it. I do feel like I did have a part in popularizing this guitar.
>
> — Doug Marks

Part of the thrust of wanting to speak with Doug for this book was that I realized what a massive influence he had on me in terms of the entrepreneurial spirit he was projecting. He may have been the first do-it-yourself rock star I ever connected with. Doug was inspiring by virtue of showing us what was within our reach. Beyond the 100,000 guitarists in 71 countries who the ads claimed had purchased the Metal Method, I believe Doug Marks was inspiring anyone who saw those ads by showing us what was possible with hard work and an industrious spirit.

That industrious spirit was evident in the ads Doug Marks purchased for his other musical endeavor at the time, Hawk, a heavy metal band that played original music and had developed a very strong following on the Sunset Strip, packing clubs and rocking crowds with a gothic tightly arranged heavy-metal sound that featured the talents of bassist Lonnie Vencent (BulletBoys, King Kobra), and the prodigious drumming of Scott Travis, who would later find fame as the drummer for British metal masters Judas Priest. The videos I watched on YouTube demonstrate Doug's clear mastery of the techniques and approaches taught in the Metal Method course, combining hot licks from the first wave of '80s shred guitar with a clear affinity for idiomatic classic-rock maneuvers. The videos also portray an airtight, polished musical and visual ensemble giving an arena rock–worthy, highly choreographed concert performance.

> I spent a huge chunk of change, because I had made a lot [of money], and it helped that my ex-wife was involved in the design of everything with me, the fashion statement or whatever. And

> she was willing to go along with it. But I spent, over the course of about six months, around eighty thousand dollars. And it all came from my guitar lessons. That's why I did the guitar lessons in the first place. I thought that it would be a vehicle to finance a band, if I was successful. And it was successful at that.
>
> — Doug Marks

Further evidence of Doug's playing can be found on Hawk's self-titled 1986 album, which was financed through the success of the Metal Method, providing Doug and Hawk with the means to make the album (with future Guns N' Roses drummer Matt Sorum handling the recording duties) at Pasha Music House in Hollywood, the same studio where gold and platinum albums by hard-rock superstars like W.A.S.P. and Quiet Riot were recorded. In a case of foreshadowing for Sorum, a freshly signed Guns N' Roses was laying down tracks for their *Live ?!*@ Like a Suicide* EP, a pseudo-live concert recording that would serve as their opening salvo as a recording act, and was ultimately an attempt to gain street credibility under the false pretence of being an indie act. That album was released on the band's own imprint Uzi Suicide, but was actually funded by a major label, Geffen Records.

Hawk were in fact rubbing shoulders with the acts that would represent Hollywood's first and second wave of hard rock and heavy metal, finding themselves, and their sound, somewhere between these two acts at Pasha.

> When I was recording my album in Pasha, W.A.S.P. was in there recording at the same time and I interacted with [W.A.S.P. lead guitarist and fellow Jackson guitar endorsee] Chris Holmes. Guns N' Roses came at the end of my era playing those clubs and everything. When I recorded my album, they were at Pasha as well. I had heard of them, knowing that they were a Sunset Strip bar band, but I hadn't actually listened to their music until I was in the studio. And we opened up the door, and we were hearing some of their playback. I was ready to say, "Oh, these guys suck!" But then when we heard it, it was like, "Wow. This is some really, really good stuff." And they were recording or actually touching up the live EP, which I guess they did as their initial thing before *Appetite for Destruction*. Those guys were just starting out and very

poor. As a matter of fact, there was a time when they had all their guitar cases there, and I didn't have a pick. And I thought, "Oh, this is good. I'll open up their guitar case and borrow one." Not *one* pick in any of the cases! They probably shared a pick at that point. [*laughs*] I didn't know any of them, but I remember in this room where they stored tapes, Axl Rose had a keyboard back there and he'd be working on keyboard parts and everything.

Axl was a very quiet guy. I don't know that I ever even spoke with him. But their bass player, Duff [McKagan], would come into the studio, because he knew who I was because of the Metal Method ads, and he would watch us. He was really friendly. So, I had interactions. Matt Sorum [who would go on to record and tour with Guns N' Roses for their *Use Your Illusion* double album cycle] he did the album with me and Hawk and also helped me with some drum programming, because I wanted to be as efficient as possible when I went into the studio. He laid down all the drum parts in a night for the entire album. It's kind of funny. When I told you the story about sticking our heads out the door and hearing Guns N' Roses in the studio? It was me and Matt Sorum sticking our heads outside. I was with Matt the first time he heard Guns N' Roses.

— Doug Marks

Nostalgia recently led me to put down US$29.99 for a blast from my rock-magazine-reading past — the Metal Method 1983 — Legacy Course. This course is a freshly digitized and remastered version available as a download from a company, and a guitarist, who was as inspirational and influential as any of the players I have mentioned in or talked to for this book. That first version of the Metal Method course featured detailed, well thought-out pedagogy that walks aspiring musicians through every step of the process of playing heavy-metal guitar.

The Metal Gear section addresses equipment and gear selection, including detailed, hand-drawn graphics that illustrate all parts of the electric guitar, proper guitar-string gauges and how to string a guitar, and how various effects color the sound, as well as advice on amplifiers and how to set up your guitar for optimum performance.

Reading through the Metal Primer section made me yearn to go back in time and reclaim the hours I lost playing through any number of beginning-guitar methods — ancient books, written and shoved down my throat by heavy-metal hating teachers that made me suffer the emotional disconnect of struggling through "Yankee Doodle Dandy," "Tom Dooley," "Red River Valley," or any number of god-awful folk songs that, while at some point had their time for being culturally significant or entertaining, frankly bored the living shit out of me. (To be honest here, my amazing guitar teacher in my hometown of North Bay was Brian McDowell who, when made of aware of my burning ambitions, put me on a righteous — if a bit heavy-metal deficient — path of classical-guitar study that has helped my career immeasurably. Thank you, Brian!)

My God, Doug, you had laid it all out there for me! How to tune the guitar, how to read guitar tablature — a system for reading music that foregoes the medieval complexities of standard notation and replaces them with numbers that relate to string and fret numbers. After all, I didn't really need to harmonically analyze a Bach lute suite, I just needed to play "Crazy Train"! There are carefully detailed instructions on how to play barre chords, how to bend strings, how to play the rock friendly pentatonic scales that could have unlocked the majesty of rock and the mystery of roll for me. And that's not to mention the dizzying array of licks, tricks, riffs, techniques, chord progressions, and yes, a Metal Theory booklet that can be applied to all genres of music to make one a more comprehensive musician. These lessons all came with audio cassettes (and in later years, video cassettes) that featured Doug performing the musical examples with an authentic heavy-rock tone and all the chops, technique, and feel of a heavy-metal master. Considering everything was typed out, the hand-drawn diagrams, and the all-analog recording of hundreds of musical examples, it must have been a staggering amount of work.

The thought of being able to learn and to actually perform the techniques I was reading about as I graduated to devouring '80s guitar magazines was a thrill. The words that described these techniques leapt out of the pages of interviews with my guitar heroes and the Metal Method ads with almost as much fury and fire as they jumped out of my stereo speakers — hammer-ons, two-hand tapping, sweep picking, pinch harmonics, dive bombs, speed picking, power chording — truly visceral verbiage.

Throughout the '80s and early '90s, Metal Method would see a great deal of evolution. Nitro vocalist Jim Gillette — a man who could shatter glass with his operatic vocals — was brought on and offered a course on heavy-metal singing, and guitar virtuoso Michael Angelo Batio — inventor of the over-under guitar technique, a master shredder par excellence, and no stranger to the pointy guitar himself — was brought in to satisfy the next wave of over-the-top, technique-hungry students who were feeling the need for speed in an increasingly competitive guitar community.

Ultimately, I did learn many of the techniques taught in the Metal Method, but I can't help but wonder how much further ahead I'd have been as a rock musician had I the wherewithal to lobby my parents hard to take me down to the bank, cash in my savings bonds, create a U.S. money order, and mail it off to the magical P.O. Box address located in the incredibly exotic sounding Studio City, California.

Doug would go on to feature another Jackson RR in later advertisements, a 1986 model that I had the pleasure of hearing him play during the course of our interview. Doug was also an endorser of Carvin guitars, a San Diego–based, family-owned company that dates back to the 1940s and was founded by Lowell C. Kiesel. In 2015, the Carvin Corporation split off the guitar business to a new company, Kiesel Guitars, named in tribute to the founder who had passed away in 2009. Kiesel continues to make electric guitars that range from traditionally classic to ultra-pointy, and points in between. Some of these models are based after models Doug himself endorsed, and that were featured in Metal Method ads and videos, including the Ultra V. In the 1970s, Carvin carved out a niche in the musical instrument world by selling directly to the public via mail order, which allowed for customization options that were as easy as checking off what you wanted and needed, not unlike the à la carte options offered in a Metal Method ad. The following description of the Ultra V comes from the Carvin Museum website, a veritable font of '80s guitar goodness with plenty of point!

> The Ultra V was a totally unique instrument. It took some design cues from the V220, as well as the Gibson Flying V and Jackson RR models, but had a unique and classy shape that still looks fresh today.
>
> The body and neck was constructed from eastern hardrock maple, as were all Carvins of the era, and the ebony fingerboard was inlaid with standard mother-of-pearl block inlays. Electronics consisted of an M22 in the neck position, and an M22SD in the

> bridge position, with single volume and tone controls and 3-way pickup selector. The Kahler Pro tremolo was standard. Base price of the Ultra V was $569. Koa wood was available for $40. Pearl finishes were available for $20. Black chrome hardware was $20, and gold hardware was $40. Dual-to-single coil and phase switching could be added for $30. It was even available as a lefty for an additional $30. The HC19 hardshell case was $79.
>
> — Carvinmuseum / Kieselmuseum.com

The V220 that inspired the Ultra V is a guitar I have been hunting for many years. I first saw one in the hands of Starship ax slinger Craig Chaquico in a full page Carvin ad, and its blending of V, Explorer, and Star facets made it an all-round (and slightly more rounded!) pointy classic.

> The V220 was a guitar that was ahead of its time. It had a totally unique look, and was destined to become one of the most popular models Carvin had offered. With MTV and other music video outlets, the V220 was seen everywhere, and was made more popular by the resurgence of Jefferson Starship (now just called Starship), whose lead guitarist (and future Carvin signature model inspiration) Craig Chaquico was often seen with one of his many V220s.
>
> The V220 was made using the same craftsmanship and materials as Carvin's other guitars. The body and set neck were hardrock maple, and was available in black, white, red or clear finishes. Curly maple and koa were also offered. Electronics consisted of an M22 pickup in the neck position, and an M22SD pickup in the bridge position, with dual volume, single tone, coil splitters and a 3-way pickup selector switch. Chrome was standard on the Schaller mini M^ tuners and B6 bridge or Kahler tremolo. MOP dot inlays were standard on the 24-fret ebony fingerboard.
>
> Base price on the V220 was a very reasonable $399. With the Kahler Pro tremolo, it was $549. Koa wood was an additional $40, and curly maple was an additional $125. Gold hardware was $50. The HC19 hardshell case was $69.
>
> — Carvinmuseum / Kieselmuseum.com

Other '80s rockers who were known to rock a V220 include former Megadeth lead guitarist Marty Friedman, who played one in his virtuosic shred-metal duo Cacophony with the equally prodigious Jason Becker, who also played Carvin guitars, including his famous numbers DC200 superstrat-style guitar that featured a multicolored humbucker in the bridge, single coil in the middle humbucker in the neck position, and the actual numbers for each fret inlaid in various colors on the fingerboard. A tribute version of this guitar, also available in his popular Bluey finish, and a black and white yin-yang design was made available by Kiesel and offered with the traditional Carvin logo as an option. Becker is a guitar hero not only for his amazing playing and compositional skills, but also for the fact that while his playing career was tragically cut short by ALS at the height of his career after securing a gig with Van Halen frontman David Lee Roth, the loss of his physical capacities has not dimmed his spirit as he continues to compose and inspire to this day.

Marty had the following to say about his relationship with Carvin and, just prior to that, Hurricane guitars:

> Well, Hurricane — a very nice company. But at that time, I was completely homeless, and Jason was still living with his parents. So, the first company that offered us guitars, we were like, "Sign us right up!" If it's a guitar, we can play the damn thing. We'll make it work. They were taking us out to dinner — we were just such an easy mark. And actually, Jason's guitar was pretty good, but my guitars were pretty much unusable.
>
> Carvin was a big step up for us. We got an offer from Carvin, and I remember us being very excited because it was a really solid company, and they made cool shapes. So, I was like "This is almost as cool as my Jackson." And it was kind of a unique pointy shape, and I liked that a lot. And the people at Carvin were just absolutely fantastic. I remember that being a big step up, our first real, real solid endorsement.

Did Marty remember anything about the way that guitar felt to play?

> I never cared about how any guitars feel and that's true to this day — I can't tell the difference between any of them. As long

> as the guitar stays in tune, I'm playing it. I've never really been one of those "thin neck, fat neck" people who complain about all these things. "The scale was this, frets are that . . ." Maybe my fingers are just not that sensitive, but I couldn't tell between any two guitars. Or even if I could tell, it wouldn't really affect the way I played very much.
>
> — Marty Friedman of Megadeth

Paul Hackman, guitarist for Canadian hard-rock institution Helix could also be seen playing a V220 in Helix videos from the band's 1987 Capitol Records release *Wild in the Streets*. Turns out it was a "gift" from his guitar partner, Brent "The Doctor" Doerner:

> Fuck. Carvin gave me that guitar for a dollar. I liked it so much, I gave it to Paul, and sadly, he fucking played it on stage. I didn't like it because the neck was too fat. I had played it for about a day, and then I gave it to Paul. Sadly, he liked it.
>
> — Brent Doerner of Helix

I have clear visions of seeing Helix play my hometown arena, Memorial Gardens, in 1987 on the *Wild in the Streets* tour, and watching Paul on stage with his red V220 (as I recall, he was also in possession of a black V220 with white binding), trading licks and choreographed stage-maneuvers with the good Doctor Doerner, as vocalist Brian Vollmer, bassist Daryl Gray, and the recently deceased (and greatly missed) drummer Greg "Fritz" Hinz brought every one of my rock-n-roll dreams to life right in front of my eyes. Much later, I would join the band as a bassist for a short spell, although I would leave shortly after for a job touring the world with Nelly Furtado. However, I continued a very strong writing, recording, and co-production relationship with Helix and singer Brian Vollmer, and would perform with the band from time to time, giving me an opportunity to share the stage with each of the Canadian rock-n-roll heroes mentioned above. Everyone, that is, except for Paul Hackman, who would tragically die in an accident when the band's van veered off a steep mountain highway and plummeted down a 40-foot embankment on July 5, 1992, in Kamloops, B.C. He was only 38 years old, but left an enduring legacy of great songs, albums, and performances that inspired many young Canadians. While I never had a chance to share the stage with Paul, I did have a chance to work with Helix on their most recent album, *Scrap Metal*, which features newly recorded versions of unreleased songs that he wrote for the band. Through the magic of technology, we were even able to use some of Paul's guitar work on the newly recorded tracks, which means I have been on recordings with every member of the classic lineup. I consider it a rock-n-roll blessing and will always associate the Carvin V220 with Paul's fiery performances. I hope one day to acquire one in tribute to his influence on me.

As Doug Marks himself mentions on the Metal Method website, he has since updated much of the material in the course, and the Legacy lessons are really there to serve as a nostalgic trip for those students lucky enough to have benefitted from Doug's heavy metal pedagogy, and, for people like me, a chance to experience that which was so tantalizing, yet just out of reach, during our youth. It's kind of funny to think that despite Doug Marks having played such a pivotal and inspirational role in the development of the person, player, artist, and teacher I'd become, that I'd never heard him play a note until very recently. Of course, I was not surprised to hear that he was a fiery, fluid player with a great style and command of the instrument back then, just as he is now.

I thoroughly enjoyed my chat with Doug Marks for this book, and I believe there is a connection between us that is rooted in the concept that our dreams ultimately brought us to a place where rock n roll meets education. Beyond the pursuit of fleeting commercial success in the recording and touring side of the music industry, we both found a place where we can take the intrinsic joy that happens when playing an instrument and share it with others. For me, it is in various elementary schools within the Toronto Catholic District School Board as an instrumental and vocal music teacher. For Doug, it is on the MetalMethod.com website, through his private instruction, and during those glory days of the glossy rock magazines of yesteryear, where he shared space alongside the guitar greats of heavy metal's golden era. With his Jackson and Carvin guitars, he inspired me to try to look as cool as he did in this noble pursuit. At the age of 52, I'm *proud* to say that I'm still trying, Doug, and I think I'm just a Carvin Ultra V or V220 away from really nailing it.

CHAPTER 7

TWISTED SISTER AND THE POINTIEST GUILD GUITARS

If you have read either of my previous books or have ever engaged in a conversation with me about the origins of my commitment to a life as a rock-n-roll guitarist, you know that it really begins with one band — Twisted Sister.

Twisted Sister has always represented empowerment to me. As a sensitive, awkward preteen lacking in physical stature and self-confidence, the band's infectious anthems, outrageous image, and overt middle-finger-thrusting attitude helped me rage against any number of machines and take on enemies real or imagined.

In many ways, Twisted Sister empowered and inspired me in the same way that the electric guitar empowers and inspires me to this day. Turns out I like my rock bands the same way I like my guitars — misshapen, sharp, and outrageous! I would even go so far as to say that Twisted Sister is the band equivalent of a great pointy guitar, a colorful tool of creative expression, and a mix of defiant anger and over-the-top fun that can be weaponized if necessary.

Revisiting the Marty Callner–directed videos for their commercial breakthrough, 1984's multiplatinum *Stay Hungry,* fills me with the same passion and excitement that was displayed when these veterans of the '70s New York tri-state bar circuit spat in the face of the disco and new-romantic eras with their NFL linebacker–meets–New York Dolls visual aesthetic and early glam rock–inspired sing-along anthems. It's pure, Sick Motherfucking magic: a world where teenage-rampage rage meets Looney Tunes–inspired comedic lunacy; where simple '50s-inspired song forms, early AC/DC, and Judas Priest inform proto–heavy metal riffage; and where two-note power chords provide a bed for the roaring and soaring, hypermelodic and hyperactive alpha-male vocal delivery of the great Dee Snider.

Hot on the heels of heavy metal's commercial acceptance in 1983 (a result of breakthrough albums by Quiet Riot, Def Leppard, and Mötley Crüe, all of which featured pointy guitars), Twisted Sister built on the foundation of their own hard-fought acceptance into the major–record company big leagues with their Atlantic Records debut, *You Can't Stop Rock 'n' Roll*. The band fully dominated the airwaves with *Stay Hungry* with its more radio-focused sound that — for better or for worse, depending on which band member you spoke to — provided sweet, midrange frequencies, which cut through the tiny speakers on TVs and radios around the world, delivering impossibly catchy and heartfelt anthems composed by Dee Snider right at the apex of the MTV era. Fortunately, the band had among its ranks a secret weapon in Suzette Snider, a talented fashion designer and creator of the famous Twisted Sister bone logo, which adorned the band's *Stay Hungry* album. Her flamboyant, neon designs were a combination of Vivienne Westwood's punk-boutique rebelliousness and '70s Times Square–drag queen chic. With this look, which included the garish application of enough lipstick, face paint, and rouge to make Divine blush, Suzette Snider had created visual shock and awe melding perfectly with the hilarious video treatments referencing the high jinks of Bugs Bunny, Wile E. Coyote, and the Road Runner. The sense of teen rebellion was honest and heartfelt and, while it frightened many a parent in the era of satanic panic and the PMRC (Parents' Music Resource Center), it had much more to do with Mel Blanc than it did with Anton LaVey.

I work with a company called Guitar Nut Tees, who create licensed, custom shirts (and pillows!) with designs featuring the guitars of iconic rockers including Steve Vai, Bruce Kulick of Kiss, Rudy Sarzo of Quiet Riot, Reb Beach of Winger, and the two guitarists of Twisted Sister, Eddie Ojeda and Jay Jay French. My wife ordered me some pillows from GuitarNutTees .com, including one with the famous guitars used by Eddie Ojeda during Twisted Sister's commercial heyday. My proud posting on social media of this Christmas acquisition prompted a response from company owner Aaron Greer, which led to a quick friendship based on our mutual love of '80s rock. It also led to a business relationship, as Aaron was kind enough to add me to his roster of clients. My own very pointy signature Godfrey guitars, the Exquire SK-1, SK-2, and the Voltez Mini-V, and my less pointy, but undeniably rock n roll, Reimer Montreux guitars are now represented in this hallowed hall of flashy axes. Obviously, to be included in such esteemed company is an honor. Sweet rock-n-roll dreams do come true, and in this case, they come with a high-quality and comfy pillow.

> I was born in the late '70s and grew up in the '80s. We got MTV when I was about seven, and I was glued to it. Twisted Sister was one of the first bands I saw. The power of "We're Not Gonna Take It" and "I Wanna Rock" — if you hear those songs as a kid, they get into your DNA. While I've always loved bands with a theatrical look and performance, it was Twisted Sister's music that truly made me appreciate them. Later in life, I gained an even deeper respect for them, especially their incredible perseverance as a band — something I didn't fully understand as a kid.
>
> — Aaron Greer, Owner, Guitar Nut Tees

As a young fan, I was always drawn to the sound of distorted electric guitars, and the instruments sported by Jay Jay French and Eddie Ojeda in the videos for "We're Not Gonna Take It," "I Wanna Rock," and "The Price" immediately caught my eye in the same way that the steel-enforced, Leslie West– and Jimmy Page–inspired '70s classic-rock licks coming off their fingerboards tickled my ears.

Eddie Ojeda's most famous axes of that golden video era were his Charvel pink-and-black bull's-eye guitar and another Charvel emblazoned with the Twisted Sister logo.

> That was the first bull's eye guitar made by Charvel, a new company at the time. That guitar was on the cover of their first catalog too. I never expected the great reaction that it got. It was modeled after our Sound City Cabinets where we painted the

> speaker cones pink and black. I used it so much that it needed to be re-fretted two or three times. Grover Jackson called me up at one point and said he wasn't able to re-fret it again and it was best to retire the guitar. I could have had a new neck put on but at the time I got an offer from a guitar collector who wanted to buy it. I wasn't with the band anymore and it wasn't playing right so I sold it. I still have the 1985 Twisted Sister logo guitar that was one of the first ones with the pointy headstock and 22 frets. I prefer the 22 over the 21 frets on the bull's eye guitar. That extra fret makes the difference. I also like the extra room at the top too, versus the 24 frets on my B.C. Rich.
>
> — Eddie Ojeda of Twisted Sister (Interview, Charvel.com.)

Prior to his affiliation with Charvel, Ojeda could be seen and heard rocking an Ibanez Destroyer and B.C. Rich Mockingbird and Bich guitars.

> As far as guitars went, I had several different guitars in the early days. I had a couple of Ibanez guitars, and then when B.C. Rich guitars came out I started playing those for quite awhile. I had a Mockingbird that I really liked and played for a while, I also had a B.C. Rich "Bitch" that was custom made for me and I was using that as well. Shortly after that, Charvel Guitars emerged on the scene with the Custom Strat type guitars. I ordered my first guitar, which was of course the bull's eye guitar, that has become synonymous with Twisted Sister, and that I used in oh so many videos and played throughout the world with. Once I got that, I was just using it all the time, it just felt like a god in my hand, it was just one of those things, just the way it looked, it was just so cool looking. So many people made so many comments and it just really fit the band very well. Shortly after that, after I had that guitar for about a year, they made me the Twisted Sister logo guitar. Throughout the whole Twisted Sister era I basically used those two guitars, I just went back and forth between the two of them. I had two other guitars on the road with me but I didn't really use them much, it was

> basically the two Charvels. The bull's eye guitar has a Duncan Custom pickup in it, with a pre-amp boost but I didn't really use it much as far as the pre-amp boost went. The Twisted Sister logo guitar had an EMG pickup in it. So, they sounded different but they both had a really great sound to them so that's why I used those two guitars exclusively.
>
> — Eddie Ojeda (Kozidos: The Band, loscocidos.wordpress.com.)

For the recording of *Stay Hungry*, Ojeda stuck to his two main Charvels, while Jay Jay played his '78 Les Paul Custom, which had been adorned with an ostentatious pink paint job courtesy of Steve Carr, a New York–based luthier who came to prominence for bringing to life an early version of Gene Simmons's now famous ax-shaped bass. Carr also helped Kiss guitarist Ace Frehley create his iconic rocket-launcher and smoke-bomb guitars, as well as the "New-York-Groove" guitar that lit up and featured a silver finish and Ace's name inlaid in pearl on the fingerboard. Carr also created a star-shaped guitar that was actually star shaped for Paul Stanley, which saw minimal use because of its poor tonal qualities, and a very cool mini Explorer with a flame-maple top for Ace Frehley that was used on Ace's star turn, "Talk to Me" on Kiss's power-pop inflected *Unmasked* album.

Jay Jay also employed his '74 Ibanez Destroyer on *Stay Hungry*. Carr had repainted the guitar black and added a pearl-inlay dragon on the lower-right bout and "Twisted Sister" lettering on the headstock. Both this Destroyer and the pink Les Paul Custom were outfitted with DiMarzio Super Distortion pickups.

> My Ibanez Destroyer was an exact copy [of a Gibson Explorer]. Ibanez did the Flying V and the Explorer, in exact Korina, back in 1975. The story goes that four hundred guitars of each model came into Port Newark, and then Gibson somehow was able to sue them for violation of registration copyright because of the trademark scimitar headstock. The first batch of Ibanez Korina Vs and Explorers were really beautiful guitars. And my Destroyer is a first-generation Ibanez Explorer [copy], which I

> then had painted black and put the dragon inlay on it, and it became a famous guitar of mine for a long time.
>
> — Jay Jay French of Twisted Sister

On the other side of the country in California, two young guitarists, Eddie Van Halen and Chris Holmes, would also get their hands on these high-quality Explorer copies. The Ibanez Destroyer (model 2459) was used extensively on Van Halen's debut album, *Van Halen I*. While Eddie Van Halen is most closely associated with his Frankenstrat, his Kramer superstrats in the '80s, and signature models for Ernie Ball, Peavey, and EVH in the latter part of his career, it's a 1975 Ibanez Destroyer that lights up tracks like "Runnin' with the Devil," "You Really Got Me," and "Jamie's Cryin'."

I found an interesting piece of information on the highly informative VanHalenGear.com website that may dispel a myth about the wood used on these Destroyers:

> These guitars were made in Japan at the Fujigen factory from 1975–1979. The body wood was made from Japanese "Sen" and referred to as "Sen Ash." However, Eddie Van Halen and Chris Holmes both originally thought they were made of korina due to the advertisements Ibanez used, but "Korina" was just the name of the finish. It features an epoxy finish which easily chipped, and most of these guitars you see today show extreme chipping over the years.
>
> The pickups were Maxon "Super 70s" and featured "Star" tuners. Ed would eventually replace the tone/volume knobs with ones from his Stratocaster. The guitar features generally characteristics of a Gibson Explorer: Set neck construction, 22 frets, fixed bridge, etc.
>
> Something very rare about Ed's destroyer is the neck joint. Ed's Destoyer was an extremely early version with bulkier set neck joint when compared to later 1975 versions.
>
> Ed eventually cut up the destroyer and turned it into the "Shark" which it is most known for now days. Ed replaced the nut with a brass version, removed part of the body, changed pickups, and of course striped it with his famous red/white

> scheme. Unfortunately, this dramatically changed the tone of the instrument in Ed's disfavor. In fact, Ed disliked the sound so much he asked Chris Holmes if he could borrow his to record the "Women and Children First" album in 1980.
>
> (VanHalenGear.com)

> I loaned him my Ibanez Destroyer. I loaned him mine, and I had [Eddie's Shark Guitar] for about six months, that actual guitar, the actual one. I had that for a long time. I wanted mine back. [*laughs*]
>
> — Chris Holmes of W.A.S.P.

I wondered if this was, in fact, the origin of the star-shaped guitar design that companies like Jackson/Charvel and DiMarzio would go on to manufacture and market. Holmes is famous for playing a number of star-shaped guitars and, when I was first discovering hard rock and metal, was the first guitarist I can recall seeing play one. Since he was also a friend of Van Halen's, it made sense to ask him who he thought came up with the design first.

> There have been stars going on since '80. George Lynch [from Dokken] had one early on; Van Halen was the first guy I saw playing one. He cut his Destroyer into a star. He made the first star ever. He had an Ibanez Destroyer, and he cut a "V" out of the back. [Actually], he didn't cut it. He drilled holes and then sawed in between the holes. It changed the sound of his guitar. . . . He had the first star. I don't know who designed the star after that. It could have been a company called Mighty Mite. It could have been them.
>
> — Chris Holmes

Eddie Van Halen's almost universal influence on rock guitar is clear and obvious, but it was heartwarming to hear of his influence on Chris, who would also go on to fame as a guitar hero. When asking Chris about his own lead-guitar style, and in particular one lick that I have heard him use to great effect on a number of classic W.A.S.P. tracks, it was clear that this was an influence born not out of idol worship, but out of friendship and respect.

> I learned that scale or pattern from Ed. A lot of things I learned, I learned from him. One time he was at my house. I used to live up by his parents, really close. We were smoking Thai weed, and we were fucking around with my Marshall, and we had it cranked. And the windows were down, and Ed goes, "Hey, man. You probably wanna close the windows with your neighbors?" I said, "Ahh, fuck the neighbors." [*laughs*] And he was playing my guitar. Right? And I was [thinking], *Man, this is cool. I hope the neighbors think it's me playing.* [*laughs*] When you grow up with somebody and you've known them before they ever got a record deal or were famous or whatever, you just think of things a lot different.
>
> — Chris Holmes

Destroyers were made by FujiGen Gakki, a Japanese instrument manufacturer that made guitars for Ibanez and performed OEM (original equipment manufacturer) services for other brands like Greco, Yamaha, Tobias, Dean, Fender, Gibson, and more. Like the Matsumoku factory, FujiGen Gakki was located in Matsumoto, Japan. The company still exists today, operating under the FUJIGEN name, where it manufactures car dashboards for Toyota, tools and utensils, and still makes guitars for Ibanez, G&L, and many other brands, along with its own FGN-branded guitars.

Ibanez.fandom.com shares the following intel on the Ibanez Destroyer:

> The Destroyer style debuted in 1975 with the model 2459, which was a copy of the Gibson Explorer. Ibanez called its copy the "Destroyer" and used provocative taglines like "Explore the Destroyer" to evoke its Gibson inspiration. The initial copies were discontinued in early 1978 when Gibson sued over trademark infringement, a lawsuit that was eventually settled. The series was revived as the Destroyer II series which was introduced for 1981. The shape of these models were altered slightly to keep the lawyers at bay.

We will get into the lawyers and lawsuits in a bit more detail in the next chapter when we hang with Def Leppard guitarist Phil Collen, who, alongside

Iron Maiden guitarist Adrian Smith, is largely responsible for the widespread popularity of the Destroyer II. But in the meantime . . .

When Steve Plunkett, a successful songwriter and composer for TV and film who also found arena-rock fame with the band Autograph, was playing the Hollywood scene with his band Wolfgang in the late 1970s, alongside bands like Van Halen and Quiet Riot, he was also lured by the charms of the Ibanez Destroyer.

> I had one of those too, which I absolutely loved. The Ibanez was much more comfortable than the actual Gibson Explorer. I never liked the Gibson Explorer. I remember borrowing one and playing it one night at a gig, and the neck was just so fat. My hand hurt for two days. I never liked those big baseball-bat necks, and that's what the Explorers have. But the Ibanez had a thinner neck. The pickups weren't as good. It didn't quite have the bite, but I stuck some DiMarzios in mine.
>
> — Steve Plunkett of Autograph

Let's get back to the guitars I first saw Twisted Sister slinging on TV and in magazines. While the pink-and-black swirling bullseye guitar that Eddie Ojeda played in the "We're Not Gonna Take It" video had me hypnotized, the wobbly, angular Gumby-esque guitars that Jay Jay French had slung from his shoulders were never actually played on the album. Of course, as we will see multiple times in this book, that is often the case; a guitar that holds a certain preferred sonic quality for a recording may not have the desired visual appeal for a concert or video performance. Of course, this would have shattered me as a young and naive music lover, as I took all of the new heavy-metal information being pumped into my brain and soul as gospel truth.

But as a *slightly* more mature 52-year-old professional musician, I have made some of the same professional choices myself, opting for a flashier ax with which to express my innermost, choreographed rock-n-roll fantasies on screen and stage, when a different guitar was used in the recording studio that had superior tonal qualities.

That's show biz, baby.

I asked Aaron Greer why the guitars that he celebrates in his T-shirt and pillow designs resonate with him and his customer base.

> Growing up watching MTV, seeing the bands I loved, and hearing their music was incredibly powerful — especially for a young, impressionable mind. Although I started on drums, I was always drawn to the guitar. I didn't just love hearing them — I loved seeing them. These unique instruments were unforgettable, and nearly every popular band had a guitarist with a signature guitar, often immortalized in their videos. It was a special time in music, full of fun and excitement. To this day, seeing these guitars connects me to that same sense of joy and wonder — the feeling of being a kid, dreaming of music, and believing anything was possible. That's what these designs mean to me, and I hope they resonate with others in the same way.
>
> — Aaron Greer

In Jay Jay's case, the guitars in those Twisted Sister videos were the stunning Guild X-79 Skyhawk models. These guitars look like a Gibson Explorer on a magic mushroom trip, simultaneously pointy and droopy, a stretched out, rubbery pop-art fantasy of a guitar design.

Guild was founded by Alfred Dronge, a Jewish immigrant who was raised in New York City. Dronge was an accomplished guitarist and banjo player who worked in music retail and eventually opened his own music store. After World War II, Dronge gave up the store and began importing Italian accordions. Building on his success and connections, he founded the Guild Guitar Company in 1952. The Epiphone company was moving the production of its instruments to Philadelphia due to problems with local unions, and Dronge was able to attract luthiers who wanted to remain in New York. Guild grew and eventually moved production to larger premises in Hoboken, New Jersey.

As guitar-based pop music became popular in the 1960s, demand for guitars increased. Corporations were beginning to diversify their holdings and, much like the CBS acquisition of Fender in 1965, Guild was sold to Avnet, Inc., an electronic parts producer. On the electric guitar side, Guild became perhaps best known for its hollow body and semi-hollow body electric guitar models, such as the Starfire, the Granada, and the Aristocrat. These guitars, by sound and design aesthetic, were perfect for jazz and the cleaner side of electric rock and pop guitar playing — a far cry from *Stay Hungry*!

As the '80s ushered in new sounds, styles, and a greater focus on visual presentation, Guild came out with a number of models that definitely got the point across that this was a company on the cutting edge of razor-sharp guitar design. It was Mark Dronge, son of Guild founder Alfred Dronge, who would sway a recently spurned Jay Jay French into becoming a Guild man.

> In '84, the peak of the band, everything was just going crazy, and I went to my first NAMM [North American Music Merchants] trade show, and two things happened. Two completely separate weird conversations took place at that NAMM show. Conversation one was with Marshall amps, whose distribution company was based in Long Island. So, they knew us because we're a Long Island band, and we would go to the Marshall factory to get our amplifiers worked on by a couple of the guys who worked there, the Franks brothers, Kenny Franks, and Tony Franks. They would do custom tube stuff. We really felt like we were inside with them, you know? Marshall's working on our amps! They're putting in the 6550 tubes, they're putting in the EL34s. You know, our amps are being tweaked by the Frank brothers at Marshall!
>
> And Marshall was famous for never giving anybody anything free. That was the whole thing with Marshall. You gotta pay. You know, Jimi Hendrix said, "I don't want anything for free. I just wanna know they're gonna work anywhere in the world."
>
> So here I am, at the 1984 NAMM show, walking down the hallway past Marshall, and they all see me. "Jay Jay, come in here, man!" I walk in and they go, "Hey, we're so proud of you guys, man! We've been watching you guys for years, man. We are so impressed that you guys made it. And you know what? We're gonna give you six Marshall stacks!" Okay. Wow. So here you are being anointed by Marshall. Fucking anointed. I mean, what else can you say? People ask me, "What's the high point of your life?" Or, "What moments are among the high points of your life?" That's one of them, for sure. That's something most people don't understand. They will never understand what it means to have Marshall tell you "We think you're one

of the greatest bands in the world. You're super hot!" So then, on the other hand, I walk over to the Gibson booth, thinking, *Hey, here I am! So, what are* you *gonna give me?* And this was the response . . . .

"Where do you live?"

"Manhattan."

"Do you know the stores on 48th Street?"

"Yeah, I've been buying guitars on 48th Street since 1966."

"Cool — go there and buy one. They have great retail prices."

That was Gibson's comment to me. That was it. It was off. I walked away from the booth really angry, and really upset. That's my fucking guitar — I've been playing Les Pauls since 1970.

But, anyway, they said to me, basically, go fuck yourself. Then I was walking down another aisle, and I run into a friend of mine who was with the president of Guild, Mark Dronge, and he introduced us. I told him my brother, who is much older than me, actually owns a Guild acoustic guitar, which was one of the first guitars he ever bought, at Manny's, in 1959. And then I told him, "I can't fucking believe what Gibson just did to me!" And he goes, "Gibson said that to you? I'll give you anything you want. Come to Guild." So that was it. I came to Guild. And they gave me the yellow-and-black, and the red-and-black X-79, and then they gave me a Strat-style guitar, and then they gave me an Explorer-style guitar. They just kept giving me guitars. They just did advertisement after advertisement with me. I was thrilled. They treated me really well. Mark died, I think, a year or two years ago [May 11, 2022]. Rest in peace. Wonderful man. Guild was great; Gibson didn't do shit. The whole pointy guitar thing was happening anyway. The Guild wasn't necessarily pointy as much as it was futuristic looking, though. The X-79 Skyhawk had that weird look.

— Jay Jay French

The X-79 that Jay Jay French favored first appeared in 1981 and featured an offset double cutaway, asymmetrical mahogany body with a fin-like bottom bout that gave the guitar an almost Gumby-esque appearance. Of course, French had his finishes customized in hot-rodded stripes in combinations of yellow and black, and pink and black, perfectly in synch with the trash and technicolor aesthetic that Twisted Sister was dealing in.

Other pros who wielded an X-79 (if only in magazine ads) were Rossington Collins Band guitarist Allen Collins, better known for his stint in Southern rock legends Lynyrd Skynyrd, K.K. Downing of Judas Priest, and Ian Hunter's band's lead-guitarist Robbie Alter, who did use it for recording and touring purposes. However, it was another East Coast guitar legend who arguably gave the X-79 its second greatest amount of exposure.

Little Steven Van Zandt is a man of many talents. Best known as guitar foil and right-hand man to Bruce Springsteen in the E Street Band, he is also a solo artist and producer. On top of that, he has garnered acclaim as an actor for his roles in *The Sopranos* and *Lilyhammer*, is the founder and supervisor of syndicated and satellite radio show Sirius XM's *Little Steven's Underground Garage*, owns a record label, Wicked Cool Records, and has many other artistic and altruistic endeavors to his name.

My good friend and noted author (plus a former co-worker at the Queen Street location of Tower Records in Toronto in the '90s) Robert Lawson has written a wonderfully detailed book about the man entitled *Solidarity Forever: The Art and Soul of Stevie Van Zandt*. He is a writer of incredible detail and skill, and I knew there was no better person to tell the story of Stevie's dalliance with these pointy Guild wonders.

> When Little Steven Van Zandt was prepping his second solo album, 1984's *Voice of America*, it was time for a change in gear. For years, as a member of Bruce Springsteen's E Street Band, and on his own debut Men Without Women 1982–83 tour, Van Zandt depended on his 1957 Stratocaster, a 1965 bright red Strat and a '67 Strat. But when Van Zandt's bandmate Jean Beauvoir showed up to rehearsals with two brand new custom Guild X-79s, Steven wanted them immediately. Beauvoir had a sponsorship deal with Guild at the time and designed the guitars himself.

> The main one has a black and white zebra stripe paint job with two EMG humbuckers, a Kahler vibrato and Dunlop strap locks. This eye-catching axe can be seen in both Van Zandt's "Out of the Darkness" music video and Springsteen's "Glory Days" clip. It was also used for many 1984–86 television appearances such as Rockpalast '84, *Late Night with David Letterman*, the Amnesty International benefit from Giants Stadium in '86 and the December '86 Concert for Peace in Tokyo, Japan.
>
> A spare, with burgundy zebra stripes, went out on the road with Van Zandt in 1984, but very rarely was ever seen on stage. In the years since 1986, the more familiar black and white Guild X-79 has been loaned out to various Hard Rock Cafe displays while the burgundy spare remains in storage.
>
> (Robert Lawson, *Solidarity Forever: The Art and Soul of Stevie Van Zandt*.)

Hard rock fans will recognize the name Jean Beauvoir for his connections to Kiss as a cowriter, session bassist, and background vocalist, with involvement on such '80s classics as "Uh! All Night," "Who Wants to Be Lonely," and "Thrills in the Night." His eclectic résumé also includes membership in the Plasmatics alongside Wendy O'Williams, and working as a producer for the Ramones. With his platinum blond mohawk and striking stage presence as a performer, Beauvoir seems well suited to the X-79s perception-twisting shape.

It's fun to note that Guild also had a model that was an exact mirror image of the X-79, the X-80 Swan or Skylark. Other equally intense and even pointier Guild models created in the '81 to '88 time frame included the X-82 Nova, the X-84 V (used to shocking effect by Mötley Crüe's Mick Mars in the "Too Young to Fall in Love" video), the X-88 Flying Star (apparently codesigned by Mick and similar to the X-84, but with variations that included the ever popular DiMarzio humbucking pickup option), the zany bolt on–neck X-97 V (the "V" presumedly referring to the Gibson Futura- and Moderne-inspired split headstock), and perhaps the most striking and forward thinking Guild model ever, the X-100 Bladerunner.

David Newell and Andrew Desrosier were the designers of the X-100 Bladerunner. I had a chance to ask David about the genesis of this unique instrument, and how his innovation not only inspired great rock-n-roll performance art, but also played a part in one of the music industry's most culturally significant moments.

> David Andrew Guitars [sometimes called David Andrew Design Research] was named for myself and Andrew Desrosiers. My relationship with Andrew [Drew] started circa 1982. Drew was a local hotshot lead-guitar player in the Albany, New York, area and was also known as *the* guitar repair-paint man in the area. Drew also dabbled in making guitars. A mutual friend hooked us up one day and we hit it off. I mentioned to Drew my favorite design was the Gibson Explorer, and that I wanted one but it was out of my price range. He told me we could make one if I bought the wood and parts. I bought a hunk of rock maple for the body, a Schechter solid rosewood neck, and all the other parts to make a guitar. We went to a local music store in Albany, Drome Sound, and we traced a Gibson Explorer on the wood. Days later I showed up at his house and he wasn't home. His girlfriend, Terry, let me in and I saw a modified guitar shape drawn on the wood. It kind of looked like an Explorer, but I asked Terry, "What are these triangle shapes for?" She said that Drew had mentioned that he was thinking of cutting those out to make holes in the guitar. Well — *boom* — the light went off in my head and I said "That's it!" I took the wood to my dad's woodshop in his basement and I cut the perimeter profile and all those holes out in the wood. I was ecstatic! I brought the wood body back to Drew's house and he said, "What did you do? I was only thinking about doing that." I said, "No, this is it man!" He was not very happy at first but a few months later, after he completed the final body design that made it to production, we were all very happy and excited. The first Bladerunner body was born. Drew was a true artisan. RIP. Shortly thereafter, we applied for a design patent and it was awarded two years later. Then began the search to license it to an existing company.
>
> I showed up backstage at a Twisted Sister concert in Albany, New York, one day with the Bladerunner prototype in a cardboard box. I met Jay Jay French and Eddie Ojeda. Jay Jay French

> was very kind to me. They let us in and they loved the guitar and used it during their sound check. Jay Jay later said, "You gotta meet somebody — Mark Dronge from Guild Guitars. He's going to love this guitar." Jay Jay literally went to the payphone at the venue, called up Mark Dronge on the phone, and he handed me the phone. A week later I was down there in Mark's office in New Jersey showing him the prototype, and then suddenly we're meeting up in Rhode Island at the factory where Willy, the German guitar builder, was making plans about how he could tool up to produce this crazy-shaped guitar body. One month later I was back in New Jersey looking at Guild's first prototype X-100 Bladerunner, as they called it. Wow was it nice. It had that high-end look and feel.
>
> — David Newell, David Andrew Guitars

The X-100 Bladerunner was played by a number of prominent MTV guitar heroes back in the day, including Mitch Perry of Heaven, MSG, Edgar Winter, and Cher fame.

> The Bladerunner — interesting story behind that guitar. Flashback to mid-1985, and I'm walking past Manny's Music in New York City. And Heaven [an Australian rock band Mitch was a member of at the time] was about to shoot a video for "Knockin' on Heaven's Door." Now, up until then, I'd been endorsing Charvel guitars. But *everybody* was now playing Charvel guitars, and as I was walking past Manny's I saw this Guild Bladerunner, and it just looked so whacked out. I went into the store and I had a couple of friends who worked there. And what's funny is the guy who I asked about the guitar was Andy Hilfiger. His brother was Tommy. Andy is basically the salesman. He and his brother Billy were both higher ups at Tommy Hilfiger, but both of them came up through Manny's, back in the day. Andy got a hold of Mark Dronge at Guild, and Mark said, "Go ahead and give him that guitar." And I literally walked out of Manny's with the Bladerunner. I was only gonna use it for the video just because it looked so radically

> different. I just wanted something that no one else was using. Now, the funny thing, I was also on my way to a Frankie Miller session because I was playing guitar on his record *Dancing in the Rain*. And my Les Paul was there, and I showed up with this weird-looking guitar. And, you know, it had EMG 81 pick-ups, so it had a really biting sound. We ended up using the Bladerunner on the Frankie Miller record — it's all over "Do It Till We Drop." I used it in the Heaven video and used it in the Michael Schenker videos and on tour with MSG. Then B.C. Rich made me one, which is insanely beautiful. I mean, it's in perfect condition, and it's like blue snakeskin paint the whole way around. It's a badass instrument.
>
> — Mitch Perry of Heaven

Autograph guitarist and lead vocalist Steve Plunkett was another prominent Bladerunner player; he played a Ferrari red X-80 in the future-friendly videos for "Turn Up the Radio" and "Send Her to Me" from Autograph's 1985 gold-selling album *Sign in Please*. Plunkett's X-80 was the perfect guitar to deliver the hard rock–meets–power pop sights and sounds that featured robots, spaceship-inspired soundstages and lasers, and mail-order mannequin groupies who came to life after assembly.

The members of Autograph (Plunkett, lead guitarist Steve Lynch, drummer Keni Richards, bassist Randy Rand, and keyboardist Steven Isham) were all veterans of the Hollywood scene, playing in bands like Wolfgang and Silver Condor in clubs like Gazarri's and the Starwood alongside bands like Quiet Riot and Van Halen. Drummer Richards was a jogging partner and friend of Van Halen frontman David Lee Roth, who, upon hearing Autograph's demo tape, invited the unsigned band to join them as the support act on their massive 1984 Tour, a break which ultimately led to a major-label recording contract with RCA Records.

> [I played] a Les Paul custom for the whole Van Halen tour, and for [recording] the first album [*Sign In Please*] that was all my Les Paul Custom. But right after that, before the record actually came out, we did a New York guitar show where we had a little booth, and that's when the Guild people approached us. I had

always been a huge fan of Guild guitars. I played one in high school and they just have a different feel to them. I love the necks on Guild better than on any other guitar. I like a nice thin neck, and Guilds used to be thin. They showed me what they had, and I really loved that X-80, because it was kinda pointy and weird and different, and that's what I was looking for. So that's what I played in most of the early *Sign In Please* shows until one day they brought me an X-100, probably a year later. Nothing sounded as great as that guitar. It had EMG pickups — you plug them in, and they sound great. I wanted that sound. I think we were in New York playing the Ritz, and they met me in the hotel ahead of time and brought me that white Bladerunner. Right. I'd never seen anything like it and it looked so cool, and it wasn't heavy because it had the holes [in the body]. When I finally cranked it up, through my amp, it was like, "Wow, this is awesome," and the neck was perfect. It's like probably one of the greatest necks I've ever had. Everything about that guitar was perfect for me. It had the Kahler tremolo, which I wanted, and I didn't use the tremolo. I had it locked down, and I liked that it would stay in tune. What was so great about the Bladerunner also were the paint jobs. They would paint the insides of the [body] cut outs a different color — I thought that was really unique. The look, the neck, the pickups, the bridge — that guitar was, to me, the perfect live rock guitar.

For some reason, the X-80 and the Bladerunners really spoke to me. The minute I would open the case, I would get a vibe just from the guitar before I would even put it on. And that's what I was looking for, especially back in those days. Both of those Guild models were really my thing. I could have played a Les Paul (I always had a great Les Paul in the truck), but I didn't want to because it wasn't the same vibe.

— Steve Plunkett

Undoubtedly, the most famous guitarist to take the Bladerunner for a spin was Aerosmith's Joe Perry. No stranger to pointy and adventurous guitars (Perry was an early adopter of the B.C. Rich Mockingbird and Bich models in the 1970s), Perry famously used the guitar in the video for one of music's most culturally important moments.

The 1986 collaboration between Aerosmith and hip-hop pioneers RUN DMC on a rap remake of the former's '70s hard-rock classic "Walk This Way" had ramifications for both bands: Aerosmith saw a renewed interest that fueled their phenomenal late '80s comeback, and RUN DMC crossed over to a predominantly white MTV audience.

> I think the cultural impacts of Aerosmith joining up with RUN DMC were monumental and controversial for the times. Both bands brought together two sides of the music world that were miles apart prior to that and I think that the Bladerunner, as Joe Perry put it when he was asked about the guitar's use in the video, and I'm paraphrasing here, was a sign of the times. It was edgy, it was controversial, and it was different, so it aligned with what Aerosmith was doing with RUN DMC [by mixing rap and hard rock].
>
> — David Newell

That X-100 Bladerunner guitar now hangs in the Met (Metropolitan Museum of Art in New York City) as part of the *Play It Loud: Instruments of Rock & Roll* exhibit, which celebrates instruments of cultural significance and impact. The exhibit features iconic guitars played by Jimi Hendrix, Jimmy Page, Eric Clapton, Jeff Beck, Eddie Van Halen, and many more. In the following interview, Perry discusses the Bladerunner's inclusion in the exhibit.

> I was really honored to think a guitar I played would have enough gravitas to make it into the Met. There are a thousand great guitar players out there who have contributed to the last 50, 70 years of rock n roll. To be asked to have even one guitar in that display is a real honor. The guitar I picked — I'm sure there are plenty of Les Pauls and Stratocasters and those guitars that have played a big part in my career in the studio and on the stage — but that guitar was in a video that was pretty pivotal.

The music [Run DMC] were making, I saw it as being the next step from blues. It's blues, hip-hop and rock — it's elemental and rhythm-oriented and the lyrics are talking about day-to-day stuff. To me it was a very logical leap from the blues to hip-hop and rap. And then to work with the guys who were right on the cutting edge of it was exciting to us. We got the phone call from Rick Rubin. They were a little skeptical about it, I know they were using some tracks of ours just as they were using other rock tracks — Zeppelin, whatever — to create their beats. But it was another thing to cover a song by a hard rock band. Rick Rubin had said in an interview a couple months before that he thought "Walk This Way" was proto rap. And we were like, "Wow, okay, thank you." We never thought about it like that, but I guess you could see that. And when we got the phone call it wasn't totally out of the blue, but it was, "Well let's try it, we'll see." They didn't even know if they were gonna put it on the record. "Let's go into the studio and see what comes from it." I brought my guitar, we put some stuff down, and Rick said, "You know, we should really get some bass." And I said, "I can play bass on it, I just need a bass." And one of the cats who was hanging out said, "I got one back at my apartment." He went back to get it, and it was one of the Beastie Boys, because they were hanging out with Rick and watching what was going on. So I used his bass, put it on the track and that was it, it was fun. We went back on the road and got a phone call not too much later — "Well we really like the song and want to do the video." I figured, again, this is not supposed to be just us [in the video], but any garage band, any rock band, to signify that's what's on one side of the wall. I figured at that point in rock n roll some of the most popular guitars were the pointy guitars, and the Bladerunner, you couldn't get any farther away from the classic Les Paul or Stratocaster look. It's got holes in it! It's oddly shaped. Oddly enough, it's a good guitar to play. It's fun to play, once in a while I take it out and use it in the studio. But visually, it's a statement.

— Joe Perry of Aerosmith

(*Billboard Magazine*, April 30, 2019.)

> Quick story about how that guitar actually got into the video. My good friend of 40 plus years Jay Abend, who owns Guitarfetish.com, was the driving force in getting the Bladerunner in the now legendary video. I got Jay hooked up with Mark Dronge from Guild early on in the process. Jay, the brilliant guy, he became many things to Guild including their artist relations rep, photographer, and ad agency during the '80s. Jay was asked by Dronge if he could bring by a few guitars to this video shoot in Queens. Jay's stories from that shoot are legendary. He had a couple of the Bladerunners — a black one and a white one — in the trunk of his car. Jay showed up in Queens where they were filming and showed the black one and a white one and maybe a pink one to the director. And the director saw these Bladerunners and said this guitar is perfect for this video or something to that effect. I want that black one in it and the rest is history. And that's the real story.
>
> — David Newell

Like Joe Perry, Newell felt incredibly honored to see his design hanging in the Met:

> It gets me all choked up just thinking about it. Forty-plus years ago, when Drew and I finished the prototype guitar, we were standing in Drew's kitchen having a couple of beers admiring our handiwork. I remember looking at Drew and it was said between us that one day this guitar design was going to be in a museum. Now when we said that we were thinking that it was going to be next to Fonzie's jacket at the Smithsonian, you know, we were thinking big. When I came to learn that this guitar was going to be in that exhibit at the Met and subsequently at the Rock & Roll Hall of Fame, it brought me to tears immediately. It really did. It was also very emotional for me as I knew I could not share this monumental experience with Drew, which still weighs heavy on my heart.
>
> When I went to the Met to see it in person I just stood off to the side as I did not identify myself to anybody that were

> walking by the exhibit. I just listened to what people had to say about the Bladerunner and how they remembered it. That was very meaningful for me to hear the stories and comments. To know that Drew and I had a hand in this was just so moving and emotional for me. I keep coming back to those same words because that's really what it meant. I felt a deep sense of pride and accomplishment knowing that Drew and I had a little part in the history of rock n roll, which in a lifetime, is a big deal to me. I'm very happy the way it all turned out. I always say it was displayed in the Met for the art and it was displayed at the Rock & Roll Hall of Fame for the music.
>
> — David Newell

Moving back to Twisted Sister, a number of custom pointy guitars made appearances in videos and on concert stages for the difficult albums that came in the wake of *Stay Hungry*'s success. The follow-up, 1985's *Come Out and Play*, was another album of rebellious anthems. Snider's *Warriors*-influenced album art and theatrical concert staging was highly inspired, if not ultimately inspiring enough to connect with fans who were now having their attention divided by the multitude of hard rock and heavy metal bands that were washing up in the wake of the first wave of the '80s commercial hard-rock boom. It would have been wonderful to see more of Jay Jay's custom graffiti-painted Guild X-88 (albeit with what looks like a X-82 Nova headstock) in the video for "Be Chrool to Your Scuel," a gross-out take on B-movie zombie kitsch and '50s rock-n-roll rebel rock. The video and recording had more star turns than an episode of Hollywood Squares, with the track featuring performances by Billy Joel and Clarence Clemons on piano and saxophone respectively, a rockabilly guitar solo by Brian Setzer of Stray Cats fame, and colead vocals from the godfather of shock rock himself, Alice Cooper who also made a cameo in the video.

With a suitably crazed appearance from '80s comedian Bobcat Goldthwaite, and a zombie band with members of the rocking dead playing Flying V– and Explorer-style axes till their fingers, and everything else, bled, there was a lot of competition for screen time, which didn't leave much time for the actual members of Twisted Sister to show off the guitars *they* were playing. To be fair, it would have been a bit weird to see Jay Jay miming along to the clean as a whistle twang of Setzer's solo while plucking his ultrapointy Guild. But when you did catch a glimpse, man, did it look cool.

> "Be Chrool to Your Scuel" had a really aesthetically heavy look to it, which is why I liked having the Guilds that I played in that video.
>
> —Jay Jay French

Hell, you can't even *see* what guitar Ojeda is playing in the video. And unfortunately, only very grainy, fan-made video footage exists as evidence of the elaborate stage production that was mounted for the tour to support *Come Out and Play*, a tour that was unfortunately cut short due to poor ticket sales. We can see that Jay Jay's pointy Guilds were in full effect in the rare visual captures, as was a very cool custom Kramer displaying the *Come-Out-and-Play* artwork that Dee dons for a song. It looks like Eddie gets into the Guild action with the more traditional, Strat-shaped Aviator model, this one in fire-engine red. It was last seen as a listing on the instrument-retail aggregator Reverb .com, ultimately going for the hefty price of over $8,000 from London Vintage Guitars of Denmark Street.

The *Love Is for Suckers* album from 1987 features a red-hot, ultraslick production job by producer Beau Hill, and, for all intents and purposes, was really supposed to be a Dee Snider–solo album. The record features a fair amount of "additional" guitar by Winger's Reb Beach, and it's hard to know just how much of French and Ojeda's sonic fingerprints actually ended up on the album.

However, in the video for the wickedly catchy "Hot Love," French and Ojeda are seen in full-flight performance mode amidst a cavalcade of hot-rodded cars in a setting that plays upon movie tropes ranging from '50s drag-strip racing to *Cool Hand Luke*–inspired sexual anticipation, all delivered in a somehow wholesome way that made me feel that such a lifestyle could be safe enough for me to participate in while staying in the good graces of my loving, yet very religious, family. Eddie's guitar in this video is a white Jackson Kelly explorer, festooned with vibrant pop-art splashes while Jay Jay rocks a jet-black Strat-style Jackson.

The overall look and sound of Twisted Sister during this era is very professional and entirely appropriate for what was happening in the music industry at the time; but, alas, they just didn't feel like Twisted Sister anymore, a feeling undoubtedly amplified by the departure of long-time drummer A.J. Pero prior to recording *Love Is for Suckers*. He was replaced for the album and tour by New York drumming legend Joey Franco.

Of those many pointy and painted wonders, I asked Jay Jay how many could still be found in his collection:

> You know, so many guitars have come and gone. I have to tell you, it's like when you can't afford one, you don't have one. And when you don't need a guitar, you got 50 of them.
>
> Every guitar company's handing you a guitar. You know, "Please play this!" So I was playing all these wacky guitars. For *Come Out and Play*, it was primarily the Guild X-88 — the pointy one. That was the one that was painted like graffiti by the guys who did the graffiti on the back cover of the album. Those guys did an amazing job.
>
> And then, Kramer and Jackson started giving me guitars — I think on *Love Is for Suckers*. I don't know if I played them on the album. I know that we didn't do a very long tour. It was a short tour to promote that record. And then they all disappeared. I mean, I had no guitars left. I had no Guilds, no Jacksons, nothing. I mean, I had the Guild with the graffiti and the *Love Is for Suckers* guitar. And then my brother one day says to me, about five years ago, "You know, I got a guitar of yours in my closet." I asked "Why?" He said, "Because I had a costume party and I needed to go as you and you lent me some clothes and the guitar." And I said, "What are you talking about?" And he opens his closet door and there's my stage clothes from 1985 in a shopping bag on the floor, like, the yellow and black, the ones you see in all the videos. My yellow boots in the bag, which I hadn't seen, and there's the freaking Guild guitar, the old yellow one, which I played briefly. And that was it.
>
> I was a part owner of a pizza chain in New York in the late '80s, and they went out of business. The owner disappeared, and for all I knew he was dead, but I found him about six months ago in Florida. I remember having one of my striped Guilds up

> on the wall. [I asked him,] "You don't have that, do you?" And he said no. I think he probably still did but didn't wanna give it to me — he paused a little too long. And I said, "Well, the Long Island Music Hall of Fame is looking for some guitars to put up on display, and that was an important guitar."
>
> — Jay Jay French

While fans who followed Twisted Sister in their club days of the '70s may have pictures of Ibanez Destroyers, B.C. Rich models, and a pink Les Paul Custom dancing in their heads, my fondest Twisted Sister–guitar memories will always involve Eddie Ojeda's Charvels and Jay Jay French's Guild X-79s; So much so that, when the following listing came up at my favorite guitar shop, the historic Twelfth Fret on Danforth Avenue in Toronto, I knew I had to have it. Mirroring the knowledge of their awesome staff, their website had the following listing that lent the guitar historical gravitas, which helped justify my most recent bout of guitar acquisition syndrome (GAS).

> Here we have a fairly rare bird — the Guild X-79 Skyhawk in white, produced in Westerly Rhode Island from 1981 to 1986, this one dating to 1984. The construction of this model is simple — the body and set neck are Mahogany, with an un-bound, 24-fret Ebony fingerboard. Those last few frets were very rare at the time!
>
> Founded in 1952 with many skilled workers from Epiphone, which had moved from New York to Philadelphia in a move to break a strike, Guild had long been known for archtop and steel string acoustic guitars, but thinline and solidbody electrics were in their catalog, too. Guild had made odd shaped guitars, including the S-200 Thunderbird seen on the cover of *Electric Mud*, the 1968 psychedelic album by Muddy Waters. The Guild X-79 Skyhawk took things further with exaggerated points on the body and almost completely unrestricted access to the 24-fret neck.
>
> For many years including the entire period of production for the X-79 Skyhawk, Guild used serial numbering systems specific to each model. Guild X-79 Skyhawk serial numbers started with

> AD and six digits, with the first being around AD100000. The last known serial in 1986 was AD101790, so approximately 1790 were built.
>
> This Guild X-79 Skyhawk is in overall good condition with a few chips and dings to the finish, to be expected on an almost 40-year-old guitar that's been used as intended. Fret wear is light, and as Guild used a medium-jumbo fret wire there is plenty of metal left yet.
>
> The original hardshell case is included.
>
> (The Twelfth Fret, 12fret.com.)

The benefit (and danger) of having such a well-curated shop filled with knowledgeable experts and mouth-watering guitars is that the staff can fill in all the historical technical information that I can't seem to keep in my brain. All I knew when I saw this listing was that I had to have the guitar. While the plain white paint job did not inspire me the same way Jay Jay's yellow-and-pink-with-black-stripes custom finishes did, holding that gloriously asymmetrical combination of wood and wire in my greedy little hands confirmed that this guitar had to be mine. It didn't hurt that the guitar was surprisingly small, as light as a feather, extremely resonant, and easy to play. It afforded me a number of sonic options; the powerful Guild humbucking pickups gave me all the power and sustain I needed for crunching power chords and soaring solos, while also cleaning up very nicely for sweet, chiming-bell-like tones — a very well made and versatile guitar that I've used on a number of recordings. Of course, when I covered the early Twisted Sister classic "I'll Never Grow Up, Now" (first released as an independent single in 1979, and later resurfacing on the 1985 major label re-issue of 1982's full-length debut *Under the Blade*) for my Crash Kelly–covers album, *Mïxx Täpe Vol. 1*, the X-79 was the guitar I had to use. I realize that Jay Jay wouldn't have been in possession of that model when he recorded the original, but why nitpick when it comes to inspiration? I really felt that using that guitar imbued the track with the spirit of not only what I love about the sound of Twisted Sister, but also what the spirit of the band has come to represent in my life.

Another arguably less appropriate way in which the influence of Twisted Sister worked its way into my professional life was during my time playing guitar with Grammy-winning pop star Nelly Furtado. Nelly was a

Gibson-endorsed artist and, as a result, I acquired my own endorsement with Gibson. Thanks to the high-profile arena shows and appearances on television programs like the *Tonight Show*, *Late Night with Jimmy Fallon*, and performing at the 2010 Winter Olympics, Gibson was more than happy to let me select a few models. I made selections that were appropriate to fulfill the sonic requirements for the gig. A white Les Paul Custom (a nod to Randy Rhoads), a Songwriter Deluxe acoustic guitar, a tobacco sunburst 335, a Gibson Firebird (a classic pointy choice that was a nod to Def Leppard's Steve Clark), and a Les Paul Goldtop Tribute with P-90s. These all met with the approval of the music director, who had voiced some concerns with the guitars made by the company I had previously been endorsing, B.C. Rich (more on that later).

During my introduction to Gibson, it came to my attention that they had gained ownership of the Kramer brand in 1997. As an avowed Eddie Van Halen fan, this thrilled me to no end, especially when I saw the '84 Model, based on the classic Kramer Barettas that were designed to be Van Halen's signature models, and would later emulate the droopy headstock design of Eddie's Ibanez Explorer (which became the Shark Guitar after he famously customized it by chopping a large piece of wood out of the body). When I looked into acquiring one, I was thrilled to see that they offered an '84 Model with a bull's-eye finish, and the red-and-black version they had was close enough to Eddie Ojeda's pink-and-black bull's-eye Charvel to make me grab one (they were kind enough to also send me a white-and-black bull's-eye Model); both were outfitted with a single Seymour Duncan JB humbucker and Floyd Rose. I never did get to sneak the bull's-eye guitars on stage with Nelly, but I did rock a few arenas with a Ferrari-red '84 Model, a little nod to 5150-era Sammy Hagar. However, that red-and-black bull's-eye was the guitar I used on an audition that landed me a gig in *Dee Snider's Rock & Roll Christmas Tale*, a holiday musical based on the music of Twisted Sister featuring lots of pointy guitars and heavy metal shredding, which just happen to be a few of my favorite things. Those pointy guitars happened to be ESP (and their budget line LTD) models, not the Kramer that I used to audition. The guitars were a variety of ultrapointy flying Vs wrapped up like Christmas presents. We'll talk about ESP guitars soon enough, but it sure was fun going through the catalog with Dee himself to select which ones we were going to use for the show. I guess Santa found a way to get me the flying V that I wanted for Christmas back in 1985 after all!

Twisted Sister followed a trajectory traveled by so many of their peers. They fought it out in the clubs, managed to secure a record deal, and defied the odds stacked against them to achieve megasuccess, only to see it diminish for any number of reasons (changing market tastes, creative or marketing miscalculations, inner-band dynamic struggles). However, as die-hard New Yorkers, when the call came to support the victims and first responders of 9/11 through a benefit concert, the classic *Stay Hungry* lineup answered the call to reunite. From the power of that performance, it became clear to the band members that Twisted Sister was an indomitable music force still with unfinished business.

Now, many bands reunite. But I can't think of many other bands who come back to climb their way back to the top of the mountain the way Twisted Sister did. Unlike Aerosmith, who returned and had massive commercial success through support from radio, video, and album sales, Twisted Sister became a headlining European festival act, playing to crowds of hundreds of thousands of people, through the strength and integrity of their live performances, as well as a carefully cultivated plan to not oversaturate the market, or play in diminished situations. Fortunately, years of hard work and grinding it out in the clubs, theaters, and arenas of the world had the band more than prepared to meet the challenge head on.

> We came back in 2003 after being dormant for 12 years, and played 125 of the world's biggest festivals — we coheadlined Wacken with Slayer. Most American metal bands can't do that because they aren't heavy enough.
>
> You gotta deliver that shit. You have to fucking deliver, and you've gotta be great. You have to make those fans walk out that night going, "What a fucking great festival!" "What a great show!" That's how you have to leave it. And, you know, I would say to people, we may not *be* the best musicians in the world, but by the time we're fucking finished with you, you're gonna *think* we're the best musicians in the world, baby. That was how it was, man.
>
> You know why we did that? Because our agents told us to do that back in the bar days. Because if you wanna make more money, you have to blow those other bands off the stage, get a

better reaction from the fans, build up your fan base. Whatever the fuck you gotta do, you do it. And that's what we did. We were driven to blow other bands off the stage.

Our motto was "Look like women, talk like men, play like motherfuckers."

And it was like we tried our best to demoralize every band we could, and it had nothing to do with personal relationships, or how great I think other bands are. It's just my job is to fucking wipe the floor with your fucking sorry ass and to make people know that. And that's all that matters to me. At the end of the night, I walk off stage at two in the morning with a hundred thousand people screaming, and singing "We're Not Gonna Take It."

I love the theatricality of it, but it wasn't just that. When people ask us what kind of band we were and use the description of "hair band," which is a derisive phrase anyway, [we say] we were a bar band from the '70s that made it in the '80s. That's really what we were. We were a hard-bitten bar band, a really war torn, battle proven, freaking bar band that knew how to annihilate people while just looking weird. And that was the deal.

You know, do I look back and go, "We should never have had [that image] to begin with. Could I be [in the] Rock & Roll Hall of Fame by now if we didn't look like that?" I don't know the answer to that question, but I don't know if the band is truly respected for the monster that it was, for the *live* monster that it was.

— Jay Jay French

Twisted Sister continued destroying festival crowds night after night until, in 2016, when they said adieu to the world and left on a high note as headliners on their Forty and Fuck It World Tour. Jay Jay may not have been playing his Guild, Jackson, or Kramer pointy guitars, opting instead for rock-solid Epiphone Les Paul workhorses, including his own signature model sporting a — you guessed it — pink finish, but maybe it doesn't matter what guitar he was playing, or what guitar any of us plays for that matter. What matters is the feeling it inspires within the player.

When people ask me, "How important is the gear?" this is what I say:

You have to feel good with what you play. You have to feel good with the gear that you're playing. If buying a new guitar inspires you to play better, then buy that guitar. If putting new pickups in makes you feel better about how you're playing, and it's inspiring you to play better, then buy those pickups. If you think you're gonna buy your way into Jimi Hendrix world or buy your way into Stevie Ray Vaughan world or buy your way into B.B. King world, no — I'm sorry. It's in the fingers.

You shouldn't wanna sound like any of them. You should want to sound like you.

— Jay Jay French

CHAPTER 8

DEF LEPPARD, RACER X, AND THE POINTY GUITARS OF IBANEZ

Pointy guitars are often associated with "shred," a musical style and heavy metal subgenre defined by hyperspeed highly technical guitar playing that became a popular movement in '80s hard rock and metal. Over time, shred has become adopted by a veritable sea of young, nimble-fingered prodigies on all social media platforms, emboldened by the never-ending pool of resources available for them to learn from. We've come a long way from the days of dropping the needle on the same groove of a vinyl record over and over again, to try to figure out what the hell Randy Rhoads was playing on "Over the Mountain," even if we did have the help of guitar tablature, as well as Doug Marks and his Metal Method back in the day.

At the living, beating, 64th-note bleeding heart of mid to late '80s shred (and '80s hard rock and metal in general) are a number of Ibanez guitar models; high performance instruments with very thin necks, a flat radius that allowed for ease of playing, and the Ibanez Edge tremolo system, an elegant refinement (and some would say improvement) of Floyd Rose's double locking system. These Ibanez guitars were, from a visual point of view, stylistically amplified versions of the Fender Stratocaster, and with the endorsement of masterful guitar players like Steve Vai (Jem series), Joe Satriani (540 Radius, which would evolve into the JS signature series), Paul Gilbert of

Racer X (Iceman, RG series, the PGM and FRM signature series, and various custom models), Richie Kotzen (RG series), Vinnie Moore (VM1 series), and fusion king Frank Gambale (540S series) would go on to become known as the "Kramer killers," taking the superstrat crown away from the American company that had ruled the early to mid-80s with celebrity endorsers like Eddie Van Halen, Richie Sambora of Bon Jovi, and Mick Mars of Mötley Crüe.

Along with the Ibanez-loving shredders mentioned above, known largely for the prowess displayed on their instrumental albums (although Vai and Gilbert would also scale the mainstream charts and pack arenas in multiplatinum acts like David Lee Roth, Whitesnake, and Mr. Big), more mainstream Ibanez hard rock endorsers such as Joey Allen and Erik Turner of Warrant, C.C. DeVille of Poison, Reb Beach of Winger, Harry Cody of Shotgun Messiah and Tracii Guns of L.A. Guns were setting their 8- to 16-bar solo slots ablaze in the studio and on stage in their successful bands' pop-metal confections. While the above players were, for the most part, associated with superstrat-style instruments, Reb Beach had two signature series that definitely fit the pointy mold, the RBM Voyager series, which combined a Strat shape with a V cutout at the base of the body, and the decidedly pointier WRB3, which fit well with Winger's progressive take on pop metal and the futuristic artwork of their album covers.

> The WRB3 is a solid body electric guitar model introduced by Ibanez in 1990. It is a signature model of American guitarist Reb Beach, who is best known for his work in the rock band Winger. The WRB3 was made in Japan by FujiGen.
>
> The WRB3 has a unique body style which Beach designed himself. It was inspired by models such as the Gibson Explorer/Ibanez Destroyer series; it also bears a slight resemblance to Ibanez's XV series of the mid-1980s.
>
> The WRB3 features a mahogany body bolted to a maple neck with a 22-fret rosewood neck with pearl dot position markers. Components include active EMG pickups with a humbucker at the bridge and single coil-sized humbuckers in the neck and middle positions, and an Edge double locking tremolo bridge.
>
> The guitar was available in candy apple red or a special Winger graphic print. Only 100 of the graphic print WRB3s were

> produced, with each one numbered and signed by Beach. Three guitars were also built for Beach himself, all of which he was forced to sell "for rent in the 'dark time' we try not to remember."
>
> The WRB3 is the only Reb Beach series model that used the WRB naming convention and the modified Explorer body shape. In 1991, two new models with the "Voyager" body, the RBM1 and RBM2, were introduced. The WRB3 was available worldwide in 1990, but discontinued outside of Japan after that year. It was available in Japan until 1992.
>
> (Ibanez Wiki, Ibanez.fandom.com.)

The Steve Vai–designed Jem series came out in 1987, complete with a recessed lion's-claw tremolo cavity, an innovation that allowed the player to not only lower the pitch by depressing the whammy bar, but also raise the pitch by pulling up, making for wild and wider vibrato action and sound effects. The Jem also came with a monkey-bar grip handle cut out of the upper body for twirling the instrument overhead should one so desire. (Vai was, and is, a master showman with a limitless supply of stage maneuvers that physically express the drama in his playing style.)

Jems were primarily constructed with basswood bodies, maple necks, and rosewood, ebony, or maple fingerboards with ornate tree-of-life vine inlays. The Wizard-profile maple necks were thin and flat, offering a 25.5-inch scale length and 24 frets built for speed and access to the screaming high notes that would inevitably punctuate every solo on the de rigueur power ballads and stadium anthems of the time. The Jem was loaded with DiMarzio Evolution pickups. Guitar companies will often indulge an artist's desire for custom pickups made by outside companies, and DiMarzio's were often the pickup of choice.

The RG series also came out in 1987 and was the next evolutionary step of the Roadstar guitar series, which itself had evolved from the Blazer series. This was Ibanez's popular, early '80s souped-up take on the Stratocaster. Where the Roadstar had softer, wavier curves reminiscent of a Fender, the RG series had razor-sharp horns and a slim profile that shed some of the Jem's ostentation while forsaking none of the build quality or performance design. Both the Jem and the RG would go on to live in many incarnations and in various series aimed at differing performance needs and budgets.

The Universe series introduced the concept of the seven-string guitar to many aspiring Vai acolytes in 1990, with an added low-B string that was incorporated to extend the scalar range of the instrument and accommodate Steve Vai's expansive melodic and harmonic concepts. It was the first mass-produced seven-string guitar. Later on, bands like Korn would use their Universe models to create nu metal, forsaking the technical flurries of the '80s and early '90s in favor of aggressive and dissonant riffing blended with hip-hop-infused grooves and vocals that would inspire the next generation of guitarists. The Universe was given its own model name but shares many design elements with the Jem in terms of specs and performance.

The headstocks on the Jem and RG models were a holdover from Ibanez's Pro Line series (Vinnie Moore's signature series guitar was also based on this line), and aside from the sharp horns on the body, there was not much pointy about these models. But Ibanez did take a stab at the truly pointy market with some killer V, Explorer, and Star variants in the mid-80s.

The PR1660 was a Jackson Rhoads–inspired beast with Ibanez's own V5 pickups designed to "increase midrange and power" and came in a classy polar white or in your face cherry-ice finish.

The X series represents the pointiest of Ibanez's shred sticks, with the most adventurous being the XV500, a guitar the company claimed to be the "shape of the future," with its shark-like offset-V and Explorer hybrid body, all bevels and points, its geometry simulating the motion of a fin cutting through water. Ibanez went to pains to explain in its 1985 catalog that the instrument's radical look did not come at the expense of playability and offered access to those upper frets so coveted by the virtuosic seekers of the screaming high note. I love the aesthetic of this guitar, but it does feel a bit cartoonish in its extremity, perhaps a step too far into that exalted future we talk about so much in this book. Or, maybe with the right artist endorsing its merits, it might have gone beyond its modest production run of 1400 guitars.

Much more popular were the DT380 and DT350 models. DT stands for Destroyer and represents Ibanez's modified take on the Explorer design. The 1985 DT380 offered splashy graphic designs that included red-and-black zebra stripe, the ubiquitous Rising Sun Japanese flag graphic, and the dangerous-looking barbed-wire finish. The DT350 more closely resembled the iconic Jackson/Charvel Star. The DG350 was a further evolution on this design, and replaced Ibanez's Pro Rocker trem system with their more stable Edge bridge. The RR series was Ibanez's take on Jackson's ever popular Randy Rhoads model. A 1986 Ibanez catalog blurb provides the motivation, target audience, and specs behind these flashy axes.

> Heavy Metal and Hard Rock music demand an instrument that is visually exciting, powerful and quick playing.
>
> The Ibanez X Series has always upheld that tradition with its Rocket Roll and Destroyer models. Our hottest pickups are used on the RR250 and DG350 guitars resulting in tremendous sustain and crunch. Fast action necks with large frets and precision tremolo systems provide the tools necessary for cranking out power chords and lightning-fast single note flurries. The new DB800 bass pushes out thunderous bottom end with two new Ibanez low impedance pickups coupled to an active 2 band EQ system. Wide tonal variations are possible with this simple to use system.
>
> The 1986 X Series has the crunch and flash to put you in the spotlight.
>
> (Ibanez 1986 Electric Guitars and Basses catalog.)

Back in chapter 7, we discussed the Ibanez Destroyer in its nascent form as a faithful, mid-70s copy of Gibson's original Explorer. So, in an attempted feat of literary reverse engineering, I'll now take you back to the genesis of Ibanez's presence in the pointy guitar world.

With the high level of demand in the late '60s and early '70s for electric guitars, escalating prices, and the decline in quality level exhibited by American companies like Fender and Gibson, lesser-known companies and entrepreneurs saw an opportunity to jump into the guitar market.

Harry Rosenbloom of Bryn Mawr, Pennsylvania, was the owner of Medley Music, a shop that sold handmade instruments. Struggling to keep enough inventory due to demand and the time it took for American manufacturers like Martin to deliver quality instruments (sometimes up to three years), Rosenbloom formed a company called Elger Guitars, and began importing instruments from Japan's Hoshino Gakki company, who were making instruments under the Ibanez brand. Hoshino Gakki bought Rosenbloom out of Elger in 1971, and the company became Hoshino (USA) and ultimately Ibanez.

Post-World War II suspicion towards any product made in Japan in the United States led guitar companies to brand their guitars in a way that would hide the origins of their production. Hoshino Gakki had been importing classical guitars from Spain in the 1920s from guitar maker Salvador Ibáñez, and in 1935 Hoshino launched the Ibanez brand. Rosenbloom brought instruments from Hoshino into the American market under the Ibanez banner to quell any consumer concerns that might arise.

Under the Ibanez name, the Hoshino company had been manufacturing high-quality copies of Gibson guitars in the FujiGen factory, including the Rocket Roll (model 2387), a version of the Flying V, and the Destroyer (model 2459), a copy of the Explorer. They even went so far as to bring to market the infamous Moderne shape that Gibson had abandoned (model 2469). While the Rocket Roll and Destroyer copied Gibson's headstock designs, the 2469 (referred to as the "Futurist" in some circles) did not, and therefore it isn't considered a *direct* copy.

As we discussed earlier, players like Eddie Van Halen, Chris Holmes from W.A.S.P., Jay Jay French and Eddie Ojeda from Twisted Sister, and future Autograph frontman Steve Plunkett were falling under the spell of these very well-made (if not entirely up to classic-Gibson levels of build quality), and much more affordable, instruments.

> By the early 1970s Ibanez USA was an up-and-coming guitar maker who happened to be very good at copying famous American models and selling them at often ridiculously cheap prices. At first, all of the so-called "lawsuit era" guitars were rather cheaply made using inferior materials, and really only resembled classic guitars visually, but by the mid-1970s companies like Ibanez, Takamine (acoustics), Greco, Fernandes, and Burny were making Martin, Gibson and Fender replicas that often rivaled and sometimes even surpassed the models that leading manufacturers were producing.
>
> (Adirondack Guitar blog, www.adkguitar.com.)

The story of how headstock designs came to be considered defining factors in trademark eligibility is rooted in a legal suit brought forth by Gibson against Ibanez for their highly regarded copies of Gibson's classic Les Paul, instruments that would become known as "lawsuit era" guitars.

> The term "Lawsuit Era" gives the impression that Gibson, Fender, and Martin were taking companies to court every time a replica or copy was produced, but the truth is that lawsuits were very rare. The most famous Lawsuit Guitar, and one of the only guitars to actually prompt Gibson to go to court, was the Ibanez Super Standard Les Paul copy produced in the mid- to late '70s with "open-book" style headstocks featured on all Gibson models at the time. Ultimately, Gibson's parent company and Ibanez USA settled their suit out of court and Ibanez revised the headstock designs. As a result, Ibanez improved the quality of its instruments, using higher quality tone woods and creating a number of set-in-neck and arch top solid body designs like the Artist AR 325, the Iceman, the Destroyer, and later the RG series guitars introduced in the '80s and '90s that are classics to this day.
>
> (Adirondack Guitar blog, www.adkguitar.com.)

A 1977 Ibanez guitar catalog proudly announced the company's aspirations toward higher-quality builds and innovation.

> Here's the new Ibanez Artist Series. There are more models, more improvements and more new features than the competition has introduced in the last ten years. The Ibanez Artist Series is a result of our commitment to bring you the state-of-the-art in electric guitars.
>
> But rather than just exotic gimmicks, every feature of an Ibanez Artist guitar is designed first to be practical. From the classic 2618 to the new Artist EQ every new feature is tested and retested with the help of leading guitarists such as Bob Weir, Steve Miller, George Benson, Jim Messina, Jerry Garcia and many more.
>
> (Ibanez 1977 catalog: The Artist Series.)

The Artist 2617, 2618, and 2619 were solid body, double-cutaway guitars that featured the prominent Gibraltar bridge and tailpiece, jumbo frets, Super 80 humbucking pickups designed to be "hot, clean and sensitive with exceptional presence from bass to treble cast in a special compound to suppress feedback," VelveTune machine heads with "exclusive torque adjustment for light or firm action," and the "half and half" nut, which was half bone and half brass, a combination that purported to provide a more balanced tone between open and fretted notes. These guitars varied in detailing and options, and bodies were made from either ash or mahogany, with the necks being made of rock maple.

Semi-acoustic electric models like the thinline Artist 2629, 2630 models, and the Florentine cutaway Artist 2635 jazz box featured maple bodies and necks, ebony finger boards, gold hardware and fretboard inlay options that were fully aimed at the "classic and classy" crowd.

One original design from 1975 would become very closely associated with Paul Stanley of Kiss, eventually becoming his most famous signature model instrument.

At the beginning of Kiss's career, Stanley was a Gibson (or at least Gibson-inspired) man, rocking the space age inspired shapes that were most appropriate for his Starchild persona. Stanley played Vs, Explorers, Firebirds, and the more conventional L6-S single cutaway (although it shared the same headstock shape as a Flying V, which made it an outlier). With those guitars, Stanley would go on to forge a guitar style that would become one of the most imitated in rock n roll. While Stanley can throw down a classic and melodic solo with the best of them, it is his work as a rhythm guitar player that has been the focus of his six-string (and sometimes 12-string) efforts.

> Early on, I realized that I didn't want to be the flashy lead player. As much as I admired them and wanted much to be like them, I became much more involved with being a rhythm guitarist. Very often, rhythm guitar was looked at as what you do before you can play lead. And there were certainly consummate guitar players who, yes, they could play lead guitar, but that wasn't their wheelhouse, really.
>
> Whether it was Keith Richards or Pete Townshend — or even David Crosby or one of the greatest right hands ever,

Richie Havens — that was more fascinating to me: not what the left hand was doing, but what the right hand was doing.

— Paul Stanley (*Guitar Player* magazine, December 2023.)

In 1977, while on tour with Kiss in Japan, Stanley was approached by Ibanez, who provided him with a guitar that, after a few name changes, would come to be known as the Iceman.

> The 2663 is an Artist series solid body electric guitar model introduced by Ibanez for 1975. It was made in Japan by FujiGen. It was also referred to as The Flash or the Iceman Std.
>
> Although these were grouped with the Artist series, they have a very different body shape than the typical Artist guitar. This shape was developed by Hoshino Gakki in partnership with Greco (whose version was called the Mirage), Daiwa and FujiGen. The Iceman name was not used until 1978, but these 2663 models are considered part of the Iceman lineage. The 2663 features a mahogany top on a mahogany body mated to a set-in 3-ply mahogany neck with a 22-fret ebonized rosewood fingerboard with binding and pearloid parallelogram position markers. Components include a tune-o-matic style fixed bridge, a stop tailpiece with stylized chrome "ashtray" cover, a pair Ibanez Super 70 humbucking pickups with special covers and individual volume and tone controls, a bone nut, speed knobs, and Smooth Tuner machine heads. The output jack is mounted on the face of the guitar. The 2663TC is a related model with a single triple-coil pickup mounted at the bridge. The 2663SL is a similar model with a sliding triple coil pickup. The 2663 was discontinued after 1977 and replaced for 1978 with the similar IC200.
>
> (Ibanez Wiki, Ibanez.fandom.com)

The body looked as if someone had given a Gibson Firebird a curved, pointed base and Rickenbacker-like hooked lower horn, providing a deep easy-access cutaway, and it had a long and

> pointy headstock. It was resolutely original and unashamedly attention-seeking.
>
> (Tony Bacon, *The Ibanez Electric Guitar Book*, 37.)

According to Bacon, Stanley was given an Artist 2663 guitar in April of 1977, and a prototype of a personal model was made in July of that year. In 1978, the Ibanez PS10 was launched, and soon was in the hands of one of the members of the "hottest band in the world." The most famous variation of the PS10 could well be the custom made cracked-mirror front, which proved to be an effective tool for reflecting the stunning lights, lasers, and explosions that were part and parcel of the Kiss arena-rock experience. The relationship with Stanley would also prove to be an effective marketing tool, capturing the imagination of young Kiss fans who saw their own bright future in the pyrotechnic, blood-spitting, teen-anthem magic of a Kiss concert.

> The first real guitar I ever bought was an Ibanez Iceman that Paul Stanley played on the Love Gun and the Alive II tour and the Dynasty tour. It was just the most original design I had ever seen and I saw him play it on the tour, which was the Love Gun tour. I was like, I have to have that guitar. I have to, someday, I have to. I saved up every penny I had and there's a music store in New Jersey that is about forty-five minutes to an hour north of where I lived and they had one there. I think it was like $450 or something like that. And I had like $425 in cash and another $25 in quarters and I went up there with all of it and I didn't even have a license yet. I think I was like fifteen or sixteen at the time. A friend of mine drove me up there and I bought it and I still have it to this day. I'll be buried with that. [*laughs*]
>
> — Dave "Snake" Sabo of Skid Row
>
> (*Glide Magazine*, August 2014.)

Tim Welch is one of Canada's top film and TV composers, as well as one of the country's finest session and live-rock guitarists. His impressive list of credits includes his own Capitol Records recording act National Velvet, as well as Alannah Myles, Carole Pope of Rough Trade, Michael Monroe of Hanoi Rocks, and Sylvain Sylvain of the New York Dolls (who was so impressed with

Tim's playing that he had him deputize when he couldn't make a Toronto gig with the Dolls at a last-minute stadium show with Mötley Crüe and Poison). Tim made his debut with the New York Dolls in front of fifteen thousand people with no rehearsal, just an intimate knowledge of the band's music, and the perfect, authentic rock-n-roll attitude to pull off such an endeavor. The

New York Dolls and Kiss have both played key inspirational roles in Tim's career, as did their usage of Ibanez guitars. Tim has been a mentor to me, and I'm proud to count one of Canada's greatest guitarists as one of my best friends. I asked Tim to comment on a few special Ibanez instruments that make up part of his well-earned collection of 96 guitars.

> I had an El Degas Les Paul copy, and I needed to step it up to something that looked cooler. I was flipping through either *Guitar Player* or *Creem* magazine [and] I saw Sylvain Sylvain from the New York Dolls. There he was with his Ibanez Rocket Roll looking all cool and playing in Japan in front of seventy-five thousand people. I'd already been into Paul Stanley's pointy guitars and his custom made Vs. This little shop in the neighborhood, I see it in the window, three hundred dollars. I was making maybe twenty bucks a week at the time. I paid the guy like eighteen bucks a week until I paid it off. Seeing Sylvain in the ad is what made me buy it. Thirty, forty years later, I had the opportunity to play with Sylvain, and the first thing he said to me was "That's my guitarrrrr!" [*laughs*] I love that guitar, and it was the most uncomfortable thing to play sitting down, as anyone with a flying V knows. It keeps sliding off your lap, but I didn't give a shit at all. You know, I had the longest guitar strap that made it impossible to play a barred F chord on the first fret, where you end up doing some wrist gymnastics. That guitar means a lot to me. After playing with Sylvain, I remember at the end of a tour, I said, "Syl, will you sign my guitar?" And, no one had a Sharpie. So, I pulled out my penknife. I went, "Well, here, just, you know, do it with this." He'd been working at it for a while, and I was like, "What's he doing?" Then he handed it back to me, and says "Timmy, how's this?" And it was the *whole* back of the guitar. Each letter's like four inches long. "SYLVAIN." I'm looking at it, and then he says, "What am I sitting on? Oh, I'm sitting on my Sharpie!" [*laughs*] I had the front signed, but it's right where your forearm rests, and now I can't play it anymore because I'll rub my dear friend's signature off. I cut that picture out because I used to collect ads from *Creem*

magazine because I knew I would never be able to afford these things. Those ads were like my wish book.

When I was like 16, I went on a road trip specifically to go to House of Guitars in Rochester, N.Y. And I was looking at Gibson TV yellow Les Paul Juniors because of Johnny Thunders. They were going from eight hundred to one thousand two hundred bucks at the time. And I think I brought maybe four hundred bucks. And I was like, I can't do it. Behind the counter, they had the PS10. The year it came out, I guess, so it was '77, I think, when it came out. It was the first time I had seen one [in person] and it just took my breath away. It was like, "I'm going to have one of those one day."

Many years later, I found one that was shipping from Southern California. It arrived on my birthday. My sister was on the phone [with] me singing "Happy Birthday." I'm all happy opening the case — and the neck had snapped. Right at the body. Really nasty. And all the binding had rotted off as well. Which was not mentioned in the ad. I had bought it on Reverb, and they were great about it. I got like half my money back. But this thing sounds awesome. My friend Scully who is Geddy Lee's guitar tech, was Jeff Beck's guitar tech, and right now he's out with Steve Vai and Joe Satriani, he played it and he said, "You'll be hard pressed to find any Les Paul that sounds as good as this. You *look* like an idiot, but it sounds great. [*laughs*] It's a huge guitar, so you can see how big those Kiss guys are when you see that guitar, it's huge. It's a big piece of real estate. When you see it on Paul, it just looks like a normal guitar.

A year later my late mother is at St. Michael's Hospital in Toronto with brain cancer. Her surgeon and I started talking about bands. He has one, he has a PS10. He's going to sell it. He goes, "I don't play guitar. I just bought it off my lawyer friend who also doesn't play guitar. He just kept it in a glass case at his house. And now I have it. Now I'm keeping it in a glass case in my house." And he goes "Yeah, I'll sell it to you." He was a Dalbello fan as well. He said that the first owner, the lawyer, he kept it at his place in the glass case, and the only people who played it were

> some strippers that this guy invited up. And they dropped it, so it had one mark on the tail. [*laughs*] He said, "No real guitar player has ever touched this guitar." It was a '78 and I was like, "Yeah, I'll take that!" It was perfect. I believe my mother got that for me. Because she knew. She watched me grow up with the Kiss posters on the wall. I still think that my mother bought it for me.
>
> — Tim Welch of National Velvet

The original PS10, which was available from 1978 to 1981, came with three-tuners-per side pointy headstock, a bound rosewood fingerboard, pearl block markers, 22 frets, a "Paul Stanley" inlay at the 21st fret, a black, pearl-bound body, two coverless humbuckers, three controls (two volume, one tone), a three-way selector on body, a side-mounted output jack, a chrome-plated pickguard, and six-saddle bridge plus a separate, customized tailpiece, and a truss rod cover with Stanley's signature.

Paul Stanley's use of the PS10, previously known as the Iceman, made an impression on two young hotshot guitarists, Paul Gilbert and Bruce Bouillet, who would both leave their small towns in Pennsylvania and Indiana respectively and meet up at Hollywood's famed Guitar Institute of Technology (GIT). They would eventually join forces in Racer X, one of the highlights of Mike Varney's Shrapnel Records label, the home for high-speed, technically demanding guitar work. Racer X quickly earned a cult following for their shred-heavy style and wild, neon-painted custom Ibanez guitars, combining neo-classical, post-Yngwie Malmsteen chops with anthemic, head-banging Sunset Strip anthems.

A native of Vincennes, Indiana, Bouillet moved to Los Angeles to attend the Guitar Institute of Technology, where he caught the attention of Paul Gilbert, who was an instructor at GIT at the time. He joined Racer X in 1986 as the second guitarist, contributing to their landmark album *Second Heat* (1987), which was loaded with over-the-top dual-guitar harmonies, technical brilliance, and a nod to the arena rock bombast of bands like Van Halen, Judas Priest, and Ozzy. Bouillet also appeared on the band's acclaimed live albums *Extreme Volume Live* and *Extreme Volume II Live*, helping solidify Racer X's reputation as a premier shred metal act. Bruce was also a member of the Scream, a band that also featured one-time Mötley Crüe vocalist John Corabi, as well as Bruce's Racer X bandmate and the Mars Volta bassist Juan Alderete.

> I think I just got back from seeing my first concert, and I was like, "Well, I know what I want!" I had seen Judas Priest opening for Kiss. It was a great concert. Being 12 years old, I was just blown away. My first electric was a Lotus Les Paul copy. I believe Lotus might have been Japanese. It was just a bolt-on neck Les Paul, and I'm assuming it was pretty cheap. This would have been 1979, and I rapidly traded it up for an Ibanez Iceman. There was one in the local music store. I grew up in Vincennes, Indiana. I was born in Memphis, Tennessee, but grew up in southern Indiana. Real small town. It was probably, like, fifteen thousand people, with one or two small music stores, but a big music scene. A lot of musicians in that town and some big names passed through there over the years. But I moved up pretty quick to the Iceman. And, obviously, seeing Kiss, that was on my radar.
>
> — Bruce Bouillet of Racer X

Many small-town rock-n-roll guitarists dream of leaving home and trying to make their mark in the big city, but very few actually take the leap and risk the almost certain poverty and existential crises that await.

> Honestly, where I grew up, my high-school band got fairly big. We won the Miller Rock to Riches contest back then in our area. Here I am in high school, and I'm already on the radio.
>
> Things were moving in the right direction, but I remember seeing that we sorta hit a wall. We were doing covers and some originals, which was a great time. But I remember my parents setting me down and saying that high school was coming to an end, and what are you gonna do?
>
> And I literally was thumbing through *Guitar Player* magazine. And there was an ad in there about M.I. [Musicians Institute. And I thought, you know what? They're not gonna be real keen on me going to Los Angeles right away, and I want their support. I didn't wanna take off and say, "Screw you guys. I'm going anyway." I wanted my family's support behind me.

I told them, "Look, there's a school in Los Angeles. It's really based around guitar, but they still teach music." Of course, my mom, being a professor at a college, one of her first questions was "What kind of credits do you get out of this?" But they saw that I really wanted to do it, and I was willing to work and pay for it and save money up for it. So, that was the plan. But my plan really was that if I go to this school, I'll have the backing of my mom and dad. I'll have their good blessings to go, and I'll be in L.A. where I know that's the place where all the players were migrating to or coming out of. I just knew that the good players were there. And, obviously, you're seeing Randy Rhoads. You're seeing Eddie Van Halen, Jake E. Lee, Warren DeMartini, George Lynch. All the premier dudes are all sort of coming out of this L.A. scene. And I'm like, well, that certainly is the place I wanna go.

I had a bunch of people saying they were going with me. And, of course, when the day came, it was only me at the airport. Nobody else went, which is sort of the reason why I went.

The school, to be fair, was excellent. It was the old school above the Hollywood Wax Museum right on the boulevard. And it was wild. I mean, you'd be up there in these cramped spaces — it was like a fire trap up there! It was scary because, I mean, it was old, old Hollywood. You know, these old buildings. There were obviously great teachers, and there were so many people from all over that you could connect with. And, obviously, the first person I saw play was Paul. I walked in, and he was doing his performance for his end of the year credits to graduate.

So, really, I saw the first incarnation of Racer X doing *Street Lethal*. I remember bumping this guy next to me, because the place was packed. And I go, "How old is this guy?" And he goes, "Seventeen." [All] I could think of was, like, I knew it. Everybody would be younger and better out here! I just knew it. I didn't know I was seeing, like, *the* guy at the time. You know what I mean? But as soon as they finished, everybody went back to their classes. I went straight up to the stage and was like, "Hey, man. That's *something*, what you just did. I know you're teaching here, so I wanna get in with you — I would love to take

> some lessons from you." And he became my private instructor and the rest you know, sort of fell in place.
>
> The first album [*Street Lethal*] was already recorded, so he already had one in the oven, and when it released, he gave me a copy and said, "Hey, man. We're thinking about adding another guitar player. Why don't you go learn the album and come back, and we'll do a rehearsal?"
>
> And I remember getting back to my place and putting the album on and going like, there's no way I'm getting this gig. I didn't know where to begin. Like, where do you begin with something like that? You know, we're talking about a time where there's no YouTube, no internet, no tab, no nothing. It was a cassette, and I got what I could. And then, a lot of those techniques, I could see him do in class. Like, I could watch him play, so I had an idea. And, obviously, he was playing some of the songs in class too, so I would just take notes. "*That's* the chord that I can't figure out. Oh, *there's* where he puts his hands on that part. And he was, of course, the nicest guy in the world when I went to go sit with him and just go through the songs. Every part I came up to, if it'd be like, "Yeah. I'm not sure what's going on?" [Paul would say,] "Oh, that's hard to hear on the album. This is really what it does." He was really accommodating on that part of it.
>
> — Bruce Bouillet

Racer X was a band that held endless fascination for me in my early years of playing, and I have come to realize that they represented a combination of all of the facets that made up my aspirations and dreams as a guitarist. They were incredibly proficient on their instruments but also played with a sense of reckless abandon and fun. They wore flashy clothes, had big rock-n-roll hair, and incorporated shocking neon colors in their stage shows, and on their self-customized and -painted instruments. For all of their virtuosity, they actually had a very punk rock, DIY feel to them. They seemed to be having such a great time, and were always candid in their interviews about the reality of their situations; there was no bullshit, rock-n-roll artifice with Racer X. They were just a group of guys who valued great musicianship but also held the theatrical and anthemic aspects of the arena-rock dream close to their hearts. They weren't afraid to put in the hard work to live the champagne life on a six-pack-of-beer budget.

I asked Bruce to put these facets into context for me and describe what role his perception of pointy guitars played in the bigger rock-n-roll scheme of things as he embarked on his journey from Indiana to Hollywood.

> You know, the pointiest guitars in, like, '79, were the V and the Explorer. I do remember seeing as a kid on TV on Saturday-morning cartoons, there was some kind of rock show that came on near the afternoon, and the two guitar players were rocking Dean Explorers with double pointy headstocks, and it was, like, wow.
>
> Before I moved to Los Angeles, bands like Molly Hatchet were starting to break, and Cheap Trick with Rick Nielsen had the famous checkerboard Hamer Explorer, so I saw a lot of that. But right before I moved to Los Angeles, Jackson was making its appearance. At the start of the '80s — '81, '82 — you had Ratt and Mötley Crüe, that era of music starting to happen; Dokken, that sort of metal type stuff going on. There were all the classics still, Maiden and Priest and all that, but a lot of the new '80s California bands, the L.A. bands.
>
> And then there was the classic Jackson ad where they had Steve Vai, Spacey T., Jake E. Lee, I think. They were all doing the Jackson thing. It was that Jackson/Charvel club. And they had the pointy headstocks — they went full pointy on this!
>
> I was enthralled with that as a kid, who wouldn't be? If you were playing metal and you were seeing that, it was like, man, these guitars must be filled with magic powers of some sort because why else would everybody be playing them? I don't think I ever owned a Jackson or a Charvel. I liked them, but I don't think I had the money when I moved to L.A. I invested my money more toward a half-stack Marshall.
>
> I did totally Frankenstein a bunch of guitars. I totally ruined my older brother's '74 or '75 Tele, which was a beautiful Tele, but I painted it fluorescent green, and I put a pointy headstock

on it. And that would be the first Racer X guitar, honestly. That was the one I joined with. And, it did not play well either. I didn't know what I was doing, but, you know, who did really back then as a kid?

But, you know, everybody saw Eddie Van Halen building these guitars, and it's like, "Well, the neck just screws on. I've got that tool to make that happen." You know what I mean? And "Yeah, this routing doesn't look perfect either. So let me route a pickup in the back of this Tele!" When I met Paul Gilbert, he had a unique situation where his dad was a guy who would build stuff. They would build stuff together — a really interesting person, really nice guy.

When I met Paul, he didn't have a real expensive guitar. He had these old Epiphone Wilshires that he had routed and hand-painted and put stickers all over them. I remember distinctly walking into M.I. and watching him play for the first time and going, like, wow. He's one the best rock dudes in the school, and he's got the cheapest guitar out of everybody — but it sounds insane! And I was coming from a background where my dad was an artist and he was a woodcarver and a painter. So there were plenty of woodworking tools around. I destroyed a lot of guitars as a kid. And I feel bad about some of them — I don't wanna mention the dates of them! But, you know, you can only imagine for a kid in 1979, a '60s guitar was not a big deal! It was like, well, that's an old junker. No. It'd be like saying, "Yeah, I got a 2011 right now." Nobody's that impressed!

So, yeah, there were some trial and errors, but I did hit it off with Paul in that [respect]. We and Jeff Martin, the singer in Racer X, we built the stage, and we would build risers with lights. We would build backdrops. It was a pretty hands-on band.

One of the first things I remember, painting guitar bodies fluorescent colors in the basement parking garages of our Hollywood apartments. It's a great memory. We had a lot of fun, doing stuff not a lot of people were doing. It was easier to go buy something stock off the shelf — that was nice.

— Bruce Bouillet

Eventually, a certain Japanese guitar company, hungry to find the hottest new players to ply their wares, came knocking to take Racer X's DIY aesthetic to the next level of performance.

> At first, Paul was playing those Coronet and Wilshire guitars. They had such an unbelievable access on the high frets, it was like an SG, how the final fret meets the body. It's got that great, easy access up high. So, I thought, "I like that guitar too. That's a great guitar. Why don't we have a couple of them made?" And he was like, "Well, Ibanez will make us a couple of them." And so we had a pink and a green one made, and those were the first — that was early on for Ibanez. That was when Ibanez was still considered a rogue Japanese guitar company — they hadn't had the big endorsees yet. They were just getting Steve Vai and Satriani on board. And we were two of the early guys. I think they had Vinnie Moore. They didn't have the Jems and all that designed yet.
>
> They were like, "Oh, they want some custom Wilshires!" I know they probably felt a little funny because they had just got sued by Gibson earlier and lost, right? So I'm sure they were, like, *thrilled* to have these two guys coming in and saying "Hey, make us some more of these Epiphone copies for us." [*laughs*] But they did it, and they played great. A lot of people were probably trying to request them because they obviously had the Ibanez headstock, and they didn't wanna make them. They didn't wanna get into that territory. And then directly after that, they made us two more guitars — they were sort of a combo. It was the back end of a Destroyer and the front end of the Iceman. They made us one of those each. I would think those guitars are pretty rare at this point because there was only two of them made — a pink one and an orange one.
>
> And, I did have a second Wilshire made by them, an orange one because I broke my green one. And I still have it. It's tucked away where it's still intact, 100 percent. The other ones escaped me at some point or another. I think I sold the orange Destroyer to somebody, actually, from Canada. On the premise that you gotta sell it back to me for the same price, you can play it for the

next how many years you want and show it off or whatever. But sell it back to me. And then somebody about 10 years ago said, "Hey man. You know that thing's up on eBay and it's up around eight thousand dollars right now?" And it was like, "Well, I ain't got that kind of money to get it back."

The guy obviously choked on the deal. It went to somebody — it went to a surgeon somewhere. So I know it went to somebody that's not gonna repaint it, you know what I mean? It's gonna stay intact, and I think the guy is a big Racer X fan.

So that at least made me feel pretty good. It went to a home where it's not gonna get destroyed, or, you know, cut up or repainted and all that.

You have to remember, my whole tenure in Racer X was only about 14 months. It was like the end of '86 to the beginning of '88. It might have been about 16 months maybe if you add it all up, but it wasn't much more than a year and a half, from beginning to end. It just happened so quick.

You just think like, well, of *course* we're gonna have some custom guitars! You know, this is *great*! Things are right on track. And you didn't really think of the value of them either. Like, oh, wow, these are kinda one offs that live on and carry on. You just don't think about it at the time.

I asked Bruce if he could take me back in time into the studio with Racer X when they were recording *Second Heat*, the follow up to *Street Lethal* on Shrapnel Records and Bruce's first full-length album studio recording experience.

This is an LP. It's a long play. And Mike Varney [Shrapnel Records founder and producer] had very cheap budgets. And really, that was the thing that actually made it great. As weird as that sounds, we got up to Prairie Sun Recording Studios, which is north of San Francisco, about forty minutes or so. It's out in the middle of, like, just open land, nowhere. Of course, there were horses. There was no walking from the place, there was nothing to walk to. You had to drive to get anywhere because it was so secluded, and so far out in the country.

We get there, and Mike has [Shrapnel artist] Tony MacAlpine in studio B finishing his second record. And what was cool is that George Lynch showed up to play on Tony's album while we were there. I'm out recording it with a tape deck out on the back deck, bootlegging it as he's playing on record. What guitarist is *not* gonna do that?

We did three days of preproduction with Mike, and it was in this basement of the house there. So it was a concrete room. I will straight up just say it — it was not great sounding at all. It was in a concrete basement, really loud and echoey. And we did three days of preproduction, and we went straight into recording. We recorded the bass and drums in one day, and then I think there was a track left over the next day or two, and we finished it the next day.

But all the bass and drums [were recorded together], and Paul played a scratch guitar with them. Most of those songs on *Second Heat* weren't cut to a click track either. That's the thing that's amazing. "Sunlit Nights," one of the slower songs where you have a long intro, obviously had clicks on [it], but Scott [Travis, currently the drummer for Judas Priest] didn't really need a click. He had such a built-in metronome in him, it was truly something. I didn't think about it. I just thought, well, this is how you make a record. I didn't know that. That's talent. We all prided ourselves in being great players. That was our goal. But you just [thought], well, I guess that's how it's supposed to be.

And then we started vocals, and Jeff [Martin] would sing during the day, and Paul and I would fire up guitars.

I think we started immediately [after basic tracks were recorded] and put rhythm guitars on so Jeff could start singing. The night shift, we would go in as soon as Jeff got tired of singing, then Paul and I would immediately go into guitar mode. I think we spent two days recording the guitars. It was a very low budget. As we were finishing a song, they would move the song to studio B and mix it while we were cutting vocals during the day and cutting guitars at night.

Paul and I would get up, and we would work out the harmony solos. We didn't even have the stuff worked up when we got up there for the most part. We were working up the solo stuff in the mornings while Jeff was going to sing, and then, we would go in, and it was really cool. We had two guitars we used. We used his pink Coronet or Wilshire. I think it said Telly Savalas on the top of the headstock he had put stickers on. It had one pickup. It was a DiMarzio Super Distortion, wired in parallel. It was like two single coils sitting next to each other, basically, and wrapped in aluminum foil and stuck back in. And then we had a guitar made by Wayne Charvel himself when he was going to start a new company.

He had sold Charvel, and he was going to start a company called American Guitars. He made a really dark purple, almost bluish looking Wilshire guitar, of course, and it had the headstock with American Guitars on it. And I remember it got knocked over, and it broke a chunk of the headstock off.

But those were the two guitars we used. And we used, two 50-watt '70s Marshall heads, fairly old ones too. I believe they were, like, early '70s. And we split them with a BOSS Chorus pedal, not engaged, but just a BOSS Chorus pedal to split the signal into a HUSH II C unit, which is stereo, into two heads, into two cabinets, and miked them with Shure SM57s. We used Marshall speaker cabinets with, I believe, 30-watt Greenbacks in them.

And we sat in the studio, and, literally, we sat next to each other behind the console with the engineer. And Paul would record a take and hand me the guitar. And I would do my part and hand him the guitar back, and we would do the same guitar, same amps, and everything. And that's when I really realized, like, wow — listen how different our tone sounds, and it's the exact same gear. You can hear it on that song, "Heart of a Lion." He starts it. And then I come in. And the two tones are totally different. Mine has a fatter, darker sound. His has a less fat, more trebly sound.

I kept looking at our fingers, and I'm like, well, it kinda makes sense because I've got fatter, shorter hands, and he's got these really long, thin, violinist hands. That made an early impression on me. That's the same guitar, same amplifier heads. I mean, he's handing me the guitar. I just tune it. That's all I did. I tune it and play. And it sounded so different. Now I don't know if the engineer was tweaking the EQ, but he wasn't tweaking it when we were handing [the guitar] back and forth because he would have had to redo each time. He might have tweaked it on the mix a little bit, but you could hear it in the studio. And we cut everything in two days, or two nights, into the early morning hours. I believe that's about it, about two and a half days.

And, I remember we were kinda running out of time. We didn't have much money, so we didn't have any food either. We were running out of food.

There was the famous incident where, well, I don't know if we wanna print this, but Juan Alderete had worked at Pepperidge Farm cookies up in the Bay Area.

So we drove out one night, and there was a storage locker they had where they stored a lot of stuff that was being shipped. And we were getting these cookies come hell or high water, and we've loaded up a car full of cookies. I remember I've got a picture of myself eating Pepperidge Farm cookies, and I don't think I ate cookies again for 12 years after that. It was like I was so sick of eating sugar, but it did get us to the finish line.

And, what was so cool about it for [my] first record, it was only three or four days tracking and done.

There was no time to really second guess. I remember some of the individual solos when we were cutting them in the studio. You didn't have a whole lot of time to go, "I don't know what to do here." You had to try something, and if it didn't work Paul might throw a suggestion. "Hey. What about that one lick? That works." There wasn't a lot of time to over-think. You just did it. You tuned. You did it. And I remember distinctly, it was around, I believe, around the holidays, almost

> Christmas. And, there was a game room, it had a Star Wars pinball machine that would always randomly say all these Star Wars phrases: "Use the force, Luke." I remember getting some rough mixes of "Scarified," "Heart of a Lion," "Moonage Daydream," and something else. And I remember listening to it, and I just was, like, "Man, my friends back at Vincennes are gonna freak out when they hear this!" I was just so small minded at that point. It didn't really dawn on me that this was gonna be a thing that goes out to the world. It was, like, wait till my bros I've been hanging out with and growing up with in my hometown hear this. They're gonna go, like, "Wow, dude. I don't know what's in the water in L.A., but you better keep drinking it!" But I do remember being pretty impressed. Like, wow. The sound — everybody was so good. I mean, Scott Travis was unreal. So was Jeff Martin, then with Paul Gilbert, you know, it didn't dawn on me that I'm playing with one of *the* guys, you know?

And why did a band with so much going for it not make the jump to the major label world?

> Well, we were showcasing for big labels. We had some showcases for CBS or Sony, they came out to a couple, and a lot of the labels were coming out. But at that time, we lacked a manager. We managed ourselves. We got so ripped off when we were first starting to sell out clubs, until we finally said, "Hey, man. Y'all are making, like, a ton of money, and we're just getting peanuts on these shows, but we're packing them in." And, you know, we started getting paid more at that point.
>
> I think a manager would have really made it happen. We were getting calls. I was a roommate with Juan already. We had a house in East L.A., and, we were getting calls from, like, New York, Limelight, Chicago, Miami. "What is it gonna take to get you guys to come out here and play?" We were getting requests. When you get a little older and start realizing, like, man, the clubs were even calling us. You just don't think about it at the time.

I think what the problem was it was a little too over the top for most people. I think if somebody came in and said, "You know what? You guys should really toughen up your sound a little bit more, go all black and toughen up your sound. Get a little more thrash, man."

I mean, we really had all the tools to become like another Metallica type thing, [but] where it was the most extreme players in the world in one band. I think we probably would have had a different outcome. But no. . . .

We did actually have some hooky songs. "Heart of a Lion" even though we didn't write that one, it was still a massive hook song. It was just confusing. We didn't draw girls to our shows. We drew an all-guy crowd basically back then. It was like going to a hard metal show. You saw more guys than you saw girls, but we had an image that was reflecting bands like Poison that were drawing mostly women. So it was a confusing thing.

And then at the same time, Mike Varney had us under contract for another album. He was holding that, if somebody wanted to come and say, "We wanna sign you guys," I think there was too much being asked to get us out of the contract. Unbeknownst to me. 'Til recently, I didn't know.

At the same time, Mike was actually putting Mr. Big [the multimillion album selling supergroup that featured Paul Gilbert, bass virtuoso Billy Sheehan, vocalist Eric Martin, and drummer Pat Torpey] together on the backside. And so I thought that was a little . . . It was probably good business wise. I don't know if it really did him any good financially because he really wasn't on the receiving end of that, but it was more of, like, you receive more favors and whatnot.

At about the same time, we did the live album [*Extreme Volume Live*]. The live album was to get out of the contract. And there was a second album that came out from those shows.

So, by the time we were doing that, Mr. Big was starting to form behind the scenes. I think there was a point where we already walked in on Billy and Paul by accident somewhere.

They had gotten together at M.I. or something, and Paul was up there. Juan was up there and walked in on him and came back to the rehearsal room and was like, "Bro, there is something going on." And, at that point, it all came out. It wasn't the greatest of endings. Even though we ended at the top of everything, which was kinda nice. We didn't have a decline.

Our last show was a sellout at the Omni in Oakland and probably one of the greatest shows ever. It was one of those shows when you look down on the crowd and people had bed sheets painted with Racer X hanging over the balconies, and people had signs, and people had album covers in the audience.

It was like one of those old-school shows, like when you see the back [cover] of Kiss *Alive!* where they've got the dudes with the Kiss sign, and it's like, yeah! When people used to bring signs and paint themselves up or whatever. It was an absolute amazing show even though we knew it was the last one.

We stayed friends and, as a matter of fact, when Paul finally got the Mr. Big album back from mastering, I got the call immediately. "Hey, you wanna come hear it?" And it was like, "Absolutely I wanna come hear it." I remember going up to his apartment in L.A. and he put it on. And I was like, "Yeah." I knew it was a good move for him. I mean, obviously, that band was gonna be big, just on the hype alone coming out that they had a lot going for them. But you could tell it was gonna have a bigger success rate. They had Atlantic Records behind them, so that was a big thing.

But it wasn't too much longer after that that that we [Bruce's new band the Scream, which featured onetime Mötley Crüe vocalist John Corabi] scored the deal with Hollywood Records. So, financially, we all were still doing pretty good. Scott got the Judas Priest gig immediately and we were super proud of that because that's stepping into the biggest shoes you could almost get. And it's like, there you go. You're in, man. You did it, and he's retained it to this day.

But I guess we [Racer X] left enough of a mark that it's still lingering out there today. I still see on a daily basis these 12,

13-year-old, even younger, kids from around the world playing "Scarified."

— Bruce Bouillet

The beauty of the rock-n-roll dream is that it has so many different levels of opportunity, and the scope of what constitutes "success" can be very wide-ranging. Bruce Bouillet and Phil Collen are both associated with pointy Ibanez guitars, and both have achieved impressive levels of recognition. While Phil's stratospheric level of commercial success with Def Leppard puts him in a different league in terms of popularity, I put them both on a similar plane in terms of personal influence. One could draw the same parallel between Sylvain Sylvain and Paul Stanley, albeit with different nuances.

Def Leppard have been known to employ a number of pointy guitars in their melding of hard-rock histrionics, disciplined pop-song-writing sensibility, and forward-thinking approach to record production. Steve Clark slung his Gibson Firebirds low and to dazzling musical and visual effect and — along with his former guitar partner Pete Willis (*On Through the Night* through to the recording of *Pyromania*) and bassist Rick Savage — played a role in the widespread popularity of Hamer Guitars through their high-profile use of that company's Standard guitar and bass models. The band also played and endorsed Hamer's Blitz and Scarab.

Clark also used Dean Guitar's Les Paul–Explorer hybrid Cadillac, as evidenced in the use of a red-wine finished model in the video for "Me & My Wine." According to this letter to dealers found in the 1983–84 Dean catalog re-introducing the model, Steve's association with the brand was valued.

For 1984 at DEAN. GUITARS "the Cadillac is back."

Due to popular response according to Dave Perdue, National Sales Manager at DEAN GUITARS "we have re-introduced our flagship guitar, the Cadillac."

The DEAN Cadillac features three humbucking pick-ups, special seven ply body binding and five ply headstock binding, a twenty-four-fret ebony fingerboard with block inlays, a deeper cutaway to allow access to the highest fret, and is available with the KAHLER LOCKING TREMOLO SYSTEM. This model is one of the DEAN GUITARS chosen by DEF LEPPARD to allow them to keep the "heavy" in heavy metal.

(Dean Guitars catalog, 1983–1984.)

Around the same time that the Leppard's were hitting their commercial stride with the *Pyromania* album in 1983, their future and present guitarist, Vivian Campbell, from Belfast, Northern Ireland, was beginning his journey to international recognition with former Rainbow/Black Sabbath vocalist Ronnie James Dio in the band that bore the late, great singer's last name. Campbell was, and is, a fiery player whose blinding speed was matched with an equally red-hot attack and intensity inspired by fellow Irishman Gary Moore. He is most closely associated with Gibson guitars, particularly his "7297537" Les Paul (he refers to it by its serial number), a wine-red Deluxe model whose mini-humbucking pickups were replaced with DiMarzio's hottest pickups of the time, the X2N, the main guitar on the first two classic Dio albums *Holy Diver* and *The Last in Line*. However, Campbell was also known to demonstrate a penchant for the point, and was a valued endorser of Charvel, B.C. Rich (for a short, and reportedly less than happy, time), Aria, and Kramer guitars.

The NightSwan was Vivian's signature model guitar for Kramer. Created for him while he was a member of Whitesnake(the vehicle for ex-Deep Purple vocalist David Coverdale), which had found multiplatinum success with its *1987* album, thanks to a sonic and visual makeover tailor-made for the late '80s. The NightSwan was designed by Texan guitar builder Buddy "Blaze" Webster and based on his own company's Shredder model. Like a number of talented independent guitar builders, Blaze would go on to partner with and work for bigger companies like Kramer and Dean. The companies would benefit from the uniqueness and ingenuity of the builder, while the builder would reap the fiscal benefits of working with a large company with much bigger manufacturing and distribution resources. Blaze is known for having designed the artwork on Pantera guitarist Dimebag Darrell Abbott's Dean-from-Hell ML model, which Abbott had won in a guitar competition. Abbott had at one point pawned the instrument, but Blaze purchased the instrument from the pawnshop secretly, modified it, and passed it to artist Craig Patchin, who repainted it blue with lighting bolts coming from the center of the body.

Blaze would go on to work with Dean Guitars (then under the business control of Elliott Rubinson's Armadillo Enterprises) on a series of replicas after Dimebag's shocking murder at the hands of a deranged fan durning a 2004 concert. He would also issue a lawsuit in 2018 against Dean Guitars and the estate of Dimebag Darrell, claiming that a replica model had been sold without due credit and compensation to Blaze. However, a judgement was handed down in favor of Dean and the estate (Consequence, December 2018).

For Def Leppard fans who came to the band via the ubiquitous videos for tracks like "Photograph," "Rock of Ages," and "Foolin'" from their 1983 breakthrough album Pyromania, there is one pointy guitar to rule them all: Phil Collen's Ibanez Destroyer DT555.

Whether it was black leather he was sporting, or a pair of tight white strides offset by a funky polka-dot top with the sleeves rolled up and unbuttoned halfway down his chest, Phil Collen was every bit the platinum-haired rock god, and his Ibanez Destroyer became a drool worthy object of desire for aspiring young guitarists. As an Ibanez print ad in the November 1982 issue of *Guitar World* magazine proclaimed, "You won't find an Ibanez Destroyer at the local polka club."

The DT555 was essentially a Destroyer II, the aforementioned Explorer-shaped guitar that was designed to deviate from the original Ibanez Destroyer after a now famous lawsuit between the Norlin Corporation (who at the time owned Gibson) and Elger Guitars. Collen had been rocking a Destroyer II with his pre-Def Leppard band Girl; other guitar luminaries, such as Adrian Smith and Dave Murray from Iron Maiden, and Richie Stoots from the Plasmatics, also armed themselves with Destroyers in their respective rock-n-roll duties.

> Last year we re-introduced the Destroyer II Series by popular demand. The updated Destroyer II became an even bigger hit than its predecessor. The bold and aggressive shape has tremendous sustaining power and a fullness of sound unlike any other instrument.
>
> Power chords have real power and searing leads flow as fast and as hot as you can handle them. The V2/bridge and Super 58/fingerboard pickup combination give you enough versatility to rock and roll any way you like.
>
> (Ibanez X Series Brochure, 1982.)

Iron Maiden, and Smith in particular, were early adopters of the Destroyer II series, so I reached out to Nico Falco, an expert on the music of this legendary British heavy-metal institution. Falco is one of the growing legions of top-shelf guitar players who are making an impact as social media influencers. His Licks of the Beast YouTube channel has thousands of devoted followers, and he is an expert on all things Iron Maiden, especially when it comes to the guitars used by their trio of axmen (Adrian Smith, Dave Murray, and Janick Gers).

Iron Maiden's music played a huge role in my life and in shaping me as a guitarist. So, the idea of paying tribute to them — one way or another — was always floating around in the back of my mind.

In March 2020, when it became clear that the COVID lockdown wasn't going to be a quick thing, I decided to start an Instagram page. I figured I'd post short videos of myself playing parts of Maiden songs — riffs, solos, harmonies — just to have a record of all the time I'd spent learning their stuff since I was 14. Since it was going to be all Maiden, I landed on the name Licks of the Beast.

At the time, I thought it'd be a fun little project for a few months. I didn't share it with friends or family or post about it on Facebook. It was just for me, and maybe a few random people who might stumble across it.

But surprisingly, it started to catch on. People really connected with what I was doing, and soon I started getting requests for full-song covers — which just wasn't practical on Instagram. My wife, Sara, suggested I start a YouTube channel. I shot that idea down at first, but she made a pretty compelling argument, so I gave in. We launched the channel in August of that same year to accommodate the longer format.

Since then, it's grown way beyond what I expected. I've expanded into full-song covers, tutorials, gear reviews, and even some general music discussion. Eventually I started covering other guitar legends like Randy Rhoads and George Lynch. Now Licks of the Beast has become this awesome little community of people who are passionate about heavy metal and guitars — and honestly, I couldn't be happier with where it's gone.

Adrian Smith played a red Ibanez Destroyer — basically their version of a Gibson Explorer — during the *Number of the Beast* and *Piece of Mind* era, around 1982, '83. The model was a Destroyer II DT300FR, which was originally made for the Japanese market only. These guitars were built at Ibanez's FujiGen factory in Nagano, Japan, and they were seriously top-tier.

The original Destroyer series was discontinued in 1978 after a copyright lawsuit from Gibson, and in '81 they came back

> with the Destroyer II line. That included the DT300, the similar DT50 (aimed at the overseas market), and the DT400, which had a flame-maple top, sunburst finish, and cream binding. Dave Murray played the DT400 for a short time too — you can spot it in the *Beast over Hammersmith* video.
>
> I always thought Adrian and Dave looked totally badass on stage with those guitars. I own both a DT300 and a DT50, and they're definitely among my favorite guitars.
>
> — Nico Falco, creator of Licks of the Beast

Patrick Pentland is a guitarist, vocalist, and songwriter for one of Canada's most popular bands, Sloan. Deftly blending power-pop, punk, and post-punk influences with classic hard rock sensibilities, Sloan are recognized for their great guitar sounds. I caught a glimpse of Patrick wielding an Ibanez Destroyer on his Instagram account and had to reach out to see what would inspire a player who can comfortably hang in the hippest of indie-rock circles to rock such a pointy ax. Turns out, he not only plays Destroyers, he references them in his band's songs!

> Adrian Smith using one in "The Number of the Beast" video was for sure why I wanted one in the first place. I was a big Maiden fan when I was in my early teens. Saw them on three consecutive tours in Halifax, although he used a Canadian Lado the first time I saw them and never used a Destroyer. Cronos from Venom also played a red Destroyer bass, and I was into them too.
>
> I have a 1984 DT150 fire-red guitar and a 1983 DT600 fire-red bass. I got the guitar from a former girlfriend about 13 years ago, and the bass I picked up recently at Paul's Boutique [a vintage guitar shop based in Toronto's Kensington Market neighborhood]. In fact, I found the bass at Paul's the day before our single "Dream Destroyer" was released, like it was a sign. What are the chances that I'd find the sister bass the exact same color and era of such a unique, hard to find guitar right as a single referencing Destroyers was released? So, I had to get it. We'll be using them both on our upcoming Canadian tour.
>
> Playing a guitar like the Destroyer is sort of a tribute to my past, or the players and music I listened to when I was first

> playing guitar in the mid-80s. I'm sure most people write off Destroyers as "pointy" guitars, and that's it. But mine, at least, sounds like a chainsaw with a jet engine. And looks badass.
>
> — Patrick Pentland of Sloan

One of the young guitarists influenced by Phil Collen's DT555 was legendary L.A. punk guitarist Pat Smear, who has played with the Germs, Nirvana, and is currently a member of the Foo Fighters, playing alongside fellow pointy-guitar lovers Dave Grohl and lead guitarist Chris Shiflett. Turns out not even the hippest of punks could resist the charms of Collen's three-humbucker equipped flame-thrower during those days of *Pyromania*.

> Pat Smear from Foo Fighters had one. Pat saw us play at the L.A. Forum in 1983. So he got one of the, you know, original ones. So when we did the Taylor Hawkins benefit show at the L.A. Forum, I got my original one, which was in the Rock & Roll Hall of Fame in Cleveland, and had it sent out for the gig and surprised him so he could play that when we jammed together. So that was nice for me, and he freaked out about that. That was really cool — Pat's great.
>
> — Phil Collen of Def Leppard

As cool as they look, did Phil ever actually use all three pickups on that Ibanez DT555?

> No, it was more for show, really. I was a huge fan of the Les Paul Customs with the three pickups. Peter Frampton had one. Al Di Meola had one. So did Brian Robertson of Thin Lizzy. When I got Ibanez to customize a basic Destroyer, they put all of that stuff on it. They put my name on it and all that. I had a Kahler tremolo put on it originally, it still sounds incredible. It's shocking how great it sounds whenever you plug it in. I've got a Jackson one now [the X-stroyer] — it's like [the original] on steroids. It's the Robo Cop of the guitar world. It's got a kill switch. It's got three DiMarzio X2N pickups, which are really powerful. It's got a Floyd Rose tremolo, all titanium stuff. And it really sounds incredible.

All of those guitars, you know, the flying-V guitar, the Ibanez Iceman, it was really more of an image thing with a lot of them. It was like trying to be a bit different, especially in the '80s. These guitars were a little like some kind of sci-fi weapon. And I think that was the whole idea, to be quite honest!

I've got an old Ibanez flying V, before they were doing legit guitars, they would do knockoffs in the '70s, and this thing is the best flying V I've ever played. This thing is an absolute beast. It's in England, so every time I go there, I pull it out. It never ceases to amaze me. It feels just beautiful. I mean, it's a vintage guitar now, a mid- to late '70s Ibanez. I got that that whole idea from Michael Schenker.

And what was it about that Ibanez flying V that spoke to Phil?

You know, it was an ax. It was a battle ax. It was sci-fi. It was post-pubescent boys getting guitars that looked like something out of a Marvel comic. Playing that flying V had a connection to a lot of other things. I think that's the reason you get into it in the first place.

Really interesting story. I was with Paul Stanley about six months after they'd done their last gig [December 2, 2023, at Madison Square Garden, New York]. And we were just talking. He said, "Hey, I've got my guitar. Do you wanna check it out? I actually had played it in the '80s when we (Girl) opened up for Kiss. He let me play his Ibanez Iceman, the original one that's got blood all over it. It's got the shards of mirror. And I said, "I've got my Ibanez Destroyer right here." We took a photo with each other's guitars, which was really, really cool, us with these two Ibanez guitars. I think his is from the '70s, and I think 1980 is when I got mine. And, again, it's that thing — the boys want to look like superheroes, and the guitar is like their weapon.

But I really did like the sound of those guitars. I used to love Michael Schenker's Flying Vs, Explorers, Modernes; all those Gibson guitars had a really great sound to them. They were made of a lighter wood, and they would resonate. So, there was more to it than the look, it was a sound that kind of leant itself to playing hard rock. And obviously that's where it went.

I noted to Phil that both Matthias Jabs and Michael Schenker, current and former members of the Scorpions, have a sweet upper-midrange sound, a lead violinist-like tone that comes from their Explorers and Flying Vs respectively. Did he think the shape of the instruments helped with acquiring that singing, stinging style?

> With both of those guys, their hands have a lot to do with it, but you're absolutely right. Those guitars have a quality that makes them sing. You know what I mean? Every time I play a flying V, or my Destroyer, or my X-Stroyer, it really sings. It's partially the wood, obviously. I don't know about the shapes — maybe the body mass and stuff like that. They are not really conventional, you know, like a Tele or a Strat or a Les Paul or something. They are definitely in a class of their own. In Girl, I was mainly using a Les Paul custom with DiMarzio Super Distortion pickups. I'd read about them because when I was geeking-out about American guitar players like Al Di Meola and Rick Nielsen (the American guitar players were playing DiMarzios), and I read that they were supposed to be great, so I got one. Just a year into playing — I was 17. They weren't very common. Years later, I met Larry DiMarzio and we've actually worked on a bunch of stuff. He's great.
>
> Without sounding name-droppy, I have to say this. I got to meet Eddie Van Halen when I saw Van Halen on their first U.K. headline tour. My mom got me this Fender Strat for my twentieth birthday, and I fucking loved it. I was talking to Eddie, and I'm, like, geeking out, and I said, "I got this Strat for my birthday and I love it. What would you do to it?" And he said "Honestly, you are not gonna be happy until you put a humbucker in there."
>
> So that was it. I heard it straight from Eddie. I went and chopped it up and got a DiMarzio in there. That's my main sound

on the *Hysteria* album, that Strat with the humbucker in it. It's on pretty much everything, "Pour Some Sugar on Me," the song "Hysteria," everything.

We were doing demos in Ireland, and Mutt Lange [the producer on Def Leppard's first three albums] had a Charvel. And I literally just started playing it and I said, "I love this guitar!" And Mutt said, "Let me get in touch with this guy, Grover Jackson." He gave me his number, and that's where that started off. I did play Jacksons on *Hysteria* as well. I've got my very first Jacksons around '85–'86 — the crackle one and the Bela Lugosi one. They were done at the same time. They do appear on *Hysteria* — the lead riff on "Pour Some Sugar on Me," and a couple of other things — but mainly everything was done on the Strat with the DiMarzios. [The Strat also] had a Kahler on it.

Interesting story, my friend Rudi Rivière was a guitar player from London, I've known him since we were teenagers. He knew this guy who did repairs and was making this tremolo arm that you didn't need to cut into the body. That was Dave Storey, the guy who invented the Kahler, and he actually installed it, so it really worked well. He was just working out of a little shop in London. That Bela Lugosi Jackson guitar used to have a Kahler on it, but I use Floyd Roses now. That guitar still sounds amazing.

As we saw with Racer X, Ibanez were clearly a company who had no problem customizing guitars to meet the needs of their artists, at any stage of their careers. In the case of Phil Collen, their support of a young artist at the beginning of his career was rewarded with the exposure of their instruments at a massive global scale.

I was in Japan with Girl. We were doing our first tour, and the Ibanez people came to a show in Japan and they said, "Oh, this is our catalog." And I said, "Wow. Could you customize this guitar [the Destroyer]?" And they said, "Yeah." And they got it to me pretty quickly, actually. I think it arrived in London just a few months after. And that was my original one. They customized it for me, and Dave Storey put the Kahler on it.

Phil joined Def Leppard in 1982, and that customized Destroyer would go on to be featured on some of the '80s most iconic tracks. How much was the guitar used, Phil?

> That's all of *Pyromania*, all the solos. That's the "Rock of Ages" solo. It's "Photograph." It's the "Foolin'" solo. It's "Stagefright." Mainly the solos but even some of the rhythm stuff. On "Rock! Rock! (Till You Drop)," I played my Les Paul, the one with the DiMarzio in it. But everything else is the Destroyer. My guitar went directly into a 50-watt Marshall head, and it wasn't the master volume one. It was just the regular volume 50-watt. And, again, you know, that was a Michael Schenker thing. I loved his tone and that's what we got. Literally no effects, just straight in, with the volume at about eight, and that was it. Then we literally plugged my amp into the 4-by-12 cabinet that Mike Shipley, the engineer, had been meticulously miking up for the last nine months, plunked the amp on top, plugged the Ibanez in, and just went for it. The first solo I did was "Stagefright."
>
> And, it sounds great. I just heard it the other day and thought, "Wow. This is killer." It's unbelievable. It leaps out of the speakers.

As a listener and fan, I was never sure who was responsible for the magical layering of guitar frequencies on *Pyromania*. I marvel at how guitars can sound so clean yet so powerful at the same time. It *feels* like it should be roaring with distortion —in "Photograph" there's not even a power chord underneath the chorus — yet it still feels like it's kicking you in the face.

> That was all Mutt. If you want to be a global presence as a rock band, [overly distorted guitar] turns certain people off, but you can still get power. We would multitrack like crazy. You know, there's the old story, "Oh, Def Leppard records chords just one string at a time," which we did on one section of the song "Hysteria." But, you know, even stuff like that, you couldn't hear notes very clearly if there was too much distortion. It would kind of cancel notes out. It would sound nasty.

So, he would use a universal notch filter to get rid of some really high-end stuff. But it was kind of clean on most of the rhythm stuff. When I first joined and plugged in, that wasn't the case. It was just like, "Yeah, crank this thing up!" But even then there weren't effects pedals, and [there] wasn't a master volume amplifier. It was the pure clarity of the guitar and the amp. There was something very pure about that. But, yeah, I think it allows you to be able to multitrack stuff up.

On the next album, *Hysteria*, we recorded everything direct through a Rockman, basically [a headphone amplifier designed by Tom Scholz of the band Boston that replicated the sound of a distorted electric guitar with chorus and delay effects]. We had such massive low end with the kick drum, the snare, and the bass, and even the bass sequencers and keyboards, and those frequencies were there all the time. You didn't want the guitars to get in the way of the vocals, you know? They share a sonic thing sometimes, especially if you multitrack backing vocals.

To keep the size of everything, you have to kind of put everything into a sonic perspective. Mutt was very good at that. It was making clarity with the guitars. We had three settings on the Rockman, clean, crunch, or distorted, and we'd just flow between those three. And it seemed to work out great. Again, really multitracking, some songs had 16 guitars: single string, root-note things, chords, inversions, playing different parts. It was very much orchestrated, which was just from me and Steve Clark listening to Queen albums. The main vocal melody's gotta come through and everything has to back it up. Same with song writing. The song is king and you have to keep it that way, you have to keep it on its throne.

The timbre and texture, and the overall approach of Def Leppard's background vocals, was almost punk rock in its intention and intensity.

Again, that's a Mutt Lange thing. There were a lot of American bands doing great vocals, and even bands like the Sweet, they had wonderful harmonies. But we wanted to sound more like the

> Sex Pistols or Slade or the New York Dolls, [which were] all very yobby and shouty, like a real football chant. We wanted to do that. You don't want to sound like session musicians; you want to sound excited. You want the blood to start flowing. Same with the guitar playing. I love Steve Jones. I love Johnny Thunders. And that's the way that they approach the guitar — they smash you in the face. And that's why the vocals have to be that way.
>
> Mutt absolutely understood. But he wanted us to be a cross between Queen and AC/DC. AC/DC couldn't really sing — they didn't have *singers* in the band. Queen obviously did, but we wanted to make a cross between the two, and make it sound like Slade. Does that make any sense? So, you'd be chanting and shouting, but you'd be doing it in tune, with that kind of perspective.
>
> A lot of people can't do that. There's a rock voice that people are not very familiar with. You know, there are loads of guys that sing really high, but they haven't got that *rock* thing that kind of that makes you wanna get into it.

One of the great treats when my band had the opportunity to open some dates in Canada for Def Leppard was to hear the individual timbre of each of those background vocals when the band was sound checking. It was an opportunity to hear each individual voice, but also to see how their sound comes together elementally to make that special Def Leppard vocal blend.

> I remember when I discovered that we had it. When Steve was in the band, you know, he could sing, but he didn't really *sing* sing. Vivian Campbell, he's a great singer. So after a few years, we'd done this acoustic session in London, and I went into the control room. I'm like, "What's that? What are those vocals?" And they're like, "That's you guys." We had just recorded. And I said, "Well, what have you done to it?" And they said, "We haven't done anything." And it was the blend. It was the chemistry of the blend, and you get there after singing together for a certain number of years. You kind of ebb and flow with each other. Years ago, when he was alive, I'd met Phil Everly a few times.

> And I would say, you know, "You and your brother, what's that all about?" He said, "Well, look, we learned to sing from the same guy. We had very similar body types, and we were singing together from the get-go." You have this chemistry, almost like an ESP, that develops. If you've ever been fortunate enough to have that kind of joy when that happens, it's pretty amazing.

The chemistry between the members of Def Leppard, be it in the studio or on stage, is undeniable. And in those early days of Phil's journey with the band, a major element of that chemistry is the Ibanez DT555. With the image of that guitar forever a part of my association with Phil, I wondered who were the pointy players that most moved him to become the icon he is.

> Well, Michael Schenker, you know, I love his technique and his sound and his vibe. And Eddie used to play an Ibanez Destroyer. You know, he kind of Frankensteined that up as well. They would be my absolute top two, right at the top, you know. No one compares to them for that, as far as I'm concerned. Both of them had the supreme vibrato and the fuck-off approach to everything and the great tone. You can't go wrong with those two.
>
> — Phil Collen

CHAPTER 9

B.C. RICH GUITARS – WARLOCKS, BLACK WIDOWS, AND BIRDS OF PREY

In 2002, I had a vision for a musical project that would represent everything I love about rock-n-roll music, a band that would strike a perfect power chord with fans of '70s glam, FM radio rock, and early '80s Sunset Strip pop metal.

Crash Kelly enjoyed a number of dream-come-true opportunities, but ultimately, achieved very little commercial success. Close, but no cigar — but you can keep the cigars, I had pointy B.C. Rich guitars. Indulge me in a bit of backstory of those glory days, the kind that can pass you by in the wink of a young girl's eye. But only if you let them.

Crash Kelly's debut album, *Penny Pills*, was recorded on a shoe-string budget with two very talented musicians, Craig McConnell and Ky Anto, and was initially released by RCD Music, a small label run by Chris and Rebecca Case. Chris and Rebecca are two wonderful people who would take on the thankless job of managing the band, and who worked tirelessly to help move Crash Kelly through the various hurdles of the music business, helping us to grow into viable contenders.

Penny Pills was an album that mixed bravado and vulnerability in equal measure. The riffs were inspired by Kiss, Aerosmith, Alice Cooper, T. Rex, Cheap Trick, Mott the Hoople, Mötley Crüe, W.A.S.P., and the Sweet — big, masculine energy dressed in drag — with the lyrics being spat out like bloody

Chiclets after a hockey fight. But these words were also laced with the insecurities of a self-loathing lapsed Catholic (that's me), romanticizing his own anguish. This anguish was largely a result of my failed first marriage attempt at 24, a union that was ultimately annulled by the Catholic Church, just like it never happened. But of course — divine erasure aside — it did happen, and writing and recording *Penny Pills* helped me process (or cover up, as needed) the heartache and humiliation that came with the divorce through sticky, power-pop melodies and loud, dirty, in-your-face electric-guitar tones. Out of marital failure, I found a new desire to rekindle the rock-n-roll flame that a changing musical landscape in the '90s had seemingly tried to snuff out. It was raw and honest, and that was reflected in the guitar tones as much as in the lyrics. It's an album I'm very proud of, warts and all. Good art can come out of a place where you feel like there's nothing left to lose. As arrogant as that may sound, I feel like with *Penny Pills*, I made something akin to a genuine cult classic. It was pure and, with a small following of people, it connected.

The album was licensed to T.B. Records, a small English label run by Mark Thomas and Neil Bennett, and we toured the U.K. and Ireland with great bands like the Quireboys, Enuff Z'Nuff, and Skid Row. Championed by my late, great rock-n-roll brother and A&R representative Brandon Stratton, we signed an American record deal with Liquor and Poker Music, the rock-n-roll imprint of independent heavy-metal heavyweight label, Century Media. We became label mates with legendary underground bands like Hanoi Rocks, the Hellacopters, and Backyard Babies. A major highlight for me (just ask anyone who has had to endure my recounting of this story over the years), was securing the opening slot on a few legs of Alice Cooper's North American Dirty Diamonds Tour, the manifestation of the arena-rock dreams I had held for so long.

Crash Kelly released albums all over the world, including three domestic releases in Japan. What a thrill it was to see the Japanese pressings of our albums with the famed obi strip, and the incredibly detailed bio notes in Japanese script! We received critical acclaim and features in hip publications like the *Village Voice* in New York and *LA Weekly*. Doug Brod (an incredible author and someone who has become a dear friend) described the band as "pre-owned Camaro rock that still runs like a charm" in a review he wrote for *Spin* magazine back in 2005. We recorded two albums in Los Angeles with ex-Guns N' Roses, Heart, and MC5 guitarist, Gilby Clarke, at the production helm. I would eventually play in Gilby's solo band for a tour of South America, and he continues to be a mentor and good friend, and he is a rock-n-roll classic in every sense.

Crash Kelly was born of the frustration of every out-of-reach, unfulfilled teenage dream that had grown inside of me up to that point, including the many times I was denied a very pointy guitar with which to play out arena-rock fantasies in front of my bedroom mirror. The glorious results of a mis-spent 15 years of sick-to-my-stomach desperation, aspiration, and unfulfilled ambition.

I had moved to Toronto in 1991 at the age of 18 years old, fully puffed up on the promises of '80s corporate rock marketing — neon-flecked guitar-magazine ads and music videos with bands running around steel multileveled stage structures, all ramps and platforms lit up by a thousand blazing lights and lasers. And within that very year, a band named Nirvana came and seemingly removed the value of all of my foundational dreams. Even though I loved Nirvana, and many of the other bands of the '90s that came in their wake, I could never truly be a part of that scene. My love for the pageantry and visual romance of the flashier hard-rocking music of the '70s and '80s was undying, and a beat-up pawnshop Fender Jaguar just wasn't going to cut it for me. While I did try and adapt my playing style, gear, clothes, and haircut throughout the '90s, with varying levels of success, it just wasn't who I was.

In being truly honest with myself for once in my life and in having nothing to lose, I finally felt free and able to write songs I truly wanted to write, create the band I always wanted to be in, and — most relevant to this book — allow myself to play the forbidden guitars I had always wanted to play. When I stopped worrying about making it on any terms other than my own, I managed to get my turn at bat.

Crash Kelly never did sell a lot of records, and our level of success was cult level at best, but I had a wonderful taste of the rock-n roll-dream. And I did it playing B.C. Rich guitars, instruments that perfectly married my '70s and '80s rock-n-roll aspirations.

> The first time I sat there going, "Pointy guitars — that's kinda cool," was with B.C. Rich. And I'm going back to the '70s. Growing up during that time, Les Pauls, Strats, Teles, those were the accepted shapes, and I always loved them. It wasn't until I

> saw Aerosmith in the Sergeant Pepper's movie, where they were playing the villains, [and] both Whitford and Perry were playing B.C. Rich guitars. One guy's playing a Mockingbird, and the other one's playing a Bich. I think Whitford was on the Bich, and Perry's with the Mockingbird.
>
> That was the first time, you know, you saw these really angular pointy shapes. B.C. Rich really went to town. They're definitely geometric, and the edges, they were all pointy and angular.
>
> If Joe Perry and Brad Whitford were playing those, I was like "This is cool!" Suddenly you start seeing all these other '70s classic-rock guys playing B.C. Rich guitars, and then B.C. Rich slides into the '80s.
>
> — Paul Riario, tech editor, *Guitar World*

B.C. Rich guitars first entered my consciousness through Mötley Crüe's "Looks That Kill" video, which first hit the airwaves in early 1984. Set against a post-apocalyptic stage set at A&M studios in Hollywood, the video features a literally captive audience of women who were cajoled into cages by the band members themselves. The whole thing now looks like Kiss, Mad Max, Conan the Barbarian, and the Solid Gold Dancers thrown into a blender.

Today's pure camp, however, was yesterday's shock and awe, and the effect of seeing the Crüe with their makeup, custom-designed studded-leather outfits, knee-high hooker boots with stacked heels, and B.C. Rich guitars left a lasting impression. Mick Mars wielded a white Warlock, while Nikki Sixx pummeled a black Mockingbird bass, and the asymmetrical points and angles screamed heavy-metal excess. I would later go on to recognize B.C. Rich's stunningly pointy guitars in the hands of '80s heavyweights like Blackie Lawless and Randy Piper of W.A.S.P., Megadeth's Dave Mustaine and Chris Poland, Slayer's Kerry King, Lita Ford, C.C. DeVille of Poison, Tracii Guns of L.A. Guns, Pete Friesen of Alice Cooper, and many more.

B.C. Rich arguably represents the most famous examples of the wild shapes and extreme pointiness associated with hard rock and heavy metal guitar in the late '70s and '80s, even though they started as one of the first boutique electric-guitar shops aimed at tonally discerning studio-session pros. While it can be said that B.C. Rich's most famous models might share tonal characteristics with classic Gibson models, I would argue that outside of the design concept of asymmetry, classic B.C. Rich models like the Seagull, Eagle, the Mockingbird, the Bich, the Warlock, and the Ironbird come from a unique place of visual and structural inspiration.

While heavy metal and hard rock would ultimately be the genre most closely associated with the brand, B.C. Rich guitars were initially adopted by and geared towards outlier guitarists from a wide variety of musical backgrounds; players looking for a something different in a boutique, high-performance instrument. Some of those illustrious players include session greats Dick Wagner and Steve Hunter (Lou Reed and Alice Cooper); Neil Giraldo (Pat Benatar); Carlos Alomar (David Bowie); jazz guitarist Robert Conti; and Rick Derringer, who designed his own pointy model for the company, the Stealth.

> It was Thin Lizzy. It was Alice Cooper. It was Joe Perry. It was a departure from the same old same old. It was all built on a legacy of players from the '70s. Gary Moore played B.C. Rich. Phil Lynott played B.C. Rich for a minute. Neil Giraldo from Pat Benatar, he played Bichs and Eagles. Tons and tons of players.
>
> — Bill Xavier, CEO, B.C. Rich Guitars (2020–present)

> There was a time in the late '70s and early '80s when the softer, rounder guitar shapes that were developed in the 1950s and '60s seemed not only old hat but utterly uncool. Sharp, pointy, ax-like and aggressively weapon-esque shapes defined the electric guitar's future, at least for anything rock or metal. And as of about 1976, that meant not Gibson or Fender, but B.C. Rich.
>
> The radically styled and appointed guitars of this California maker looked, felt, and sounded "rock." And for a good part of the era when hair was big and trousers were tight, B.C. Rich's guitars appeared on about as many arena stages as those of the big-name guitar makers that had come before. But if you take the story back a couple decades further, the roots of the B.C. Rich operation can be found in a far tamer breed of guitar making.
>
> (Dave Hunter, *Guitar World*, 2024.)

Crash Kelly was the vehicle that enabled me to secure a guitar company endorsement with B.C. Rich guitars. I can't overstate the significance that the relationship with B.C. Rich had on my life in forming the person I am today. Playing classic B.C. Rich models like the Mockingbird and Bich gave me an identity as a performer. When I played them in concert, I felt like I was holding a magical musical weapon in my hands, one with which to fend off any insecurity or self-doubt I may have felt as I transitioned to bigger stages. I could finally honor the rock-n-roll fire inside of me that had to burn.

A very kind and generous man named Ted Burger, who is also a great guitarist and friend, took a chance on bringing me and my Crash Kelly guitar partner (and best mate), Allister Thompson, into the B.C. Rich fold, providing us not only with some of the iconic B.C. Rich models that we will investigate in this chapter, but also a wealth of amazing promotional opportunities, including appearances at the famed NAMM show in Anaheim, California, generous features in the B.C. Rich product catalogs, and a full-page advertisement that ran in *Guitar World* magazine, shot by famed rock photographer John Harrell. At the time, Ted was an artist rep for B.C. Rich and their parent company, Hanser Music Group. Today, he is the president of that company, and while Hanser licensed the B.C. Rich brand to Praxis Musical Instruments in 2016 (who in turn sold those rights in 2018), he is forever a part of the long history that started with a man named Bernardo Mason Rico.

The B.C. Rich guitar story was born out of the small Candelas guitar shop in Los Angeles, when Mr. Rico purchased it in the mid-1950s and hired luthiers from Paracho, Mexico, to craft handmade guitars for mariachi, classical, flamenco, and folk musicians. Rico's son Bernardo "Bernie" Chavez Rico, an accomplished guitarist who studied with flamenco great Sabicas, also became involved in the guitar-making process, and as Los Angeles's burgeoning folk-music scene grew, Bernardo's Guitar Shop (formerly known as the Valencian Guitar Shop and Casa Rico) developed a reputation for guitar repairs and the production of steel string acoustic guitars.

Bernie made his first electric solid-body guitar in 1968, which led to initial small-run production efforts of guitars and basses modeled after the Les Paul and the Gibson EB-3 starting in 1969. In 1972, Bernie and employee Bob Hall developed a model that would become known as the Seagull, which became the company's first marketed guitar production model in 1974. The name "B.C. Rich" has a few origin stories, one suggesting that it was adopted when shop employee Mal Stich switched up his usual phone greeting of "Bernardo's Guitar Shop" with the catchier "B.C. Rich." Another story is that the inspiration came from musician and friend Bobby Rich, who adopted the stage name Roberto Rico, and that Bernie simply reversed the process and anglicized Rich's name for his guitars. Perhaps the truth lies in some combination of both, but the result was a name that rolled off the tongue and guitars that flew off the racks, particularly in the visually obsessed 1980s.

High-end, production guitars with the qualities and attributes of custom guitar builds were the name of the game with B.C. Rich. Customers could request special fingerboard inlays or custom pickups (DiMarzio pickups were the standard company choice, while Guild and Bartolini pickups were also employed), but they were still production guitars, with the electric guitar parts and materials being sent to a facility in Tijuana, Mexico, to be initially assembled, and then picked up by Bernie once a month and brought back to California to be painted and finally finished off.

Mal Stich worked as a luthier, shop foreman, and at one time was the vice president of B.C. Rich during its ascendancy in the guitar industry. In Joe Charupakorn's excellent 2011 article for *Premier Guitar*, Stich describes that B.C. Rich guitars truly earned the handmade designation in those early days.

> When Stich says early B.C. Riches were handmade, he means it in the truest sense of the phrase. He recalls that there were no machines in sight inside the shop — only band saws, belt sanders, block planes, spoke shaves, files, and special guitar knives that the luthiers made themselves out of highly carbonized metal. "The guys would literally go out and buy a metal slab that was probably a quarter inch thick, and they would cut it, shape it, sharpen it, and make a handle for it — usually out of mahogany. People would walk in and go, "Where's your machinery?" and we'd go, "Sittin' right there," and point at a knife. Then they'd go into the paint shop and guys would be water-sanding, finishing

> coats, and buffing by hand. When they cut the blanks, the sides would be glued on and wrapped with cord like in the old days, when they made violins and wrapped them with cords in France in the 1500s. They would tap shims between the cord and the wood to make it as tight as possible for the glue joints, which were always superb. The guitars would go through a process of being marked out with a pencil and a template of the shape of the guitar — we had aluminum templates and later plastic — and then they would do a cutout on a band saw. From there, the necks would be handcarved using what I call a "Mexican guitar maker's knife," and they just hacked the [expletive] out of it. It would start out with a hammer and a chisel — *bam, bam, bam* — making the neck. Then they would go to the knife, and finally to a spoke shave. These guys could knock out a neck in about 20 minutes.
>
> ("B.C. Rich Beginnings," *Premier Guitar*, 2011.)

Once the woodworking part of the guitar-building process was completed, the next step in the assembly process was the final step, the hardwiring of the electronics. These electronic parts were also made by hand, and the circuitry involved in these early B.C. Rich designs offered a wide variety of tonal options to the discerning player.

> Noted luthier Neal Moser, who had developed a reputation as the go-to guy for hot-rodding guitar electronics, joined the company in 1974. Over the initial dinner meeting at Bernie's house, Moser sketched out the circuitry and layout for a new design on a piece of cardboard. He soon went to work for B.C. Rich as an independent contractor. His dinner-table design — which consisted of master volume and tone controls, a built-in preamp, a 6-position Varitone, and coil taps — was implemented on the production Seagull guitar.
>
> B.C. Rich's electric offerings were originally equipped with Guild pickups, but the company later switched to DiMarzios, which Stich says, "added a whole different reality to the guitars. The Guilds had this '50s or '60s sound, whereas the DiMarzios

had a new sound to them. They also worked better with Moser's circuitry."

(Joe Charupakorn, *Premier Guitar*.)

Moser's influence on the success of B.C. Rich is expansive, from his innovative electronic work, which offered players a wide variety of tonal options, to his eye for design and impeccable craftsmanship as a luthier.

Neal Moser started back in 1974 as an independent contractor with them. A lot of people get confused. He was never actually an employee at B.C. Rich. He was always an independent contractor, and his very first role was doing electronics and setups, which he continued to do from '74 till he left in '85. In '74, when the Seagull came out, he developed the electronics for that, which are now famous. And over time, those electronics evolved into the Mockingbird electronics and then, of course, the Bich electronics, which has the biggest circuit with all the switches and knobs and everything, Varitone and whatnot. He played a pivotal role, not just with the electronics and the setups. I mean, his setups, I don't think there's anybody alive today that does a better guitar setup, or better fret work than Neal. I think he told me he's done, like, over fifteen thousand fret jobs and setups. I've always read in business books if someone does something ten thousand times, as long as they're doing it the right way, they become a master.

Neal Moser is a certified master luthier. During that period, he was also helping design guitars. They started with the Seagull and then he helped to revise that into the Seagull II, which eventually evolved into the Eagle, another famous model.

— Zach Gunter, Neal Moser Guitars

The first originally designed guitar Bernie created after taking a step into the electric realm came three years later, and was called the Seagull. Featuring thunderous humbuckers, four simple knobs, and an impressive spike protruding from the

> guitar body, the Seagull was B.C. Rich's first foray into creating uniquely shaped guitars. Though the fabled tone may have sold the Seagull, it was definitely the shape of the body that first captivated players. As the company grew, more and more prominent guitarists sported Seagulls, including Dick Wagner, who is famous for his work with Alice Cooper and Aerosmith.
> (Jack Smith, "History of B.C. Rich Guitars," Gear Vault.)

While the single-cutaway Seagull now seems fairly conservative compared to the more outlandish B.C. Rich shapes that followed, it did have one visually striking, yet decidedly uncomfortable, protruding point on the upper body that tended to poke into a player's torso at certain angles.

The Eagle was the next evolutionary design step, an asymmetrical double cutaway a bit more akin to a Stratocaster, but with a longer, sharper upper horn and shorter, more rounded lower horn (similar to the Seagull). It mixed the Les Paul double-cutaway shape (like an SG) with a Stratocaster's more flowing and stretched curves, while also representing a move towards increased edginess and attitude in the horns and headstock.

> I was born a guitar nut, always exploring and getting excited about new brands and models. My brother and I saw Dick Wagner [Alice Cooper] with some B.C. Rich models, and we freaked. By the late 1970s, when Bob [Kulick, Bruce's brother] and I joined Meat Loaf for the Bat Out of Hell Tour, Bob found a koa Mockingbird. It was awesome, and for a while I had one as well. Remember, Todd Rundgren did the guitar work on the *Bat Out of Hell* LP, so my 1963 Fender Stratocaster was more appropriate for the parts I was asked to perform. After the Meat Loaf tour was over, I found a natural maple Eagle Supreme with cloud inlays and ebony neck. It was gorgeous. It became my main guitar with the band Blackjack featuring Michael Bolton as the lead singer. I used it for the Billy Squier LP titled *Tale of the Tape* as well. By late 1984, I was the new guitarist for Kiss. I toured for the *Animalize* release, with two Charvels and a black B.C. Rich Eagle, sadly stolen from the Kiss warehouse in 1988.

> It was the one non-Floyd guitar I would perform with, great for the vintage songs in the set.
>
> — Bruce Kulick of Kiss and Grand Funk Railroad

In 1976, the same year that the Eagle officially took flight, the Mockingbird also got its wings. Fittingly, the first official Mockingbird reportedly went to Aerosmith guitarist Joe Perry, by way of famed sound technician and noted guitar afficionado Robert "Nitebob" Czaykowski. Nitebob, whose credits also include Led Zeppelin, ELP, the New York Dolls, Steely Dan, the Ramones, and more, plays a key role in the dissemination of the B.C. Rich brand throughout the rock world thanks to his introducing the Mockingbird and Bich models to the Aerosmith camp.

> The first pivotal point in B.C. Rich's rise to widespread recognition came in 1976, when sound engineer Bob "Nite Bob" Czaykowski picked up a maple-bodied Mockingbird — the first one ever made — for Aerosmith guitarist Joe Perry. "All of a sudden, B.C. Rich was on the map," says Stich. "In my opinion, if it wasn't for Nite Bob, B.C. Rich would have been another flash-in-the-pan guitar company."
>
> (Joe Charupakorn, *Premier Guitar*.)

> Our sound man, Nite Bob [Robert Czaykowski], hooked me up with a lot of guitars back then. B.C. Rich was making some guitars that didn't look like Les Pauls or Stratocasters, and there was a quality of build that I liked. There was something about the Mockingbird and the Rich Bich, and Brad bought one, so we were a couple of the first guys to use them. I remember being in the studio around then, and the phone rang, and the secretary said, "Joe, phone call for you." It was Lou Reed. I'd never met him, and he called me, saying, "I saw a picture of you with this guitar . . ." That guitar has a distinct sound that doesn't work for some things, but it sounds great on others. It has a really cool thing about it, almost like a flange thing. It's really amazing, though it doesn't work for everything.
>
> — Joe Perry (*Guitar World*, October 2024.)

> The early B.C. Rich guitars were the ultimate Southern California guitar of the early '70s, in my opinion. Handmade by super skilled craftsmen from Mexico in East L.A. Totally handmade, no CNC machines, they even made their own tools. Each one was slightly different. They listened to what the players wanted and incorporated a neck thru design and custom electronics.
>
> — Nitebob (Medium.com.)

Conceived by bassist Johnny "Go Go" Kallas in 1975, the Mockingbird received its name from Moser, who wanted to keep the tradition of aviary-themed model names going.

> Our standard Mockingbird guitar is available in maple neck and body with rosewood stripes or koa neck and body with maple stripes. 24-fret, 2-octave, rosewood fingerboard with diamond shape genuine mother of pearl position markers and rosewood headplate. Hardware features include: B.C. Rich Quadmatic® Brass Bridge, brass truss rod cover, genuine bone nut, Grover Imperial 109 C machine heads, 24% nickel frets, and Straplok System. Electronics include our standard circuit; Master volume, pick up selector, six position varitone, preamp with preset controls, phase switch, dual sound switches, and master tone. DiMarzio PAF, Super Two or Bill Lawrence L-500 pickups.
>
> (B.C. Rich 1982 catalog.)

The Mockingbird balances classic inspiration with an extreme and striking amalgam of points, angles, and flowing, curvy lines. It takes the concept of double-cutaway guitar to a very different place, with a long, sharp upper horn that swoops upward, while the lower horn (initially shorter, as per Kallas's original design, and then refined to be longer in later incarnations) curves downward, creating the Mockingbird's defining contrast. The bass-side body wing extends outward in a wide sweep, and the treble-side wing is more compact and angled upward. Further separating the instrument from guitar designs that came before, the waist of the Mockingbird is highly offset, and has a deeper lower cut. The combination of body lines combining sharp and soft elements give the guitar an aggressive, yet carefully sculpted feel. The headstock originally followed B.C. Rich's signature 3+3 tuner layout, with later models adopting the pointier "widow" headstock, made famous on Blackie Lawless's signature Black Widow bass in the '80s, and incorporated on various B.C. Rich models in the company's later, more metalcentric, years.

The Supreme was the top-of-the-line B.C Rich instrument and featured mother of pearl cloud-shaped fret inlays that became a defining design feature.

> The Supreme is available in the Mockingbird or Eagle body styles. The supreme comes with a koa neck and body with maple stripes or maple neck and body with rosewood stripes. The 24 fret, 2 octave, ebony finger board and rosewood headstock are bound in white celluloid. Position markers are genuine mother of pearl cloud shape inlay as is the R logo on the headstock. Hardware features include: B.C. Rich Quadmatic® Brass Bridge, brass truss rod cover, genuine bone nut, Grover Imperial 109 C machine heads, 24% nickle frets, and Straplok System. Electronics include our standard circuit; Master volume, pick up selector, six position Varitone, preamp with preset controls, phase switch, dual sound switches, and master tone. DiMarzio PAF, Super Two or Bill Lawrence L-500 pickups.
>
> (B.C. Rich 1982 catalog.)

Gilby Clarke may be most closely associated with the Gibson Les Paul and Fender Telecaster, but Rick Derringer inspired him to acquire his first B.C. Rich guitar, a Mockingbird Supreme. His fellow guitarist in his days with Guns N Roses, also fell under the spell of the Mockingbird.

> I have an affinity that goes back to when I first started playing guitar. My first good electric guitar was a B.C. Rich Mockingbird. I eventually graduated to Les Pauls. But I still have a soft spot in my heart for B.C. Riches, and they sound good — the old ones sounded real good.
>
> — Slash of Guns N' Roses (*Premier Guitar*, November 27, 2018.)

Pete Friesen is a Canadian guitarist, composer, and educator, currently residing in the U.K. Pete made his name playing guitar with Alice Cooper, touring in support of the platinum-selling *Trash* and *Hey Stoopid* albums in the late '80s and early '90s. Pete would go on to play guitar for Scottish band the Almighty, as well as Iron Maiden–frontman Bruce Dickinson's solo band.

I became aware of Pete after seeing the *Alice Cooper Trashes the World* live-concert video. Watching Pete play his B.C. Rich koa Mockingbird (with neck-through body and distinctive, thin strips of walnut wood "stringers" running alongside the neck and body for structural support and visual accent) was highly impactful on me. In the context of Alice's highly theatrical live show, Pete's Mockingbird suggested visual modernity, while his tasteful,'70s-inspired playing brought a spoke to the traditions of early arena rock. I was equally taken with Tracii Guns's use of a similar Mockingbird in the L.A. Guns video for "Rip and Tear," where Tracii's culminating solo coda burns with a shred-like intensity while also retaining a decidedly classic rock tone and pentatonic, bluesy feel. The combination of koa and walnut is said to enhance sustain and resonance, and it also gives the guitar that special boutique feeling.

Pete's story speaks to the aspirations, dreams, and struggles that I myself have felt and encountered, and it was a thrill to speak with this native of Sudbury, Ontario (a mere hour and a half from my own hometown of North Bay) and hear how his pointy guitar brought him to the world's stage.

> The Mockingbird was my main guitar, and I'll tell you how I got that. My dad dropped me off at the Greyhound bus station in Sudbury in the dead of winter to Toronto . . . I think it was Sam's Music, maybe? I had twelve hundred dollars stuffed in my sock because I thought if someone's gonna rob me, they wouldn't look at my sock. [*laughs*] How naive is that? And I tried every Strat and every Les Paul in the place, and they all had baseball bat necks. And I just didn't like them. And then I saw this guitar. I thought, *God, it's the maddest looking thing I've ever seen*. And it had a nice thin neck. I really don't have big hands, so I quite like a thin neck. It was definitely one of those situations when you try a guitar and you go, "Okay, yeah. I

have to have this." That was the Mockingbird. I took it down to L.A. That was my guitar in L.A., the Alice gig, I played it quite a lot. I got a second one too. I bought a second one in a pawnshop in L.A. It was like a nice sort of cherry tobacco color. This is the maddest thing, I finished [studying] at GIT [the Guitar Institute of Technology], and I was answering ads in papers, going around, trying to find a band. And a guy [I met] who's a bass player, who I had brought a little demo tape I made on a four track to. I didn't end up being in his band. He calls me up six months later. And he says, "I'm going down to audition to be in an Alice Cooper video. Would you like to come along? We can learn a song together, so we seem a bit more organized."

We learned a New York Dolls song called "Chatterbox." How random is that? I don't know why we chose it. But, being always hyperorganized, he gave me the number to call to get myself on the list. I called the guy and asked if there was going to be an amp there. He goes, "What kind of amp do you have?" I say, "A Marshall half stack." He asks, "Can we rent it off you for the day, and for how much?" At this point, I'm starving, and my mind is going, *Oh shit, I don't wanna overcook it.* What do I do? I said "Fifty dollars." And he was like "Done." I was like, *Oh my god. It's like groceries for a month!* So, I turn up early and set up my amp. It's a cattle call, hundreds of guys are coming through the door. And I just think, *Alright, I ain't got a chance here. This is gonna be a total roll of the dice.*

I go in. We do our thing. I leave, and I have to stay around until the end because I need to pack up my amp once everyone is done. As I'm packing up, a voice behind me goes, "Yeah, that was pretty cool. Do you play bass?"

I turned around, and it was Alice! What do I say? I just went "Yeah. Yeah, I play bass." And I got a call the next evening. They said, "Okay, we have a guitar player we like, and we wanna use them, but we'd like you to play bass in the video. Are you up for that?" And I'm like, "Yeah, of course." And they said, "We really like your guitar. Would you mind if the guitar player played your guitar?"

And that was the beginning of that Mockingbird having a life of its own. I said, "Yeah, of course!" I borrowed a bass from a guy in the apartment next door and learned the bass line. In the "Poison" video, I'm playing bass. Mike Hollywood, clearly not his real name, was playing guitar, and he's playing the Mockingbird.

We got paid a hundred dollars each. We had a party with my friends when I got to watch myself on MTV and was like, oh, amazing. And I thought that was that, and I went back to being in my cover band. You know, we did our first gig at the Whisky to, like, eight people. And then I got a call saying, "The single's done really well in the U.K. We want to do another single and video ["Bed of Nails"], and Alice wants the same band. Are you up for it?" I said, "Yeah, sounds good."

At [the video shoot] Alice says "You play guitar, don't you? We're having auditions for the touring band. Would you like to audition?" I was a huge fan. I love "School's Out," "Welcome to my Nightmare," "Killer." I loved the sort of rawness of it.

It's funny how life works out because the reason I got the gig was, in the '80s, everyone was doing the flashy thing. You know, the song "Eighteen" has that unison bend at the beginning. Everyone was trying to flash it up and turn it into something else. I came in and played it note for note, and they liked that. They wanted two guys. They had Al Pitrelli, the guy who could do the Steve Vai thing, and they wanted the guy who would play it the old school way, like the record. So that's how I got to audition to be in the touring band, and I ended up playing guitar with Alice Cooper. It's funny how things work out.

— Pete Friesen of the Alice Cooper Band and the Almighty

The most famous and bestselling B.C. Rich model is the provocatively named 10-string Rich Bich, later shortened to Bich, and now known as the

B Legacy, adjusted for changing times. The Bich offered rock players the option of chiming, chorus-affected sounds courtesy of the doubling of the top four strings, leaving the lower two strings free for harmonically unencumbered power-chording better suited for players using a high level of distortion or overdrive. Many players opted to remove the top strings and play the Bich as a conventional six-string. Iconic users include the aforementioned Aerosmith duo of Joe Perry and Brad Whitford, Dave Mustaine of Megadeth, former Runaways and solo guitar legend Lita Ford, Randy Jackson of Zebra, and Craig Chaquico of Starship.

> The Rich Bich features our one piece through the body hee-less construction maple neck with koa body or a maple neck with maple body. A 24-fret, 2-octave rosewood fingerboard with genuine mother of pearl cloud position markers accent the rosewood headplate with mother of pearl R logo on head-stock. Easy access tuning: the E, A, D, G, B, E tune on the head while the octave D and G and the unison B and E tune at the butt. Standard hardware and electronics include: B.C. Rich Quadmatic® Brass Bridge, brass truss rod cover, brass pick up frames, Grover Imperial 109 C machine heads, Straplok System, genuine bone nut, 24% nickle frets. Master volume, rhythm pick up volume, pick up selector, twin preamps with preset for each, six position varitone, phase switch, dual sound switches, and master tone set. Standard pickups are DiMarzio PAF, Super Two or Bill Lawrence L-500.
>
> (1978 B.C. Rich catalog.)

The Bich will always hold a special place in my heart, as it was the first model I received as an endorsed B.C. Rich artist. It was handed to me at the Rock & Roll Hall of Fame in Cleveland, where I was a contestant in *Guitar Player* magazine's inaugural Guitar Hero contest, performing in front of celebrity judges like Steve Lukather, Joe Satriani, and the staff of *Guitar Player* — no pressure! While I didn't win the competition, I walked away with an instrument that encompassed the spirit of the music that inspired me. While mine was a 6-string 2005 NJ Classic re-issue, I would eventually land a treasured 10-string model as well.

Designed by Neal Moser, the 10-string Bich is a throwback to his earliest foray into guitar building, when he modified a six-string Yamaha acoustic to a twelve-string with his father's help in 1964. The Bich adds unison D and G strings and octave B and E strings strung in the opposite direction from the other six strings, with the additional tuners arranged along a diagonal cut below the bridge. The body shape eventually changed slightly, featuring a shallower cut where these tuners attached to allow for a Kahler tremolo. The Bich also added a second preamp to Moser's already complex electronics.

(Elizabeth Hanson, "B.C. Rich Origins and Evolution," Reverb.com.)

In 1977, while Bernie was in Japan, Moser went into the wood-shop one day and crafted the company's edgiest design to date — the 10-string Bich. According to Stich, when Bernie returned to the shop and saw the new project, he got upset and yelled "You guys don't design guitars without me!" The model's name stems from a trip Moser and his wife made to the county fair. "They noticed some girls wearing charms on their neck-laces that read 'Rich Bitch.' They agreed that would be an ideal name," recalls Stich. "Of course, the 'T' was dropped."

(Joe Charupakorn, *Premier Guitar*.)

It's rare that a woman would point out an attractive woman to her husband, but Earleen Moser pointed out a woman that was very good looking, and she was wearing a necklace that said "Rich Bitch." That's when they named it the Rich Bich. Some people tried to say that they called it a Bich because it was so hard to tune the 10 strings, but that really wasn't the case.

— Bill Xavier, CEO, B.C. Rich

I was a B.C. Rich endorser and collector for years. I first started working with Bernie Sr. and Jr. They made me many cool Biches and Mockingbirds. I left for years but came back twice. B.C. Rich was, and is, very special. With Moser's electronics you

> can have a Strat sound, a Les Paul, and over 40 different tones at your fingertips. Now we know why guys like [Rick] Derringer and [Neil] Giraldo played these.
>
> — Jack Frost of Savatage and Aldo Nova

> The Bich is Neal's design. The story he told me, and I hope I get the details of this right, is that Bernie Rico had to go out of town. I think he had to go to Japan because this was maybe about the time that they were looking into doing the NJ series [a foray into more cost-effective, offshore production models built in Nagoya, Japan]. Bernie was out of town, and during that time, Neal sketched out the Bich guitar, because he wanted to do this 10-string idea. He told me he sketched that and it came together very quickly. The Bich was just one of those things, an almost divinely inspired design. When Bernie came back, I can't remember if it was just a drawing or if Neal had actually built the guitar, but I guess Bernie was pissed. He was like, "That's the last time anybody does anything while I'm not here!" He eventually cooled off and realized, hey, this thing is really cool, and people might like it. And it went on to be the bestselling B.C. Rich design of all time.
>
> — Zach Gunter, CEO, Neal Moser Guitars

As we have seen with other guitar companies, a growth in popularity and demand comes with a need to satisfy customers looking for instruments with differing options at various price points. By 1980, the Son of a Rich (a bolt-on Bich), the Nighthawk (a bolt-on Eagle), and the Phoenix (a bolt-on Mockingbird) were introduced. Strat-like tremolo systems also made an appearance, where previously hard-tail bridges had been standard issue on all models.

The '80s also brought forth the guitar that would truly usher in B.C. Rich's heavy-metal era. The pointier-than-thou Warlock model came on like thunder in 1981, the same year the swerving, curvy, Wave design was introduced. Where the Wave functioned as a slimmer and somewhat swooshier evolution of the Eagle, the Warlock truly was its own beast. (Not to be confused with the Beast model, the Warlock's evolutionary cousin, designed in the '90s by Brian Hoffman of the death-metal band Deicide.) The Warlock was a resurrection of a 1969 design that Bernie Rico had conceived at a drafting table.

> This was the only guitar I ever designed at a drafting table, using straight-edges and French curves. It was lots of curves going into straight lines. At first I thought it was the ugliest guitar I'd ever designed.
>
> — Bernie Rico (B.C. Rich 2008 catalog.)

> Be among the first to come under the spell of the new B.C. Rich.
>
> Designed by master guitar builder Bernie Rico the Warlock is a departure for B.C. Rich, an angular shaped mahogany body bound in white, spellbinding in visual appearance yet sinfully comfortable to play. It features our 1 piece thru-the-body mahogany neck, reversed headstock with rosewood headplate and fingerboard with dot position markers. Standard is a single humbucker pickup, tremolo and simple electronics with preamp. Available in all standard and custom finishes the Warlock is a sight to behold. Let the magic of the Warlock feed your creative desire and unleash sounds previously unknown to mere mortals.
>
> The Wave, designed by Bernado C. Rich and introduced originally into the European market in 1981, turned a lot of heads. The popularity of its uniquely carved body led to its quick availability to U.S. guitarists. The Wave embodies all the qualities of a B.C. Rich guitar; uniquely hand carved body combined with the finest hardware and state-of-the-art electronics.
>
> (B.C. Rich 1981 catalog.)

The introduction of the Warlock in 1981 marked the beginning of B.C. Rich's rise to iconic status in heavy metal. Its looks owe more to the Bich than to the Seagull, Eagle, or Mockingbird, and it foregoes the graceful curves of earlier models in favor of aggressive angles. The confluence of B.C. Rich's far-out

> designs and the emerging hair metal culture of the late '70s and early '80s helped cement the brand's place in the market, with unmistakable designs, player endorsements, and appearances by several B.C. Rich guitars in the movie *This Is Spinal Tap*.
>
> (Elizabeth Hanson, "B.C. Rich Origins and Evolutions," Reverb.com)

When '80s hard rock and heavy metal fell out of favor with the onset of the '90s grunge movement, so too did the pointy guitars of that era, at least in the world of mainstream, commercial rock. It's reasonable to assume that the comedic associations of B.C. Rich guitars with Spinal Tap's hilariously poignant portrayal of dim-witted, drug-addled, herpes-ridden metal musicians did not help matters. However, over time, the lines between ridiculing parody and hilarious homage have been blurred, with many of Spinal Tap's tropes becoming a celebrated reminder of the over-the-top fun of the era.

> The wild shapes of B.C. Rich guitars also attracted the attention of the producers of *This Is Spinal Tap*. Stich put some guitars together for the production, and in so doing, unwittingly became responsible for adding a new phrase to popular music's cultural lexicon. "There was a meeting in my office to loan the guitars and basses. I was playing with a volume knob Larry DiMarzio gave me that went to 11. I showed it to them and explained why it went to 11." The producers used it in one of the movie's classic scenes, and the idiom soon became immortalized in the vernacular of guitarists and rock fans the world over.
>
> (Joe Charupakorn, *Premier Guitar*.)

The Warlock — with its jagged, beveled edges, sharp contours, off-set cutaway horns, and V-inspired notches at its base — is aptly named; it looks like it could have been conjured out of bat wings and battle axes by a wizard who saw a future informed by hair spray, leather and chains, and adolescents screaming for vengeance, shouting at devils, and worshipping metal gods in volume-soaked hockey arenas. The Warlock looks like a weapon, an amulet for the modern-day warrior with a mean strut and swagger.

> Indeed, [the Warlock] would have never been made were it not for a guitarist working at his shop by the name of Spencer Sercombe. Mr Sercombe, later of the Glam Metal band Shark Island, eventually convinced Mr Rico to put it into production in 1981, and the B.C. Rich Warlock quickly took off amongst the burgeoning heavy metal community. Its outlandish, outrageous and ostentatious design was not a weakness or a blight but instead was its selling point, and musicians such as Lita Ford, C.C. DeVille, Mick Mars, and later Kerry King all played B.C. Rich Warlocks at some point in their careers. Before Slash would become known for his Gold Top Gibson Les Paul, he would commonly play a B.C. Rich Warlock as well as later playing a Mockingbird. Unlike most aspects of Glam Metal, the Warlock managed to endure and many guitarists in the 2000s such as Mick Thomson of Slipknot continue to play it to this day.
>
> (Jake Blakey, Gough & Davey blog, June 2023.)

In the hands of guitarists and bassists like Craig Goldy of Dio, Nikki Sixx of Mötley Crüe, Lita Ford, Bobby Dall of Poison, Kelly Nickels of L.A. Guns, and in the early days of Guns N' Roses, even the famously Les Paul-toting Slash, the B.C. Rich Warlock represented both glamorous flash and a hint of danger. It was high-life fun in low-life society, glorious and trashy excess, rock-n-roll rebellion on a stick (or at least as big a stick as you could carry, even if you weren't planning to speak all that softly). However, when thrashed upon by players like Kerry King of Slayer, Max Cavalera of Sepultura, Dave Mustaine and Chris Poland of Megadeth, and Chuck Schuldiner of Death, B.C. Rich guitars, particularly the Warlock and Bich, could also represent something entirely different — violence, venomous political protest, and anger. These and other guitars were the tools of the new thrash, death, and black-metal movements; movements that would disparage the wimps of the Sunset Strip. In these bands, B.C. Rich guitars were weapons designed to kill hair-metal poseurs on sight. There was one group of B.C. Rich users that seemingly appealed to the glam rockers and the thrashers — or at the very least, could hang on a bill with any of them.

W.A.S.P. were an act that embodied the most extreme version of the Sunset Strip's sense of theater, with shows that involved pyrotechnics, flaming band logos, dripping raw meat, naked women tied to torture racks, and B.C. Rich guitars helping to provide the electric soundtrack to this dark theater of the mind. W.A.S.P. performed with a burning intensity that could send shivers down the spine of even the most hardened thrasher, but their highly accessible songs were reminiscent of vintage Kiss and Alice Cooper set to stun.

> I saw their first show at the Troubadour, and when the "W.A.S.P." sign with the butane and flames lit up we all got a suntan. I saw the first night they played, and, apparently, they toned it down for the second night. It was *way* too hot!
>
> — Gilby Clarke

While we will see soon enough in this book that lead-guitarist Chris Holmes would remain a faithful Jackson guitars man throughout his tenure in W.A.S.P. (and who remains so to this day), band leader Blackie Lawless (who started on bass and would switch to guitar), guitarist Randy Piper, and future bassist Johnny Rod all played B.C. Rich guitars and basses during W.A.S.P.'s commercial and artistic heyday.

> You see, how I got my endorsement with Jackson was like this. Blackie goes, "Oh, I'll get you your endorsement." So, we go out to Charvel, and Grover Jackson just about told Blackie to get fucked in a way. You know? He almost laughed at him. Because Blackie thinks he knows everything . . . [that's] the way he is, the way he presents himself. [Grover] wouldn't give him a deal. Like, he didn't *say* get the fuck out of here, he just said no. Blackie went to B.C. Rich and did get a deal with Randy Piper. B.C. Rich is a Les Paul–scale length, which is shorter, not a Strat scale length, which is longer. I like the longer Strat scales. At one point, Bernie Rico wanted it to be like Kiss. On a few of their albums, it says, "Kiss uses all Gibson." Blackie and Bernie Rico wanted W.A.S.P. to do that. In fact, in '95 when I came back to work for W.A.S.P., one of the roadies goes, "Chris, here's Bernie's number. I was out getting something for Blackie, and he wants you to call him." I didn't call him. About two weeks later, he goes, "Chris, Bernie wanted to talk to you. Why didn't

> you call him?" I said, "I don't know. It's something that I would have fucking *died* for years ago, but I don't really give a fuck about it now. I don't care." And then he's like, "Well, he promised he'd make you anything you wanted, any kind of guitar." I just said, "You tell Bernie I really appreciate it, but I can only play one [guitar], you know?"
>
> — Chris Holmes of W.A.S.P.

Through the album cycles for their self-titled debut, *The Last Command*, *Inside the Electric Circus*, *The Headless Children*, *The Crimson Idol*, and beyond, Blackie Lawless would come to be identified by his use of the custom spider-shaped Widow bass he designed (the headstock of which would be seen on future B.C. Rich models) and the Warlock electric guitar, which he used when he switched to guitar after the departure of Randy Piper for 1987's *Inside the Electric Circus* album. While Randy was only in the band up until the end of the *Last Command* tour, his strikingly original B.C. Rich custom made guitars, replete with wild airbrush finishes and sculpted protruding elements ensured that he would forever be cemented in the minds of metal fans as one of W.A.S.P.'s most important and memorable band members. According to randpiper.net, his wild custom guitars came with thematic names:

> Skull and Crossbones was a Warlock model, and was featured in the music videos for W.A.S.P. hits like "L.O.V.E. Machine" and "I Wanna Be Somebody"; the Rivet was another air-brushed Warlock, decorated with bolts and chains and used in horror film *The Dungeonmaster*; Pipes, a twisted creation made from real exhaust pipes, had built-in smoke canisters (videos of Piper performing with it during iconic shows at the Lyceum Theatre in London, U.K., and the Irvine Meadows Amphitheatre in Irvine, California are online); the Texas Longhorn Demon was made famous by MTV heavy rotation hits "Wild Child" and "Blind in Texas"; and the disturbingly realistic Stripper, wore a bustier and fishnets but little else. A Piper said on his website, "If I had my way, I'd play a different guitar for every song — one that relates specifically to that song."
>
> — RandyPiper.net

> You look at the paint jobs that became a characteristic and an identifier. Your paint job was just as important as the shape of your guitar. . . . I mean, you look at W.A.S.P. and Blackie Lawless. It wouldn't be Blackie without that really pointy guitar, and whatever [else] they had.
>
> It really became a signature of who you were, a signature of the player. I think I said that in a review once. There was a time during the '80s the guitar was just as signature as the player. You could line up 10 guitars from the players of the '80s, and you could pick out the player just by looking at the guitar.
>
> — Paul Riario

Don "Screaming" Leaming is the man who airbrushed and helped sculpt these inspired axes, and his story provides insight into how he helped turn iconic guitar shapes into stunning six-stringed canvases for his imagination.

> I met Randy Piper through B.C. Rich. I've always been an airbrush artist ever since I was 11 years, 12 years old. My dad was a painter, and I worked in a paint shop with him. I saw those '70s vans and said, "I have to paint some of those." So I got to doing airbrush work. And, then I worked in a paint store, and I bought my first airbrush. I just started doing silhouettes, and then I'd do silhouettes with a little bit more shape to them, until I worked my way into doing portraits and stuff like that.
>
> I was in a band back in the late '70s. I don't know if you know what a disco destruction is? We were playing rock and roll, and we hated disco. Disco destruction is when you play a disco record on a record player and then you smash it with a guitar. We were playing some party and somebody was slipping us some drugs that we didn't know about. And the party kinda went to hell in a hand basket. The bass player picked up my 1964 Gibson SG with a Bigsby whammy on it and threw it against the wall because he thought it was the disco destruction guitar. About the time it hit the wall, he goes, "Oh, shit. Wrong guitar." I tried fixing it, but those Gibson's, you know, once the necks are broken, they're broken.

So, anyway, I started building. What I did is I took the entire guitar apart and I go, "Oh, this is just a piece of wood with some routing and some holes drilled in it." You know? I said, "I can do this." I started buying a couple necks from old beat guitars and built them new bodies and build them onto the necks. And then, the other guitar player and I decided we're gonna go to Hollywood to make it big. So, we bought this old ratty van and drove it all the way down there from Portland, Oregon.

I had seen B.C. Rich guitars and thought, "Oh, those are some pretty cool shapes. I need to go talk to them about a job or something while I'm down here." I went in there and Spencer Sercombe was the general manager at the time, and I talked to him. He saw some of my work and said, "Well, you know, we got a couple of guitars for you to paint in a few months if you can make it down here." I had to go back to Oregon because I was broke. We sold the van, I flew home, and my partner stayed down there.

I ended up going back to B.C. Rich. I flew down and painted three guitars. I did one of the Warlocks. I did a flying V for Paul Stanley, it was just zebra stripes. It wasn't a B.C. Rich V, it was a Hamer V. Paul was endorsed by B.C. Rich at the time, I believe, but he had this old Hamer V and he wanted zebra stripes on it. If somebody famous like Paul Stanley brought a guitar in, you're gonna do what he asks.

I also did a Bich with some stars and galaxies on it. That's how I got working with B.C. Rich. Bernie Rico was there, and Neal Moser was working there at the same time. Randy Piper was endorsed by B.C. Rich, so he came in and said, "I have some ideas for some crazy guitars." He says, "I used to have this old Strat that had bolts on it, and I want to do an airbrush job on a Warlock with rivets and bolts." That was the first guitar we did together.

And then I did a skull and crossbones guitar, and then we started sculpting guitars. We did the Pipes Guitar, the [Texas Longhorn] Demon Guitar, and the Stripper Guitar, all sculpted. I had a friend, Scott Child, who was a wood sculptor, and he

> carved and sculpted the pipe guitar and the naked lady guitar, the Stripper Guitar. I watched how he did it, and after that I said, "Hey, friend, I appreciate you, but I know how to do it now, so I'm gonna start doing it from now on." [*laughs*]
>
> — Don "Screaming" Leaming

Don proved himself to be very successful at interpreting what the various artists he was working with were trying to convey with the artwork on their instruments.

> When [Randy and Blackie Lawless] told me what they want, I thought, "There's gotta be other bands out there that like the same stuff." So, I kept my art in that vein, as I was presenting it to other artists. I did a guitar for Rick Derringer, who designed the Stealth guitar, and I painted one of those with floating TVs in space, and he liked it, so they gave it to him. I did the back of a neck for Dave Mustaine of Megadeth on one of his Bich guitars when he was endorsed by B.C. Rich. David Ellefson in Megadeth, he had a Mockingbird bass that was painted like a fighter jet with the teeth and some eyeballs. I did a Geezer Butler bass. The one that he played at Live Aid. He only played it once, it was an Ironbird, and he hurt his hand on one of the points, so he said he'd never play it again. [*laughs*] I did it in yellow first, and then just as I was about to finish it, I got a phone call from Geezer, and he says, "I want it in black." So, I had to repaint it.
>
> Kiss was doing a giveaway. I did five different Mockingbird-model giveaway guitars with the Kiss logo. I did one with zebra stripes and one with tiger stripes. I'd fade the color from the top to the bottom, stars and rainbow colors, I did two of them like that. And I'd go, okay, those are getting boring. So, I did a rivet and bolt Kiss logo.
>
> — Don "Screaming" Leaming

Sometimes, in the name of artist relations, Don would be called upon to apply his artistic talents to other areas of work.

> I painted the Blackie Lawless saw-blade codpiece that says "I Fuck Like a Beast." That's my work. I did also a couple of them that didn't have saw blades on them. Here's a funny story. Blackie brought the codpiece in and wanted to get it painted with, kind of a zebra or a tiger coloring on it. Bernie called me up in the office and says, "I got a job for you." And I walked in there and Bernie's wearing the codpiece on his head!
>
> And I tell him, "Man, it doesn't go on your head, it goes down between your legs!" [*laughs*] That was funny. We had a good laugh about that. I did two sets of shin guards for Chris Holmes. One pair that he wore on stage [to get] trashed, and another that had like skull-and-cross bones on the knee part of it for photo shoots.
>
> Once I did that rivet bolt Warlock for Randy Piper, Bernie saw it and he goes, you know, we have a guitar called the Ironbird that we need to do rivets on.
>
> — Don "Screaming" Leaming

The Ironbird was introduced in 1983, the same year as the Rick Derringer–designed Stealth, and was created by Bernie's son Joey Rico. It could be argued that it was B.C. Rich's first instrument intentionally designed for the heavy metal scene. The Ironbird became a favorite among extreme metal guitarists like Chuck Schuldiner of Death and Trey Azagthoth of Morbid Angel, but was also a favorite in the arsenal of less heavy but equally rocking sonic fare like King Kobra, Kiss, Shotgun Messiah, and Canada's Brighton Rock.

> When we first got our record deal with Warner back in '85, I had just purchased a B.C. Rich Ironbird. It was one of the first in Canada, and it's one of the rarer ones, because it's one piece. Ninety-nine percent of the time, if you find an Ironbird, [it usually has] bolt-on necks and stuff like that. I stumbled upon it at Steve's Music in Toronto. I said, "What the hell is this?" I always loved the Mockingbird, but that was pretty out of my price range at the time. When I saw the Ironbird, [I said,] "I have to have it, that's going to be the guitar I'm known for." I said, "You gotta hold it for me," and they said, "First come, first

> serve." Shit, I live in Niagara Falls! The next day, I drove back up to Toronto with my drummer and bought it on the spot. It was fifteen hundred dollars, which was a lot of money back then. This was one of the first ones, if not the first one, that was available in Canada. 0057 is the serial number on it. I still have it. If you watch our very first video, "We Came to Rock," that's the guitar I'm playing. Because it was one of a kind, when I would play places, people would really make a big deal about the guitar because nobody had seen one like that yet. I wanted to be known as the guy with the B.C. Rich, because it was a one-of-a-kind guitar, and I loved the way it looked.
>
> — Greg Fraser, Brighton Rock

> I did explore the Ironbird model, first ordering one slightly larger in a custom red design. I posed with it, but soon realized it was too large. I had them resize it, closer to their stock shape, but I asked for a custom design, a blue, black, and silver graphic. It was featured on the Asylum Tour.
>
> — Bruce Kulick, Kiss

Don Leaming helped make his name around the Hollywood scene with his airbrush work on the Ironbird.

> I started doing rivets on Ironbirds. And I would go to shows around Hollywood and stuff where people were playing that guitar, and they would come up to me and go, "You know, I had to get really close to that guitar to find out that it was airbrushed because I thought it was real metal with real rivets in it." I get the same thing with the Pipes Guitar from Randy Piper. People ask me how I wrap the metal around the wood. I say, I didn't, I airbrushed it. It's all sculpted. That was the first sculpting guitar we did.
>
> I drew up five different designs of bent pipes, you know, and how they would fit on and where the pickup would be in the bridge and all that. And, you know, one of them actually

said "W.A.S.P." in bent pipes. What's funny is that I drew up all those, and then for the very last one I drew up, I said, "I'm just gonna do something abstract, that doesn't look like anything." And that's the one he happened to like, so we just added one other pipe coming out off the bottom of it.

Were there any tonal considerations when creating artwork for these guitars?

Well, the pickup and the bridge are pretty much in the same place on every guitar I do. When I do artwork on a guitar, it's normally a single pickup guitar, so there's a lot more room. If you look at all those sculpted guitars, they're pretty much all the same. Now and again, they might have two pickups in there if they really wanted to get different sounds out of it. But for the most part, the Pipes Guitar and the [Texas Longhorn] Demon Guitar, and the Stripper Guitar were all just single pickup guitars with one volume knob and that's it.

And how did these ornate guitars sound?

Well, they sound good because, we were using the same kind of wood that they use for all their other guitars, the mahogany. I started using mahogany for all my sculpted stuff because, number one, it had a nice even grain, and it wasn't splitting on me like orange padauk would. I like doing things out of that, but when you're using a hammer and a chisel, sometimes it will split, you know, and you get slivers. But the mahogany, it's a nice even grain wood and I could sculpt it without getting slivers and having it break off.

And that's the first the reason why I used mahogany. B.C. Rich used it for their guitars, and that's a good tone wood, so let's just use that. And for the most part, they were all neck throughs. That's where your sound comes from, the strings and the neck going all the way through the body. So, you know,

> you've got all that tone wood there under the pickup and the bridge and everything else. And the wings are also made out of mahogany for the most part. You've got all that tone wood, and I figured, if it's good enough for them, it's good enough for me.

Don's run at B.C. Rich ended in the spring of 1985, another casualty of the cost-saving measures and tactics involved in offshore mass-production guitar building. But his legacy endured, and would ultimately see him return to working on iconic B.C. Rich shapes with Neal Moser Guitars.

> From '81 through to, I don't know, February, March, April of '85. I guess they credit me with starting to airbrush stuff on guitars. I don't really know if I started it or not. I know that that's what I wanted to do, and so I just ran with it. I think I was one of the first people to do sculpted guitars. I guess the Jackson 5 had some guitars that looked like a baseball glove and other things that might have preceded my stuff, but I wasn't aware of them at the time. I wasn't inspired by them. I did my own thing, and then I saw these things later on.
>
> I quit B.C. Rich because I had a run-in with the general manager at the time. That's not Spencer Sercombe. It was a new guy. I'm not gonna mention his name. He promised me that if I lowered my price on the Rivet Guitar, he'd have a hundred of them for me to do. And that just never came about. After I had lowered my price, I said, "Look, you're not getting me all these guitars. [He said,] "They're coming in. They're gonna be in next week, they're coming from Japan." And he kept saying that, kept saying that, kept saying that. I went and talked to Bernie, and Bernie said, "I have to go along with what my general manager says," and I said, "Okay, then I'm out of here. I just did, like, 20 guitars at the lower price, and if you're not gonna have these other guitars for me, I wanna get paid the full price for all those 20 guitars I just painted for you." And the general manager goes, "No. I'm not gonna do that." "Look, you're ripping me off, so I'm out of here."
>
> — Don "Screaming" Leaming

Of course, Bernie was aware of the trends that were happening with companies like Jackson/Charvel and Kramer, and he saw the success that they were having with superstrat model guitars. The ST model was the B.C. Rich solution and was released in 1985. In 1987, two former employees of the original San Dimas era of Jackson/Charvel, graphic artist and luthier Dan Lawrence and master builder Glenn Matejzel (who now work together at boutique company GMP Guitars), came over to the join B.C. Rich, now working out of a factory in El Monte, California, and designed a refinement of the ST that would come to be known as the Gunslinger. Dan's work as a custom graphics artist has graced instruments belonging to an endless list of guitar luminaries, including C.C. DeVille, Mark Kendall, Paul Stanley, Vinnie Vincent, Steve Vai, Michael Sweet, and Bruce Kulick.

> By 1987, Bernie Rico knew that the EVH Floyd Rose craze was not going away. He needed to get competitive. I loaned him my 1963 Fender neck from the Meat Loaf days since he was asking about my preferred choice of neck shape. I don't think he ever got it as close as I hoped but the ST III was born. Sadly, I never got that neck back, I loaned it because it needed a new rosewood fingerboard! I posed with his new creation, a ST III model in a Ferrari red color. It looked really cool; a modified superstrat with a new headstock design, a departure from his neck-through instruments. Even though I was loving my ESP M-1 models, this ST III had a race car vibe, and then I had a thought. Since my main outfit for the Crazy Nights Tour and video was a radioactive suit why not coordinate the ST III guitar with the outfit? The luthiers at B.C. Rich in California filled the two pickup holes since I only wanted one humbucker, and then added the radioactive symbols across the body as I requested. The Radioactive B.C. Rich was born! Paul Stanley got involved through the years with Bernie's guitars, and at times we both did some events to support the B.C. Rich line. But ultimately, the company never kept the popularity of the previous years.
>
> — Bruce Kulick

The offshoring of B.C. Rich electric guitars began in 1981 as a way to fend off the knock-off guitars being made by companies like Aria overseas. B.C. Rich's NJ (Nagoya, Japan) series was an attempt to import high-quality Japanese guitars into America initially under the B.C. Rico moniker in an attempt to differentiate them from the U.S. built B.C. Rich models. However, a dispute with the reed maker Rico Reeds over market confusion resulted in B.C. Rich reverting to its original name. Initially, the NJ series was built in Japan and was respected for its high standards of craftsmanship at a midlevel price.

The early NJ guitars sought to retain features of their American counterparts, such as neck-through construction, high-output pickups, and, of course, the classic pointy shapes, but in the mid-1980s, a changing of the guard saw some key players leave the company (Stich in '84, Moser in '85) and by 1986 production of the NJ series had moved to Cort Guitars' factories in Korea and China. A marketing agreement with New Jersey–based Class Axe began with the importing, marketing, and distribution of import B.C. Rich guitars, and by 1989 Class Axe had licensed the B.C Rich name and assumed control. This saw a proliferation of cheap B.C. Rich guitars released under the Platinum, Rave, and Bronze series names. While the guitars looked stunning, with bright, vibrant finishes that made those classic B.C. Rich shapes pop, reports of bodies made of layered plywood and generic lumber, poor workmanship, and inferior hardware damaged the reputation of a company that had started off making high-quality instruments in the truest sense of the handmade tradition. There is no denying, however, that these cost-cutting measures did get the guitars in the hands of young budget-conscious players.

Bernie Rico went on to form Mason Bernard guitars, with high-profile players like Mitch Perry and Tony MacAlpine signing on as endorsees. Bernie ended up regaining ownership of the company in 1993, and tried to bring the company back up to a higher standard of quality and reputation. Bernie died on December 3, 1999, and his son, also named Bernie, took over the company and turned it over to the Hanser Music Group in 2001.

B.C. Rich would go on to design and bring to market many more wild shapes, including the Virgin, the Virgo, the Draco, the Warbeast, and Kerry King's signature V series guitars, ever pointier instruments geared towards a new breed of extreme metal player. While some of these models go beyond my appetite for pointiness, they speak to a different generation of players and are an important part of the company's legacy.

For this book, I spoke with two men who are endeavoring to not only capture the glory days of B.C. Rich, but also to take Bernie Rico's vision to new places. In 2025, Bill Xavier is the CEO of B.C. Rich Guitars, and today, the company endeavors to honor its classic design legacy while also moving forward with innovations that can keep pace with the demands of today's highly developed shred community.

> Today, we're making all of the old shapes and we consider that to be the Legacy series, which really pays tribute to anything that we did from '69 to the late '80s. We're doing the Mockingbird. We're doing the Eagles again. We're doing the Warlock, obviously.
>
> — Bill Xavier

The current demand for these classic model shapes has been fueled by the use of a Warlock in the *Stranger Things* TV series. In the finale of season 4, Eddie Munson, a high-school headbanging outsider becomes a hero as he shreds along with Metallica's "Master of Puppets" in the Upside Down. This iconic scene made pointy guitars relevant with a whole new generation of kids in much the same way as the show made '80s music like Kate Bush's "Running Up That Hill" a smash hit again, almost 40 years after its initial release.

> We had huge success with *Stranger Things* — that was massive for the brand. That one placement probably [will keep] us relevant for the next decade or two. It's the gift that keeps on giving.
>
> We have the Extreme series, which was made for the young shredder kids who are on Instagram, because the Instagram kids are the guitar heroes of today. Then we have the Prophecy series which is us doing whatever we want to do. We just keep experimenting with different things, like different pickup configurations.
>
> We're doing a series of guitars that are true handmade, made by Moser. Those guitars are amazing. The made-in-America

thing is so important to us, so we have that happening as well. We're fighting the good fight, like all the other good guitar companies are.

— Bill Xavier

I asked Bill what the current B.C. Rich mission statement was.

Back in the day [the mission statement] was "Shapes that rock." I worked with B.C. Rich from 2006 to 2016. In 2020 became a partner and part owner of the company, which doesn't give me license to say I know it all because I definitely don't; there are people out there that have forgotten more than I know about B.C. Rich. For me personally, my mantra is "commitment to excellence." I'm stealing a tagline from football, the [Las Vegas] Raiders. We've been reinventing, which, by definition, is to change something so much that it appears entirely new.

When I say commitment to excellence, I think that one of the things that didn't work for B.C. Rich was that there was a period of time when the company was just mass producing $199, $299, $399, Chinese-made guitars. There's still money to be had in that business, but when we acquired B.C. Rich from the Hansers [Hanser Music Group], we drew a line in the sand and said we are no longer going to have cheap guitars. Our cheapest guitar now is $899, and that's a Gunslinger. One of the only bolt-ons we make. Everything else is neck through body. Our starting point really for a guitar is $1200 to $1300 for an end user, so we have basically disenfranchised people that wanted to buy a cheap B.C. Rich for $199.

I think that it's fair to say that we've inspired. There's some element of B.C. Rich DNA in other "shape" guitars. In a B.C. Rich catalog I did one year, we had a picture of Kerry King from Slayer playing in front of a humongous crowd, and it was just the back of him. There was no denying that he was playing a B.C. Rich.

— Bill Xavier

Zach Gunter is the current CEO of Neal Moser Guitars, a custom guitar company that also serves as the current B.C. Rich custom shop. As a young shredder and guitar collector, Zach fell under the pointy spell of Neal Moser's work, before and after his time with B.C. Rich, in such a deep way that it led him to apply his entrepreneurial skill set to buy the company that Neal had been running himself. He kept the legendary luthier on board, ensuring that the high-quality legacy of Neal's work with B.C Rich, and beyond, carries on into the future.

> I had been doing the Gunter Collection, which was my business before this, and that really just started out as my guitar collection. I started playing when I was 13 and just got obsessed with it, and I started collecting pretty hardcore, like, five, six years ago. Ever since I was a kid, I always loved B.C. Rich, and through doing research on that, I discovered Neal Moser. And once I discovered Moser's website, you know, probably back in 2004 or something like that, that was it for me. I was like, "Those are the coolest guitars I've ever seen." That was back when Neal was building them all himself.
>
> You know, it was basically a one-man operation. And there were very, very few of these things out there in the world and even fewer of them out in the wild. Like, you just never saw a Moser for sale. It was, like, custom order only — they were not in dealers or anything like that.
>
> So, I never had a chance to even play a Moser. I just rolled over pictures of them online and, you know, dreamed about one day owning one.
>
> And then when I started collecting, I got the fourth 10-string Bich that Neal made after he started Moser. They called it Moser Custom Shop back then. It's got black limba wings and ebony stringers, maple neck. I think he actually built it for the NAMM show back in, like, 2006.
>
> And, basically, it just changed my view of guitars. Up until that point, I've collected Gibsons and Fenders and ESPs and Jacksons. I've always been a metalhead too. I've owned a bunch

of high-end custom-shop stuff from every metal guitar brand. But once I played this guitar, it was just so different. It's got a big chunky neck, and it doesn't have giant jumbo frets.

And there's just a lot of the equation that on paper — as a heavy metal guy and a guy that likes to play Yngwie kind of stuff — you wouldn't think it would be the right guitar for me. But when I played it, I was like, "This is the best playing guitar I've ever picked up."

I just got obsessed with the brand at that point. And I started collecting. Anytime I could find a used Moser somewhere, I bought it. And what I noticed was every single one of them did not disappoint. They were all just perfect. They are as close to perfect as a guitar can be.

There's no such thing as a perfect guitar.

Compared to any of the competitors, Jackson, ESP, all that kind of stuff, it was just a cut above. I'm a car guy too, I always thought of it like this: B.C. Rich is sort of like Lamborghini, and then Moser is more like Pagani or Bugatti. It's just that next tier. Once I collected a few of those, I fell in love with them, and I almost stopped collecting other brands at that point.

I was just trying to find Mosers. So much has happened in the last few years, I have trouble remembering exactly how it happened. I've always been a businessman; at this point I qualify as a serial entrepreneur.

I've started companies, I've sold companies, I've bought companies. Guitar was always like a hobby, really. But I have a tendency to turn hobbies into businesses because it keeps life fun. I had sold one of my other businesses totally unrelated to music, and I had all this money. I was like, "Alright. What's next?" You know, what am I gonna do? I thought it would be fun to start a guitar company and build guitars. It just seemed like a fun idea, but kind of a pipe dream, but then I got thinking. Maybe I should just try to buy an established brand.

I got in touch with Neal, I think it was maybe through Facebook, because he's very active on Facebook. And I said,

> "Hey, I'd like to chat with you about your business." And he said, "Yeah. Sure."
>
> So, I called him one day and said, "Hey, man, big fan, love your work. Every guitar I've ever played that you built has been just amazing. I think your brand has a lot of potential. Would you be interested in selling your business, full stop?"
>
> I'm sweating bullets because I don't know this guy. I don't know if he's gonna tell me to go fuck myself, get offended, or whatever. There was a moment of silence, and then he said, "I'm still listening." We had a great conversation, and the rest is history at this point.
>
> — Zach Gunter, CEO, Neal Moser Guitar

While I will always feel some regret for not playing B.C. Rich in my gig with a pop superstar, I will always be grateful to Ted Burger, Bill Xavier, and everyone at the company for the support and kindness they showed me over the years. B.C. Rich was with me on my first arena shows, during my first fully fledged American tour, and in my hands in my first appearances in *Guitar World*, *Guitar Player*, and *Hit Parader* magazines. The pointy guitars of my dreams were with me when my rock-n-roll dreams came true, and they still hold a treasured place in my guitar collection. From Joe Perry, Mick Mars, and C.C. DeVille to Pete Friesen and Tracii Guns, B.C. Rich and the players who rocked them loom large in the pointy-guitar hall of fame that resides in my heavy-metal heart.

CHAPTER 10

KRAMER AND ESP GUITARS – THE WINDS OF CHANGE

Like fingers on a fretboard, a theme that has been running up and down this book is how ideas from the past are brought into the future with renewed vision. For guitar makers, that means building on the traditions of the classic luthiers who preceded them and bringing models to market in ways that honor the best of what has come before while feeding the appetites of the present and anticipating the curiosities of the future.

For artists who have experienced success, there is a similar challenge to stay current and contemporary while also (hopefully) retaining your core audience; to find new fans to replace those who have moved on.

I'm a lover of the theater and pageantry of arena rock, which has been deeply influenced by both the music and stagecraft of Alice Cooper and Kiss. It's generally accepted that both of these acts released their most highly regarded work in their '70s heyday, even though their legends would grow as they performed for many decades to follow.

While Alice arguably holds the upper hand in terms of critical recognition, Kiss's work in the '70s has profoundly influenced countless numbers of aspiring players in multiple genres. When Gene Simmons and Paul Stanley put their makeup back on in 1996 for a reunion tour with original members Ace Frehley and Peter Criss, Kiss became cool again, and so long as that makeup stayed on, their popularity endured. However, there was a time when the band deemed the makeup to be a creative anchor that dragged the band down into the abyss of faded glory. New upstarts like Mötley Crüe and Ratt may have taken their stadium rock cues from the elders in Kiss, but they were connecting in a meaner, leaner, more street-savvy way that was resonating with '80s kids.

Kiss had to adapt in the '80s, and they did so in a way that is finally beginning to receive its due appreciation. They removed their makeup and brought in new guitarists who could compete in the decade of shred, but they also maintained the traditions of classic songcraft that built the Kiss brand.

When we think of creative high points, original Alice Cooper group efforts like *Love It to Death*, *Killer*, and the formidable *Billion Dollar Babies* come to mind, as do Alice's solo efforts with *Welcome to My Nightmare*, *Goes to Hell*, and *From the Inside*. With the albums that followed, we start to see a commercial and artistic decline that seems to dovetail with Alice's now well-documented battle with addiction. Regardless, '70s classic tracks like "Eighteen," "Under My Wheels," "Be My Lover," "No More Mr. Nice Guy," "Elected," "Only Women Bleed," and "I Never Cry" have firmly established Alice Cooper, the band and the man, as major contributors to the great rock-n-roll songbook. It would take a few flops, a stint in rehab, and a redirection of his addictive personality into the world of golf for Alice Cooper to find his commercial footing again in the mid-1980s.

For Kiss, appreciation for their early albums like the self-titled debut, *Hotter than Hell*, and *Dressed to Kill*, was dramatically increased with the release of *Kiss Alive!*, which captured the band's bombastic in-concert experience on wax, bringing classic songs from their first three albums like "Deuce," "Strutter," "Black Diamond," "Firehouse," and perennial party classic "Rock and Roll All Nite" to life in a way that the arguably sterile production on their previous studio releases had not. Following up with classic LPs like *Destroyer*, *Love Gun*, and *Rock and Roll Over* and *Dynasty* saw the band riding high until they ultimately became victims of their own success, saturating the market with all manner of merchandising propaganda, and forsaking their previous rock-n-roll edge for attempts at power pop (*Unmasked*) and progressive concept rock (*Music from "The Elder"*) that left fans cold.

A reputable attempt at a hard-rocking return with *Creatures of the Night* still wasn't enough to keep the commercial fires burning, and inner turmoil saw the departure of founding members Peter Criss and Ace Frehley. An attempt to carry on with new members Eric Carr and Vinnie Vincent complete with new makeup identities initially stalled, and dramatic steps needed to be taken if Kiss was going to continue being competitive in the changing sonic landscape that was the 1980s.

After years of listening, I'd be hard pressed to disagree with the critical assessment that the '70s material represents the best years for both acts. I consider the work that Alice and Kiss did with producer Bob Ezrin on both *Billion Dollar Babies* and *Destroyer* to be the ultimate commercial and artistic realization of both bands' larger than life concepts. That being said, my introduction to both of these bands came in the '80s, and my love affair with both Alice Cooper and Kiss started in that decade.

Kane Roberts was the guitarist chosen to be Alice Cooper's song writing partner and creative foil on 1986's *Constrictor* and 1987's *Raise Your Fist and Yell* albums. He also helped Alice mount his Nightmare Returns comeback tour in 1986. As Alice's music director for the tour, Kane is the architect of the sound that defined Alice's return to hard rock, a deft blend of the classic arrangements of Alice's '70s heyday and the '80s heavy-metal tones and attack that were capturing young audiences at the time. To this day, an Alice Cooper concert reflects Kane's influence; he was able to honor Alice's past, while also bringing it into the future with a heavier, guitar-forward approach.

The story of how Kane got on Alice's radar in the first place harkens back to a special time when the music business was a thriving world of possibility and opportunity, and speaks to the power of chemistry.

> I was with a publishing company at the time called Screen Gems, and I was doing demos all the time. Somebody said, "You got any action?" and I said, "No, not really." [*laughs*] And they said, "Are you sending your demos anywhere?" So, I started sending them out, and this guy named Don Paccione worked there, and he sent my tape to Bob Ezrin, who was looking for a writing partner for Alice. They'd gone through a few of them, but one of the things they were very sensitive about was whether or not they partied, they drank, or they smoked weed, or [how they were] attitude-wise. Alice, he's got an evil sense of humor, you know, a very intense guy, but he's also very sweet. Ezrin called

> me to New York, and I go there and I'm sitting down in front of him and, he's got this big chair and this big, black mahogany desk. Behind him is a big picture window, you know, with Manhattan in the background. And, you know, I swear he gave me a lawn chair. [*laughs*] I was, like, looking up at the Wizard of Oz, you know? [*laughs*]
>
> And he said, "Kane, I believe you're one half of a great writing partner." So, you know, I felt like I was meeting with the drill sergeant at first. We went back into the room, where the posse was. It was Ezrin; Shep Gordon [Alice Cooper's manager] was there. There were other people, all kind of intense guys, and Alice. Within five minutes, Alice and I were best friends. Didn't make any sense. And they noticed. So that day, Alice and I went to Upstate New York to a studio and worked a little bit. The working relationship seemed easy, and then everything just, you know, rolled out from there.
>
> — Kane Roberts of Alice Cooper

The Nightmare Returns Tour and resulting concert video, combined with the anthemic and powerful songs from *Constrictor* and *Raise Your Fist and Yell*, set the stage for Alice's smash-hit *Trash* album (to which Kane also contributed) in 1989. With hits like "Poison" and "House of Fire," a star-studded roster of guest artists, including Jon Bon Jovi, members of Aerosmith, songwriting from Joan Jett, Toto's Steve Lukather, and the melodic firepower of superstrat-wielding session ace John McCurry, helped *Trash* set the course that Alice follows to this day, as he continues to make well-regarded records and pack large concert venues.

Kane Roberts's talents as a fleet-fingered and inventive lead guitarist and songwriter with a penchant for uber-catchy rock riffs were enhanced by an imposing visual presence. With his muscle-bound physique, Gold's Gym cut-off t-shirts, and custom-made machine-gun flame-throwing guitar, he evoked Sylvester Stallone's character in the hit Rambo movies, a franchise of flicks that left so many teenage boys in the '80s longing to be a fugitive from the law.

Kane's look was the perfect foil to Alice's larger than life aura. Seeing Alice the man become Alice the stage performer is a transformative phenomenon unlike anything I have ever experienced. When my band Crash Kelly supported Alice Cooper on a tour in 2006, I can remember the distinctly terrifying experience of having the man pass me in the arena hallway on the way to the stage in full costume and makeup, pinning me to the wall with the intensity of his pre-show presence. The humble, funny, kind, and generous man who we'd seen earlier in the day at catering had now been replaced with a dark, all powerful, villain from another dimension.

According to Kane, my reaction was not surprising.

> There were times on tour where it became almost like a culture of violence on stage. Now, I'm not talking about for real, or that it was promoting anything like that. But I would play some heavy chord, and turn and look at [Alice] and go, "That's not the same guy that I was looking at literally 20 seconds ago." He does get fully engaged. It's just really intense, a sort of intensity controlled the moment. I don't care how big the crowd was.
>
> Our first big show was at Joe Louis Arena [in Detroit]. We'd done maybe two before that, little venues to sort of warm up. It was New Year's Eve, and it was broadcast on MTV. It's a sold-out Joe Louis Arena. The band, [which included future Winger frontman, Kip Winger, on bass], we're all guys who had never done any of this stuff before. There wasn't one member that had done anything like this, okay? The only guy was Alice. So, we're kinda hyperventilating in the back. Alice sings the first lines of "Welcome to My Nightmare," and the crowd explodes. During the strains of the keyboard intro, because the whole point was to make it sound like the classic Alice and then to just sort of bust it apart, we all climb up on stage, still nervous. Alice then kicks this gate down and comes out, and all the nerves went away because he just commanded the audience in every moment, and you just get pulled along by this expert beast of a musician. It's kinda crazy.

Kane also shared one funny story (depending on how dark your sense of humor is, I suppose) about the one time where the theater of the mind, which Alice was such a masterful purveyor of, didn't have quite the effect that was intended.

> Alice, was always 100 percent into it, and if you watch him, you know, he's really delivering it. It didn't always go the way it was planned. There was a show in Italy, during the *Raise Your Fist and Yell* tour, a pretty big venue. There were a lot of people on the floor in front of us, in the house. There's a song [we performed] called "Gail" where a prostitute walks out during the performance — it's part of the drama. And he's singing the song, and then he goes up behind the girl. And the music has to be the backdrop for this soundtrack. And he's got this giant knife. And every place that we went, he would go up to her like he was going to stab her and then wouldn't do it, and he'd look at the audience and go, "Should I?" and the crowd would explode.
>
> In Italy, he holds the knife over this really hot girl, and then he looks at the audience, and they go, they're like, "No, don't do it!" So, he tries it again, and it's louder this time: "NO!" [*laughs*]
>
> So finally, the whole thing is he has this knife that shoots blood, cuts her throat, and a riot breaks out! And guys are, like, running on stage. One crew guy pushes some guy off the stage. The guy grabs his shirt and pulls him into the crowd. There are all these fists going everywhere.
>
> Unbelievable. I was such a mental case there. I went to the edge of the stage because the energy just really caught me and guys were grabbing my legs and everything. I mean, not romantically. [*laughs*] People were freaking out. I just thought it was interesting because it's the only time that ever happened where the crowd went antithetical to what his intended purpose was. I thought it was kinda interesting. [*laughs*]

Seeing that Joe Louis show on MuchMusic here in Canada was my introduction to the music of Alice Cooper. With ears trained and raised on the guitar tones that were happening at the time, Kane's playing and approach was like a gateway for me to understand and appreciate the brilliance of Alice's music. Of course, years later, I would learn to love and cherish the brilliant sounds and playing on those classic early albums. But at the time, I craved the high-octane energy that was coming from the heavily distorted amplifiers and pointy guitars that Kane was wielding onstage.

Kane was an Alice Cooper fan in the '70s and also a contemporary of the hot heavy metal and hard rock sound of the '80s, with both facets informing the music he wrote with Alice.

> Now there's obviously a "job" aspect in working with Alice Cooper, it just never *felt* like work. The job aspect of it was to conceptualize where he was in this moment of history, you know, with his own timeline, and then what's been going on with Van Halen, Ozzy, and these massive powerhouses. I said to him, "You don't wanna come back like you just survived rehab. You gotta come back like this sort of nuclear version of yourself. You don't wanna be an oldies-but-goodies band. That's not the way. Even if you're doing the older stuff, we have to sort of remodel it." And he was 100 percent into it, the *heaviness* of it. And one of the reasons was he knew he could do it live — "Welcome to My Nightmare" with the heavy chords I put in there. I think that's one of the reasons why it worked and why we worked together so well. Bob Ezrin [legendary producer of Kiss, Alice Cooper, Pink Floyd] was there for a couple of the writing sessions to see what this kid's gonna do with Alice or whatever. And then he left, and Shep [Gordon, Alice Cooper's manager] said, "Just write." They flew us around the United States so we could write in different cities and they even flew us to sit down and do some playing with [original Alice Cooper band members] Neal [Smith] and Dennis [Dunaway], which I thought was really cool. They were such rock stars. You look at pictures of Neal back in the day, or Dennis with the bass down to his ankles. It's just all iconic stuff. And, you know, you strive to do that, but when you're right there in front of the real deals, it's humbling. But I think it really does inspire you to be a better player.
>
> I wasn't a professional musician until after the first Alice tour. I caught the jet stream.

Kane's reverence for the work of the original Alice Cooper band has clearly informed the authenticity in his own contributions to the Alice legend. It's my belief that Kane's refinement of the rockier, riffier elements of those early classics were key to making the Alice Cooper concept work in the '80s and beyond. As much as I now appreciate the more psychedelic, experimental side of albums like *Love It to Death* and *Killer*, I would not have been as receptive to these qualities as a young fan weaned on Ratt and Mötley Crüe. That being said, Kane's playing, a result of studies in jazz and classical music, also has a sophistication and diversity that allowed him to be able to interpret the more evolved musical dynamics in Alice Cooper's diverse catalog.

> My playing is greatly influenced by all sorts [of music]. If you listen to my solos, they don't sound like anybody else. My experience, as a kid growing up, was Jimmy Page, Led Zeppelin, and all that stuff. But then, you know, I studied jazz and there were certain musicians I got obsessed with and I learned what they were doing, so it just became sort of an expansive kind of thing. I remember I was at this seminar with this Black jazz drummer named Art Blakey and somebody said, "How do you make it in the music industry?" And he said, "You have to have faith." Faith that if you work hard enough and you get a level of greatness, the world will beat a path to your door. I'm not saying I'm great. I'm saying there's nobody else on the planet that woulda hired me but Alice Cooper. This big muscle guy with the guitar — this is not gonna happen. [*laughs*] And he found me somehow.
>
> The funny side to the story is that I thought I was the shit on the guitar. [*laughs*] I was in Boston just, like, chewing everybody up, you know. There are some great players there. I'm just saying, I felt like I was one of the absolute best. And I came to California, and there's thousands of guitar players that were just so fucking amazing. [*laughs*] It was a humbling experience. But then right away, you just get down to the work of it, out of respect for the instrument, and for Alice and for the faith that he had to work with me.

Tying back into our story's premise, there are two guitars that are forever linked with Kane Roberts during his early days with Alice Cooper, his custom-made machine-gun guitar and his Kramer Voyager, one of the company's pointy delicacies.

> Amazing. Both amazing instruments. The gun guitar — I'm sitting at Shep Gordon's management company, which I was now part of. Somehow, this kid, this army brat that made guitars, got in touch with him. He described what he had, and Shep said, "Yeah, come on in." So, you can see how Shep's brain works. It infiltrates everything that's going on with Alice in a very positive way. The fact that he saw that I would be a good writing partner and the bonding as friends, because that's what Alice needed coming out of rehab. So, the gun guitar, you know, the kid shows up, and I go into the conference room. There's this giant anvil case. He opens it up, and I just went, "Oh, my God." I couldn't believe the way this thing looked. And I'm thinking, *This can't play well.* [laughs] *There's no way.* So, I pick it up and the neck felt pretty good! He said, "Let's go outside. I'll show you what it can do." We go outside and he arms it, [using] these different switches. He said, "This is what you gotta do. Point it in the air and pull this trigger." So, I pulled it, and it shot this rocket up in the air, it exploded, and this little guy floated down with a parachute! And I said, "I don't know if I wanna do that." It was, like, very Spinal Tap. [*laughs*] And then he showed me the "flame-thrower." So right away, and I have to be honest with you, Sean, I was completely clueless on the Rambo comparison. That there's this guy with, like, black curly hair and weighs well over two hundred pounds just from lifting [weights].
>
> I'm probably wearing a tank top. And I'm shooting it going like [*in a Sylvester Stallone type voice*], "Oh, it's good." [*laughs*] I didn't get the Rambo thing. And you know, it's funny because, I started seeing it in different publications. You know, they'd be talking about Alice's new guitar player, Kane "Rambo" Roberts. And I'd say to Alice, "What the fuck is that? Why am I getting that?" And he'd say, "Have you looked in the mirror? All you need is a headband!" [*laughs*]

In a chat with Andrew Daly for *Guitar Player* magazine, Kane shared that hitting the right chords and playing the right parts wasn't the only thing one had to pay attention to when playing a flame-throwing guitar.

> "At the end of my solo," he says. "I had to flick a switch to make it shoot flames. I had to do it at the appropriate time — and, hopefully, away from the audience." "Hopefully" was the operative word. And in one memorable instance, Roberts didn't stick to his carefully prepared script.
>
> "We were at a theater, and it didn't shoot flames the night before," he recalls. "So I did the dumbest thing: I looked back at the drummer and ended up pointing it at the audience And when I turned around, the flames were shooting into and out over the crowd!" He laughs. "I wasn't paying attention!"
>
> — Kane Roberts (*Guitar Player*, April 3, 2025.)

Fortunately, with two hundred pounds of pure muscle on his frame, Roberts was able to manage this unwieldy six-string weapon with aplomb.

> Yeah, what a great guitar, even though it was cumbersome, a very heavy guitar. I'm glad I was able to handle it in that regard. Soloing on it was just a blast, you know, because that was the whole purpose of it, was to shred on the thing, and it was great for that. The guy's name is Rick Johnson, and he was like 19, and he said, "I'm an army brat, so I was always around weapons, and then I started learning how to make guitars."
>
> I saw a guy with a gun guitar that shot flame in one of the Road Warrior movies [Mad Max franchise], and now Rammstein's taken it to, like, this nuclear level. It's pretty cool. I'm not saying I'm responsible, but there's a little bit of an influence there.
>
> — Kane Roberts

Just as iconic (at least in the mind of this scribe) is Kane's Kramer Voyager, one of the company's pointy guitars that is often overshadowed by the massive success of superstrat models.

> The Voyager that I got was so perfectly shaped, and it has a little extra width to it. My hands are big, so it just fit. It's a guitar that I just never got tired of playing. [Before that] Les Pauls are what I played. There's no tremolo bar, and I decided I wanted to try that. Before I went on tour, Kramer visited me, and I played a whole bunch of guitars. They gave me a few guitars, and that one ended up being one of my all-time favorites. I asked for Seymour Duncan "Jeff Beck" pickups. You don't even really have to do anything to them to get them to sound fucking hot if you have the right amp and everything.
>
> — Kane Roberts

The Voyager was Kramer's take on the star-guitar shape that Eddie Van Halen had popularized with his modified Ibanez Destroyer shark guitar, and was one of a few pointy guitar models from a company that made its biggest mark with superstrat models like the Pacer and the Baretta (both of which gained worldwide popularity through the endorsement of Eddie Van Halen). The Challenger was a flipped or mirror image of the Voyager, and the Vanguard and Condor models were Kramer's versions of the Flying V and Explorer respectively. Both the Voyager and Vanguard would get more extreme makeovers in the mid-80s, as pointy guitar culture hit its apex. Today, the Voyager is represented through artist models in both its traditional (Tracii Guns Gunstar) and modified (Lzzy Hale signature) forms.

> There's something to be said about the Kramer Vanguard or the Voyager that are super pointy. There are some things about the rigidity that you have to compensate for, mechanically, when you play, and it alters the way you think about certain things. I think that's the beauty about these kinds of guitars. When you wield one, the differences in the body shape and the tensile strength of the strings, and the way it plays causes you to think about different parts, about different ways you can layer your guitar parts, which I think is a beautiful thing.
>
> — Aljon Go, product manager,
> Gibson Brands, Kramer, and Epiphone

An entire book could (and should) be dedicated to Kramer's complete dominance of the electric guitar market in the '80s, although *A Step Ahead and Two Steps Back: The Life and Death of the Original Kramer Guitar Company, 1976–1991* by Michael Plunkett gives a great insider's view into the company's inner workings. With Kramer being more deeply associated with the superstrat phenomena, this summation based on Justin Beckner's well-researched "A Brief History of Kramer Guitars" gives us a timeline.

Kramer began as a partnership between Gary Kramer and Dennis Berardi, (along with former Norlin VP Peter La Placa, luthier Phil Petillo, and investor Henry Vaccaro) after Kramer's partnership with Travis Bean went sour. Travis Bean guitars were notable for their use of aluminum guitar necks and a unique forked headstock design, and early Kramer guitars built between 1976 and 1981 also shared these traits (albeit with wooden inserts placed in the neck to reduce weight and give the guitars a more traditional feeling). The XL-5 featured a body shape that resembled a melted down B.C. Rich Bich, and the XKG-10 looked like the tail fin of a vintage Cadillac. By '81 Kramer started moving more toward wooden necks, and the first of these instruments came out with Fender-style headstocks, which were eventually changed to the famous pointy beak headstock due to a cease-and-desist order issued by Fender. As a cost-saving measure like those seen numerous times in this book, production of components was moved overseas to Asia, with Gotoh handling tuners and vibrato-bar systems, and neck manufacturing being outsourced to ESP (Electric Sound Products) in Japan. These components were then sent back to the Kramer factory in Neptune, New Jersey, for final assembly. Eddie Van Halen's innovative whammy-bar work had inspired a great demand in the market for vibrato guitar systems, and Kramer partnered with German inventor Helmut Rockinger to design locking systems that could keep the instrument in tune. The original Kramer Pacer (with the Strat-style headstock) came with a Rockinger trem that was marketed as the Edward Van Halen Tremolo.

In 1982, Kramer switched to locking-system originator Floyd Rose, and became the only company to offer the original Floyd Rose system on their guitars, manufactured by German company Schaller, who also built components for Kramer during the '80s. Along with the securing of Eddie Van Halen (thanks to a chance meeting on a plane between Berardi and Van Halen's management) as an endorsed artist, this created the perfect storm of demand for Kramer guitars. Superstrat models like the Pacer, launched in 1981, and the Baretta (with the banana-shaped headstock modeled after that of an Ibanez Destroyer), launched in 1983, were closely associated with Eddie (think of his iconic 5150 guitar), and these variations on the traditional Strat design became some of the most coveted guitar shapes on the market. Floyd Rose came out with his own series of guitars through Kramer, and these were some of the pointiest guitars ever brought to market, with the Triax and the Enterprize looking more like alien spacecraft than anything resembling a traditional guitar.

The popularity of Eddie's famous striped graphics, as well as the custom guitar work that was coming out of California at the time, undoubtedly inspired Kramer to explore a slew of flashy paint jobs and hot graphics, with airbrush artists like Dennis Kline creating beautiful "guitart" finishes with countless variations on the de rigueur animal-print, fantasy-art, snakes-n-skulls, pin-up-girl themes that were prominent in hard rock culture at the time.

Other famous '80s guitarists like Mick Mars of Mötley Crüe, Vivian Campbell of Dio, Whitesnake, and Def Leppard, Dave "Snake" Sabo, Jeff LaBar of Cinderella, and many more MTV icons were playing Kramer guitars on stage and — more importantly from a marketing standpoint — on screen. Kramer developed artist signature models with the likes of Bon Jovi's Richie Sambora (a cross of the older Pacer shape and the newer contoured body shape that Kramer had been developing), Elliot Easton of the Cars (an exaggerated Strat shape with longer horns), Paul Dean of Loverboy (a double-cutaway body shaped with a more squared off horn, based on Paul's earlier signature guitar designs for Odyssey and Hondo in the early '80s; built at the Larrivée guitar factory in Vancouver), and Vivian Campbell of Whitesnake (The NightSwan, designed by Buddy "Blaze" Webster and discussed earlier in this book).

> Many of the guitar players who favored Kramers were in the hard rock and pop metal bands that had become popular in the mid-80s as interest in punk and New Wave began to wane. Centered in L.A., this rock movement mostly featured guys in tight glam Spandex outfits with long, ratted and teased poofy hair. "Hair bands!" Catchy melodies, a hard backbeat, and lots of rifferama.
>
> (Michael Wright, MyRareGuitars.com, January 1, 2011.)

> MTV and Kramer went hand in hand, and so did all of those artists that boomed in popularity during that time. The pickups were great, they were Seymour Duncans [from 1986 onwards], and then you had the Floyd Rose, which was exclusive for Kramers at the time. If you wanted to dive bomb, and you wanted to get all the pyrotechnics and all that flash of that era, playing guitar like a gunslinger — that's why they called it the Baretta! It was definitely like a sure shot, that your way to number-one-hit stardom is to play Kramer. That's what was drilled into our minds as kids, and into all of those artists that endorsed that brand.
>
> — Aljon Go

Kramer was flying high until a combination of changing tastes — Eddie Van Halen's defection to Ernie Ball guitars, the rise in popularity of the Steve Vai– and Joe Satriani–endorsed Ibanez, Slash's use of the Les Paul, the advent of grunge, and a series of financial blows, including a lawsuit from Floyd Rose — took the wind out of their sails. Fortunately, the brand has been resurrected and brought back to prominence under the Gibson umbrella.

I asked current Kramer product manager Aljon Go which players he thought best represented the brand:

> Eddie Van Halen, rest in peace, was obviously number one but there are so many others, you know, and they're all signature artists. Richie Sambora, Vivian Campbell, Paul Dean, all those guys that had those guitars back in the day. Mick Mars, Snake Sabo, Jeff LaBar from Cinderella (rest in peace) — all of these players were amazing ambassadors, and for those who are still with us, they continue to be ambassadors for Kramer. I just spoke to Reb Beach recently, and we reminisced about some cool times he had with his Kramer. So, a lot of those old Kramer guys are still just amazing and they have a lot of really nice things [to say] and fond memories about Kramer, and I appreciate that. Next year is gonna be Kramer's fiftieth anniversary, and I hope that, they're with us and supportive of the journey of Kramer for the next 50 years.
>
> — Aljon Go

As mentioned earlier, I was lucky enough to be endorsed by Kramer Guitars for a period of time. Some of the prizes of that relationship were two '84 Barettas adorned with Eddie Ojeda–inspired bull's eye graphics, a Jersey Star (based on the Richie Sambora signature model), and a Snake Sabo signature model. These are all superstrats adorned with various versions of the Kramer logo, and which feature either a banana (hockey-stick) headstock or a classic pointy one.

My only truly pointy Kramer guitar is my Gorky Park balalaika guitar. It's a guitar that represents both a landmark musical festival and stunning duality: Eastern communism meeting Western democratic values, wasted rock stars preaching sobriety, and Kramer Guitars at both the highest and lowest points of its powers.

> Behind every guitar there's some sort of story, but they usually aren't as rich as the one behind the Kramer Gorky Park! Not only was this guitar associated with one of the big flash-in-the-pan pop metal bands of the late 1980s, it symbolically and almost literally marked the end of Kramer, as the largest guitar company in the world was crumbling just like the Iron Curtain!
>
> (Michael Wright, MyRareGuitars.com, January 1, 2011.)

The Moscow Music Peace Festival was a two-day rock concert held on August 12 and 13, 1989, at Moscow's Central Lenin Stadium, drawing about 100,000 fans and millions more through pay per view broadcasts. The festival was organized by American manager Doc McGhee through his Make a Difference Foundation (an anti-drug/alcohol organization that was court mandated as a condition of his bail for illegally importing marijuana into the U.S.). It was presented as a cultural exchange promoting world peace and anti-drug awareness, coinciding with the Soviet Union's era of glasnost. The lineup featured major Western acts — Bon Jovi, Mötley Crüe, Ozzy Osbourne, the Scorpions, Skid Row, and Cinderella — performing in the USSR for the first time, alongside the Soviet band Gorky Park.

The festival was criticized for its dubious motives, as well as the hypocritical nature of a group of hard-partying, drug- and drink-addled American musicians coming to lecture a Russian audience about the dangers of substance abuse. However, a kinder view of the festival could see it as a symbol of changing East–West relations at the end of the Cold War. The festival is said to be, along with the fall of the Berlin Wall, the inspiration behind Scorpions worldwide smash hit ballad Winds of Change.

With many of the guitarists playing Kramers (Sambora, Mars, LaBar) or Kramer factory–made Spector guitars and basses (Scotti Hill, Dave "Snake" Sabo, and Rachel Bolan of Skid Row), Kramer was the de facto representation of American rock n roll, the creator of instruments of hope and freedom, promising that the "Nothin' But a Good Time" vibes of America were now within reach of a rock-deprived Russia.

> Enter Mother Russia. About the same time Kramer began importing guitars, 1985, Mikhail Gorbachev took control of the Communist Soviet Union and began a process of liberal reforms. Among those were a toleration of underground music such as rock and a relaxation of travel restrictions.
>
> In 1987 singer Nikolai Noskov, Sasha Minkov on bass, Sasha Lvov on drums, and Jan Ianenkov on guitar formed a rock band called Gorky Park, after the big public Moscow park named in honor of Maxim Gorky. The band was able to travel to the U.S. and soon acquired champions including Frank Zappa and Kramer advocates Jon Bon Jovi and his axeman Sambora. In 1989 the band's self-titled album debuted and they scored three successive hits and MTV rotation, the first popular Russian hair band.
>
> (Michael Wright, MyRareGuitars.com, January 1, 2011.)

> The band Gorky Park was pieced together by Stas Namin, an early Russian rock performer and the grandson of a former chairman of the Supreme Soviet Presidium. Thanks to some contacts he had made in the West, Namin got Gorky Park a U.S. recording contract with PolyGram and helped put together the Moscow Music Peace Festival where the band and two other Namin-connected Soviet groups shared the bill with five Western entries: Bon Jovi, Osbourne, Mötley Crüe, the Scorpions and Skid Row.
>
> (Robert Hilburn, *Los Angeles Times*, September 3, 1989.)

> Probably through the Sambora connection, Kramer's Dennis Berardi became interested in the band and formed a management company to handle them. The Kramer Gorky Park was intended to be a promotional item in support of that effort.
>
> (Michael Wright, MyRareGuitars.com, January 1, 2011.)

> The bridge to America and PolyGram Records came through Namin's link with New Jersey-based manager Dennis Berardi. With the help of a good word from Bon Jovi guitarist Richie Sambora, a long-time friend of Berardi, Gorky Park got signed by PolyGram Records. The group, which is expected to tour here late this year, is already getting exposure on MTV.
>
> "We realize the Russian thing is going to get the band a lot of attention in the beginning, but that only lasts for a couple of weeks," Berardi said backstage at Lenin Stadium. "After that, the band will have to prove itself."
>
> (Robert Hilburn, *Los Angeles Times*, September 3, 1989.)

As for the Gorky Park guitar, it sounds and plays great, despite the obvious cost-cutting measures that went into its Korean production.

> Built for Kramer in Korea and introduced in 1989 or early 1990, the Gorky Park had a cool balalaika shape and graphics and signature of the band. Balalaika. Russia. Geddit? The guitar really wasn't all that bad, actually. It has one hot Seymour Duncan humbucker and a licensed Floyd Rose.
>
> (Michael Wright, MyRareGuitars.com, January 1, 2011.)

> Unfortunately, the Gorky Park arrived just in time to see everything crumble. In 1989, the Iron Curtain came down, as Berliners attacked the Berlin Wall and dismantled it. I still have a piece in a box my parents gave me as a present! Gorky Park returned to the exuberance of liberation in Russia. Alas, the enthusiasm for hair bands in the U.S. was also beginning to crumble as alternative rock represented by the Seattle Sound was coming on. Lastly, Kramer Guitars itself had become a

> house of cards and was beginning to crumble. Bad management and other bad things began to undermine it — it probably didn't help that Berardi was off focusing on Gorky Park. By the end of 1990 Kramer Guitars also collapsed.
>
> (Michael Wright, MyRareGuitars.com, January 1, 2011.)

When I saw a Gorky Park Kramer at the Twelfth Fret Guitar Shop in Toronto, the $400 they were asking for it quickly flew out of my bank account. Just seeing the guitar brought me back to a time when crazy dreams of rock stardom and world peace seemed like wild fantasies that were still possible, if you were willing to live on a prayer and surrender to the winds of change; dreams that would be deemed out of touch in today's world of AI generated content and political strife but seemed somehow within reach back then.

> Gorky Park, the band, continued to be popular in the former Soviet Union, but became mostly a footnote to '80s rock and guitar history. Today these guitars show up every so often and can actually trade for quite a bit more than the clearance price! In the early 2000s the Kramer name was sold to Gibson by its owner, Henry Vaccaro, a former principal in Kramer, in order to finance the now-defunct Vaccaro Guitars venture. Like the Gorky, modern Kramers are budget imports, but with no connection to the former Soviet Union!
>
> (Michael Wright, MyRareGuitars.com, January 1, 2011.)

Getting back to the "hottest band in the world," I was familiar with Kiss long before I ever heard a single guitar lick, thanks to the media saturation of their over-the-top image. It wasn't until their run of '80s albums like *Lick It Up*, *Animalize*, *Asylum*, *Crazy Nights*, and *Hot in the Shade* came along that I discovered them as a musical entity.

When Kiss lost the makeup, they may have had their moment of visual identity crisis (with Gene Simmons in particular struggling to maintain his identity as the Demon while sporting outfits that could make Joan Collins blush), but they were successful in navigating the modern production landscape of commercial '80s hard rock, bringing in a succession of great players who could maintain the anthemic integrity that the band was built on. Bolstering the sonics with the mandatory guitar pyrotechnics and sounds, which players like Randy Rhoads and Eddie Van Halen had introduced, was a key component in this plan,

Vinnie Vincent had been heavily involved in the writing and recording of Kiss's last makeup-era album (until the makeup returned with '96's original line-up reunion), *Creatures of the Night* (becoming a full-fledged member for that album's tour), which had re-established the band as a heavy rock force after forays into disco, power pop, and progressive rock had alienated Kiss from their core fan base. It was the decision to lose the makeup and truly embrace the new production techniques of the '80s that saw Kiss hit platinum once again with the *Lick It Up* album, and Vinnie was front and center with his fiery lead guitar playing and his Jackson Randy Rhoads flying Vs. Vinnie was a very early adopter of the Jackson RR model and was the first guitarist to be offered the model from Jackson after Rhoads's death. Vincent would later have Jackson create him a signature "Double V." Two flying-V bodies, one hot pink, one glittering silver, overlaid and offset, screamed the initials of this flashy new Kiss guitarist.

While Kiss was no stranger to wild shaped instruments, the '80s did see a pointy guitar evolution for the band. Throughout the decade, Paul Stanley could be seen brandishing B.C. Rich Eagles, Warlocks, and Ironbirds, Hamer Scarabs, and custom Explorers with a variety of flashy neon and animal print finishes in videos and in concerts.

Gene Simmons continued to wield the signature Axe bass, flexing his business muscles to strike up numerous production deals with various companies throughout the years, and demonstrating his now famous trademark and copyright expertise. It turns out that the commercial rights to the word "Axe" as it relates to a musical instrument has actually been trademarked by Simmons himself.

In an interview with Guitar.com, Jason Beckner spoke with Simmons about the nature of bringing a design idea to guitar companies and to market.

> So, what is the Axe Bass, then? Well, in simple terms it's a neck-through construction instrument with a hard maple

The author with his BC Rich Bich in a guitar magazine ad circa 2005.

ALL IN SERIES: JONATHAN MANKUTA

PETE DOVE

A colourful display of BC Rich models from the collection of Jonathan Mankuta/Lita Ford with her Double Neck BC Rich Bich.

Richie Sambora

The first thing you notice about the Richie Sambora model is its unique visual design. Play the guitar and you can feel the power and presence of this hard-driving rock & roll instrument.

Richie, lead guitarist for Bon Jovi, designed his guitar with two requirements in mind. The guitar had to deliver a solid, straight-ahead rock & roll sound combined with striking stage presence. The 25-inch scale body is enhanced with gold hardware and uses the "Original" Floyd Rose™ Tremolo. Unique star-shaped pearl inlays are offered on either a maple or rosewood fingerboard. Three Seymour Duncan™ Humbucking pickups give more full-blown power than other rock guitars in its class.

Richie Sambora Model

Bridge System: "Original" Floyd Rose™ Tremolo System
Fingerboard: Rosewood or Maple
Neck: 22-fret, bolt-on neck
Hardware: Schaller strap locks & machine heads
Pickups: Two Seymour Duncan™ JB pickups (bridge & middle), One Seymour Duncan™ Humbucking pickup (Neck)
Controls: One volume control, One 5-way pickup selector switch, Two humbucking split switches
Design Features: Star inlays on fingerboard, body and headstock, Gold-plated pickup rings

Finish Options:

Black
Candy Blue
Champagne
Candy Red
Flip Flop White
Fluorescent Pink
Violet
White

Paul Dean

The Paul Dean Signature Model is a reflection of a fine player's talents and experiences on the road and in the studio. Paul Dean, lead guitarist for Loverboy, collaborated with us to design a neck-through body guitar that really goes the distance for the versatile musician.

The result . . . a no-nonsense approach in rock & roll guitar design. The Signature is constructed from the finest Honduras mahogany and equipped with Seymour Duncan™ pickups, the "Floyd" tremolo, Schaller strap locks and machine heads.

As Paul says, "It's smooth, fast and light. The construction and pickup configuration give me the quality of sound I have to hear."

Paul Dean Signature

Bridge System: Recessed "Original" Floyd Rose™ Tremolo System
Body: 25-1/2" scale neck - through body constructed of Honduras Mahogany
Fingerboard: Rosewood with dot inlays
Neck: 22 frets
Hardware: Schaller strap locks & machine heads
Pickups: One Seymour Duncan™ JB Pickups, Two Seymour Duncan™ Vintage single coil pickups
Controls: Three on/off switches, One volume, One tone

Finish Options:

Black
Flip Flop White
Flip Flop Red
Flip Flop Blue
Fluorescent Pink
Harvest Yellow

Vivian Campbell

Created by Vivian Campbell and Buddy Blaze for Kramer, the NightSwan transcends traditional electric guitar designs.

The sleek, contoured body balances perfectly with the 24¾" scale length neck. Carved from hard rock maple, the 24-fret special radius neck gives access to two octaves of fast playing power. Constructed of the finest Honduras mahogany with an ebony fretboard, it resonates with a warm, solid sound.

The NightSwan is the only production model guitar to have an ultra-slim #1 locking nut giving easier "bend" to the strings. It is the first production model to feature the Seymour Duncan "Full Shred" pickup, a smooth distortion pickup with extreme clarity.

NightSwan

Bridge System: "Original" Floyd Rose™ Tremolo System
Body: 24-3/4" scale rear - routed body constructed of Honduras Mahogany
Fingerboard: Ebony with custom dot inlays
Neck: 24 medium jumbo frets, bolt-on neck with reverse head stock
Hardware: Schaller strap locks & machine heads
Pickups: One Seymour Duncan™ Full Shred humbucking bridge pickup. One Seymour Duncan™ JB middle pickup
Controls: One 3-way on/on/on mini-toggle switch, One volume
Options: Left-handed model

Finish Options:

Black
White
Candy Red
Lightening Graphic
Blue Sparkle
Burgundy
Polka Dot — light blue/dark blue
Polka Dot — dark blue/light blue

Model Options:

Left-handed model

Kramer guitars ruled in the mid-late '80s with a roster of high-profile endorsers.

Customization was the name of the game at Charvel/Jackson, paradise for '80s rock guitarists!

ALL ON PAGE: STEVE BROWN/VINTAXE.COM

DONALD GADZIOLA

Left: Randy Rhoads flying high with his Jackson Concorde!

PETE DOVE

Above: Randy Rhoads in full flight with his Karl Sandoval-built Polka Dot Flying V.

STEVE BROWN / VINTAXE.COM

PETE DOVE

PETE DOVE

PETE DOVE

Clockwise from Left: Vinnie Vincent of KISS, Robbin Crosby of RATT, and Chris Holmes of W.A.S.P captured in concert with their custom-made Jackson guitars.

Bottom Right: LADO guitars: high quality, made in Canada instruments that struck a power chord with great players around the world.

The Exquire SK-2, designed and built by Les Godfrey.

One-of-a-kind Voltez Mini V, designed and built by Les Godfrey.

An Edwards/ESP E-RS-145 Random Star, a signature model for Loudness guitarist Akira Takasaki.

Killer KG-Pirates Exploder, a signature model for Akira Takasaki.

The Parabellum, created and built by Havok Guitars, with custom pickups by Pariah Pickups.

A 1985 Peavey Vortex guitar the author picked up in a pawn shop in Abbotsford, BC while on tour with Lee Aaron.

ALL ON PAGE: EDWARD POND

Right: The author in concert with his Godfrey Exquire SK-1.

Below: Dean Guitars were right there at the dawn of arena rock to create instruments that provided a perfect balance of "show" and "go"!

CHRIS SURDYKOWSKI

STEVE BROWN / VINTAXE.COM

STEVE BROWN / VINTAXE.COM

> neck and mahogany "ax blade" body. Various production versions of the instrument often feature pickup configurations and tone controls that offer a wider tonal palate, but Gene doesn't want anything getting in the way, and so his personal versions feature just a volume control. Under the hood, in the 70s and 80s the Axe featured a boost, but the current models feature only EMG pickups and a preamp. The inception of the Axe Bass came from the adage of referring to a guitar as an "axe". Ever the savvy businessman, Simmons ended up trademarking the term "Axe" as it refers to a musical instrument, as well as the shape of the bass. As Simmons explains, ". . . because I owned the name and the design, it qualifies as an invention in the library of congress. My bass is the only musical instrument that is an 'invention'." By trademarking the name and shape of the Axe, Simmons was able to control who builds the instrument for him, and sure enough he's switched builders many times over the years. Gene tapped Valdez Guitars to build the first one, then Steve Carr built a few, as did Kramer, Jackson, and Cort. In the case of Kramer, Jackson and Cort, as soon as quality started to dip, a new builder would be found. As Simmons explained, "[Cort] started mass producing them and selling them for a cheaper price, obviously, so the wood was cheaper – everything was cheaper, and the paint started to crack. So, I ended that relationship and continued to make them on my own." "Everything starts with me," he explains. "I do stuff because I get excited about it and then I hope that other people will get excited about it as well. For me it was also pragmatism, because I already owned the word 'Axe' as it relates to musical instruments, so I hand-designed it, and I still have the original artwork and it looks very much like the Axe that's available today. I drew what the Axe might be.
>
> (Jason Beckner, Guitar.com October 25, 2022.)

Simmons would play many different basses throughout the '80s, '90s, and beyond including Spector and B.C. Rich. He would collaborate with the latter company on his signature Punisher bass, another pointy beast that helped Gene stay connected to his inner Demon during those make-up-free years.

When Vincent was dismissed from the Kiss fold for refusing to fall in line and sign an employee contract (it has been suggested that he demanded a share of Kiss's overall profits), his first replacement was Mark St. John, who came on board for the *Animalize* sessions, an album that continued Kiss's return to commercial good fortunes reaching double platinum sales, and yielding fan favorites like "Heaven's on Fire" and "Thrills in the Night."

As a player with prodigious technical ability and a deep theoretical knowledge, St. John had been doing guitar clinics and seminars for Jackson guitars, and has stated that he was one of 10 players suggested by Grover Jackson himself to replace Vincent. Born Mark Norton, he had first gained attention through Shrapnel Records founder Mike Varney's famous Spotlight column in *Guitar Player* magazine, a discovery vehicle for such shred luminaries as Yngwie Malmsteen, Paul Gilbert, Richie Kotzen, Guthrie Govan, and many more.

A Jackson loyalist, St. John's main guitars in Kiss were a pair of black Jackson Soloist superstrats with Floyd Rose systems, and a yellow, 1983 custom-made Jackson largely based on Allan Holdsworth's signature model, an instrument that incorporated features that would become standard in Charvel guitars, such as the swimming-pool route, which allowed easier installations of pickguards with different pickup configurations.

For all of his technical ability and musical versatility, St. John struggled to find his place in Kiss. He hadn't been a fan of the band prior to joining, and when thrown to the lions in front of huge audiences with little rehearsing or coaching, the differences in musical approach were amplified louder than the din on stage.

> Since I didn't play live with them much, we didn't rehearse for the gigs — they just threw me in front of 10,000 Kiss fans and said, "Play!" I had never performed in front of that many people. Also, Kiss songs are typically behind-the-beat and I usually play on top of the beat, so I had to listen to the drums a lot to know where we were. I rushed sometimes because I'd never played in that groove, which Gene calls "the monster

> plod." The rest of the guys had been doing this for years, but I couldn't tell what was going on half the time. The whole thing was like a huge wall of sound, with no distinction. Still, I had a great time doing it.
>
> — Mark St. John (Interview from 1990, *Vintage Guitar*, July 2023.)

While it is possible that with more time and opportunity to develop his stage legs St. John could have become comfortable with his role in Kiss, a rare medical condition made continuing on with the band impossible.

> I got arthritis. Kiss' first world tour in two or three years was scheduled and all of a sudden, the new guitar player's hand starts to swell up. That freaked them out, but there was nothing anyone could do — the show had to go on — so they got Bruce Kulick to come in. There's no hard feelings or anything; we're all still friends. But the doctor said that if I played on the tour, I could have ruined my hand forever. Before I was in Kiss, I used to do all the Paganini and difficult violin and cello pieces; then I joined a band that plays all barre chords and my hand swells up. It was really weird.
>
> — Mark St. John (*Vintage Guitar*.)

In certain circles, St. John is considered the misfit of the Kiss guitar lineage, the player who just didn't gel on a performing or musical level. However, he is at least an important evolutionary step in Kiss's development, a player who represented their willingness and desire to evolve and to compete in a new world of guitar playing technical proficiency. Mark St. John's contributions lay in his ability to *burn*, even if the fire got a little too hot at times.

> I think it was giving them a more-modern sound, so they could compete with all the guitar slingers in the other bands. Vinnie Vincent had just left and I had to follow in his and Ace Frehley's footsteps, but Gene and Paul knew they needed a guitar hero to compete with Yngwie Malmsteen, Randy Rhoads, and Eddie Van Halen. Bruce continued the contemporary style that I

> injected into the band. But after Kiss and all I've been through, I know where I stand with my own talent. I'm not very competitive these days and don't want to get caught in that trap — I just want to do my own thing.
>
> — Mark St. John (*Vintage Guitar* interview.)

Bruce Kulick had already marked his presence in the Kiss camp through his lead-guitar session contributions to *Animalize* tracks "Lonely Is the Hunter" and "Murder in High-Heels." Kulick's older brother Bob had been deputizing on Kiss recordings as a session guitarist as far back as the studio tracks included on *Alive* II, and was a frequent collaborator on other band and solo projects. Bob had even auditioned alongside Ace Frehley before the band was known as Kiss, and while the band's undeniable chemistry with Ace ultimately saw Kulick lose out on the gig, he was remembered for his great playing instincts.

Bob recommended his younger brother Bruce for a Kiss cattle-call audition back in 1982 when Frehley first left the band, and while that first attempt didn't yield a successful result, a seed was planted, and the younger Kulick would be invited back into the Kiss universe, first as a session musician, then as a temporary replacement for the ailing Mark St. John on the Animalize World Tour, and ultimately as a member of the band.

As a guitarist, Kulick represents the best of Kiss's '70s roots and their '80s gunslinger aspirations. In my book *Don't Call It Hair Metal*, I discussed Kulick's playing style in detail.

> With Bruce Kulick on guitar, Kiss had a player who embodied the best traits of previous guitarists Ace Frehley, Vinnie Vincent, and Mark St. John. Kulick was a tasteful, melodically developed player rooted in the tradition of '60s British rock who had earned his sea legs as a touring guitarist for Meat Loaf during his massively successful Bat Out of Hell tour in the '70s. Kulick was able to harness the firepower that was expected of players in the '80s and executed by Vincent and St. John in their studio performances on *Lick It Up* and *Animalize* respectively, and blend it with Frehley's more traditional approach to craft exciting and

powerful solos that were among the finest examples of a style of playing called "in and out in eight."

The best "in and out in eight" players take an allotted space of eight measures and are able to elevate a song by delivering solos that are melodic and memorable, while also providing the excitement that comes from demonstrations of technical mastery of their instrument. This can also be modified to "in and out in four" for slower tempos (for example, Steve Lukather of Toto's melodic master class on "Rosanna"), or "in and out and in sixteen" for bands that featured a particularly prodigious guitar hero (such as Steve Lynch's two-handed tapping clinic in Autograph's "Turn up the Radio," or Matthias Jabs's fleet-fingered fire in "Rock You Like a Hurricane" putting the "sing" in the "sting"). These players often didn't garner the big features in guitar magazines of the day, but they fulfilled a very important role nonetheless, and, in retrospect, their contributions to '80s guitar vocabulary were most memorable to the general music-loving population. Kulick's brilliant solos on the *Asylum* hits "Tears Are Falling," "Who Wants to Be Lonely," and "Uh! All Night" are textbook examples of the style, breaking up moments of flash and burn with soulful string bends and simpler patterns that repeat rhythmically, allowing the listener to anticipate and appreciate in a more meaningful way. Deeper *Asylum* cuts like "King of the Mountain" showed Kulick to be a master of post–Van Halen shred guitar as well, and also demonstrated his tonal consistency, conviction, and fluidity of phrasing.

(Sean Kelly, *Don't Call It Hair Metal*)

At times, I could shift from the more melodic restraint and then be super flashy too. Looking back at my faster playing, it was still melodic considering it showed speed and a certain sparkle of "look at me!" But largely the song dictated the solo work, and that has always been what playing my leads are about. Playing the right riffs for the composition of the song.

— Bruce Kulick, Kiss

I had the opportunity to ask Bruce how the musical direction he received in Kiss affected his guitar-playing approach, and in turn, his choice of musical instruments.

> Kiss required me to be competitive with the guitarists of the '80s. I know Paul and Gene loved me having a firm root in the blues, and having influences like Hendrix and Jimmy Page, I had a good vocabulary of rock riffs that fit Kiss. The shadow of Eddie Van Halen on all guitarists during that time was tremendous. They wanted me to be able to be flashy and that would require the techniques of the day.
>
> Playing a vintage Les Paul or Fender Strat would not be the ticket for success with my guitar duties with Kiss. At first, the Charvel custom-shop superstrats, with Floyd Rose tremolo and EMG pickups featuring flashy sparkle finishes were my weapon of choice. By the time the Asylum Tour came around, these guitars were my tool to speed around the neck, and if a dive bomb was necessary, so be it — they could do it all.
>
> During the first years of my Kiss tenure there was no real difference in guitars used live and in the studio. But that did evolve, with many studio guitars not being [taken] on the road because they were *that* good, my ESP M-1 Banana guitar being one that rarely was seen in public. Of course, my old Les Paul would be introduced as well to my recordings, but not ideal for touring.
>
> There was a balance of touring guitars and studio guitars as my time in the band became more comfortable. The music of Kiss kept adjusting in unique ways from album to album. *Hot in the Shade* is not *Asylum*. And *Revenge* is not *Crazy Nights*, so each LP had its own needs.
>
> When I got the invitation to join Kiss for the Animalize [World] Tour, I needed some guitars to do the work involved. I only had one Floyd Rose equipped instrument, a parts guitar, and not really what I would prefer for the tour. I went to 48th Street

in NYC, and in the window of Sam Ash was a used Charvel in metallic blue with a heavy flamed neck, nice rosewood fingerboard, and a black Floyd Rose on it. These are the gold decal, angled-headstock models, and I was impressed with the quality. The neck was a bit thinner than I liked, but that metallic-blue guitar was my best friend to get me through the tour. I really couldn't afford another guitar.

I knew I had the black B.C. Rich Eagle for some of the vintage material but I would need a back-up for the blue Charvel. Kiss kindly purchased a gold-metal flake three-pickup model, with the angled headstock and gold Charvel decal. It had EMGs and a black German-made Floyd Rose, but this one had an ebony fingerboard. The gold one had some paint issues and Grover Jackson sent a repainted body. There are some photos of it looking odd, and for the U.S. tour once I knew I was a full member of Kiss, I got a two-pickup silver-sparkle Charvel. For the Asylum Tour, and the video of "Tears Are Falling," another Charvel with a custom graphic was part of my Kisstory.

The company was getting known for the Jackson Soloist line, and I was impressed with the look and quality. Neck through beauties. And I then requested the company to do some graphics. One was the zebra-themed black-and-white Soloist, and then I ordered a candy-apple red one. Sadly, the neck of the candy-apple red was *super* thin, so I never kept it. Sam Ash received the guitar and it was easy for them to sell it even though I never played it outside of the store. The zebra one was featured with Kiss. I sold it in the early '90s, since the ESP Horizons of the late '80s were much more comfortable for me to play. The influence of Charvel/Jackson was huge, and their quality was fantastic, but I found the neck shapes weren't a good fit for me, and ESP did a better job for my preference.

— Bruce Kulick

I asked Bruce which guitar shapes and models he felt had come to best represent the power and identity of the band's recorded and live work.

That's a great question and with all the Kisstory there is, so there are many guitar shapes to discuss. I will do my best to summarize. When you think of original guitarist, Ace Frehley, you have to think Les Paul. He was easily identified with that iconic Gibson model in colors of his preference. Paul had many phases. Sometimes cool shapes like the Explorer or V, naturally his iconic Ibanez PS10, and then during *Crazy Nights*, a Steinberger guitar with decals all over it, looking like a paddle for a rowboat. Paul performed with cool B.C. Rich models as well. But clearly the PS10 would be his best connection to a shape and style of guitar. Vinnie Vincent, as you know, is [famous for] the double V from Jackson. Great choice for him.

Now for me, I played so many guitars. I started with the Charvel Strat shapes and explored custom graphics on them. I kept the B.C. Rich connection using a custom Ironbird for *Asylum*, but ESP Guitars, with their M-1 models that I continue to play, became the brand I preferred. Some of the ESPs had interesting finishes and graphics like the flip-flop blue and my multiswirl during the *Asylum* era. In 1987, I'm holding a simpler banana yellow M-1 guitar on the back of the *Crazy Nights* LP, and it became a powerhouse of sound for me to record with. But I wouldn't tour with it. So, I had ESP make me a white M-1. That guitar (with a tortoise shell pickguard like Jimi Hendrix's) did two tours, Hot in the Shade and Revenge. I then explored the ESP Horizon model and really loved how they played and looked. I used a red one, a black one, a sunburst one. Fantastic guitars.

But what about the B.C. Rich Radioactive guitar?

Very identifiable, but I didn't tour with it. I was using many shapes, different colors, and in some ways, throughout those 12 years, I was having a blast exploring whatever guitars I wanted. I would open the Hot in the Shade Tour using a Gibson Les Paul Special in black, and by the Revenge Tour I evolved with the black-and-white ESP Explorers [the ESP EX], a vintage beat up

Les Paul Junior, and of course a few M-1 Floyd guitars, blue and the white one. With the success of the Explorers by ESP I asked them to also make a Custom flying V with mirror pickguard. That one was used in South America, and I also had Gibson make me a black LP Custom that I loved and performed with when we toured internationally for dates in Japan during 1995. By the *Carnival of Souls* Kiss LP release, I am posing with a B.C. Rich Eagle Supreme in koa on the cover that I recorded with as well. My point is, unlike Ace and Paul, and someone like Slash or Angus Young from AC/DC, I lament not being identified with one guitar. I do think many fans associate the ESP Banana with me, the multiswirl, and a red Horizon. And for the MTV Unplugged performance the black Ovation Elite model got a lot of exposure!

— Bruce Kulick

Of all the companies used and mentioned by Bruce in this guitar Kisstory, ESP is one that has not yet been discussed in this book.

My friend Johnny DiFatta is a guitarist, luthier, vintage guitar historian, and owner of AXN Guitars in Hollywood, California. He creates high-quality instruments that reflect his love and deep knowledge of guitar craft, in particular the vintage guitars of the '80s. One of his most recent projects has been the design of a Bruce Kulick Asylum Tribute Guitar. An interview with Johnny from the AXN website explains the nature of the collaboration:

> "Bruce and I are friends and vintage guitar geeks. We like many of the same things in a Rock N' Roll guitar. I loved the ESP guitars he used during his era of Kiss," Johnny explains. "We went over the early 1980s ESP guitars Bruce played and used live at that time. 1980s ESP Guitars were one of my two main influences as a guitar luthier and manufacturer. The other being early, very early, Charvel Guitars with which we are both very familiar."
>
> (Johnny DiFatta (AlienXnation), AXN Guitars.)

Johnny reflects on the inspiration that tied Bruce Kulick and Johnny together.

> The ESP Bruce played live in the early Kiss days was his 1985 ESP M-1 with a Flip-Flop paint job. It's the same guitar that is hanging in the Hard Rock Cafe in London England right next to Eric Clapton's Stratocaster today. I went on to manufacture and produce a replica of that M-1 ESP. Then we developed the Asylum tribute guitar. It was a lengthy process of trial and error to get to the exact neck shape and other specifications that Bruce liked in his guitars. We got there successfully and the whole journey to completion rocked! I learned so much from Bruce and all the data is reflected in my second generation of AXN Boutique guitars that you can buy today!
>
> (Johnny DiFatta, AXN Guitars.)

Johnny's website is full of highly detailed research on the vintage '80s guitars that have inspired him, including the history of ESP, which helped me glean a fair bit of information. ESP's guitars ended up in the hands of some of my favorite guitarists, including George Lynch of Dokken, Akira Takasaki of Loudness (whose own guitar company, Killer Guitars, is a subsidiary of ESP), and Vernon Reid of Living Colour. Ron Wood of the Rolling Stones was an early adopter, and some of the most famous ESP endorsees include Kirk Hammett and James Hetfield of Metallica, each of whom have a number of signature models to their name.

> Hisatake Shibuya established ESP in 1975 along with his friends Hidesato Shino (who was previously in charge of Greco design at Fujigen) and Moony K Omote, later the founder of Moon guitars.
>
> ESP (Electric Sound Products) began in Shibuya Tokyo as what the Japanese referred to as a "Guitar Salon". The shop focused on custom, higher end-guitar components, guitar repairs and "one-on-one" custom order guitars. Shibuya's shop was also a training ground for guitar repairmen and soon became a popular stop for musicians. ESP was unique for producing multiple product lines for the Japanese, North American, and

worldwide markets. These included the Navigator, Edwards, and Grassroots line of instruments. The Navigator series remained true to classic Gibson and Fender specs, yet despite not being intended to be direct copies, they still were considered too close to be imported into the United States, and got caught up in the aftermath of the Gibson vs Hoshino lawsuit of 1978, which saw Gibson's parent company Norlin suing over use of Gibson's headstock designs.

(Johnny DiFatta, AXN Guitars.)

In 1984, ESP decided to take its replacement parts business to New York. A company representative would fly from Tokyo to visit Music Row on Manhattan's 48th Street and sell components to repair shops. During one of those trips, ESP formed a relationship with Kramer, which used ESP to "ghost build" necks and bodies. Kramer was flush with demand after the endorsement of Eddie Van Halen and needed to outsource production to keep up. That introduced ESP to the U.S. market, and in 1986 the company began selling the 400 series, which were familiar vintage designs at first, but later included original ESP designs, such as the Horizon.

(James M Brill, Reverb.)

While ESP-made parts and models were available in the United States in '84, distribution was limited. One oft-referenced story in ESP lore involves George Lynch of Dokken. The band was touring in 1985, and Lynch stopped in at the Tokyo headquarters and shop. He was already aware of ESP replacement parts but was amazed when he picked up a guitar later known as the Kamikaze model. He ordered one on the spot. That exposed more players to the unique style of ESP. While the company had relationships with players before Lynch, including Ron Wood of the Rolling Stones, who was an early adopter, the breakthrough with Lynch laid the groundwork for ESP's emergence as the premier metal guitar. Other high-profile users soon joined the ESP family with signature models at varying

> price points. The company produced KH models, named for Metallica's Kirk Hammett, and the Truckster and Snakebyte models, which are associated with the band's James Hetfield. Signature models have become a staple of ESP guitar offerings, and the company produces a wide array of them in conjunction with a large pool of international players. Meanwhile, ESP expanded its standard line to more U.S. markets to meet strong demand.
>
> (James M. Brill, Reverb.)

According to DiFatta, Hisatake gleaned corporate-culture and product-marketing experience from years working for Japanese companies like Kawai, Nippon Gakki (later Yamaha) and Fernandes Guitars, and applied this when he created the ESP Tokyo shop, a professional shop in Japan focused on creating a dialog with working musicians and interacting closely with guitarists.

> Hisatake brought in machinery to operate as a guitar retail store/workshop and they started building Navigator high-quality hand-made electric guitars. All the while ESP absorbed player level details that guitar makers usually do not notice. This led to ESP manufacturing custom order high-end guitars in Japan [around] 1979. ESP eventually moved production facilities outside of Tokyo but kept it a policy to concentrate on high-ticket guitars. In the 1970s–1980s most of the well-known Japanese guitar making companies, including ESP, were able to produce runs of super highest quality guitars and runs of lower quality guitars simultaneously. Other manufacturers that could achieve this were Tokai, Matsumoku, Fujigen, Kawai, Chushin Gakki and others. ESP did that and did it very well.
>
> (Johnny DiFatta, AXN Guitars.)

ESP manufactured high-quality replicas of Gibson and Fender guitars under the Navigator label, and also sold guitars under other brand names like ZEP-II, Edwards, and Grass Roots (aimed at entry-level players), as well as a series of guitars under the Seymour Duncan banner. In 1987, Hisatake was involved in the purchase of the Schecter Guitar Research brand, and in

1995 he purchased the Musicians Institute in Hollywood (previously called the Guitar Institute of Technology, GIT).

Of the many designs that ESP has produced over the years, the one that moves the pointy needle the furthest into the red in my heavy-metal heart is Loudness guitarist Akira Takasaki's Random Star signature model. With its star-shaped body and Danelectro-style neck and headstock, the Random Star was inspired by a custom Charvel-Danelectro hybrid that Van Halen used on their 1980 World Invasion Tour.

Akira started his own Killer Guitars company in conjunction with ESP manufacturing and marketing services. The Killer Prime and Exploder models blend the Explorer, B.C. Rich Bich, and Random Star concepts and take them in a bolder, chunkier, more extreme direction. I'm a proud owner of both an Edwards (ESP) Random Star and a Killer Exploder. Both guitars play like butter and have a wonderful acoustic resonance. Even when I'm not plugged into a stack of Marshalls, these guitars seem to pull out of me the kind of aggressive, Randy Rhoads and Ritchie Blackmore riffs and licks that influenced Akira in defining his own distinctive style.

In much the same way Loudness broke down international barriers with their progressive take on traditional '80s American and European metal, so too did Hisatake Shibuya by opening ESP locations in the United States, Germany, and Asia, ensuring that the virtues of Japanese quality in guitar making were known, and experienced, by some of the world's best players.

CHAPTER 11

JACKSON/CHARVEL GUITARS – CALIFORNIA SCREAMIN'

Throughout my conversations for this book, numerous players have referenced their special relationship with Grover Jackson, and their connection to the legacy of Charvel and Jackson guitars. Through a combination of high-performance playability and aggressive, forward-thinking design elements, Jackson proved to be the most resilient pointy-guitar brand from the '80s, weathering the storms brought on by the '90s alternative movement. By serving as a bridge between late '80s Sunset Strip–inspired commercial hard rock and the progressive thrash-metal movement, Jackson was a brand that was "cool" enough for bands making technical and aggressive music in a post-grunge world. Bands like Deftones, Slipknot, Periphery, and Black Dahlia Murder followed the lead of guitarists in Jackson-endorsed acts like Megadeth, Sepultura, Slayer, and Anthrax, all of whom (for the most part, give or take a few lean years) escaped the great culling of technically proficient guitar playing that came in a post-Nirvana, early '90s world. Of course, in 2025, cyclical tastes in music seem to be a thing of the past. All of the world's recorded musical output lies at the fingertips of anyone with a computer and an internet connection, and players of all ages are finding the music, artist, and instruments that speak to their souls, free of the aspersions that come with "going out of style." Online communities abound where musicians and music fans can share and indulge in their love of very specific genres and guitar brands and models. For example, it's quite common to find blazing young shredders on TikTok and Instagram playing their favorite '80s licks and riffs on period-appropriate pointy axes (often reissued due to their popularity) while decked out in equally period-appropriate leather, chains, and spandex, hair piled high to the sky.

One of the great joys of playing a guitar with historical ties to a specific genre or musical scene is the connection you feel to the players who were there at the vanguard. When I was asked to give guitar clinics here in Canada for Charvel and Jackson guitars last year by my friend Glen Booth, a sales representative for Fender Guitars (both Charvel and Jackson brands currently fall under the Fender Musical Instruments Corporation [FMIC] umbrella, who acquired both brands in 2001), I jumped at the chance. I saw it as an opportunity to play and demonstrate iconic instruments that embodied the performance and visual aesthetics of my favorite guitarists from my favorite era, the hard rockin' '80s. There is something magical about holding an instrument that has been informed by the input, influence, and playing styles of legendary guitarists. Playing reissues of signature models by Warren DeMartini of Ratt, Randy Rhoads and Jake E. Lee from Ozzy Osbourne, and other models made popular by '80s greats has been a true thrill. I believe this speaks to the innocent dreamer seeking communion with an idol as much as it does to the experienced musician seeking a high-quality instrument with which to create and, to that point, the many reissues we see in the modern guitar-retail market aspire to tap into both streams.

When I'm holding a Charvel, a Jackson, or an EVH guitar (the gear company started by Eddie Van Halen in partnership with Fender), I'm transplanted to the California birthplace of '80s hard rock and heavy metal that has been at the center of my musical devotion. It puts me in that spiritual space where Eddie Van Halen started a brand-new guitar movement with the eruption of molten guitar lava that burned through the first Van Halen album in 1978. I feel like I'm in a stadium somewhere, going off the rails on a crazy train commandeered by sonic engineer Randy Rhoads, or flying high like he did on 1981's *Diary of a Madman* album. It compels me to bark at the moon with the howling lupine licks that Randy's successor Jake E. Lee was tearing off in 1984, and spins me round and round like the millions of Ratt records that Warren DeMartini and Robbin Crosby were helping to shift in malls across America.

Yes, it was often a Charvel or Jackson in the hands of Carlos Cavazo when he was banging heads and rocking the girls who were rocking their boys on Quiet Riot's chart-topping *Metal Health* album, just as it was when George Lynch was breaking the chains of guitar playing mediocrity in fiery style with Dokken. Phil Collen was driving fans *Hysterical* with his Jackson Soloist and PC signature models and Steve Lynch had kids turning up the radio to try and figure out his mind-bending two-hand tapping guitar licks. Michael Sweet and Oz Fox of Stryper were divinely inspiring saints and sinners alike by tightening the bullet Bible belts on their skin-tight yellow-and-black attack spandex and delivering the virtuosic, twin guitar leads that would help define their distinctive brand of American Christian-themed heavy rock on the Sunset Strip, heavy metal's holy land.

In 2025, Charvel and Jackson guitars are like six-string DeLoreans that offer the chance to travel back to the future.

California was the breeding ground for the most famous and flashy innovators of '80s guitar-based rock n roll. With Van Halen and Rhoads blazing the path and leading the pack, an army of ferocious, technically gifted, and sonically adventurous players weaned on guitar heroes like Eric Clapton, Jimi Hendrix, Ritchie Blackmore, Jimmy Page, Mick Ronson, Michael Schenker, and Alvin Lee (to name but a few) ushered in a glorious era of excessive guitar. Long-haired hopefuls, dialed up the speed, distortion, and volume to crystallize the culture of the Sunset Strip into a flurry of two-hand finger tapping, whinnying dive bombs, sweep picking, power chords, and double-picked scalar flurries. From the hair-sprayed and eye-linered denizens of the glam metal scene to the raging thrash metal mavens that spat in the former group's collective mascara- and lipstick-sporting mugs, there existed amongst almost all of them a commonality. These sultans of strings were playing guitars custom built, assembled, or painted by the talented luthiers and craftsmen at Charvel/Jackson Guitars.

It was an era where young guitarists, with appetites whetted by the combined influence of late '70s hard rock and the hot-rod modification culture of California, were seeking tools that would allow them to express themselves in the louder, faster, and flashier playing style that would come to define 1980s hard rock. These guitar virtuosi of the "shred" era required instruments that could handle the need for speed, with compound-radius guitar necks, high-quality components and systems that could help them stay in tune while enduring torturous string bending and whammy-bar abuse. They needed pickups and electronics that enhanced tone and delivered high-gain performance while still retaining definition. On top of all that, the growing emphasis on visuals demanded by the MTV generation meant that guitars had to be as visually shocking as they were sonically rocking.

Wayne Charvel is considered by many to be the godfather of the guitar customization craze that swept the '80s hard-rock guitar scene and continues to this day. From very humble beginnings in Charvel's repair shop in Azusa, California, the groundwork for a guitar culture zeitgeist was laid.

Wayne Charvel had worked at Fender for three years before opening his shop in 1974. Charvel's Guitar Repair focused on repairs, custom-finish work, and replacement parts that would serve professional touring musicians. At the time, the major guitar companies did not offer custom-guitar work to the public, opening up a market for independent luthiers to perform after-market customizations. If a successful artist had a request for a modification, the larger companies would often turn the request over to smaller companies like Charvel's Guitar Repair. As we have discussed throughout the book, a dip in manufacturing quality from these big companies would create opportunities for luthiers inspired by the high quality of the Gibson and Fenders during their glory years of the 1950s. Out of this desire for quality and the creative and innovative minds of players and luthiers alike, wonderful combinations of mix-and-match components would come to create a new guitar revolution.

Charvel's Guitar Repair developed a reputation for providing modifications that helped guitars play at optimum levels. The shop became well known for its necks with compound radiuses and large fret wire, which allowed for speed and comfort in equal measure. Grover Jackson, an employee of Charvel, suggested moving into the business of assembling finished guitars and selling them under the Charvel brand name. Initially, Charvel used parts and bodies provided by a number of sources.

One such source was Lynn Ellsworth, a childhood friend of Wayne Charvel, who made replacement bodies under the company name First Impressions. Lynn teamed up with his neighbor Jim Warmoth in 1976 to create Boogie Bodies. When Lynn and Jim parted ways in 1980, Jim's son Ken would continue in his father's footsteps and form the Warmoth custom guitar-and-bass parts company. Though both Jim and Ken are deceased, Warmoth Guitar Products is still going strong today.

> Well, when I first started working for him, Wayne was not building necks — at least not to my knowledge. I never saw templates, machinery or anything that had to do with building necks. He had a source through, I think, Fender. We had quite a few Fender necks there because he used to do — what you could call — refurbishing. He repainted them and did whatever they requested.
>
> — Karl Sandoval ("The Birth of the Randy Rhoads Sandoval Dot V," DiMarzio.com.)

Wayne also worked with Dave Schecter of Schecter Guitar Research. Dave helped Wayne build 100 bodies in 1976 in order to fulfill a contract with International Sales Associates (ISA). Schecter had already been working with ISA with his own company and had connected them to Charvel. However, when Charvel was unable to fulfill the terms of the deal (ISA had pressured Wayne into purchasing expensive pin routers in order to meet the demands, but the cost of operating the machines and finding appropriate parts was prohibitive), a lawsuit resulted creating enough stress and financial hardship for Wayne that he opted to declare bankruptcy and sell his interest in the company to his enterprising young employee, Grover Jackson. If Wayne is indeed the godfather of after-market guitar customization in California, a sound argument could be made that Grover is the true Prince of Point when it comes to electric guitars.

Before we dive into the pointy history of the Grover Jackson run Jackson/Charvel company, we should first explore Wayne Charvel's connection to a guitarist who changed the way the electric guitar would be played — and made — in the late '70s, throughout the '80s, and well beyond.

When a young Eddie Van Halen walked into Wayne Charvel's shop, it was as much out of financial necessity as it was out of his innate sense of innovation. Eddie was looking for a guitar that could capture a sound and a feeling that was not available through an off-the-rack instrument, and he could not afford a brand-new custom build. It turns out that by venturing into Charvel to purchase an $80 body on to which he bolted a Stratocaster neck and wired-up by trial and error, Eddie would change the guitar world forever.

The Frankenstrat was Eddie Van Halen's legendary homemade electric guitar, and it would become one of rock's most iconic instruments. Originally built in '74 or '75 from mixed parts including an ash body, Fender Stratocaster neck, and a single Gibson PAF humbucker pickup, the guitar featured Eddie's now famous red, white, and black striped paint job that he applied with the used of masking tape. This DIY creation was the result of the sound and concept Eddie had in his head that would combine the sustain of a Gibson Les Paul with the whammy-bar capabilities and look of a Fender Stratocaster. The Frankenstrat defined Van Halen's early sound on classics like "Eruption" and "Runnin' with the Devil," and its success inspired the entire superstrat guitar category. Eddie would go on to work with a number of different companies including Kramer, Ernie Ball, and Peavey until starting his own EVH instrument brand in conjunction with Fender.

The components that make up the Frankenstrat have been the subject of much speculation and debate in the guitar community, and there are many forums dedicated to pursuing the chronological history of the evolution of this guitar. Eddie was an avowed tone chaser who was constantly swapping-out parts in his pursuit of an instrument that could sate his musical appetites.

> I didn't bring Eddie to Wayne's shop. He actually heard about us through the grapevine of musicians. We were probably the only custom guitar shop around. I think that some music stores back then did repairs, pickup changes, nuts and so forth. But Wayne did complete builds, refinishing, customizing of all nature — for guitar and bass.
>
> So, Eddie got wind of us. And I'll tell you, Larry, I still distinctly remember him walking through the door – seeing him for the first time. And I tell you, man, sometimes you just look at a person and say "oh, there's no way that could be a guitar player, there's no way." It's not necessarily about looks. Obviously, some of these bands came from money, when they were first starting out, and some didn't. I'm not really sure about Ed's background, but when he came in . . . he just looked like a lot of teenagers at the time. Back then, they just wore, I guess, what was clean or available. I can still picture him with his long hair: it's dark and he's young. He was wearing what looked like a really oversized shirt, like one of his dad's shirts or something, a pair of Levi's that were torn, and he was barefoot. He comes in and I'm looking

> at him, thinking, "Is this the guy that everybody keeps talking about? Eddie Van Halen? Eddie Van Halen?!" There he was, right in front of me, and I was a little nervous. I don't know why exactly, because he was just another dude from the community.
>
> — Karl Sandoval ("The Birth of the Randy Rhoads Sandoval Dot V," DiMarzio.com.)

According to VanHalenGear.com, the guitar body that Eddie Van Halen purchased to create his famous Frankenstrat guitar may have been built from a Dave Schecter template, and not from a Lynn Ellsworth template (as Eddie himself has previously suggested in various reports). However, Eddie did have Ellsworth build him a number of guitar necks, and the body of his almost equally famous Bumblebee yellow-and-black striped guitar has been attributed as a Boogie template build, although there are a few discrepancies around who did what when it comes to actually assembling the instrument.

Eddie Van Halen's Bumblebee guitar, completed in October 1978, represented another important creation, and most likely involved the work of both Karl Sandoval and Grover Jackson (who purchased Wayne Charvel's business in November 1978), and perhaps the work of other employees working in the shop at the time.

The Bumblebee had rear-loaded electronics, which negated the need for pickup routing on the front of the guitar and allowed for a flat surface. As a result the black-and-yellow stripes could be featured prominently when it debuted on the cover of the *Van Halen II* album. This design was perfect for players who wanted to have their guitars painted with graphics, and many wild and colorful custom paint finishes were on offer from Charvel/Jackson throughout the years.

The Bumblebee featured an ash Strat body and originally housed a single Mighty Mite humbucker with a Charvel brass tremolo bridge. While Grover Jackson owned the Charvel shop and provided the neck (an early Charvel pre-production neck possibly made by Jackson), Karl Sandoval was also directly involved in the construction, as evidenced by photographs of him standing with Eddie and the completed guitar.

In line with Eddie's reputation as a DIY-guitar enthusiast and restless tone-chaser, the guitar underwent multiple modifications including various pickup changes and the installation of a prototype Floyd Rose–locking-tremolo system.

The Bumblebee was used prominently during Van Halen's 1979 world tour. However, the relationship soured when Grover Jackson began making unauthorized Charvel VH-II clones without permission, leading to cease-and-desist orders and ultimately ending the relationship between Jackson/Charvel and Eddie Van Halen. In 2004, the guitar was buried with Pantera's Dimebag Darrell, who had become a friend of Eddie, as a tribute to the lifelong Van Halen fan.

> Eddie had the idea to build a new guitar with an ash body and black-and-yellow-stripe paint job, with rear-loaded electronics so there would be no pickguard. He tasked Wayne Charvel to make the original guitar, which had a maple neck, maple fingerboard and dot inlays. Other features on the first-incarnation guitar (as pictured on Van Halen II) were a standard nut, single Mighty Mite® humbucking pickup with transparent bobbins, single chrome volume knob, original Charvel® six-screw brass tremolo bridge, and Schaller® tuning keys.
>
> While pleased with the looks of the guitar, Eddie was less impressed with its tone and quickly began tinkering with it, as he was prone to do. He installed a new Boogie Bodies maple neck with a natural headstock, unfinished back (which he has always preferred) and 12"-radius dot-inlay maple fingerboard.
>
> Next to go was the Mighty Mite pickup. After selecting a DiMarzio® Super Distortion humbucking pickup, he swapped out its ceramic magnet for an alnico 2 magnet from a Gibson® PAF. He rewound the pickup by hand, dipped it in paraffin wax and put copper tape around the windings.
>
> Eddie also stripped out the original Charvel bridge, leaving its six screw holes behind. He instead outfitted the instrument with a prototype two-point Floyd Rose® bridge and locking nut with retainer bar, becoming the first professional rock guitarist to use a locking-nut tremolo system. He also swapped out the chrome volume knob with a Strat-style skirted "Tone" knob. After all these modifications, only the original body, striped paint job, screw-eye strap hooks and Schaller® tuners remained from the first version of the guitar
>
> ("'79 Bumblebee," EVH.com.)

Despite having worked closely with Grover Jackson during the '70s, Karl Sandoval remained for decades largely unrecognized for his contribution to guitar lore. However, his involvement with one iconic V-shaped instrument in particular is key to the history of flashy, customized pointy guitars.

Starting his career at Fender and later working at Wayne Charvel's guitar custom shop, Sandoval learned the fundamentals of guitar repair and custom building before establishing his own business in 1979. His key innovation was pioneering the use of Danelectro necks on custom guitars, which offered flat-radius fretboards that allowed extremely low string action and superior tremolo performance without fretting out, characteristics that became essential to the emerging shredder-style of playing.

The creation of Randy Rhoads's Polka Dot V began when Randy was talking guitars with future Dokken guitarist George Lynch (then with the Boyz), backstage in 1979. Randy was impressed by Lynch's custom Sandoval-built flying V guitar. Sandoval also worked with Lynch on his famous superstrat Tiger guitar, a 13-pound solid-maple body selected from Charvel shop scraps that evolved over decades with multiple neck and hardware configurations.

Randy contacted Sandoval, who by this time had left Charvel, and visited his garage workshop to discuss his vision of a V-shaped mahogany body with distinctive polka dots, a custom harpoon headstock that Randy sketched on notebook paper, and a Danelectro-based maple neck with bow-tie inlays. The resulting guitar featured dual DiMarzio pickups and a Fender-style tremolo system. Completed on September 22, 1979, for $738, Randy specifically requested no company logos or branding, which unfortunately obscured Sandoval's contributions to pointy guitar lore, although word of the quality of Sandoval's work did spread throughout California and he would go on to become a go-to guitar-repair and luthier resource to many stars. Along with his famous white Les Paul Custom, the Polka Dot V became Randy's signature instrument on Ozzy Osbourne's *Blizzard of Ozz* and *Diary of a Madman* albums, though Randy broke the headstock just three weeks after receiving it (which Sandoval quickly repaired).

Sandoval's modest garage workshop became a hub for Southern California's emerging metal elite, with clients including Eddie Van Halen (Karl also built

Eddie's Jerry Sewell–designed Megazone guitar, a geometric monstrosity that featured a 12-pound ash body and a Danelectro neck), Rhoads, George Lynch, Tracy G. of Dio, Rusty Anderson, and Lita Ford.

Grover Jackson borrowed money from his father to acquire controlling interest in the business and the right to the Charvel Guitars brand in November of 1978. By this point, the shop had moved to San Dimas, California, using a P.O. Box for correspondence. This address was stamped into the neckplate of Charvel guitars, becoming a defining feature of the instruments, and beginning a long association between the city and the early (and much coveted) guitars coming out of Charvel headquarters. These early "San Dimas" models fetch a considerable dollar on the vintage guitar market and have been referenced in numerous re-issue models since FMIC acquired the brand.

> Now, business is good, Wayne's crazy busy, and then you get Grover Jackson coming in — a real craftsman — and they end up working together. Eventually, Wayne has some financial trouble, and Grover takes over. And that's when Charvel really starts putting their name on these hot-rodded Strats. That's kind of the birth of the whole superstrat thing, man. Nobody was really customizing guitars before that; these guys were figuring it out as they went, hot pickups, wild finishes, the works.
>
> — Glen Booth, Canadian Business Development Manager, FMIC Specialties

> Wayne and Grover came to an agreement where Grover bought the business, in November 1978. By the end of January in the new year, Grover and his wife JoAnn Pieroth [later Jackson] had their first employee, 18-year-old guitarist Mike Eldred. Mike arrived at the San Dimas workshop one day after a tipoff from Ed Van Halen. He'd known Ed for a while, mainly through backstage guitar chats, and he'd followed Ed's progress through a series of eccentric guitars. First they seemed relatively normal — a white Ibanez, a Gold Top — but then one night up in the dressing room at the Whisky, Ed showed Mike a distinctly unusual Fender.
>
> "It was a black rosewood-neck Strat," Mike recalls, "and he'd painted a little white pinstripe around the edge. It had a stock

> tremolo, and a mint-green pickguard that he'd cut out and put a humbucker in the back. I went wow, this is so crazy — and it sounded killer! Fast forward a couple of months, again at the Whisky, I go in the dressing room and he has this black-and-white striped guitar. I'm like, 'What the fuck is that?' He goes, 'I built it myself, I got a body and a neck from Charvel Manufacturing.' I asked where they were at. He goes, 'They're in San Dimas and they sell bodies and necks.' I'm thinking OK, I gotta get one. So he gave me the phone number."
>
> Mike called Charvel and went to meet Grover to sort out the kind of guitar he'd like, handed over a deposit, and after that would make regular visits to pay off the balance. On one such occasion, and fed up with his job at a late-night grocery store that severely limited his opportunities to play music, he asked Grover if he was hiring.
>
> "Grover said to me, 'You don't want to work here, you'll mess your hands up — you're a guitar player.' I said I really needed to find a different job. So I filled in a form and I got the job," Mike remembers. "My motivation was that I just wanted to play music, but I had to put gas in the car, so I needed a job. And if I was getting a custom guitar made, what better scam is there than to go work at the place where my guitar is getting built? One, I'll probably get a break on the guitar, and two, I'll probably be able to build it myself, right there, using his tools. But then all around me, it grew really, really fast. Grover started hiring other people after me, and soon we were building so much stuff left and right."
>
> (Tony Bacon, "A Repair Shop Sparked a Revolution," Reverb.com)

Grover began making guitar bodies in house, while initially purchasing necks from Boogie Bodies. Under Grover's ownership, Charvel would supply bodies and woodworking services to companies like B.C. Rich, DiMarzio, and Mighty Mite (both of whom were selling guitar kits for DIY enthusiasts, along with various parts and — most famously in the case of DiMarzio — pickups). Prior to this, DiMarzio was acquiring their bodies from Boogie Bodies, as was Charvel. Both DiMarzio and Mighty Mite were also providing pickups for Charvel guitars. There was a close connection between these smaller, independent companies, sometimes as collaborators or mutually beneficial product providers, and sometimes as competitors, vying for pole position in this new guitar race. Jerry Sewell was a childhood friend of Grover Jackson's from his hometown of Chattanooga, Tennessee, and was brought into the Charvel fold when Grover acquired controlling interest of the company. As an employee of Grover, Jerry was initially making guitar bodies for Mighty Mite guitars but would reportedly leave Charvel to work for Mighty Mite directly.

> The team at the San Dimas workshop by the railroad tracks did indeed expand beyond the original trio of Grover, JoAnn, and Mike. After hiring Tim Wilson and Mike Shannon from a local firm called Woodworkers, they made guitar bodies for Mighty Mite and later for DiMarzio. And soon they had a set of Charvel guitars ready to show off to the music trade at the June 1979 NAMM show in Atlanta. "Probably the very first Charvel guitars that were sold on any kind of real commercial level were sold at that show," Grover recalls. "We sold them to some of our good friends from the Anvil days, a music shop called Veneman Music in the DC area. At that stage, these were Strat-style guitars in mahogany, oil finished and not painted."
>
> (Tony Bacon, "A Repair Shop Sparked a Revolution," Reverb.com)

We were all looking to make our guitars better with better components, especially considering Gibson and Fender's well-established production issues.

I found and contacted Wayne because I liked his brass Les Paul jack plates. I really thought those were great and I even started selling them. I must have replaced fifty of the plastic ones while I was working on 48th street — his brass ones made so much more sense. I ultimately met him at a NAMM show, a year or two later.

I also started ordering some bodies from him around '78, just Strats and Teles initially, but we added Explorer and

V-shaped bodies by '79. Then Wayne was suddenly out of the picture and Grover Jackson was the owner in charge.

JoAnn became my sales contact at Charvel, and soon became Mrs. Jackson. She told me that they had necks in addition to bodies, which totally fit my plan: I was already buying brass bridges from Stars Guitars in San Francisco and had designed the DiMarzio 250 and 500K pots. So, with the addition of bodies and necks, DiMarzio would be able to offer our dealers a full line of high-quality replacements parts that could be used to build a guitar or improve any Gibson or Fender.

When Grover's first shipment arrived, the bodies were good, but the necks didn't meet my expectations. Luckily, I was friends with Stu Spector, who was making basses in Brooklyn and using the DiMarzio Model P as his main pickup. He and his partner, Allen, agreed to build my necks and we spent months together (several days a week) fine-tuning every detail: I changed the traditional Fender fingerboard radius from 7.25" to 9.5" and opted for the larger frets that I preferred. They had Strat-style headstock shapes and were all maple in the beginning, with my favorite vintage Fender-style '57 V-shape profile and rolled fingerboard edges.

I also made a few changes to Grover's Strat-style bodies, so that they were felt more like what Fender produced in 1960 — those cuts were wonderful and felt better when playing in a standing position. I requested that they be made from only one or two pieces of wood, and that they only be finished with a sealer. This way you could do anything you wanted: paint them, keep them natural, etc.

— Larry DiMarzio ("The Birth of the Randy Rhoads Sandoval Dot V," DiMarzio.com.)

In my previous book, *Don't Call It Hair Metal*, I expounded upon the virtues of the first Mötley Crüe album, *Too Fast for Love*. On the back of that album,

Mick Mars is holding a guitar that I was never able to identify, an ultra-pointy beast with a shape that fell somewhere between a spider and a star. A brief mention in an excellent and informative documentary entitled *The Original Charvel Gang*, directed by former Charvel employee Paul Gervasi, helped me to discover that the person who designed and built that guitar was Dave Jellison, a prominent film and TV director responsible for over a thousand commercials, whose experience in a number of creative milieus has informed his success.

> Born in Memphis, Tennessee, David immediately began pursuing a career as a small, hollering infant. He was an instant success, and decided to move to Hollywood to find an industry that rewarded infantile behavior.
>
> He found it: The Music Industry. After surviving a soul-charring stint in that sociopathic hellshow, he escaped to the relative safety of advertising. Along the way, David designed guitars for Mötley Crüe, studied film at the Art Center, photography at Otis Parsons, and toured with Van Halen for four years as an Art Director . . . all without going to rehab. At the conclusion of his rock and roll career, David retired his mullet and began directing music videos, but soon switched to commercials after discovering that the catering was vastly superior.
>
> (David Jellison Bio, PersuaderMedia.com)

Dave Jellison's creative journey began in San Diego's vibrant music scene of the late 1970s, where he played in bands like Bad Reputation and Aircraft alongside future stars including Jake E. Lee from Teaser, Ratt, and Ozzy Osbourne. Dave's transformative musical moment came when Van Halen's debut album hit the scene. Jellison and his friends rushed to buy it at two o'clock from Licorice Pizza and played it three times straight, completely stunned by Eddie Van Halen's revolutionary guitar work that was, as Jellison said "so far beyond anybody else's skill set." When fellow San Diegan and future Ratt star Stephen Pearcy pioneered the move to Los Angeles in early 1980 and began playing venues like the Whisky, it set the wheels in motion for a core group of about 20 musicians from San Diego to follow suit. Among these hopefuls were future guitar stars Robbin Crosby, Jake E. Lee, and Warren DeMartini, all of whom would go on to achieve multiplatinum success. Jellison joined this exodus and within three weeks found himself in Ratt, which had just lost its bass player, and thrust into the electrifying Sunset Strip scene. As he describes it, the period was perfectly captured in the Mark Wahlberg film *Rock Star*, a period from 1980 to 1984 when legendary venues like Gazzari's, the Troubadour, and the Starwood represented a long-haired, leather-clad, drug-addled field of dreams.

His path to guitar craftsmanship began when he saw that Eddie had mentioned Charvel guitars in the credits of the first Van Halen album, and he reached out to the company about having a bass made (despite having no money):

> Grover had split from Wayne Charvel. I think it was 1978, but I contacted him in '79. I drove up there to a shop in a little industrial park, and I laid out the bass design, you know, flame pattern and everything. And he said, "Yeah. It'll be six months before you get it." I go, "Good, because it'll be six months before I can pay the rest of it off."
>
> I'd gone up there a couple of times for design meetings from San Diego to see Grover in San Dimas. San Dimas is about 40 or 50 miles outside of the center of L.A. It was just an industrial park that he could afford to set up a wood shop in. I kept going up there. I had worked construction in San Diego, but I didn't know any construction companies in Los Angeles. So, I said, "I'll ask Grover for a job, then I'll design and build guitars on the side." I had all these ideas for guitars.
>
> —Dave Jellison

Jellison was initially rejected by Grover Jackson, who "didn't hire band guys." Jellison persisted by offering to work a day for free, impressing Jackson with his detail work on necks — one of the most challenging parts of guitar construction involving extensive sanding and fretting. This led to a grueling schedule. However, Grover fostered a welcoming environment that felt like "the cool rock club," a generous, creative atmosphere where innovation could thrive, and he also understood exactly what would appeal to rock musicians.

> That was it. I lived in Hollywood and had to drive to San Dimas. It's an hour drive. Work started there at seven. I worked for

> Grover from seven to two thirty in the afternoon. Then I would work on my own guitars between two thirty and six thirty because you don't wanna drive back to Hollywood [in traffic] at that time. Ratt's garage that we practiced in was in Culver City. I would leave San Dimas at six thirty and get to the Ratt Cave, as we called it, at about seven forty-five. And then we'd rehearse eight to ten. I'd drive home and my girlfriend, who was going to school, worked at this fun curio shop in Century City called Heaven, and she would work till ten. So, basically, both of us would leave at six in the morning and return at ten thirty at night and then go back to bed.
>
> That was that era. I just started building guitars and basses, and I played them in Ratt. People came up and said, "Hey. Where'd you get that?" I'd say, "I made it, and I can make you whatever you want." So, I started this business of designing and building these instruments. (Robbin) Crosby saw my shit, and was like, "Where'd you get that?" Charvel was now just blowing up. So (Ratt) went to Grover Jackson and they did all the custom work.
>
> — Dave Jellison

Jellison observed some of the harsh realities of the scene. A good example was the financial state of the ascending musician. Mötley Crüe were so broke they couldn't afford the $350 he was charging for the guitars they were modeling on the back of their debut album.

> They couldn't even afford to buy the fucking guitars. They were on per diems, it was like six hundred and fifty dollars a month, but at the time, I'm like, "You're getting six hundred and fifty a month? Fuck, you're *rich*!" [*laughs*]

Jellison's guitar-design philosophy centered on pushing creative boundaries:

> How eccentric of a design can I make and still have it playable? I built a dozen instruments. One shaped like tommy gun, the blood bass [an Explorer-shaped model with a blood-splattered

> paint job made famous by Van Halen's Michael Anthony], a Megazone bass. I didn't wanna repeat myself. I kept trying to find new ideas and new things to create.

Arguably his most famous contribution to guitar building is the Jack Daniels bass he designed for Michael Anthony. The path to that instrument's creation reads like an idealized version of the American dream. Through a combination of creative impetus, hard work, connections, perseverance, and luck, Jellison found success that extended beyond his days working for Grover Jackson and applied his abilities to a number of different creative pursuits.

> My girlfriend's best friend was a girl named Tawny Kitaen [an actress and model perhaps most famous for her performance in Whitesnake's "Here I Go Again" video]. She was going out with Robbin Crosby who had not yet moved up [from San Diego], but she moved up. Crosby was still in San Diego playing in a band called Mac Meda and then he moved up and lived with his brother-in-law in Manhattan Beach.
>
> Tawny at that time had broken up with Robbin and was going out with Pete Angelus who was an art director and a lighting designer for Van Halen. Pete and I became roommates and he's like, "I want you to go on the road with us."
>
> In the intervening time, after a year of working at Charvel, and after I quit Ratt, I went to Vidal Sassoon [hair-styling school]. My girlfriend [who was studying at Vidal Sassoon] thought it would be a good creative outlet. I was still able to build [and] I would work one day a week at Charvel for Grover. At that point, he and I were friends, and he would let me have the run of the shop, basically. So, I would still make guitars for band guys in L.A., while going to the Vidal Sassoon school.
>
> Van Halen was prepping for the *Diver Down* tour and Pete said, "Why don't you come out with us? I need somebody. We'll start you on the stage." I started as a stage tech laying down the flooring and, you know, all the other stuff that you need on stage to get ready.

> The lighting department for Van Halen was always the most difficult because you leave the bus at six thirty in the morning, you get back on the bus at three in the morning, and you would not stop working in that time frame.
>
> It was because the system was so big and so complicated. I started out on stage and three weeks later, they had fired so many lighting people that they didn't even have other people to pull in. So, they said, "You're on the lighting crew." I said, "Okay." And they kept firing people throughout the tour till by the end, I was the lighting crew chief. I was in charge of the lighting system.
>
> I had a break [from the tour], and I did the 1983 NAMM show that was in Atlanta. I created and designed Charvel's backdrop for all the guitars, this whole system.
>
> While I was on tour with Van Halen, I became much more involved in the art direction side of it. I didn't have any time off. We toured South America. We did the US Festival. I was just basically on staff with those guys nonstop. At the end of the *Diver Down* tour, Mike Anthony said, "I wanna have a design, something that's like a signature instrument. And he drank Jack Daniels. So, I said, "Why don't we make a Jack Daniels bass?"
>
> And he's like, "You can do that?" I go, "Yeah. We sure as fuck can." [*laughs*] I met with Grover, and I laid out the design. And, so that's how the Jack Daniels bass came to be. And that was the last instrument that I designed. [Jackson/Charvel] built it. I designed it. I designed all the dimensions, the specs, the look, and where all the controls go and stuff like that. But Grover physically built that.

As we have seen, the specifics of "who did what" on some of the iconic instruments in Charvel/Jackson's history can become cloudy:

> A lot of people have laid claim to a lot of shit. And I'll give you an example. That Jack Daniels bass is in the Rock & Roll Hall of Fame. I'm listed third in line for the design when I did the whole fucking thing. The whole thing was my idea, and what happens is that gets filtered out, but at least at least I got a mention.
>
> — Dave Jellison

Along with superstrats, there were several other body shapes coming out of Charvel during the San Dimas era, including Telecasters and Explorers, as well as a guitar inspired by Eddie Van Halen's modified Ibanez Destroyer, the Star.

> The first time I ever really saw a Star model was one that Charvel made. That was like Eddie's shark guitar where he chopped up the middle. My first Star was from Wayne Charvel's shop. I forget the guy's name who made it — he was a guitar maker who worked for Wayne Charvel. I think I got it for like forty dollars, just the body, and then I put a left-handed Strat neck on it and painted it yellow.
>
> — Chris Holmes of W.A.S.P.

The San Dimas telecaster maintained the traditional Telecaster aesthetic while incorporating Charvel's hot-rodded appointments and modern hardware, appealing to players who wanted the classic Tele look with contemporary performance capabilities. San Dimas–era explorers and flying Vs represented Charvel's take on the aggressive Gibson shapes but with the company's signature fast, bolt-on necks and modern electronics. The connection between Charvel and the development of Jackson guitars also stems from this period's experimentation with radical body shapes. While many players, including Steve Vai (who famously borrowed a Grover Jackson–built sunburst finished superstrat with a unique humbucker-single coil-humbucker configuration and painted it green while on the road with Alcatrazz in Japan) were content with an outlandish paint scheme on existing Charvel models, some wanted more.

Eddie Van Halen's stripes and Randy Rhoads's polka dots kickstarted a trend of instrument personalization that allowed a player or band to be linked to the instruments they were playing, another marketing tool to be used in the highly visual '80s. The most recognizable and requested paint jobs included George Lynch's Bengal Tiger stripe and Warren DeMartini's Blood and Skull and the Japanese-themed Rising Sun, driving home the point that in 1980s California (and to every guitar playing kid around the world who wanted to be there), the looks were just as important as the hooks.

Aside from his ground-breaking and breathtaking guitar work with Ozzy, Randy Rhoads would also become known as a design visionary for one of, if not *the* most famous pointy guitar models of all time.

On December 23, 1980, while on a break from Ozzy's *Blizzard of Ozz* tour, Rhoads visited Grover Jackson at the Charvel workshop with a sketch he'd drawn on a cocktail napkin.

This collaboration resulted in Randy Rhoads's first Jackson prototype: a white, pinstriped, asymmetrical Flying V–inspired model built largely by shop foreman Tim Wilson. The guitar had a maple neck and body with neck-through construction, an ebony fretboard, medium frets, a Stratocaster-style tremolo system, and Seymour Duncan pickups. The resulting white, angular, asymmetric instrument was nicknamed "the Concorde" because it resembled the supersonic airliner of the same name, with some saying that Rhoads named the guitar after the aircraft because he actually flew home from the U.K. aboard the Concorde in late 1980. This prototype became historically significant as not only as a further evolution of pointy guitars, but also as the first instrument to bear the Jackson logo. Jackson, cautious of alienating customers with a confusing, unusual design, was hesitant to place the Charvel name on the instrument and instead put his own name on the pointed headstock, thus founding Jackson Guitars as a separate brand.

> Here's where it gets good — Randy Rhoads comes along, right? He wants something completely different, way outside of what everyone else was playing. So, Grover designs this insane V-shape, totally radical. But he's thinking, "If this thing doesn't fly, I don't want to drag the Charvel name through the mud." So, he sticks "Jackson" on the headstock instead. And of course, it takes off— Randy Rhoads, Ozzy, boom!
>
> — Glen Booth

> Grover had made a few earlier through-neck V-style guitars for an Italian guitarist, Vic Vergeat. But Randy's was the first with a Jackson logo on the head rather than Charvel, Grover apparently thinking he didn't want this unusual design to clash

> too obviously with the developing Charvel line. Around March '81, Randy took delivery of his new Jackson, which had a pointy offset-V body finished in white with black pinstripe detailing. There was a vibrato bridge, two humbuckers and four controls, a block-inlay board, and Grover's take on a droopy Explorer-style headstock. Randy immediately put the instrument to good use, but soon he was thinking about a more extreme design. Randy told Grover that people would ask if his white guitar was a butchered job on a real Flying V. "So now he wanted something more sharkfin-like," Grover says.
>
> (Tony Bacon, "A Repair Shop Sparked a Revolution," Reverb.com)

With a clear distinction between the companies, Jackson would become the pointier sibling known for neck-through construction, while Charvel maintained its status as the more traditional bolt-on neck instrument of choice.

Randy wasn't completely satisfied with the first design and re-designed the next prototype because he felt the shape of the Concorde wasn't distinctive enough from the traditional Flying V (apparently spurred on by questions from fan's asking if the guitar was simply a modified Gibson V). His solution was to elongate the top "horn" of the instrument so that the body bore more resemblance to a shark's fin. With its black finish and gold hardware put together by Mike Shannon, this guitar was meant to become the third of Rhoads's iconic flying Vs to be used in concert.

Tragically, Rhoads died in a plane crash in March 1982 before two other refined guitars were completed and before he could give Grover any feedback on the design of the black and gold guitar. Following Randy's death, the refined prototypes he had been working on became the foundation for Jackson's production line. These revised prototypes would become the first guitars sold to the public under the Jackson Guitars brand name. Vinnie Vincent, formerly of Kiss, was the first professional guitarist to be offered an early Rhoads guitar by Jackson after Rhoads's death. Vincent used the Rhoads model on the Kiss *Creatures of the Night* and *Lick It Up* tours from 1982 until 1984. The design's popularity led to its evolution into a full production series that would span multiple decades.

> The Rhoads guitar had established the idea for the Jackson brand alongside Charvel, and soon the catalogues were calling the operation Charvel/Jackson, with a flurry of instruments pictured inside with one or other of the brand names. The general distinction at the time was that Charvel guitars were bolt-on and Jackson guitars were neck-through-body. What became known as the superstrat style was taking shape, too, primarily as the Jackson models were offered with 24 frets (following a request from Sammy Hagar's guitarist, Gary Pihl), hum and sing pickups were arranged in various "new" combinations, and locking trems were installed.
>
> (Tony Bacon, "A Repair Shop Sparked a Revolution," Reverb.com)

Superstrat models like the neck through Soloist and the bolt on Dinky (so named for its smaller body shape) became popular with players like Def Leppard's Phil Collen, and combined the sleek, traditional body of a Stratocaster with the more aggressive, pointy headstock found on the Rhoads model. Collen's relationship with Jackson would result in his own signature guitar models.

> The very first Phil Collen model, you know, we'd actually done something that was a bit wonky. It was like the Salvador Dali clock, where it's been melted, and it curved around the back so it fit the player's body great. I just wanted something a little bit different. . . . I went to the Jackson factory, and it's not far from where I live now. But, you know, back then in the '80s, we would go there, or Grover would come out on tour, and we'd go in a drawing room, and we'd get it up on on this board and everything to draw the thing. And I remember going down there and he hacked a piece of wood up with a neck on it. I've actually still got it. It's got all these pencil marks on it. And it plays, and it's actually great. And that was the original, you know, Jackson Phil Collen model guitar. This was before I went to the PC1 [Phil's production-model

> signature guitar, launched in 1995]. And that was basically me throwing my hands up and saying, "Okay. You know what? It's so much easier just to play a Strat." With a raw kind of neck, I use giant fat necks. Now I've got these telecasters that Jackson have made me that are probably my favorite guitars I've ever had, and it's the biggest neck they've ever made. So they're really chunky. It has an ash body, and it has a DiMarzio X2N in it with coil splits. It can really sound like a clean country or jazz guitar or whatever.
>
> — Phil Collen of Def Leppard

Michael Sweet of Stryper was an early Rhoads model supporter, and has since gone on to play a number of pointy guitars of varying brands inspired by iconic Jackson shapes.

> My first and biggest influence — though I don't necessarily play or sound anything like him — was Michael Schenker, who always played a V. I loved everything about his approach: his style, his soul, and especially the fact that he played a V because it was different and distinctive. When Randy Rhoads came on the scene with his Vs — the Rhoads model and that famous Polka Dot V — I fell in love with his style too. The fact that he also chose to play a V really resonated with me. Both Michael and Randy are two of my biggest influences, and I think they subconsciously contributed to my decision to play Vs. Dave Meniketti from Yesterday and Today (Y&T) was another influence. He played a V back in the day on their first album — you can see it in the photos. Seeing him with that V was probably another factor in why I continue to play Vs to this day. In my opinion, he was every bit as good a player as Rhoads or Eddie or Lynch. Dave was just so awesome to watch live — an incredible singer, player, showman, with so much fire and energy.
>
> My first pointy guitar that I bought with my own money and played faithfully was a Dean explorer model [a Dean Z] from the '70s. I bought it back in the '70s, and that purchase really started my trend with pointy guitars. From there, I graduated

> to purchasing Stephen Pearcy's Gibson V. When we became Stryper, I went to Guitar Center in Santa Ana and bought an original Jackson Rhoads — white with gold hardware. The serial number on that guitar was in the first hundred ever made. No one was playing those guitars at the time except for Randy. By the time we reached *To Hell with the Devil*, Jackson made me a Kelly model with triangles on it, which became iconic for the band. Eventually, I had a reverse Rhoads custom made for me, and later I had a King V made as well. I just became a V guy through and through — I've always played Vs.
>
> — Michael Sweet of Stryper

Chris Holmes, the legendary lead guitarist for W.A.S.P., and now currently fronting his own band Mean Man, was another player who helped put the Rhoads model on the map.

> In '82, W.A.S.P. was doing a movie called *Dungeonmaster* at the Troubadour [in Hollywood]. We were filming it. And then I called up Grover. I said, "Grover, I'm doing a movie. If I use one of your guitars in the movie, can I get one?" And he goes, "Now you're talking. You're helping me promote my business."
>
> He brought the guitar down to where I was filming the movie. It was a Black Randy Rhoads V. I used their guitar in the movie. And then I went to the shop, and they made me one. I told them, "Listen, if you make me a few Jacksons, that's all I'll ever play for the rest of my life." They always gave me everything I wanted. Everything. And I never once really played anything else. I recorded every W.A.S.P. album with the black Randy Rhoads V, the first one they ever gave me — the first album, *The Last Command*, *Inside the Electric Circus*, *The Headless Children* — every solo, everything. If you saw me put a Les Paul on, you'd just laugh. It looks like a tinker toy on me because I wear the guitar low. I'm six-six, and the Destroyer is a bigger guitar. A V looks bigger too. Even though it doesn't have more wood, they look bigger, and that's why I preferred them.
>
> — Chris Holmes of W.A.S.P.

Along with the Rhoads V, Holmes played a number of Charvel and Jackson models in W.A.S.P., custom variations of the V, Star, and Explorer shapes with a variety of graphics including the Harley Davidson logo, zebra stripes, an image of Charles Manson (!), and one unique explorer-inspired shape that was created for *The Headless Children* album featuring the California Highway Patrol insignia.

> Grover said, "What shape do you want?" I asked what he had, and he pulled out a notebook with billions of shapes that somebody had drawn. I went through them and said, "Boom. That one. I want that shape." He said, "Okay, we've never done this, but cool." So he made that shape — it's never been made before.
>
> — Chris Holmes

Mick Sweda currently plays with Poison drummer Rikki Rockett's band the Rockett Mafia, as well as his own band the Hot Summers. He made his name as lead guitarist for Los Angeles based acts BulletBoys and King Kobra. His relationship with Jackson reinforces the company's willingness to explore new design methods to give the artist what they are looking for:

> When I became aware of Charvel and Jackson, I was really drawn to their Star body shape. I just love that design. I mean, I've always loved Explorers from the very beginning. But when I noticed that they had those Stars available, I thought, *Well, I don't want to have a Star like everybody else.* So I got in touch with Jackson and had them customize one for me. They beveled the edges and made it a neck-through design, which I don't think they were making at that point. I dove right into the pointy guitar thing right off the bat, I guess you could say.
>
> That guitar is really more of a prototype than anything else. Like I said, they hadn't done a neck-through before. The upper fret access isn't really that good because back then, they didn't even think about carving that area out. There were a lot of things that had to be worked out with that guitar because it was literally the first [neck-through Star] they made. My Star played really well. At the time, I was wearing it a little higher than I

> wore the Les Pauls, just because it felt more natural to have it in that position. So, it was easier to play. It had the Floyd Rose on it, so that added another dimension to my playing. That guitar is really heavy, but the lightness factor wasn't an issue for me. To me, the heavier the guitar, the better. The more weight it had, the better it sounded to me. I actually like the heaviness factor.
>
> — Mick Sweda of BulletBoys, King Kobra, and the Rockett Mafia

Both Sweet and Holmes, while on decidedly different sides of the spiritual and moral spectrum back in the day (one band renounces the Beast, one aspires to copulate like it, if certain song titles are to be taken literally), did at least share a love of Jackson guitars. They were both notorious tone chasers with signature sounds and, through tireless experimentation, ran their Jackson instruments through an interesting array of sonic manipulators to achieve massive, arena-rock ready tones.

> I'm like the OCD, ADHD musician. I'm never happy. Even if it's amazing and the best-sounding tone you've ever heard in your life, I still want to make it better. That can be a fault at times, but [what] we've done over the years, we experimented and tried things that maybe some people didn't try.
>
> I'm never happy — I mean, I'm happy, but I'm always trying to be happier and make it better. That's my thinking. The words "good enough" never come out of my mouth. If I have a killer pickup in my guitar and I love it and it sounds perfect, and someone comes up to me and says, "Man, have you heard this pickup?" I'll say, "Oh, throw it in. Let's throw it in my guitar right now." I'll try anything. Just always searching for a better tone.
>
> The first album I bought was *Boston* — the first Boston album. That's really what sent me over the edge in terms of my quest for the ultimate guitar tone. I heard that tone and I was like, "Wow." I started going out to pawnshops and trying out different gear, different amps, and different pedals on the front end and back end. That was really what did it for me. . . . That was in '76 when I heard Boston. Fast forward to like '79, and that's when I found

a Lab Series. I love Montrose, and I found the Lab Series, and I started creeping that into a Marshall. That's what changed my world. That was the Stryper tone that instantly formed.

— Michael Sweet

Sweet would go on to play in a late-era line-up of Boston — another band defined largely by their guitar tones — after the passing of vocalist Brad Delp.

Love our tone or hate it — and we get both sides of that coin, believe me — it's a very identifiable tone. Immediately when you hear it, you know it's us. And it's because of that midrange. Basically, what it is with the Lab Series: I found that head in L.A., and I liked it because Ronnie Montrose used it. You listen to that Montrose album, and you can hear just that tone. That was his own thing and very different than other players at the time, and it instantly made my ears perk up. Same with the *Boston* album, and then obviously, next level with the *Van Halen I* album. Everyone in the '70s had a straight-in mentality — old school Marshalls that had the four inputs that didn't overdrive as much. It was a different thing. Once we got into the '80s, I think people were a lot more experimental, and I was very experimental.

— Michael Sweet

I'm more into the sound — what I do for sound — more than my actual guitar playing. Fuck, who cares about shredding? Everybody shreds. But it's the sound that's the most important thing. It wasn't about all the notes. It was about making a big sound that could fill up a room and get people excited.

I always run signal one totally dry — nothing on it, no effects. Then the other side is just all effect without any dry signal, no blend. That's what makes the stereo spread. It sounds big — the frequency range is huge. It makes two guitars at once. You take maybe 27 to 30 milliseconds of slap delay. You've got the dry signal, and then the other one you bend the note a little bit. I turn the rate real slow so it's almost like a harmonizer. The

Lexicon processor in that rack I've had since '83. That's what gives you your stereo spread. It's weird how I run my sound. I've seen Steve Vai's and Joe Satriani's setups, and nobody runs it like I do. I don't know why.

Joe Floyd from the band Warrior came into our studio and hooked up my Lexicon. He said I needed two amps, so we got two amps. When I played, I went, "Woah, that's fucking happening." Once he did that, I never went back to mono again. Because of him, that's half the sound I got.

— Chris Holmes

I remember going into the pro audio department of a music store. I said, "I want to try that for guitar," talking about the Furman PEQ3, and the guy said, "You can't. That's not for guitar." I said, "Well, I don't really care. I want to try it." He goes, "Suit yourself." I hooked it up to a Marshall in there, and everyone started circling around. It was like, "Whoa, how are you getting that tone?" It was just gnarly. I ran the preamp out into a Marshall, and it was just this wall of sound. What I was doing was adding — there was a little semi-parametric on that Lab Series — I was adding between 750 and 800 hertz and boosting it all the way up. I used that for a while.

We played with Mickey Ratt when Jake E. Lee was in the band still, and I used to hide that Lab Series. They would say, "Man, how are you getting that tone?" I'm like, "Yeah, that Marshall."

I graduated eventually — around 1980, almost '81, I started using a PEQ3 made by Furman. If you fast forward to Dimebag and Pantera, he started using a PEQ3 and then moved into a PEQ4. I've heard in multiple interviews him actually say that he was inspired by our tone. It's like a half-cocked *wah* sound — very Schenkerish, but with a lot more gain. That input knob is all the way up, and that red light was staying on constantly. That was the tone. That's the sound you hear on our first album, *Yellow and Black Attack*, on *Soldiers* [*Soldiers Under Command*], and on *To Hell with the Devil*.

— Michael Sweet

We did start using different heads. On *Soldiers*, we used the Mark IIC+ Boogie. On *To Hell with the Devil*, we started using Boogies and Marshalls and even a Dumble. We rented a Dumble — didn't know it, but we rented it. That's where we started experimenting more with heads. We recorded at a place called Master Control. They were the first studio in L.A. to have this particular machine — a Mitsubishi 32-track digital machine. We were, from what I understand, the first metal band to record digitally, in the U.S. at least. We did different miking techniques [that] at the time no one was doing — like, most people were using Celestians. We were using, back in 1986 and '87, Electro-Voices, EVs. They were looked down on at the time for guitar — they were more of a P.A. speaker. But we used them in our guitar rigs. Then you fast forward six, seven years later, and Zakk Wylde used them.

— Michael Sweet

The Jackson Kelly is a heavily modified version of the Gibson Explorer that came about when Bradford Kelly approached Jackson Guitars in the early 1980s. Kelly was a guitarist for the Australian metal band Heaven, and he had previously endorsed the Hamer Blitz guitar, suggesting an affinity for Explorer shapes. The Kelly model would see increased profile and popularity thanks to Megadeth's Marty Friedman, who would go on to have his own signature series Kelly released in the 1990s.

[Around 1985] was the first time I heard Jackson existed, and it was supposedly this ultra-boutique company that makes the best guitars in the world. And they had this [Kelly] shape. I always loved that Explorer shape. So, it was kind of a no-brainer that the first time I was to buy a really good quality guitar, I was gonna get a shape that I really liked.

I think I first got into the Explorer shape, because when I was a kid, I loved the very first Def Leppard album. On the back,

> Pete Willis is playing a Hamer Explorer [a Blitz], and I was a big Runaways fan, and Lita Ford played a Hamer Explorer [a Blitz] back then. So those two just looked the coolest thing I ever saw.
>
> I became more obsessed with the look of the guitar as an accessory, which fits into your book concept. It's like a necklace or a suit or something. You know? It's part of the look. There's magic that happens when you have a shape that fits you and your personality and your body type. Nothing is cooler than standing there with a rad shape. It was the best guitar I ever played, and it's still right up there now as one of the top guitars I've ever played.
>
> I still was with Carvin when I joined Megadeth. At that time, both the other guitarists and bassist of Megadeth had Jackson, so it would just be a natural for me to get signed up with Jackson too. And I couldn't have been happier. The first thing and main thing that I did [on the signature Kelly model] was I got rid of a bunch of the knobs, and I put only one knob on it and put it far away because when I play, my hands are all over the place. I just don't have a really tight and accurate playing style. It's almost like I'm flailing around aggressively, kind of like a punk guitarist might.

Friedman's most recent Jackson signature model marries the traditional look of a Gibson Les Paul with a futuristic pointy nod in its unique headstock design.

> The only guitar shape that looks great on everybody, and it's a mystery why this is, is the Les Paul shape. It just looks great on everybody. It looks good on wild rock dudes. It looks good on accountants. It just looks like it just completes the picture. You can't take a bad picture. In terms of the headstock, it's gotta be Jackson. It's gotta be futuristic. It's gotta be modern. There has to be some sense of metal in there. It's like a little clue to the people looking at this. I might be wearing a tuxedo, but I'm still metal. That's what the headstock is all about.
>
> — Marty Friedman of Megadeth

The models that came after the RR speak to the success and popularity of the angles and geometry that helped define it. The King V, designed in the early '80s was a more symmetrical flying V–design than the Rhoads. It became popular among metal players for its aggressive points and solid balance. It was popularized by and named after Robbin "King" Crosby of Ratt and has been a weapon of choice for thrash metal innovators like Scott Ian of Anthrax and Dave Mustaine of Megadeth, and later model variants were seen in the hands of modern metal merchants like Corey Beaulieu of Trivium and Phil Demmel of Machine Head. The King V is actually a modified version of the Double Rhoads, a customized guitar for Overkill guitarist Dave Linsk that was built for players of larger physical stature. This is the instrument that Crosby played most, with the King V being a scaled down version of the Double Rhoads. The King V had shorter wings, and unlike the Double Rhoads, was made available as a production model.

The Warrior's angular, modernistic design made its debut in 1990, and was designed by Mikey Wright, then head of Research and Development at Jackson. The Warrior, a five-pointed beast with a pointy headstock and four body horns, pushed the boundaries of guitar aesthetics with lines directly inspired from the headstock popularized by Jackson on the Rhoads model. It represents the most extreme body design in the Jackson arsenal.

Amir Derakh is another musician from San Diego who had enjoyed success over the decades as a guitarist, producer, and engineer with bands like Rough Cutt, Jailhouse, Orgy, and Juilen-K, to name but a few. Amir has also designed a number of guitars and has worked closely with Jackson over the years.

> "I always liked really unique guitars, and seeing some of these other guys that were using these guitars, like Randy Rhoads, that inspired my choice to use something different." Before joining Rough Cutt, Amir already owned "a Star body Charvel that probably was made in San Dimas." When Rough Cutt manager Wendy Dio helped connect him to Grover and JoAnn Jackson, he "just really hit it off with them," and, as has become a theme in this story, was welcomed with open arms. "They really liked me, so we started making some guitars, some custom guitars, which in the beginning were not free, but they gave me an

> amazing deal." Amir's experiments included painting guitars like fighter planes.
>
> "I started painting them like fighter planes. The dad that I grew up with was an Air Force pilot, he flew a B-17 in World War II, and I have [this] thing for military stuff and fighter planes — I love military stuff. So, I started doing these fighter plane paint jobs, which, up to that point I don't think anybody had ever done. So that kind of became my theme. And, you know, a lot of those early guitars were made from scraps, B stock and things like that. Like I said, the first one or two guitars I had payment plans on them. But then at a certain point, Grover and JoAnn kind of pulled me aside and said, 'Look, you're touring a lot, we want to get you a couple more guitars so that you've got enough guitars, because you're touring a lot.' And I was like, 'Oh, well, you know, I can't really afford that.' And they're like, 'No, no, don't worry about it. And actually, don't worry about whatever you owe us on the guitars that you've already got. We're giving you a full endorsement.'
>
> "I started to learn how to make guitars, because he started teaching me at that point. What they used to call the 'Bone Room.' And I picked out some things, and he kind of explained why this one was better than that. Two of my favorite guitars that I ever made with them were those two guitars which were actually made from rejected parts, rejected bodies, and rejected necks."
>
> — Amir Derakh of Orgy and Julien-K

The most innovative idea to come out of the relationship came out of an idea that, perhaps, two necks were better than one. Amir's double-neck guitar journey began with inspiration from icons Alex Lifeson and Jimmy Page, prompting him to propose the idea to Jackson, but the idea was initially met with reluctance,

> I just always thought it'd be so cool to have a double neck guitar. [The Jacksons] were like, "Nah, no, we don't — that's going to be pretty hard. I don't think we could do that." At the NAMM convention Bernie Rico of B.C. Rich stepped in: "I really wanted

> to make a double neck, but Jackson didn't want to do it." [Bernie Rico] said, "I'll make you a double neck. They won't care."

After checking in with Grover, who gave his blessing for the project to go forward with B.C. Rich, a beautiful Warlock-shaped double neck, painted like a British Harrier jump jet by Glenn Matejzel was unfortunately stolen from the B.C. Rich plant in a major theft, and a Polaroid picture taken by Glenn after it was painted was the only proof of its existence. After hearing of the theft, Grover Jackson reversed his stance:

> After that happened, the Jackson people, Grover, Darla, and JoAnn, they all got word of what happened to Bernie, which, of course, was horrible, and they felt bad. One day, JoAnn called me up [and says,] "Grover wants to talk to you." He goes, "Come down here and make your stupid double neck."

Amir, Grover, and Mike Shannon improvised the design from spare parts:

> We had like a couple of strat bodies, basically, kind of laying on top of each other. . . . I was like, "What if, you know, crazy idea, but what if the bottom neck had a reverse headstock, and the top one had a normal headstock?" And we kind of cocked the necks out so that they could connect. And so we laid it out with the neck pieces and body pieces. Mike Shannon said, "I can make that work." He goes, "I'll put an hourglass piece of wood in the headstock tops, so that they connect." So he made a little cut out, almost like you do corners on furniture. He figured out a way to basically lock them together. So we did that. And I [suggested] that the shark inlay should be reversed, so that it looks kind of like it points.

The tuner layout was refined by borrowing from B.C. Rich's innovative design for the Bich:

> "Why don't we kind of rip off the B.C. Rich, so we can send the six strings back to the back of the body." On my design the

> tuning knobs were actually hidden behind the body, and you wouldn't see them, and if you stuck it on a guitar stand or it was standing upright you wouldn't bump the tuners, which is the way that I wanted it. When they actually went into production — and I don't know why they did this — they changed that. Somebody thought that wasn't a good idea, that you need to see the tuners.
>
> — Amir Derakh

Famous musicians who played Amir's Jackson double-neck design included C.C. DeVille of Poison, Canadian guitar hero Jeff Healey, and Adrian Smith of Iron Maiden.

> I was really flattered that, you know, people took to the design. I'm sure they didn't make a lot of them. I don't remember how many they made, but I would guess it was definitely less than 100. So probably, you know, 50 to 70 is my guess, maybe.
>
> It's really disappointing that Jackson has never given me credit for any of that, and they've actually made some of those guitars. It's like special sales, and it's caused some online outrage. You know, people are just like, "What the hell, like? It doesn't say anything about you here." Even Mike Shannon, has come out, in a movie [*The Original Charvel Gang*] and talked about designing the guitar, and he gave me full credit for everything. And you know, it's just like [Jackson] won't acknowledge my designs, yet they still use them and sell them.
>
> And the thing is, it's not even about the money for me, because I know how much money you make doing this. It's not a lot. It's about just being cool, you know, like, hey, this is an homage to my design. You know, they take my ideas and they kind of move the things around on the guitar, and then, you know, oh, it's a Harrier fighter plane, double neck, you know, whatever, created by Dan Lawrence. And it's like, okay, well, this was entirely my idea. And Dan, you know, he's great, and we work together really well. And these designs,

> you know, they started with me, but we worked together to create it. So, he had input as well, as did Mike Shannon in creating the guitar. So, I'm not like, "Oh, I did this all soup to nuts," but it was my idea initially; it's my design. They just don't acknowledge that.
>
> — Amir Derakh

Amir was one of a rare number of artists who found success in the '80s hard-rock milieu as well as in the post-grunge era with his band Orgy, signed as the first act to Korn vocalist Jonathan Davis's Elementree imprint on Reprise Records. Orgy struck gold and platinum with their mix of electronic, industrial, goth, and nu-metal elements. This new musical environment provided Amir with an opportunity to further explore his guitar-design innovations.

> When I started doing the thing with Orgy, I really didn't want to play *just* guitar again. I wanted to play guitar synth, and I was only interested in using really weird guitars. Donnie Wade [marketing manager for Jackson / Charvel] approached me and said, "Look, I really want to get you back to Jackson." And he's like, "What do I have to do to make that happen?" [I said,] "Well, you know, I really like this Roswell guitar. It seems like you guys can do some really crazy stuff, so I want to do something crazy."

The Roswell was Jackson's late '90s sci-fi take on the Randy Rhoads model, the apparent result of a dream by then-marketing director Charles Perrino. The Roswell's aluminum body was shaped like the famous Star Trek logo, and featured crop circle fretboard inlays.

> I took that Roswell guitar and turned it into a Roswell Star, and that was the first thing we did, which is also very pointy. The first few of those Roswell Stars were painted with chameleon paint, which changes colors when you look at it. My very first Charvel was this purple Star body. And when I came back to Jackson, I re-created a modern version of that . . . It all kind of came full circle.

Another pointy innovation of Amir's around the same time was the Disruptor model, which was "inspired by a mix of Vox Phantom and Star Wars aesthetics."

As has been the case with every company we have looked at, success breeds demand, which requires greater production capacity. In 1985, Grover aligned with Texas-based International Music Corporation while moving the business from Glendora to a 28 thousand square foot facility in Ontario, California. This new business situation saw guitars made in Japan being issued under the Charvel brand, and Jackson guitars remaining as a U.S.-made brand exclusively.

Perhaps the most cherished of these new Japanese instruments were the Charvel Model series built in the Chushin Gakki factory in Nagano. The six unique guitars built in the superstrat mold included features found on USA-built Jackson Custom shop instruments, all with pointy headstocks brandishing the Charvel name.

Grover Jackson left Jackson / Charvel in 1989, going on to work with companies like Washburn, B.C. Rich, Friedman, and his own GJ2 brand. Wayne Charvel launched Wayne Guitars with his son Michael in 1999, offering custom shop instruments inspired by classic Charvel models.

In 1997, Charvel / Jackson was acquired by Akai, and ultimately landed with Fender Musical Instrument Corporation in 2001, where they remain today. Master builders like Dave Nichols, Joe Williams, "Big" Rob Knowles, and Pasquale "Pat" Campolattano carry on the traditions of pointy guitar excellence passed down from the Jackson / Charvel originators, crafting everything from meticulously detailed early Charvel throwbacks, to fully customized modern metal machines.

> [With the dawn of Jackson / Charvel] now you've got this whole new lane for guitars. The cool thing is it was always a custom-shop vibe. Guys would ask, "Can you do this graphic? Can you throw these pickups in?" and the answer was always "Yeah, why not!" Shark-fin inlays, compound-radius boards — Jackson and Charvel were the first guys doing that stuff. I mean, it was all hand-built, and it still is — a two-year wait list for a Custom Shop Jackson now.

> Some of those old luthiers are still kicking around, passing the tricks down the line. Really, the whole Do-It-Yourself and modding scene? It started with these guys. That Southern California hot rod mentality — strip it down, build it back up, make it your own. Charvel and Jackson, man, they weren't just building guitars, they were inventing how rock guitars could look and sound. And honestly? They still are.
>
> — Glen Booth

Through the success, failures, trials, and changes that have marked decades of presence in the guitar market, Grover Jackson's relationship with his employees and the artists he worked with is undoubtedly the beating heart of Charvel/Jackson's story of innovation. Wayne Charvel and Grover Jackson's careful accommodation of and attention to the needs and desires of guitarists over the course of the company's history have resulted in music that will resonate for years to come.

> I think what makes a successful working relationship is exactly that — relationship. If you're getting with a company based on just how much gear you can get, you need to re-evaluate, because that's not going to be a good relationship. It should be about working together to help one another, working to create better gear, something innovative, something new, something better sounding, something that plays better.
>
> — Michael Sweet

CHAPTER 12

LADO, GODFREY, AND THE POINTY GUITARS OF CANADIAN ROCK

As a proudly Canadian guitarist, I have been fortunate to work with a number of my home and native land's greatest artists, many of whom I grew up listening to. Lee Aaron, Coney Hatch, Helix, and Honeymoon Suite often provided the soundtrack to sun-drenched days on the beach, sweat-drenched nights at the high-school dance, and booze-soaked parties deep in the wilds of the Northern Ontario bush. Video didn't necessarily kill the radio star in the '80s, but it's almost impossible to separate songs like "Whatcha Do to My Body," "Wild in the Streets" or "Wave Babies" from the videos that made these Canadian idols seem larger than life. Most of these celluloid clips featured the bands in some kind of performance environment, wielding visually striking pointy guitars of some brand or another. While these groups, and others like Platinum Blonde, Haywire, Saga, Toronto, and Brighton Rock, were playing the major American or Japanese guitar brands, one Canadian guitar brand in particular was seen in the hands of all of the aforementioned bands at some point in their careers, and found in the hands of international superstars like Iron Maiden, Nazareth, and Sabaton.

> The '80s Canadian rock scene was electric, and Lado guitars were right at the heart of it. Our instruments didn't just support

the sound of the era, they helped define it. With their striking designs, powerful tone, and unmistakable presence, Lado guitars became part of the visual and sonic signature of some of the most iconic acts of the time.

Platinum Blonde was one of the first major bands to showcase Lado on national stages. Their sound was massive, their look was sharp, and the Lazer and Falcon models matched that energy perfectly. Saga brought a more progressive, technical edge, and their use of Lado guitars validated the brand among serious players looking for precision and tone.

Haywire, one of the East Coast's standout rock acts, also played a key role. They embraced Lado's blend of visual style and rock-solid craftsmanship, helping carry the brand's momentum through the late '80s and into the early '90s.

We also had strong connections with Brighton Rock, Coney Hatch, Lee Aaron, and Honeymoon Suite — artists who didn't just pose with the guitars, they played them, live and in the studio. Lado became part of their toolkit — not because of contracts, but because of trust in the instrument.

— Joe "Lado" Kovacic, owner of Lado Guitars

JOE AND SUSAN KOVACIC

JOE AND SUSAN KOVACIC

Lado Guitars was founded by Joe Kovacic, a luthier who trained in Zagreb, Croatia before immigrating to Canada in 1968 to work for Turner Musical Instruments, a distributor for Gibson guitars. Joe started Lado Musical Inc. in 1973, opening a retail shop on Kingston Road in Toronto, where he not only built Lado guitars, but also held an exclusive repair contract for Canada with C.F. Martin Guitars. Lado was named after a professional Croatian folk-dance group. Joe had built a double bass for the group, and in turn received permission to use the Lado name on his instruments. The word Lado is synonymous with good, love, and dear, and Kovacic would come to be known by the nom de plume Joe Lado to the artists who played his highly regarded handmade instruments.

I asked Joe, and his daughter Susan Kovacic (who I thank profusely for her time and efforts in helping convey her father's story) to share the Lado Guitars mission statement:

> There really isn't a formal one, but informally, after 55 years of crafting, I'd most likely create one today like this:
>
> Lado Guitars exists to create instruments that do more than play — they speak. Built by hand, powered by imagination, and made to push boundaries, each Lado guitar is a fusion of old-world craftsmanship and forward-thinking design. We build iconic tools for players who want to sound different, look different, and feel connected to something real. Every curve, every fret, every finish — made with purpose. Played with passion. We build not for trends, but for legacy — one guitar at a time.
>
> In fact, part of our marketing branding tagline in the '80s and '90s, which was in our brochures said: "Handcrafted quality ahead of its time."
>
> —Joe "Lado" Kovacic

JOE AND SUSAN KOVACIC

And what was it that Lado guitars had that other companies were missing?

> According to 90 percent of the musicians who've played them, it's the neck. Lado guitars are renowned for having some of the fastest, smoothest-playing necks out there — thanks to Joe's expertly crafted fingerboard radius and ergonomic design. But the real magic goes beyond just feel.
>
> Lado was never about cookie-cutter production. From the very beginning, it was all about custom craftsmanship — building guitars and basses to the exact specs of the musician, not just rolling out standard models. Every instrument was a one-of-a-kind creation, fine-tuned for tone, feel, and presence.
>
> There were even periods where basses surged in popularity over guitars — and later, Tele-style Lado models found their moment too. But regardless of style or era, one thing stayed consistent: quality.
>
> Another signature element? The neck-through-body construction. Unlike bolt-on necks, this design runs a single piece of wood from headstock to strap button, giving Lado instruments unmatched sustain, stability, and resonance. Players notice it immediately — the tone is richer, the notes ring longer, and the instrument feels like an extension of their body.
>
> Only the finest woods made the cut — from rare and exotic species to top-grade 5A Canadian birdseye and curly maple, much of it aged since the 1970s. But it wasn't just about what you could feel — it was also about what you could see. Lado's signature transparent finishes were designed to highlight the natural beauty of the wood, not cover it up. Every grain pattern, every ripple in the figuring was put on display like a piece of art. That level of material selection and visual craftsmanship gives each Lado guitar not just a voice of its own — but a soul that can be seen, heard, and felt.
>
> — Joe "Lado" Kovacic

Through the decades, Lado's top models shifted based on era, style trends, and price points. In the early 1980s, the more rounded, traditionally shaped, boutique-styled Falcon and Solo models were bestsellers, especially among Canadian rock musicians. After 1983, following the exposure from Iron Maiden's use of Lado guitars, forward-thinking Earth series (with its aggressive, pointy, Explorer-esque design) gained international attention and became a flagship model. In the 1990s, popularity shifted to the Golden Wing, and then the more aesthetically traditional Rocker and Classic model lines, which appealed to players seeking refined tones and exquisitely grained woods.

> Design is always flowing — I'm never without a pen in hand, always scribbling. Like a fashion or industrial designer, inspiration doesn't keep office hours. Whether I'm sitting at the table before dinner, walking through the woods, or standing over a workbench in the shop, I'm sketching — curves, edges, wild shapes. It's instinctual. It's constant. I've always had a vivid imagination, and I truly dream guitars. Some of my most iconic designs started not on a blueprint, but in a dream — or in that quiet space where creativity takes over. Guitars aren't just something I build — they're something I feel. Nature inspires me. Architecture inspires me. Emotion inspires me. I see a hawk in flight or a piece of stained glass, and instantly I'm thinking: how could that line, that motion, become a guitar? Guitars are my life — I live them, breathe them, and see them in everything around me. That's how Lado designs are born — from raw passion, imagination, and the drive to turn inspiration into something a musician can hold in their hands.
>
> I've never been interested in following trends — the goal was never to fit in, but to be ahead of the times. I didn't want to make just another standard guitar. I wanted to build instruments that looked different, felt different, and played different — guitars that would push boundaries and spark imagination, just like they did for me. That's the spirit behind every Lado design.
>
> —Joe Kovacic

Having one of the world's biggest heavy metal bands use Lado instruments in their videos and live concert appearances gave the brand a massive promotional boost, and helped bring Lado guitars to international attention.

It was a turning point that catapulted the brand onto the global stage — especially for the Earth and Lazer models. Andy Curran from Coney Hatch was the connection — he brought the Iron Maiden guys to the shop on Warden Avenue in Scarborough, Ontario, and that's where it all started. We began working together, and while the band wasn't officially endorsed, Lado guitars made appearances during the '84–'85 World Slavery Tour, which was immortalized in the *Live After Death* home video. Lado guitars were also used in the "Aces High" and "2 Minutes to Midnight" music videos (Steve Harris on the Unicorn bass and Adrian Smith on the Earth and Lazer models) and are often seen in photo shoots and appearances from that period of time.

The Lado Earth and Lazer models were one of the brand's more visually aggressive and iconic models from the 1980s, often associated with the glam and hard rock scenes of that era. Its name, styling, and edge were very much in line with the bold, futuristic branding that set Lado apart.

That kind of visibility — even brief — was enough to light a fire. Suddenly, players around the world were asking about Lado. The Earth model in particular took off, and it cemented our reputation for bold, distinctive designs that could hold their own on the biggest stages. And honestly, that momentum has never stopped. I'll never forget how down-to-earth the guys were — Steve Harris, Adrian Smith, Dave Murray — no ego, just great musicians with a real love for their craft. We connected over guitars, not business. They were generous with their time, curious about the builds, and genuinely interested in the work being done in the shop. One of my fondest memories was having them over at my home during a gathering with a few other artists who had become close friends over the years. It wasn't about celebrity — it was about connection. We shared stories, laughs, and time with family. That kind of experience stays with you. Even after all these years, I still have deep respect and admiration for them. Their humility and authenticity left a lasting mark — not just for what it did for the brand, but for the kind of people they were.

— Joe "Lado" Kovacic

> Adrian Smith was the main guy using Lado guitars in Iron Maiden. He played a few different Earth models during the *Powerslave* tour in '84–'85, and later used a Lazer [a variant of the Earth] on the *Seventh Son of a Seventh Son* tour in 1988. It was a stunning guitar, equipped with a MIDI controller, and really stood out on stage, even though he only used it during the song "Can I Play with Madness."
>
> Steve Harris and Dave Murray also played Lado instruments during the *Powerslave* era.
>
> Steve had two different Lado basses. One was the Condor, which had this almost medieval-looking body shape, and the other was the Unicorn — Joe's take on the Firebird shape. That one shows up in the videos for "Aces High" and "2 Minutes to Midnight."
>
> Dave Murray had a Lado superstrat-style guitar, but his was more of a traditional Strat shape, so no pointy horns or headstock. Definitely more subdued compared to Adrian's Earth models, but still a very cool guitar. I've only seen it in a few photos so I don't think he used it very often.
>
> — Nico Falco, creator of Licks of the Beast

> At the end of the day, many of these artists — including Iron Maiden, Saga, and Nazareth — already had official endorsement deals. But they added Lado guitars to their personal collections because they loved how they played and sounded. That's the difference: when a guitar is chosen not because of a logo on a headstock, but because it inspires the person holding it.
>
> — Joe Kovacic

Joe wasn't content to simply rest on the endorsement of world-famous players to spread the word about his instruments. He was willing to put his money (and a substantial amount of it) into creating a monument to a dream he was chasing, one that inspired him to manifest the ideals of his craftsmanship on a massive scale. Lado Guitars held the Guinness World Record from 1987 to 1991 for building the "largest built, and presumably the loudest playable electric guitar," a 14-foot, 3-inch tall, 309-pound "Earth" model guitar.

> It started with a dream — literally. One night, I envisioned this colossal guitar, and by the next morning, I was in the shop, fully locked in. Within 24 hours, the concept was designed. I called over my foreman, John Bradley, handed him a drink, and said, "Get ready — we're about to make history." We laid out a 20-foot cardboard cutout, stood back, and pulled up the current Guinness World Record. I looked at it and said, "We're going to beat this — and we're going to do it our way." It was part ambition, part engineering challenge, and part artistic statement.
>
> I've always believed guitar-making is equal parts craft and imagination — and this was the ultimate test. Not just to go big, but to go bold. And just like every Lado, the world's largest electric guitar wasn't just built to impress — it was built to play. A fully functional, handcrafted instrument — just on a much grander scale. We started calling our vendors for parts, sharing our vision and to share in the history making — from sourcing piano strings for the scale and working with suppliers for custom bridges, machine heads, and other hardware. In the end, we spent over twenty-five thousand dollars just on parts alone. But for me, it was never about the cost — it was about proving what was possible when vision, skill, and a little audacity come together.
>
> — Joe Kovacic

Lado's success was largely based on their desire and ability to customize, going to great lengths to not only source and provide high quality parts and components, but also to meet and exceed the specific requirements of the individual player.

> Customization at Lado is never just about specs — it's about understanding the soul of the musician. Every build starts with a conversation, not a template. I want to know who they are, not just as a player, but as a person. What kind of music do they live and breathe? Are they on tour, in the studio, or writing at home? What inspires them — sonically and visually?

We talk about the guitar they're currently playing — what they love about it, what they don't. Then we get into the feel: What kind of neck fits their hand best? What's their ideal weight balance? Are they drawn to certain woods, or curious to try something new? The answers shape everything from the tonewood to the pickup configuration, the scale length, even the color and finish, which, for many, is just as emotionally important as the sound.

The hardware, electronics, wood, and aesthetic are all open for discussion, and every choice is made together. Sometimes I'll offer guidance if I know a certain combo will bring out a better tone or feel, but it's always in service of their voice, not mine.

Some musicians come in with a clear vision. Others only know how they want it to feel when it's done. That's the beauty of it — we build the guitar around them. No two Lado customs are the same, because no two musicians are. And when they pick up that final instrument, they don't just feel like they're holding a guitar, they feel like it was built for their hands, their music, their story.

And that's when I truly know we got it right — when the messages start coming in. Emails, photos, social media posts from musicians pouring out their excitement. Some say it feels like holding a new baby. Others call it life changing. It's not just a guitar to them — it's their guitar, built from the ground up with heart, intention, and soul. Moments like that remind me why I do this. It's not just about building instruments — it's about creating something meaningful, something lasting. And every time, it's worth every hour, every detail, and every bit of the wait.

— Joe Kovacic

John Albani is a successful record producer and photographer in Nashville, Tennessee. In Canada, he is best known as the cowriter, coproducer, and virtuoso guitarist who served as the six-string foil to Lee Aaron, a multiplatinum artist who was recently inducted into Canada's Walk of Fame. For the past 12 years, I have had the privilege of playing guitar alongside Lee, and as a result, have spent a great deal of time studying John's wonderfully melodic and fiery guitar playing.

> Joe was amazing. He would watch you play; he'd sit you down at the shop, and he would say, "I know what I need to do." And he would come up with whatever he did to model that guitar for you. It literally was like an extension of your body, and his guitars were just effortless to play.
>
> I mean, I remember going to his shop, picking out the wood. I'd literally see the thing being built, and then I go pick it up and play it. You'd realize that these aren't really just guitars. These are pieces of art. This guy's an artist. You know, he's not just building guitars because it's a job. This guy lives and breathes and loves this shit, you know? Unbelievable. I remember he had this, I don't know what you call it, but it was like an aluminum thing that had bars on it, and all these little bars in the center. And he made me grab it with my hand, and it took an imprint of my hand. He used that to sculpt all my necks,
>
> There was just a confidence that I had walking out on stage with a Lado guitar and knowing how that sounded on stage every night, how it reacted to my rig, how it played, the way he would measure your hand and get those necks so everything was effortless. It was like you didn't have to think about anything. It made it so that you could walk out and you could, actually, right from the first note, really enjoy your show and have fun. You weren't fighting anything.
>
> —John Albani of the Lee Aaron Band

Andy Curran is the bassist and vocalist in "Toronto's loudest band," Coney Hatch, an ensemble that I have been a member of for the past 11 years. He is also a member of the band Envy of None alongside Rush guitarist Alex Lifeson, a Juno Award–winning solo artist, and respected music industry professional on the business side.

> I had broken a headstock off of one of my guitars, I'm pretty sure it was my B.C. Rich Mockingbird bass. Somebody said you

> should go to Joe Lado and he'll repair it for you. They said he's the best luthier in Canada. Joe said, "I can fix this, no problem." He immediately started telling me, in a proud, and confident way [*laughs*], how his guitars were better than everything else and that I should stop playing B.C. Riches, and that he should make me a guitar. I told him I always wanted an Explorer body type of guitar. Joe said, "I'm not going to do an exact Explorer type. I've got a design I think you'd like." That was what we stumbled upon. I think he called it the Earth. I might have been the first guy, like 001 or 002, of those Lado Earth basses.
>
> I had a second one done where Joe installed a Kahler whammy bar on one of my Earth basses. That was like the ultimate pointy rock stick of death with a whammy bar on a bass guitar. The first one was black, and Joe had a friend airbrush [the lips from] *The Rocky Horror Picture Show* on the top. The second one had a thinner neck and a Kahler whammy bar on the bridge. We used all Schaller hardware. I was in on all of it — watching it get done, the inlays, choosing fretboards and finishes.
>
> My all-time favorite Lado guitar that Joe made for me was the eight-string bass we called the Octavian. I still own and use it. I don't think he made very many of those. I've used it on a bunch of records. I wish I still had my Earth basses, but they were very long and the headstocks were quite heavy. I ended up gravitating towards the Octavian, which was a three-quarter scale with a shorter neck.
>
> — Andy Curran of Coney Hatch and Envy of None

I asked Andy about his personal relationship with Joe. Knowing the amazing human being that Andy Curran is, and how much he has personally mentored and helped me, his answer did not surprise me in the least.

> He was a super knowledgeable guy. We chose all the fretboards together and the finishes. I had a blast doing that with him. He wanted to know everything — different radius curves on the back of the neck, how high I wanted the curve to go. We modified things to fit my playing style. He was so thorough and

> a consummate professional. Nothing left his shop until he was happy about it.
>
> He was a stickler for detail, but we formed a beautiful friendship. We had so much fun. He has a crazy sense of humor, and we became really good friends. I probably value my friendship with him more than the guitar. When we finished the guitars, we would have a toast. He would bring out this crazy Croatian grappa, and we would have a celebratory shot. Through that, I introduced Joe to the guys in Iron Maiden and Adrian Smith, and he made some basses for Steve Harris as well. I always tried to open the door for Joe, because I thought he was a bit of an underdog and wanted more people to know about him and his guitars.
>
> — Andy Curran

Honeymoon Suite and Brighton Rock were two Canadian bands with a lot in common. Both bands hailed from the Niagara Falls region, and mixed crunchy guitars with keyboards and distinctive vocals to craft highly melodic and energized commercial hard rock. They were both signed to Warner Music Canada. And they both featured rock-solid bassists and virtuoso guitarists who rocked Lado guitars.

> Did I play Lados? Hell, yeah! Me and Johnnie [Dee, lead vocalist and rhythm guitarist] both got a bunch of guitars from him back in the day. He was all over us. Most of them got stolen in New Jersey, but I have a white flying V from him that wasn't on tour with us at the time, so I still have that guitar. [My Lado guitars] were custom made, there was one that was kind of like an Explorer meets a B.C. Rich — lots of points!
>
> — Derry Grehan of Honeymoon Suite

Bassist Gary Lalonde (one of my favorite musicians and human beings in the Canadian music scene) also played a number of Lado basses.

> Joe Lado is a master craftsman. His passion and dedication to designing and producing instruments shines through in every

> piece he creates. Working with him on bass designs has been a highlight of my life.
>
> — Gary Lalonde of Honeymoon Suite

Sheron Alton is a guitarist, vocalist, songwriter, and was a driving creative force behind the band Toronto. She is one of the songwriters behind the Heart classic "What About Love," which reignited the careers of the Wilson sisters in the 1980s. Sheron is also a designer who works in a number of disciplines. She shared what made her Lado guitars special, as well as her holistic approach to creative endeavors.

> For me, it's the neck, the wood, the sound, the type of wood used, the craftsmanship. That was it. The three Lado guitars that I have are all endorsements. Brian [Allen, Toronto guitarist] and I both had Joe make us guitars. I purchased one from him after he gave me the first guitar that he made for me. It was nice, but not quite what I wanted. It wasn't rock and roll enough for me, it was a little heavy, with a lot of wood on it. It was called the Falcon. He let me customize that, especially the neck. Every neck I had was customized, perfect, because I have really small hands. So, I got a slimmer neck so I could fit my little fingers on there. My main one was the Earth model. The Earth had a pointy design — it was a little too pointy for me, but I liked the whammy, so it had everything on it. I helped design the Lado Earth guitar with Joe — he has the prototype, and I have number two. Although my contribution was small, I always thought it should be in scale and have proper proportion, as balance is so important in design.
>
> My background as a designer extends beyond guitars to houses, furniture, clothing, and more; songwriting, for me, is just another facet of that creative drive. I've always preferred a guitar with a compact, balanced form, something that looks good and feels right — especially when thinking about how it would look on a woman. That's what I love about the Lado Earth; it feels right for me, and I think it's beautiful. Over the years, my input has been about striving for that perfect balance and simplicity. I've experimented with different whammy bars

and pickups, and certain guitars, like my Zebra, just resonate with me. Collaborating and sharing these designs has always been rewarding. To me, the heart of great design — whether in guitars, songs, or anything else — is always seeking balance and symmetry in service of a greater idea.

— Sheron Alton of Toronto

Yeah, when we first got our record deal with Warner back in '85, I had just purchased a B.C. Rich Ironbird. It was like one of the first in Canada. Our bass player [Steve Skreebs] had a Lado endorsement, and I was offered one as well. Joe said, "Hey, when are you going to play Lado?" I went, "No, I'm good. I'm happy. I'm quite happy with what I've got." He goes, "What do you play?" I go, "B.C. Rich." He goes, "B.C. Rich? I shovel snow with B.C. Rich." [*laughs*]

I said, "No, I'm good," because, you know, I wanted to be known with the B.C. Rich, because it was a one-of-a-kind guitar, and I loved the way it looked compared to all the Lados I had seen up to that point. I thought, the Ironbird kind of made me unique and I hoped it would make me stand out. That was my intention, because our record wasn't released yet. But [Joe Lado] goes, "Look, pick up anything here and try it." I said, "Okay, let me just take this one here to see how it sounds." The one I picked was a stock one. When I plugged it in, it sounded better than my B.C. Rich — I was kind of disappointed — "Shit, it sounds bigger and fatter than mine!"

He made me two Lasers [*sic*]. The first one, my blue one, had a Floyd Rose on it, and it had a weird headstock I didn't like. I said, I'd like a [different] headstock, which is the one you'll see in the videos and in pictures. For the second guitar, I wanted more of a pointy one, if you look at the headstock, it comes more to a point, yeah, and that one's spelled different, it's l-a-z-e-r. The second one is a red one. It's just got one pickup, one volume knob, and the same Lado original pickups. Now, if he builds you one, he puts like Seymour Duncan or whatever in there. But the original pickups, way back in '86, were built in Germany. The guy who built all

> those pickups either retired or he passed away, because I wanted to get a backup pickup later on, and he said "No, those are gone."
>
> — Greg Fraser of Brighton Rock

> Over the years, we've worked with a variety of top-tier component manufacturers to ensure that every Lado guitar delivers not only on craftsmanship but also on performance. One of the most notable partnerships was with ABM in Germany — I would consider the Ferrari of guitar parts. Their engineering was exceptional. They've been making high-end hardware for decades and even produced semi-hollow tailpieces for Gibson for over 50 years. Their components matched our standards for precision and reliability.
>
> We also incorporated pickups and electronics from DiMarzio, EMG, Seymour Duncan, Bartolini, Shadow, and Schaller — depending on the tonal needs and player preferences. And of course, we also crafted our own Lado pickups for artists looking for something unique and fully integrated into the build.
>
> Ultimately, the choice of components was always guided by one principle: what will best serve the musician and the instrument we're building? Whether it was a neck-through monster for stage performance or a refined studio guitar, I made sure every detail — down to the hardware — reflected the same level of care as the craftsmanship itself.
>
> — Joe Kovacic

The demand for Lado guitars, and the company's desire to grow, necessitated a move to off-shore production. Where some other companies suffered a hit to their reputation due to substandard instruments being produced, Lado was able to ensure that quality standards remained high.

> The decision to produce the Lado Hawk overseas was a strategic move — one rooted in making the brand more accessible without compromising on quality. We wanted to give music stores the opportunity to offer a more affordable line that still carried the Lado name, feel, and integrity. The Hawks were

> built in Korea and Taiwan, but every model was made strictly to my personal specifications. I personally traveled to the manufacturing facilities to oversee production, inspect craftsmanship, and ensure that each instrument met my exacting standards. It wasn't about mass production — it was about extending the brand thoughtfully, with care and consistency. The result was that over two thousand Lado Hawks were sold in Canada alone, and not a single one was ever returned. That's something we're incredibly proud of. The Hawk line proved that you could offer players an affordable option without cutting corners — a true Lado, through and through.
>
> — Joe Kovacic

Today, some 50 years down the road, Joe Kovacic continues to handcraft instruments for discerning players, collectors, and enthusiasts from all over the world, sometimes resulting in relationships that run much deeper than just that of craftsman to client.

> We're now seeing a new wave of recognition thanks to social media and online communities. One standout is Nico Falco, known for his Iron Maiden–focused YouTube channel and Instagram page, Licks of the Beast. Just eight months ago, he purchased his first Lado Earth, drawn in by his deep love for Iron Maiden and a fascination with the guitars that once shared the stage with them. When he shared it with his audience, it reignited global curiosity — the post reached thousands of fans, and before I knew it, I had more orders than I could handle in retirement.
>
> — Joe Kovacic

> A lot of it comes down to Joe "Lado" Kovacic himself. I've gotten to know him personally and I'm lucky to now call him a friend. He's a true master luthier with over 60 years of experience, and he's ridiculously passionate about what he does. What's crazy is that Joe still builds every guitar by hand — no CNC machines, no shortcuts. Even those gorgeous inlays are cut by hand! Every

> Lado is a one-of-a-kind piece, built with pride and attention to detail you just don't see much anymore. You can feel it when you play one.
>
> — Nico Falco, creator of Licks of the Beast

> Most recently, the Swedish metal band Sabaton has become part of the Lado story through guitarist Chris Rörland. Chris has been quietly building an impressive personal collection — he already owns eight Lado guitars, each one hand-selected or custom built to his preferences. What makes this especially meaningful is that these aren't promotional instruments or part of an endorsement deal — they're guitars he chose to invest in, one by one.
>
> Through that journey, a genuine friendship has also been established — built on a shared respect for craftsmanship, tone, and the artistry behind the instrument. They've spent time together discussing guitar builds, exchanging ideas, and connecting over their mutual passion for the craft. For me, it's been rewarding to see that kind of connection with a younger generation of international artists who truly understand what Lado stands for.
>
> For a world-touring guitarist like Chris, owning multiple Lado guitars speaks volumes. Each one offers something unique — different tone, woods, finishes, and personalities — allowing him to tap into a range of voices depending on the song, setup, or atmosphere. But beyond the technical, it's about connection. Musicians at that level don't collect guitars casually. They choose instruments that inspire them, that hold up on stage, and that reflect who they are.
>
> — Joe Kovacic

According to Susan, the younger generation of guitarists and influencers espousing the virtues of Lado guitars has been key to bringing the Lado brand back into the consciousness of the international guitar community.

> Many of Nico's followers — and others in the social media guitar community — were teenagers during the height of

> Lado's presence in the '80s. Back then, they admired from afar, but couldn't afford one. Now, decades later, they're successful professionals, artists, or collectors who still love the music, the band, and the era — and they can finally make that dream real. For them, buying a Lado now isn't just about owning a guitar, it's about reclaiming a piece of their youth with the instrument they always wanted. That kind of emotional full circle is something no marketing plan can create — it's pure, authentic legacy.
>
> On another note, it wasn't always the big-name artists that recognized what made these instruments special. The impact of international sales has always been an important — and sometimes underappreciated — part of the Lado story. Over the years, Lado guitars found their way into the hands of passionate players around the world through a network of international wholesalers, music stores, and one-of-a-kind custom orders. Whether it was a small shop in Germany, a collector in Japan, or a touring musician in South America, there was always a common thread: a desire for something different — something handcrafted, built with soul, and made to last. These sales weren't about scale — they were about connection. And they helped carry the spirit of Lado far beyond Canada's borders, into studios, stages, and homes across the globe.
>
> — Joe Kovacik

I believe that "reclaiming a piece of our youth" lies at the heart of the desire of many of us who are obsessed with pointy guitars. I know when I hold one in my hands, specific shapes, brands, and models take me back to times when life was easy, innocent, and fun. I'm grateful for this nostalgia, as it has helped find my own creative path in life, just as it has spurred me on to seek high quality tools of expression in the form of instruments crafted by talented builders.

One of the final conversations I had for this book was with Jonathan Mankuta, a successful American actor and writer known for his work on TV series Lost, Veep, and Hollywood Treasures. Our mutual friend (and fellow pointy guitar enthusiast) Wayne Comeau connected us to discuss his incredible collection of vintage pointy guitars, many of which have their own "rock star" history. He provided some incredible insight into the emotional drive of the truly dedicated guitar collector.

> Collecting guitars is about chasing the memories and desires of my youth. There's an unmistakable nostalgia that flavors every acquisition. [In the '80s] we were in a very unique, once-in-a-lifetime, decade of decadence and excess and craziness and great music. That music scene is very, very sentimental to me as a Gen Xer. I still have all my magazines and a lot of the clothes from back then. It's about holding onto a piece of that past — a time when music was both sonically and visually creative, excessive, and just plain fun. There's an unmistakable nostalgia that flavors every acquisition.
>
> I have over two hundred B.C. Rich guitars in my collection of over three hundred guitars. They're my favorite brand, with Charvel probably second, and Kramer right after them. Jackson is up there too. Sometimes, the thrill is as much about the hunt or the memory it celebrates as it is about the instrument itself. You're always one away from having just enough in your collection. Gear acquisition syndrome, or GAS, is very real. I just bought two guitars in the last two weeks.
>
> — Jonathan Mankuta, pointy guitar collector

While my personal collection is much smaller and more modest than Jon's, I can relate to the unmistakable nostalgia that, as he says, "flavors every acquisition" of instrument from the '80s.

> Every new guitar brings back that same feeling of opening that present on Christmas, where it's that shiny new object that's in your life, and you can't wait to play it.

Trying to reclaim that innocent feeling of desire is a thrill I can relate to; one that inspires me to keep chasing for one more hit of a magical, less complicated time in my life. Sometimes, that thrill is as much about the hunt or the memory it celebrates

> It's always the best feeling in the world. New guitar day. You know, it's like the UPS driver, if they haven't fucked it up, is like the ice cream man coming to your house.

For Jon, the established elements of what constitutes a pointy guitar provide a fundamental checklist for what inspires a purchase.

> It must have pointy headstock, it must be loud, it must have flashy colors or graphics.

Many of the guitars in Jon's collection are special not just for their design, but for the stories and people behind them.

> Some of my favorites are guitars that were owned by C.C. DeVille of Poison. I have two of his B.C. Rich Gunslingers and a custom [built by] Roman Rist. Those are huge prizes of mine because I saw him rock those guitars on stage. I have a few guitars from Warrant, including two of their Gunslingers and a bass. Those are personal favorites because I've seen Warrant a bunch of times. I own Pete Friesen's Mockingbird — the one he played in the Alice Cooper "Poison" video. That guitar made me love Mockingbirds and want a handmade B.C. Rich. I have a couple of Great White guitars from Mark Kendall. One is shaped like a shark body, and the neck is a leg with a sneaker as the headstock. It was custom made by Dan Lawrence.
>
> The crown jewel of my collection is Mom, George Lynch's original Skull and Bones guitar. It's one of the most recognized guitars of the '80s, and I have the actual original. I also have several of George Lynch's other guitars: the green "Booger" Tiger, the purple Tiger ESP, and two of his B.C. Rich Gunslingers — one with a gray snakeskin finish and one white with skull sketches. I have Andy Timmons's red Kramer Holoflash, the only factory one made with a red body. I also have a few others from Andy because I became friends with him over the years.

> I own Steve Brown's Kramer NightSwan, which was custom made for him and used on the cover of the *Trickster* album. I have Tony MacAlpine's Harlequin guitar, the one he played in the "Tears of Sahara" video. I have three Ibanez Jem 777s — limited editions in neon green, desert sun yellow, and shocking pink. I even bought one that Steve Vai gave away on a radio contest and another he raffled for charity. I have a 1979 B.C. Rich Bich 10-string that used to belong to Mike Chapman, the famous producer and songwriter. The serial number is MC1. I have a Fender Stratocaster that George Lynch played in his later years, which he modified a bit. I have a Charvel Strat with a big mouth graphic that belonged to Tracii Guns of L.A. Guns, and a modified Gunslinger of his with pink flames.
>
> A lot of these guitars represent the period when I was most inspired. The guitars were really built for shredding back then, and that was like my style. Even though I suck as a player. [*laughs*] I absolutely to this day suck, but I love figuring out riffs and stuff and noodling around. Look, I'm an actor by career, so I don't have to worry about being good or bad at playing guitar. It's just a hobby I love.

Jon feels that his penchant for pointy guitars makes him an outlier in the realm of "serious" collectors.

> No one will ever pick up a guitar and say, "I want the brightest, flashiest, pointiest guitar, the most outlandish, craziest thing you've ever seen." No one will want that again. Collecting these guitars is about keeping the spirit of that era alive — one flashy, pointy, nostalgia-laden instrument at a time.
>
> — Jonathan Mankuta

Steve Gilliss is another avid guitar collector. He is also a veteran of the Canadian Armed Forces who uses his talents as a guitar instructor to help veterans and first responders through a program I am proud to be associated with, Music 4 Mental Health, delivered through the Veterans Association Food

Bank in Airdrie, Alberta. Steve loves ESP Guitars; his James Hetfield signature ESP Snakebyte is one of his personal faves.

Through Steve's vision for helping those suffering from PTSD, I've come to see the true power of connection a guitar — pointy or otherwise — can offer.

> After 10 plus years of teaching veterans and first responders how to play guitar through group workshops and individual lessons I whole heartedly believe that a guitar isn't just six strings on wood — it's a lifeline. I've seen veterans and first responders pick it up, and with every chord, the weight they carry grows lighter. Music doesn't just heal — it transforms.
>
> — Steve Gilliss, Guitars for Vets

Steve and I recently started a business together called Rock N' Refresh, which specializes in guitar-shaped air fresheners for cars. We currently offer two models: one is based on the Derry Grehan signature "tread" model made by Canadian company Godin Guitars, and the other is based on my own signature model, the Godfrey Guitars Exquire SK. I love the blurb that Steve wrote for the packaging.

> The Exquire SK (Sean Kelly Artist Series) by Canadian builder Godfrey Guitars is the very first guitar we chose to immortalize as an air freshener. With its bold color and sharp, pointy shape, it instantly grabs attention — just as it did when it first inspired us. For many of the veterans and first responders in our program, its unconventional design has become a powerful symbol: a reminder that even when you feel like you don't quite fit in, you can still stand out with strength and purpose.

The Exquire guitar is, as its name suggests, a cross between a Fender Esquire and a Gibson Explorer in concept. It features two pickups created by Pariah Pickups, a Canadian company that specializes in pickups that emulate era-specific hard-rock and heavy-metal tones. One hidden underneath the pickguard that can be blended in via a push–pull function on the volume knob, the other is a rail-style humbucking pickup that fits the space of a traditional

Esquire single coil. The guitar is finished in a blinding neon pink, a finish color that harkens back to my love of Twisted Sister.

> So that design was really inspired by a couple of guitars I've always loved — the early Fender Esquire and the Gibson Explorer from the late '50s. My goal was to kind of blend the two. I've always seen this weird continuity between them, even though they're very different shapes. I wanted to make something that felt like it *could've* come out of that same era — something believable for the '50s — but that could also go in a completely different direction depending on how you finish it. Like, you can take an Esquire and paint it pink and it instantly feels '80s. Same with an Explorer — those guitars retro out really well. So my idea was to design something that could live in both worlds: very '50s if you want, or totally flashy and graphic if you want to push it that way. I also wanted to keep some of the purity of the original Esquire — like the ashtray bridge — but I reversed the pickup slant. Part of that was aesthetic; it just works better with the body lines. But also, if I have the option, I tend to prefer that direction anyway. On top of that, I wanted to bring in a few modern touches, like a heel-less design so you can actually reach the high frets comfortably. The idea was to get that Explorer vibe visually, but make it a little more compact — something that fits in a standard case and feels a bit more balanced overall.
>
> — Les Godfrey, Godfrey Guitars

I loved the two Exquire guitars (is one ever really enough?) that Les made me so much, I knew I needed another Godfrey in my collection. One evening, after watching a performance of Judas Priest live in concert over a few glasses of red wine, I was inspired to reach out for another custom build, a smaller flying V shape with a Kahler tremolo.

> Then with the Mini V, that one obviously pulls from the Voltez line that I make, but also from the Hamer mini V that K.K. Downing used back in the Judas Priest days. We went back and

> forth on a few ideas, but I thought it'd be fun to do a version with a black top and some pink accents that glow in the dark — just a little shred machine with a single humbucker. Spec-wise, they're all pretty similar. The bodies are poplar, the necks are quarter-sawn walnut, and the fingerboards are ebony. The Mini V is the only one that's got the Chemcast binding around the board and a Richlite black top with an acrylic underlay for that glowing look. They all use the same scale length — the only real difference is that the Mini V has 24 frets instead of 22, and it's got nickel frets instead of stainless. Other than that, they're basically built from the same DNA.
>
> — Les Godfrey

As I bring this book to a close (and in truth, it really feels more like an abandonment — I have barely scratched the surface of a topic too vast to cover in one telling), I realize that, in so many ways, my Godfrey guitars represent the main theme of this story. They draw inspiration from the great designs of the past, they are influenced by all manner of pop culture, and they speak to a meeting of the minds of the craftsmen and the player. These instruments were born from many conversations that Les and I have had over the years about art, music, life, and friendship. Make no mistake, I take *zero* credit for any of the work or inspiration that went into Les's creations, but I do know that many aspects of these very special guitars were created with me in mind. Les knows the artists I work with, and he is a fan of their work.

One of the greatest moments in my professional life, a life that has been blessed with many, was when Lee Aaron had the opportunity to share the stage with Mötley Crüe at the Festival d'été in Quebec City on July 14, 2024. In front of a crowd of 80 thousand people, I had the chance to wield my own pointy, neon pink Exquire SK signature model guitar with one of Canada's most iconic singers and a band of brothers who I consider to be among my closest friends. With my wife and two sons in attendance, I stared out at the crowd, awaiting the visual cue from the massive video screens that would flash the Lee Aaron logo across the historic Plains of Abraham, where, on September 13, 1759, the British Army and Royal Navy led by General James Wolfe successfully resisted the French militia of General Louis-Joseph, Marquis de Montcalm. That historic battle would influence the creation of

Canada. Rock n roll isn't war, but it can be a vicious game, and despite many years of performing, sometimes in front of crowds even bigger than the one I was facing on this day, I was feeling the heat of the moment.

But at 52 years old, experience has blessed me with the perspective that nerves and fear can be conquered with gratitude, and that moments like these are a blessed part of my life's vocation. As that massive screen lit up the Plains with the Lee Aaron logo, my years of "field training" kicked in, and I automatically assumed a well-studied, legs-splayed rock stance in my skin-tight jeans, leather jacket, and leopard-print boots, pointy-toed of course.

With the summer night's breeze blowing through my recently dyed head of blond-highlights (yeah, there may be more than a touch of gray underneath, but I still have my mop of curly rock locks), I turned to stare down the throngs, and laid into the opening riff of "Vampin'" — a Zep-inspired selection from the *Radio On!* album. My Exquire felt incredible in my hands, the comfort of the neck allowing me to bend and shake the strings with buttery ease. The power of its geometric lines and angles projected the spirit of every rock god I've longed to emulate, and every pointy ax I longed to possess. Throughout the evening, I was able to experience a wonderful sense of being present in the moment, soaking it all in. Every technique I'd learned from the pages of a guitar magazine or the grooves of a vinyl record informed my performance that night — a finger-tapped flurry here, a sweep-picked lick there. I was able to appreciate the notes I got right, and smile through the ones that got away from me (a few always do, but that's rock n roll, innit?)

In that first moment of riff delivery, I heard two things simultaneously — the glorious, throaty tone of my Godfrey guitar (delivered with love and passion through the massive P.A. by our gifted front-of-house technician, Tony Crea), and the appreciative roar of a festival audience primed for an evening of rock n roll. Looking over at my talented friends on that stage, I knew we were poised to win the day. John Cody on the drums, Dave Reimer, rocking his own gorgeous handmade creation, on bass, and Canada's premier rock-goddess Lee Aaron commanding the crowd like the star she was born to be, I realized that we were safe. But we weren't playing it safe. We were the real rock-n-roll deal. We were an army. And in my hands, this amalgamation of wood and wire representing all the dreams that brought me to this day, was *my Canadian-made* battle axe.

ACKNOWLEDGMENTS

To Erin, Des, and Jack Kelly for endless love and support through all of my artistic pursuits, and for making room in our house for the many pointy guitars that have found their way into our home. I love you all more than words could ever say.

Thank you to my parents, Des and Mary Kelly, for all of their sacrifices that made my life such a blessing. Love to Pam, Kerry, Jim, and all the extended family . . . special shout out to my little rockers Luci and Quinn.

My sincere gratitude to my editor, Michael Holmes, for his belief in this project, his friendship throughout, and for helping me find my way when I got lost in the forest of pointy guitars.

Thank you to Kathryn Lane for her beautifully detailed copyedit work. Your careful insights and knowledge have made this a much better book, and I am grateful for your efforts.

Thank you to the ECW team: Victoria Cozza, Jessica Albert, Jennifer Gallinger, Jen Albert, Emily Ferko, Emily Varsava, Aymen Saidane, and David Caron: I am proud to work with such talented people.

Thank you to Pete Dove, Edward Pond, George Aslaender, Chris Surdykowski, and Jonathan Mankuta for their incredible photographic contributions.

Thank you to Steve Brown (VintAxe.com), Chris Bennett, Kevin Taylor, Wayne Comeau, Susan Kovacic, Ernest Skinner, Paul Newman, Zach Gunter, and Glen Booth for going above and beyond to provide archival resources.

I would like to sincerely thank everyone who took the time to share their wisdom and insights with me for this book. It has been an honor and a privilege to share your stories.

Thank you to everyone at The Twelfth Fret in Toronto for keeping my pointy guitars in top playing shape!

RESOURCES

Adirondack Guitar. "What Do We Mean When We Say Lawsuit Guitar?" January 13, 2019. https://www.adkguitar.com/blogs/news/what-do-we-mean-when-we-say-lawsuit-guitar.

Bacon, Tony. *Flying V, Explorer, Firebird: An Odd-Shaped History of Gibson's Weird Electric Guitars*. Backbeat, 2011.

Bacon, Tony. *The Ibanez Electric Guitar Book: A Complete History of Ibanez Electric Guitars*. Backbeat, 2013.

Bacon, Tony. "A Repair Shop Sparked a Revolution: The Charvel/Jackson Story." Reverb. April 8, 2021. https://reverb.com/ca/news/a-repair-shop-sparked-a-revolution-the-charvel-jackson-story.

Barrette, Sean. *Heartstrings — First Guitars: Guitar Players & Their Stories of the Guitars That Made Them*. Published by the author, 2023.

Beckner, Justin. "A Brief History of Harmony Guitars." February 14, 2023. https://guitar.com/features/a-brief-history-of-harmony-guitars/.

Beckner, Justin. "A Brief History of Kramer Guitars." Guitar.com. August 29, 2023. https://guitar.com/features/a-brief-history-of-kramer-guitars/.

Beckner, Justin. "The Story of Gene Simmons' Iconic Axe Bass." Guitar.com. October 25, 2022. https://guitar.com/features/opinion-analysis/gene-simmons-axe-bass/.

Benedittini, Frankie. "Matsumoku Industrial Co." Vintage Japan Guitars. Accessed January 15, 2026. https://vintagejapanguitars.com/matsumoku-gakki-en/.

Blakey, Jake. "The Guitar That Nobody Expected to Succeed." Gough & Davy. June 20, 2023. https://goughanddavy.co.uk/blogs/news/the-guitar-that-nobody-expected-to-succeed.

The Blue Book of Guitar Values. https://bluebookofguitarvalues.com/

Brill, James M. "A Brief History of ESP Guitars: From Replacement to Refinement." Reverb. January 6, 2016. https://reverb.com/ca/news/a-brief-history-of-esp-guitars-from-replacement-to-refinement.

Cavazo, Carlos. *Guitar World*. November 1984.

Charupakorn, Joe. "B.C. Rich Beginnings." *Premier Guitar*. September 20, 2011. https://www.premierguitar.com/gear/reviews/b-c-rich-beginnings.

Czaykowski, Robert. "Nitebob." Interviewed by Tamra Lucid. Medium.com.

Davies, Dave. "Dave Davies: Reflections of a Kink." Interview by Dan Forte. *Vintage Guitar Magazine*. August 2023. https://www.vintageguitar.com/61338/dave-davies-2/.

Dickson, Jamie. "Roxy Insisted I Have a White Strat . . ." Interview by Jamie Dickson. Guitarist. January 3, 2025. https://www.guitarworld.com/artists/guitarists/roxy-music-phil-manzanera-50-years-of-music-guitars.

DiFatta, Johnny (AlienXnation). "Bruce Kulick." AXN Guitars. https://alienxnation.com/bruce-kulick-axn-guitars.

DiFatta, Johnny (AlienXnation). "ESP History — Electric Sound Products." AXN Guitars. https://alienxnation.com/vintage-1980s-guitar-resource-blog/2019/6/8/esp-history-electric-sound-products.

Easton, Elliot. "Driving Classic Cars." Interview by Bret Adams. *Vintage Guitar Magazine*. March 2018. https://www.vintageguitar.com/33516/elliot-easton-5/

EVH Gear. "'79 Bumblebee." https://www.evhgear.com/tribute/bumblebee.

Frehley, Ace. "I Studied Eric Clapton, Jimmy Page, Jeff Beck, Pete Townshend, the Beatles, the Stones . . . Those Guys Taught Me How to Play," The Virtual Guitar Show. Updated September 26, 2020. https://www.musicradar.com/news/ace-frehley-i-studied-eric-clapton-jimmy-page-jeff-beck-pete-townshend-the-beatles-the-stones-those-guys-taught-me-how-to-play.

Hanson, Elizabeth. "B.C. Rich: Origins and Evolution." Reverb. May 16, 2014. https://reverb.com/ca/news/bc-rich-origins-and-evolution.

Hilburn, Robert. "Meanwhile Bach in the U.S.S.R." *Los Angeles Times*. September 3, 1989.

Hunter, Dave. "With a through-neck, two DiMarzio Super Distortion pickups . . ." *Guitar Player*. March 7, 2024. https://www.guitarplayer.com/gear/classic-gear-bc-rich-mockingbird.

Ibanez Wiki. Accessed January 15, 2026. https://ibanez.fandom.com/wiki/Ibanez_Wiki.

Iconic Axes: The Instruments Used by the Gods of Six Strings. "The Edge's 1976 Gibson Explorer." October 1, 2012. https://iconicaxes.blogspot.com/2012/09/the-edges-1976-gibson-explorer.html.

Keifer, Tom. "On Johnny Winter." Interview by *Lithium Magazine*. BlabberMouth.net. July 26, 2014. https://blabbermouth.net/news/tom-keifer-on-johnny-winter-i-didnt-even-realize-how-big-he-was-in-my-life-until-after-his-death.

Kelly, Sean. *Don't Call It Hair Metal: Art in the Excess of '80s Rock*. ECW, 2023.

Kiesel Guitar Museum. Accessed January 15, 2026. http://kieselmuseum.com/.

Lawson, Robert. *Solidarity Forever: The Art and Soul of Stevie Van Zandt*. FriesenPress, 2024.

Matthes, Steve, and Joe Moffett. *The Ultimate: An Illustrated History of Hamer Guitars*. Schiffer, 2013.

McCarty, Ted. "Ted McCarty: I'm Not a Musician." Interview by Willie G. Moses. *Vintage Guitar Magazine.* April 1999. https://www.vintageguitar.com/2826/ted-mccarty/.

Mitchell, Ed. "The Guitars that Built Rock: The Gibson Firebird." *Classic Rock*. October 30, 2016. https://www.loudersound.com/features/the-guitars-that-built-rock-the-gibson-firebird.

Mitchell, Ed. "The Guitars that Built Rock: The Gibson Flying V." *Classic Rock*. Updated September 20, 2022. https://www.loudersound.com/features/the-guitars-that-built-rock-the-gibson-flying-v.

Ojeda, Eddie. Interview. "Kozidos: The Band." Accessed January 15, 2026. https://loscocidos.wordpress.com/guitar-hero/eddie-fingers-ojeda-twisted-sister/.

Ojeda, Eddie. "Twisted Sister's Eddie Ojeda Talks Charvel," Interviewed by Pauline France. Charvel. October 24, 2011. https://blog.charvel.com/2011/10/twisted-sister%E2%80%99s-eddie-ojeda-talks-charvel/.

Owens, Jeff. "The History of the Fender Stratocaster: The 1950s." Fender. Accessed January 15, 2026. https://www.fender.com/articles/behind-the-scenes/the-history-of-the-fender-stratocaster-the-1950s.

Perry, Joe. "Joe Perry Explains Choosing an Aerosmith Guitar for Metropolitan Museum of Art Exhibit." Interview by Joe Lynch. *Billboard Magazine*. April 30, 2019. https://www.billboard.com/music/rock/joe-perry-aerosmith-met-play-it-loud-guitar-8509437/.

Perry, Joe. "Joe Perry on Aerosmith's Roaring '70s and Writing 'Dream On.'" Interview by Andrew Daly. *Guitar World*. October 1, 2024. https://www.guitarworld.com/features/joe-perry-looks-back-on-aerosmith-in-the-1970s.

Persuader Media. "David Jellison: Based on True Events." https://persuadermedia.com/bio/.

Resnicoff, Matt. *Guitar World*. February 29.

Riario, Paul. "Review: Jackson X Series Soloist SL4X." *Guitar World*. February 8, 2019. https://www.guitarworld.com/gear/review-jackson-x-series-soloist-sl4x.

Roberts, Kane. Interview by Andrew Daly. Guitar Player. April 3, 2025. https://www.guitarplayer.com/guitarists/kane-roberts-machine-gun-guitar.

Sabo, Dave. "Dave 'Snake' Sabo of Skid Row." Interview by Leslie Michelle Derrough. *Glide Magazine*. August 4, 2014. https://glidemagazine.com/122089/dave-snake-sabo-skid-row-interview/.

Sandoval, Karl. "The Birth of the Randy Rhoads Sandoval Dot V." Interview by Larry DiMarzio and Eric Kirkland. DiMarzio. Accessed January 15, 2026. https://www.dimarzio.com/stories/birth-sandoval-randy-rhoads-dot-v.

Slash. "Living the Dream." Interview by Tzvi Gluckin. *Premier Guitar*. November 27, 2018. https://www.premierguitar.com/artists/slash-living-the-dream.

Smith, Jack. "History of B.C. Rich Guitars." Gear Vault. Accessed January 15, 2026. https://gear-vault.com/history-of-bc-rich-guitars/.

St. John, Mark. Interview by Pete Prown, 1990. *Vintage Guitar*. July 2023. https://www.vintageguitar.com/60781/mark-st-john/.

Stanley, Paul. "I Didn't Want to Be the Flashy Lead Player." Interviewed by Ken Sharp. *Guitar Player*. December 8, 2023. https://www.guitarplayer.com/players/the-paul-stanley-interview-2023.

Tipton, Glenn. "Hamer Guitars." Glenn Tipton Official Website. Accessed January 15, 2026. https://www.glenntipton.com/hamer-guitar.asp.

Tiven, Jon. *Guitar World*. May 1986.

The Twelfth Fret. "Guild X-79 Skyhawk White, 1984 [Used]." Accessed January 15, 2026. https://archive.12fret.com/instruments/guild-x79-skyhawk-white-1984/.

Way, Pete. *A Fast Ride Out of Here: Confessions of Rock's Most Dangerous Man*. Constable, 2018.

Wright, Michael. "Hair Bands, Soviet Russian and the 1989 Kramer Gorky Park Electric Guitar." My Rare Guitars. January 1, 2011. https://www.myrareguitars.com/1989-kramer-gorky-park-electric-guitar.

Zelinsky, Dean. *Dean News*. Summer 1981.

Zelinsky, Dean. "The History of Dean Guitars, by Dean Zelinsky." Mikes Gig. January 14, 2017. https://mikesgig.com/the-history-of-dean-guitars-by-dean-zelinsky.

INTERVIEWS WITH AUTHOR

John Albani
Sheron Alton
Glen Booth
Bruce Bouillet
Steve Brown
Chris Caffery
Carlos Cavazo
Angus Clark
Gilby Clarke
Phil Collen
Andy Curran
Jol Dantzig
Gino Del Sole
Amir Derakh
Brent Doerner
Rik Emmett
Nico Falco
Greg Fraser
Jay Jay French
Marty Friedman
Pete Friesen
Jack Frost
Steve Gilliss
Aljon Go
Les Godfrey
Aaron Greer
Derry Grehan
Frank Gryner
Zach Gunter
Scotti Hill
Chris Holmes
Michael Holmes
Dave Jellison
Joe Kovacic
Susan Kovacic
Bruce Kulick
Gary Lalonde
Don "Screaming" Leaming
Jonathan Mankuta
Doug Marks
David Newell
Patrick Pentland
Mitch Perry
Steve Plunkett
Paul Riario
Dave Reimer
Kane Roberts
Billy Rowe
Rick Savage
Reed Shimozawa
Stacy Stray
Mick Sweda
Michael Sweet
Nick Walsh
Tim Welch
Bill Xavier
Dean Zelinsky